International Conflict and Cyberspace Superiority

This book examines cyberspace superiority in nation-state conflict from a theoretical and a practical perspective.

This book analyzes superiority concepts from the domains of land, maritime, and air to build a model that can be applied to cyberspace. Eight cyberspace conflicts between nation-states are examined and the resulting analysis is combined with theoretical concepts to present the reader with a conclusion. Case studies include the conflict between Russia and Estonia (2007), North Korea and the U.S. and South Korea (2009) and Saudi Arabia and Iran in the Aramco attack (2012). The book uses these case studies to examine cyberspace superiority as an analytical framework to understand conflict in this domain between nation-states. Furthermore, the book makes the important distinction between local and universal domain superiority, and presents a unique model to relate this superiority in all domains, as well as a more detailed model of local superiority in cyberspace. Through examining the eight case studies, the book develops a rigorous system to measure the amount of cyberspace superiority achieved by a combatant in a conflict, and seeks to reveal whether cyberspace superiority proves to be a significant advantage for military operations at the tactical, operational, and strategic levels.

This book will be of much interest to students of cyber conflict, strategic studies, national security, foreign policy and IR in general.

William D. Bryant is a career fighter pilot and has a PhD from the School of Advanced Air and Space Studies, Maxwell, USA.

Routledge Studies in Conflict, Security and Technology

Series Editors: Mark Lacy, Dan Prince, Sylvia Walby and Corinne May-Chahal, *Lancaster University*

The *Routledge Studies in Conflict, Security and Technology* series aims to publish challenging studies that map the terrain of technology and security from a range of disciplinary perspectives, offering critical perspectives on the issues that concern public, business and policymakers in a time of rapid and disruptive technological change.

Nonlinear Science and Warfare
Chaos, complexity and the U.S. military in the information age
Sean T. Lawson

Terrorism Online
Politics, law, technology
Edited by Lee Jarvis, Stuart Macdonald and Thomas M. Chen

Cyber Warfare
A multidisciplinary analysis
Edited by James A. Green

The Politics of Humanitarian Technology
Good intentions, unintended consequences and insecurity
Katja Lindskov Jacobsen

International Conflict and Cyberspace Superiority
Theory and practice
William D. Bryant

International Conflict and Cyberspace Superiority

Theory and practice

William D. Bryant

Routledge
Taylor & Francis Group
LONDON AND NEW YORK

First published 2016
by Routledge

2 Park Square, Milton Park, Abingdon, Oxon OX14 4RN
711 Third Avenue, New York, NY 10017, USA

Routledge is an imprint of the Taylor & Francis Group, an informa business

First issued in paperback 2017

British Library Cataloguing-in-Publication Data
A catalogue record for this book is available from the British Library

Library of Congress Cataloging-in-Publication Data
Bryant, William D. (Career Fighter Pilot)
International conflict and cyberspace superiority : theory and practice / William D. Bryant.
pages cm. — (Routledge studies in conflict, security, and technology)
Includes bibliographical references and index.
ISBN 978-1-138-91891-7 (hardback : alk. paper) — ISBN 978-1-315-68818-3 (ebook : alk. paper) 1. Cyberspace—Political aspects. 2. Social conflict. I. Title.
HM851.B79 2015
303.48'34—dc23 2015006411

ISBN: 978-1-138-91891-7 (hbk)
ISBN: 978-1-138-89319-1 (pbk)

Typeset in Baskerville MT
by Keystroke, Station Road, Codsall, Wolverhampton

Contents

Figures

Tables

1 Introduction

The importance of cyberspace continues to grow in the modern world. Now it is not just the computer under the desk that is part of cyberspace. We are connecting our cars, phones, kitchen appliances, and even toilets to cyberspace. These connections allow increases in functionality and productivity unimaginable even in the realm of science fiction just a few years ago. Today's iPhone makes a "Star Trek" communicator look like a caveman's rock abacus, but the iPhone is the one that actually exists. Unfortunately, just like a "Star Trek" ship's computer runs amok, our devices may be working against us.

There is a dark side to this ever-increasing connectivity and functionality. Our iPhone can be spying on us and reporting our every move to a foreign intelligence service, our car might be reporting our location to an enemy, and malicious hackers can even take over our humble toilet to humiliate us.[1] Action from cyberspace is not only limited to malicious pranks. Hackers have demonstrated the ability to send potentially lethal commands to common cars, such as the Toyota Prius. One pair of enterprising hackers has demonstrated the capability to blast the horn uncontrollably, "make pathological liars out of speedometers and odometers," spoof the GPS, and even violently jerk a Prius' steering at any speed, threatening a potentially lethal collision.[2] These threats and vulnerabilities become even more magnified as you look at cyberspace systems on the municipal or national level.

Cyberspace is increasingly becoming an arena for nation state conflict. If a nation were to drop a bomb on an enemy power plant, the target nation would consider it an act of war. If the same nation sent a "logic bomb" through cyberspace causing the same amount of damage to the power grid, that is also war. The delivery method does not change the physical effect of the attack. Analysts are increasingly accepting cyberspace as a domain, or discrete region, where combatants fight, much like the domains of land, maritime, air, and space. According to former National Security Council Director for Cyber Security, Gregory Rattray, a goal of U.S. national strategy is to gain control of cyberspace.[3] The nature of warfare has not changed, but now there is a new field to fight on, much like when aircraft first opened up the air domain to warfare in the early 1900s. Although the majority of analysts have accepted cyberspace as a domain of warfare, there are some dissenting voices.

I agree with the majority of analysts who think that treating cyberspace as a domain is useful. One well known analyst that takes the opposing view is Martin Libicki who proposes that thinking of cyberspace as a domain causes cyberspace operators to apply inappropriate "warfighting" concepts at the expense of other paradigms such as systems engineering.[4] There are many reasons I think warfighting is a better mental template for conflict in cyberspace than systems engineering or any other proposed construct, but the most important is that cyberspace conflict is fundamentally human conflict in a new medium. Computers are not attacking each other and trying to steal other computer's information, people are attacking each other and trying to steal other people's information using computers. This means that the classic illustration of conflict by Carl von Clausewitz of two wrestlers dynamically reacting to each other applies as much in cyberspace as in the other physical domains.[5] I contend that thinking of cyberspace as a warfighting domain is far more helpful than thinking of it as an engineering problem and I will more fully develop this topic throughout this book. Some analysts don't argue that cyberspace is not a domain, they instead argue that war in cyberspace will not happen.

Thomas Rid's basic thesis is that "cyber war" has not happened, is not happening, and will not happen in the future.[6] Rid's thesis is completely dependent upon his definition of "cyber war," which he defines as having to include the potential to be lethal, "at least for some participants on at least one side."[7] I agree with Rid that cyber weapons will not often be the proximate cause of death, although there are a number of scenarios such as crashing a drone into a building where they could be.[8] I do not agree with Rid that the fact that people are generally not directly killed by cyberspace weapons means we should not think of conflict in cyberspace using theories from warfare. I am also not sure how relevant it is to soldiers who are killed when their positions are overrun because they lost all ability to communicate or call in fire support.

Normally, death and destruction will be dealt out through the physical domains, but that is increasingly facilitated and supported through the cyberspace domain. As a result of its importance, "war" has already started in cyberspace, although I use the term "conflict" to help identify that it is normally not as violent as in the other domains. If cyberspace is different from the other domains in that it is less violent, how else is it different? What is the basic character of this new domain?

Cyberspace is difficult to grasp intuitively because we cannot experience it directly with our senses. We can stand on the land, dive into the water, and see aircraft or satellites with our eyes. To "see" cyberspace we rely on computer screens or diagrams that provide representations, but we are not looking at or experiencing cyberspace directly. Another thing that makes cyberspace difficult to grasp is that it often operates inside or underneath the physical objects we see. According to Professor Chris Demchak, "orchestrating a national security response to cybered threats is hard because cyberspace is *hard to see physically* in any case, but especially so now as it is deeply embedded in normal societal functions."[9] Cyberspace underpins modern society and if it were seriously disrupted, only then would we understand what it had previously been doing for us. In that respect cyberspace in the modern world is like air; people take it for granted and do not think about its importance until it is no longer there. This difficulty in visualizing cyberspace makes careful definition of the domain even more important.

Connections between computing devices create cyberspace. An isolated computer sitting on a desk is no more part of the cyberspace domain than a ship sitting in dry dock is part of the maritime domain. The connections are what matter. The United States Joint Staff has defined cyberspace as "a global domain within the information environment consisting of the interdependent network of information technology infrastructures and resident data, including the Internet, telecommunications networks, computer systems, and embedded processors and controllers."[10] Although this definition has achieved wide acceptance, one common area of misunderstanding is the relationship between cyberspace and the Internet.

Cyberspace and the Internet are not synonymous, the Internet is a smaller subset of the larger cyberspace. This understanding has important implications for conflict in cyberspace, but the idea of the Internet as cyberspace is widespread. Even Libicki states that, "The Internet is basically tantamount to cyberspace; everything connected to the Internet is connected to cyberspace and, therefore, part of cyberspace."[11] Although everything connected to the Internet is connected to cyberspace, that does not make the Internet tantamount to cyberspace as there are many interdependent networks of information technology infrastructures that are not part of the Internet. Some examples include air gapped systems such as Iran's nuclear enrichment facilities, as well as embedded processors and controllers in a range of platforms, from cars to satellites. The danger in thinking of cyberspace as the Internet is that non-Internet connected devices are ignored by cyberspace defenders focused on traditional networks, when often those systems are the most critical to protect. Cyberspace is broader than the traditional Internet, but it is not useful to cast it so broadly as to include the entire electromagnetic spectrum.

One point of the definition that analysts still debate is whether to include the electromagnetic spectrum as part of cyberspace. As analysts first developed the concept of cyberspace, some policy makers included the electromagnetic spectrum as cyberspace's "maneuver space."[12] However, over time the definition has narrowed "down to the physical network infrastructure used for transmitting and storing information."[13] Sean Butler gave the principal reason for this narrowing when he stated that,

> The ability to process, store, and exchange large amounts of information rapidly, using automated systems, is the defining characteristic of cyberspace—the physical methods are superficial. In fact, its logical or virtual nature, rather than its physical mechanisms, sets cyberspace apart from other domains.[14]

I find this argument compelling and so will use the narrower Joint Staff definition from *Information Operations* for cyberspace, which does not try to include the entire electromagnetic spectrum.[15] I present a much more detailed analysis of the characteristics of the cyberspace domain in Chapter 3. Now that we have a definition of cyberspace, is freedom of action within that domain significant?

If the cyberspace domain is a key component of modern warfare, then it follows that freedom of action within that domain is important. According to Air Force Doctrine Document (AFDD) 3–12,

> Freedom of action in the cyberspace domain enables our command, control, communication, computers, intelligence, surveillance, and reconnaissance capabilities. Our modern defenses, industrial base, and global commerce, as well as that of our nation's enemies, depend on free use of land, sea, air, space, and cyberspace. Leverage in cyberspace affords influence and control across all other domains. This leverage increases our forces' access, speed, reach, stealth, and precision.[16]

In other domains, and especially in the air and maritime domains, analysts refer to this freedom of action as domain superiority.

The United States Air Force presents a clear definition of cyberspace superiority in Air Force doctrine. According to AFDD 3–12, cyberspace superiority is, "The operational advantage in, through, and from cyberspace to conduct operations at a given time and in a given domain without prohibitive interference."[17] This definition is the one I will use for cyberspace superiority and it is important to note that cyberspace superiority has an offensive and defensive component. Understanding this dual nature is critical and AFDD 3–12 goes on to provide more context and expand on the simple definition.

> Cyberspace superiority may be localized in time and space, or it may be broad and enduring. The concept of cyberspace superiority hinges on the idea of preventing prohibitive interference to joint forces from opposing forces, which would prevent joint forces from creating their desired effects. "Supremacy" prevents effective interference, which does not mean that no interference exists, but that any attempted interference can be countered or should be so negligible as to have little or no effect on operations. While "supremacy" is most desirable, it may not be operationally feasible. Cyberspace superiority, even local or mission-specific cyberspace superiority, may provide sufficient freedom of action to create desired effects. Therefore, commanders should determine the minimum level of control required to accomplish their mission and assign the appropriate level of effort.[18]

I will explore a number of important elements in this definition. The first element encompasses the different levels of cyberspace superiority.

There is a wide range of possibilities of how much advantage a combatant can have in a given domain. Note that in the AFDD 3–12 section quoted previously, there are at least two words used to discuss friendly freedom of action, "superiority" and "supremacy." There are also a large number of terms that authors and thinkers have applied to advantage in a domain that includes command, control, supremacy, and superiority. Because authors often use these terms to mean different things, it can be confusing when comparing multiple works. "Sea control," "command of the sea," "maritime superiority," and "control of sea communications" are all similar concepts, but there is no generally accepted hierarchy or understanding of how each term relates to the others. Accordingly, in this project I use the single term of cyberspace superiority, while acknowledging that there will be different levels of cyberspace superiority from near parity among the combatants, to complete domination of all of cyberspace by one combatant. In many of the quotations from other authors throughout this project, they use other terms such as "command of the air" or "sea superiority" and I have not altered them. I consider each of them to refer to domain superiority in their domain, with the addition that sometimes they imply greater or lesser domain superiority, as in AFDD 3–12, which places cyberspace supremacy over cyberspace superiority. The range of strength of superiority that a combatant can achieve brings up the related question of how much superiority a combatant needs or should seek.

A combatant should be seeking just enough cyberspace superiority to achieve their objectives, because seeking too much superiority can be counterproductive and prevent the attainment of strategic or operational objectives. For a combatant to pursue domain superiority requires resources that they could have applied to other important objectives. In addition, if a combatant seeks too high a level of superiority, there can be significantly diminishing returns for the increased resources put toward solving the problem. For example, in the air domain a combatant may be able to reduce an enemy Integrated Air Defense System (IADS) to 50% effectiveness at a reasonable level of effort, but to get to 99% degradation will normally be cost prohibitive. Temporary, local superiority may be sufficient if that is all that is required to accomplish the mission or objective. For example, when the Israeli Air Force bombed the Iraqi nuclear reactor, they did not seek air supremacy or even air superiority over all of Iraq; they simply wanted air superiority over the target and the ingress and egress corridors for just long enough to destroy the reactor. The Israelis were very successful by only seeking just enough superiority to accomplish their mission; had they attempted to gain total air supremacy they would not have been able to, and would not have been able to destroy the reactor. On the other hand, some analysts think that even limited cyberspace superiority is not a useful concept or goal for military forces.

Analysts have a wide range of opinions on the utility of cyberspace superiority as a concept. Martin Libicki is a well-known cyberspace analyst who is rather blunt when he states that, "the question of cybersupremacy is meaningless and, as such, is not a proper goal for operational cyberwarriors."[19] Owens, Dam, and Lin are slightly more circumspect and see some utility for developing capabilities, but still say that conflict in cyberspace will be very different from in the land, air, and maritime domains, which will make enduring dominance of cyberspace by the United States unrealistic.[20] Cyberspace analyst Jeffrey Carr states that the tendency of U.S. military forces to attempt to control the domains they operate in is a problem for the United States as no nation can dominate or control cyberspace.[21] Carr is afraid that the United States will pour resources into seeking an objective that is not attainable. Professor David Lonsdale concurs with Carr that a high level of cyberspace superiority is not attainable. Lonsdale looks at Douhet's definition of command of the air and states that an equivalent command of cyberspace is impossible and even undesirable, as it would require denying an enemy effective use of their information assets.[22] Not all analysts agree that there is no value to the concept of cyberspace superiority; some see it as a useful concept that requires modification when applied to the new cyberspace domain.

What these objections highlight is that cyberspace is not like the other domains, which will make gaining superiority look different, and the character of the superiority gained may be different as well. This difference in character does not release the cyberspace warrior from attempting to control their domain. According to well-known strategic theorist Colin Gray,

> To make advantageous use of an army, navy, air force, space force, and information force, it is necessary as a prerequisite to seek out and defeat the geographically similar forces of the enemy. If use of the sea is vital to us, in consequence it is vital to an enemy that he should be able to contest our ability to use the sea. The same strategic logic applies to the air, to orbital space, and to cyberspace. The technologies, tactics, and operational aims must vary with what is feasible in each unique geographical environment: the strategic logic, however, is uniform.[23]

Gray's strategic logic will drive cyberspace operators to attempt to control the cyberspace domain even if it is difficult. We should not simply ignore cyberspace superiority, we should wrestle with it to determine whether there is utility for strategists and planners in the concept.

The purpose of this book is to closely examine the concept of cyberspace superiority to determine whether it is a useful construct for thinking about and planning for nation-state conflict in cyberspace. The argument I will develop is that cyberspace superiority does provide a useful construct, but it requires significant modification from superiority in the other domains to account for the unique characteristics of the cyberspace domain. As I examine the characteristics of the cyberspace domain compared to the other physical domains, I begin to frame several important questions that shape my analysis.

The first question is whether domain superiority is a local or universal concept. In the more familiar air domain, combatants often implement air superiority through combat air patrols, or CAPs, where fighter aircraft hold a position and deny that space to the enemy. However, a single flight of aircraft cannot fly to their assigned CAP, "plant the flag" and fly home having established air superiority over the entire theater of operations. They have only established air superiority in the area of the domain that their sensors and weapons can reach and only for as long as they are in their CAP. Nevertheless, the fact that they have established superiority in their local part of the air domain also affects the overall superiority in the theater air domain, as the enemy now cannot utilize the airspace occupied by the CAP without fighting for it. So what is the relationship is between local and universal superiority in the cyberspace domain? I examined how the local and universal levels of domain superiority interacted among the physical domains and found that in the cyberspace domain, the local level of superiority is dominant over the universal level. The analysts who state you cannot gain total "command of the cyber" are correct if you restrict cyberspace superiority to the universal level. It is on the local level where realistic cyberspace superiority can be sought and won. The simple example of a CAP in the air domain also highlights another issue.

The second question is how persistent domain superiority typically is. When the aircraft return to base, what happens to the air superiority that the combatant gained? Does it continue and persist? In the case of the CAP, once the aircraft return to base, the enemy can utilize the airspace just as easily as before the aircraft set up the CAP, so there is no longer superiority in that localized area. Accordingly, the combatant will have to rotate aircraft through the CAP so that there are always fighters on station if they desire persistent superiority. What does persistence look like in the cyberspace domain? After all, if the persistence of superiority in a domain is zero, then there cannot be superiority in that domain. Does the great speed of action in the cyberspace domain result in persistence so short that it makes cyberspace superiority not worth pursuing? After looking at domain superiority theory from the other domains, and sifting through the case study evidence, it is readily apparent that superiority in the cyberspace domain tends to be transitory, unless the fact that they are under attack can be hidden from defenders. However, short cyberspace superiority can be long enough to accomplish a combatant's objectives as shown by the case studies. Looking at the persistence of cyberspace superiority over time brought up the final issue.

To examine the persistence of cyberspace superiority over time, I needed to develop some way of measuring cyberspace superiority. Simply comparing the force structures of the two sides will not tell you definitively who has, or is likely to gain, superiority. If an analyst looked only at the aircraft and systems possessed by Israel and Syria before the Bekaa Valley air campaign of 1982, it would have given no indication of the extremely one-sided air superiority subsequently gained by the Israelis. However, there are useful metrics that combatants routinely utilize to measure air superiority. What percentages of friendly strike aircraft are successfully attacking their targets? How many enemy aircraft are getting through and hitting friendly targets? Which side is losing more aircraft? Often, the indicators will be mixed and hard to read during a campaign. In a few cases, the superiority is obvious, such as when the Iraqis completely ceded the air domain and buried their fighters in the sand to try to preserve them for the future.[24] Generally, measurement of superiority in the cyberspace domain is not so simple.

Measurement of the level of superiority in the cyberspace domain is extremely difficult. The cyberspace domain is less tangible than the physical domains and it is harder to count and compare cyberspace weapons to aircraft, ships, or infantry divisions. However, many of the same concepts will apply. What percentage of friendly cyberspace strikes got through enemy defenses? How successfully are friendly defenses holding off enemy cyberspace attacks? These are the key questions that formed the foundation of a methodology of measuring cyberspace superiority. I settled on a weighted preference analytical model that is presented in

Chapter 5. As with any weighted preference model, the coding methodology is critical and is presented in the appendices.

To lay out the evidence and analysis I start by examining the elements of domain superiority and persistence of superiority from other domains in Chapter 2. I also develop a general model that links universal and local domain superiority and apply it to the land, maritime, and air domains. In Chapter 3, I examine the characteristics of cyberspace to develop the elements of domain superiority as they apply to it. I also apply the general model linking universal and local domain superiority to cyberspace. In Chapter 4, I delve into the details of local cyberspace superiority and build a model of what the key elements are and how they are related to each other. Chapter 5 explains the measurement methodology that I apply to analyze the case studies in Chapter 6. Having demonstrated how cyberspace superiority contributes to military operations, the final chapter will summarize what was learned by this analysis of cyberspace superiority. I will start by examining what elements of domain superiority I can pull from the other physical domains.

Notes

1 Trevor Mogg, "Smart Toilet Security Flaw Could Result in Nasty Surprise," *Fox News*, 5 August 2013. www.foxnews.com/tech/2013/08/05/smart-toilet-security-flaw
2 Andy Greenberg, "Hackers Reveal Nasty New Car Attacks—With Me Behind the Wheel (Video)," *Forbes*, 24 July 2013. www.forbes.com/sites/andygreenberg/2013/07/24/hackers-reveal-nasty-new-car-attacks-with-me-behind-the-wheel-video
3 Gregory J. Rattray, "An Environmental Approach to Understanding Cyberpower," in *Cyberpower and National Security*, ed. Franklin D. Kramer, Stuart H. Starr and Larry K. Wentz (Washington, DC: Potomac Books, 2009), 255.
4 Martin C. Libicki, "Cyberspace Is Not a Warfighting Domain," *I/S: A Journal of Law and Policy for the Information Society*, Vol 8:2 (2012): 328.
5 Carl von Clausewitz, *On War*, ed. and trans. by Michael Howard and Peter Paret (Princeton, NJ: Princeton University Press, 1976), 75.
6 Thomas Rid, *Cyber War Will Not Take Place* (Amazon: Oxford University Press, 2013), Kindle Location 144.
7 Rid, Cyber War Will Not Take Place, Kindle Location 194.
8 Rid is dismissive of this possibility as he assumes, "it is very unlikely that such an attack could succeed against a more complex armed military drone in the field." Thomas Rid, *Cyber War Will Not Take Place* (Amazon: Oxford University Press, 2013), Kindle Location 441. Given the government and military services' record so far in cyberspace security, to assume that no enemy could possibly penetrate military cyberspace defenses on an armed drone, seems unwise.
9 Chris C. Demchak, *Wars of Disruption and Resilience* (Athens: The University of Georgia Press, 2011), 176.
10 Joint Chiefs of Staff, Joint Operations, Vol. 3–13, *Information Operations*, 2012, II–9.
11 Martin C. Libicki, "Cyberspace Is Not a Warfighting Domain," *I/S: A Journal of Law and Policy for the Information Society*, Vol 8:2 (2012): 323–324. In the same article, Libicki discusses how some of the connections are "intermittent and asynchronous" and gives examples such as Natanz or DoD's SIPRNET. Libicki thus extends his definition of the Internet to cover many systems not directly part of the normal Internet. The problem with using this approach is that the nuance is often lost on less careful readers and there are still connected computing systems that never connect to the Internet but are part of cyberspace.

12 Michael W. Wynne, "Flying and Fighting in Cyberspace," *Air Space Power Journal*, Volume 21, no. 1 (2007): 6.
13 Thomas David McCarthy, "Traveling Domain Theory: A Comparative Approach for Cyberspace Theory Development" (PhD diss., Fletcher School of Law and Diplomacy, 2012), 56.
14 Sean C. Butler, "Refocusing Cyber Warfare Thought," *Air Space Power Journal* Volume 27, no. 1 (January–February 2013): 50.
15 There are numerous definitions of cyberspace, Daniel Kuehl gives fourteen in a single article in Daniel T. Kuehl, "From Cyberspace to Cyberpower: Defining the Problem." in *Cyberpower and National Security*, ed. Franklin D. Kramer, Stuart H. Starr and Larry K. Wentz (Washington, DC: Potomac Books, 2009), 26–27. What is common across the majority of the definitions is the idea of communication via connected computing devices. I use the Joint Staff definition as it is well known and I find it to be among the most complete without overreaching into the electromagnetic spectrum.
16 Air Force Doctrine Document (AFDD) 3–12, *Cyberspace Operations. Change 1*, 15 July 2010, ii.
17 AFDD 3–12, *Cyberspace Operations. Change 1*, 2.
18 AFDD 3–12, *Cyberspace Operations. Change 1*, 2.
19 Martin C. Libicki, *Cyberdeterrence and Cyberwar* (Santa Monica: RAND Corporation, 2009), 141.
20 William A. Owens, Kenneth W. Dam, and Herbert S. Lin, eds. *Technology, Policy, Law, and Ethics Regarding U.S. Acquisition and Use of Cyberattack Capabilities* (Washington, DC: National Academies Press, 2009), 39.
21 Jeffrey Carr, *Inside Cyber Warfare: Mapping the Cyber Underworld* (Beijing: O'Reilly Media, 2011), Kindle location 4089, chap. 11.
22 David J. Lonsdale, *The Nature of War in the Information Age* (London: Frank Cass, 2004), 184.
23 Colin S. Gray, *Modern Strategy* (Oxford: Oxford University Press, 1999), 209.
24 In the first Gulf War the Iraqis flew a number of aircraft to Iran for safekeeping. The Iranians subsequently refused to return them and they were lost to the Iraqis anyway. In the second Gulf War the Iraqis tried to preserve some of their aircraft by burying them to be dug up later, but as the war resulted in the collapse of Saddam's regime, that attempt proved useless as well.

Bibliography

Air Force Doctrine Document (AFDD) 3–12, *Cyberspace Operations*, Change 1. 30 November 2011.

Butler, Sean C. "Refocusing Cyber Warfare Thought." *Air Space Power Journal*, Volume 27, no. 1 (2013): 44–57.

Carr, Jeffrey. *Inside Cyber Warfare: Mapping the Cyber Underworld.* Beijing: O'Reilly Media, 2011. Kindle edition.

Clausewitz, Carl von. *On War.* Edited and Translated by Michael Howard and Peter Paret. Princeton, NJ: Princeton University Press, 1976.

Demchak, Chris C. *Wars of Disruption and Resilience.* Athens: The University of Georgia Press, 2011.

Gray, Colin S. *Modern Strategy*. Oxford: Oxford University Press, 1999.

Greenberg, Andy. "Hackers Reveal Nasty New Car Attacks—With Me Behind the Wheel (Video)." *Forbes*, 24 July 2013. www.forbes.com/sites/andygreenberg/2013/07/24/hackers-reveal-nasty-new-car-attacks-with-me-behind-the-wheel-video

Kuehl, Daniel T. "From Cyberspace to Cyberpower: Defining the Problem." In *Cyberpower and National Security*, edited by Franklin D. Kramer, Stuart H. Starr and Larry K. Wentz, 24–42. Washington, DC: Potomac Books, 2009.

Libicki, Martin C. *Cyberdeterrence and Cyberwar.* Santa Monica: RAND Corporation, 2009.
Libicki, Martin C. "Cyberspace Is Not a Warfighting Domain." *I/S: A Journal of Law and Policy for the Information Society*, Vol 8:2 2012, 321–336
Lonsdale, David J. *The Nature of War in the Information Age.* London: Frank Cass, 2004.
McCarthy, Thomas David. "Traveling Domain Theory: A Comparative Approach for Cyberspace Theory Development." PhD Dissertation, Fletcher School of Law and Diplomacy, 2012.
Mogg, Trevor. "Smart Toilet Security Flaw Could Result in Nasty Surprise." *Fox News*, 5 August 2013. www.foxnews.com/tech/2013/08/05/smart-toilet-security-flaw
Owens, William A., Kenneth W. Dam, and Herbert S. Lin, eds. Technology, *Policy, Law, and Ethics Regarding U.S. Acquisition and Use of Cyberattack Capabilities.* Edited by National Research Council. Washington, DC: National Academies Press, 2009.
Rattray, Gregory J. "An Environmental Approach to Understanding Cyberpower." In *Cyberpower and National Security*, edited by Franklin D. Kramer, Stuart H. Starr and Larry K. Wentz, 253–274. Washington, DC: Potomac Books, 2009.
Rid, Thomas. *Cyber War Will Not Take Place.* Amazon: Oxford University Press, 2013. Kindle edition.
U.S. Department of Defense, Joint Chiefs of Staff. Joint Operations. Vol. 3–13, *Information Operations.* Washington, DC: U.S. Government Printing Office, 2012.
Wynne, Michael W. "Flying and Fighting in Cyberspace." *Air Space Power Journal,* Volume 21, no. 1 (2007): 5–9.

2 Elements of Domain Superiority from the Other Domains

Examining other domains of warfare will yield critical concepts and elements that I can apply to the cyberspace domain. An idea of how cyberspace superiority operates does not have to start *ex nihilo*, from nothing; it should leverage the large body of work that analysts have already developed in other domains. I can pull out elements from the work of theorists in other domains to determine what elements should likely be included when examining domain superiority in the cyberspace domain. I can do this for concepts of how superiority in the domain operates, and for how it is measured. First, I will define what a domain is, and which ones I will examine in detail in this study.

For this project, a domain is a distinctive sphere of operations bounded by unique characteristics. There are many definitions of the term "domain." Thomas McCarthy identified ten in a single dictionary but narrowed the list to the three most applicable, including:

1 A region distinctively marked by some distinctive feature.
2 A sphere of knowledge, influence, or activity.
3 A territory over which dominion is exercised.[1]

All three of these apply to the traditionally recognized domains in warfare of land, maritime, air, space, and now cyberspace. Combatants have long fought over all of these domains.

Each of the domains has been the focus of struggles for control. Since the dawn of time, men fought for control of the land domain. As soon as men took to the water, they fought for control of that domain as well. The Egyptians, Minoans and Mycenaeans were building warships to contest the maritime domain in 1500 BCE[2] It was not long after the first powered flight that the Europeans fought for superiority in the air domain during World War I. The struggle in the space domain has taken a unique form, due to the characteristics of that domain, but there are no shortages of ideas and programs to seek domain superiority in space as well. One thing that has been common across these domains is that military forces have sought domain superiority in all of them.

Military forces tend to seek to dominate their domain before they attempt to affect other domains. This tendency is perfectly natural as forces focused on a specific domain such as land, maritime, or air spend most of their time thinking about and operating in that domain. Maritime and air forces generally see establishing control of their domain as a prerequisite to accomplishing other cross-domain missions, while land forces tend to see their domain as having primacy over all the others. Who is right in the continuing debates over missions is not relevant to this discussion; each domain-specific warfighter is correct that they cannot operate effectively without some control over their domain and, thus, cannot provide anything to other domains before establishing enough superiority in their own domain to operate. McCarthy looked at superiority across multiple domains and multiple theorists to determine that, "*The pursuit of domain control is the primary function of domain-centric forces.*"[3] Accordingly, I will examine those domain control theories to determine their relevance to cyberspace superiority.

Although I will examine domain superiority theories from the land, maritime, and air domains, I will not examine space superiority theory for two reasons. First, the space domain is immature and there has not been enough conflict to clarify the lessons on superiority from that domain. Second, there is no accepted theory of how the space domain operates as a medium of war. Each of the U.S. service war colleges study Clausewitz, Sun Tzu, Jomini, and others from the land domain, A.T. Mahan and Julian Corbett in the maritime domain, and Giulio Douhet and Billy Mitchell in the air domain. There are no space theorists with comparable, widely accepted theoretical works. Accordingly, I will focus on examining the other three domains.

To organize the discussion of the land, maritime, and air domains, I will examine six categories in each domain. The overall purpose of this examination is to determine what elements of domain control in each of the three physical domains might apply to the cyberspace domain. First, I will examine the physical rules, geography, and distinguishing characteristics of the domain. Next, I will examine whether theorists consider the offensive or defensive to have the advantage in the domain. After examining the balance between offense and defense in each domain, I will turn to the third area of how a combatant gains superiority in that domain. The fourth element is how a combatant can utilize superiority in the domain once gained, and the fifth is whether a combatant can expect superiority to be persistent or temporary in that domain. Finally, I will examine what measurement concepts analysts have utilized in the domain. However, before turning to the specific domains it will be helpful to examine a generic model of gaining and utilizing domain superiority.

I can build a model of generic domain superiority by starting with the interaction between universal and local superiority. Recalling that domain superiority is the ability of a combatant to conduct operations without prohibitive interference, a combatant will experience this superiority at the local level. I define local as within a given unit's area of influence, which will of course vary widely depending on the domain and type of unit. For example, a strategic surface to air missile (SAM) system may influence an area covering hundreds of square miles, while a rifle company will have a much smaller area of influence. Beyond the differences extant in different unit's capabilities, theorists in the domains I will discuss have

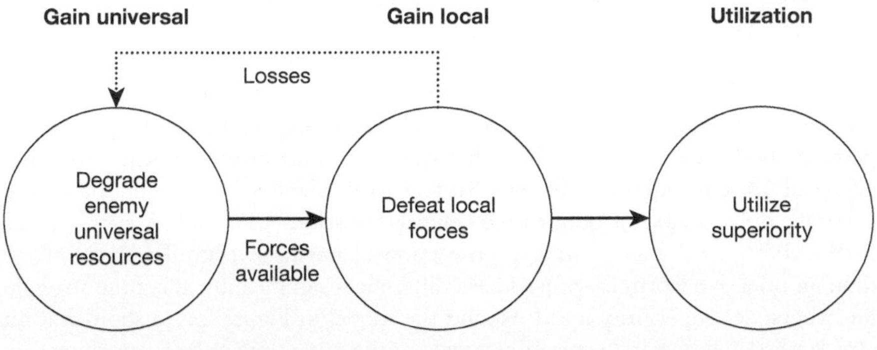

Figure 2.1 General Model of Gaining and Utilizing Domain Superiority
Source: *Author's original work*

had differing opinions on whether domain superiority in their domain was local or universal.

I posit that a combatant will experience domain superiority at the local level, but that the forces available to contest superiority will be determined at the universal level. For example, if nation A has 100 multi-role fighters and nation B has only 10, it is sensible to assume that at the universal level nation A has a reasonable level of air superiority. However, if one of nation A's fighter pilots finds themself alone in the same piece of sky as eight of nation B's fighters, it is unlikely that universal superiority will matter much in determining whether the lone nation A pilot is going to experience "prohibitive interference." As such, my general model of gaining and utilizing domain superiority is shown in Figure 2.1.

As the model indicates, there is an interaction between the universal and local levels. The universal level determines what pool of resources is available to produce local forces; any losses at the local level affect the pool of universal resources. Depending on the domain, resources may not be able to move easily from one local area to another. Once local forces have been defeated sufficiently, a combatant can then utilize the superiority gained in order to accomplish objectives designed to move the combatant closer to their desired goal or end state. The characteristics and current technology of each domain will alter the details of this general model, which lays out domain superiority from the perspective of only one combatant.

This first model only captures the process of gaining and utilizing domain superiority for one combatant; the enemy is also attempting to gain domain superiority at the same time. The enemy's attempt to gain superiority may mirror what a combatant is trying to do, or may be very different if the enemy has a different end state or a different method of connecting their means, ways, and ends. This first model will also change in the different domains based on their characteristics. One factor that this model needs to account for in the different domains is the distinction between the offensive and defensive sides of domain superiority that domains exhibit in varying degrees.

Differences between the offensive and defensive sides of the struggle for domain superiority will be particularly important with the air and cyberspace domains as they have the greatest amount of dissimilarity between offensive and defensive forces. An infantryman, tank, destroyer or submarine all can easily execute either offensive or defensive missions. In the air domain, only multi-role fighters easily perform both types of missions, while bombers and cruise missiles can only effectively execute offensive missions. Surface to air missiles, on the other hand, are generally only capable of performing defensive missions.[4] This split is even greater in the cyberspace domain, with a defensive firewall having a very different character than an offensive worm or virus. These differences significantly affect the struggle for cyberspace superiority and I expand the model in Figure 2.2 to show that an attacker is defending against enemy attacks at the same time as he is attacking.

The different characteristics of the various domains will cause this model to change somewhat for each domain. First, in some domains, the forces used for offensive and defensive actions are the same, and so the offensive and defensive circles under gaining universal superiority collapse back down to a single circle as in Figure 2.1. In the land and maritime domains, there is so much overlap that they will collapse completely, while in the air domain there will be some, but not complete, overlap. In the cyberspace domain, there will be no overlap as defensive and offensive weapons are completely different. However, there can be overlap in the use of superiority on the far right of Figure 2.2.

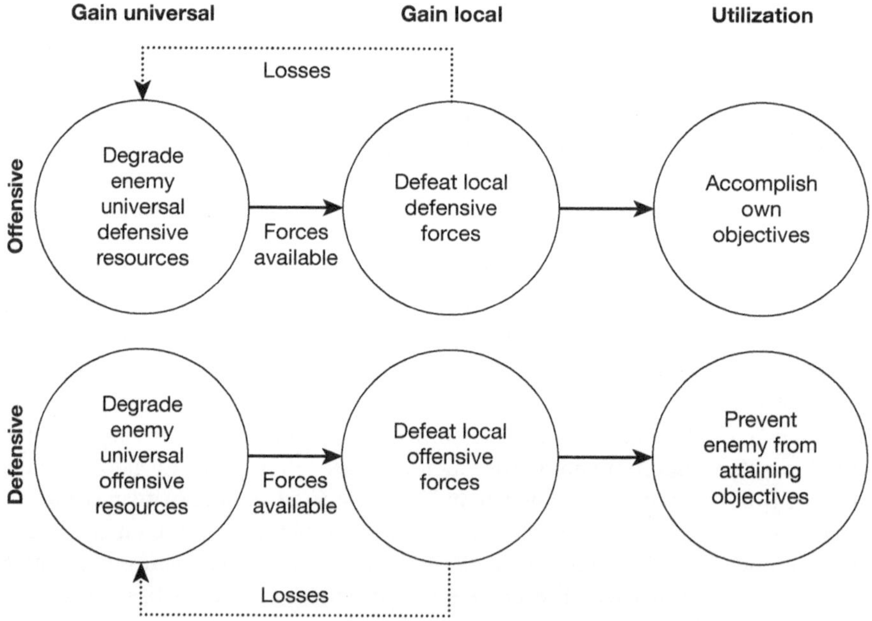

Figure 2.2 Generic Model of Domain Superiority Split into Offensive and Defensive
Source: *Author's original work*

Changes in the characteristics of the domains can also alter the amount of overlap between the offensive and defensive in utilization of domain superiority. The land and maritime domains exhibit this case as both the attacker and defender are trying to control terrain or sea lines of communication. In the air and cyberspace domains, combatants utilize offensive and defensive superiority in substantially different ways, as I will discuss in the sections on gaining superiority in those domains. Beyond the amount of overlap in utilization of forces and superiority, I will also capture the relative importance of universal and local domain superiority.

The final area of significant difference between the domains is in how important the universal and local levels are in gaining domain superiority. In the subsequent figures specific to the domains, I will illustrate this difference by the size of the universal and local circles. I determine the size by three factors. The first is how easy it is to move forces in the domain from one local area to another, the second is how much overlap there is between offensive and defensive forces, and the third is the vulnerability of those forces to attack or degradation. As an extreme example, consider a theoretical domain where a combatant could move forces instantaneously to any local area, any force element could accomplish offensive or defensive missions equally well, and forces were easy to attack at the universal level. In this case, the universal level would completely dominate and the local level would be unimportant. If, on the other hand, there was no ability to move forces from one local area to another, offensive and defensive forces were not interchangeable, and universal forces were extremely difficult to attack until they became involved in local engagements, then the local level of superiority would dominate. None of the domains are at either extreme, but they exhibit wide variation with the maritime domain being the most universal, and the cyberspace domain being the most local. Now that I have established a generic model of how a combatant can gain and utilize domain superiority, I will apply it to the land, maritime, and air domains within a broader discussion of their characteristics. I will start by examining the land domain.

Land Domain

Geography and Characteristics of the Land Domain

The land domain is the one most unlike cyberspace. It is physical, tangible, and the easiest to grasp intuitively. The most important element of superiority in the land domain is control of the land itself and the resource extraction capabilities that control brings, which combatants most often implement with "boots on the ground." The cyberspace domain is radically different in each of these areas, however, there are common elements that make it worthwhile to consider the land domain before moving onto some of the more similar domains such as maritime or air. Some of these commonalities include the interface between the local and universal levels of superiority, as well as the interaction between combatants, as they each strive to defeat the other. The differences between the land and cyberspace domains are significant enough that it is uncommon for theorists to think in terms of land superiority at all.

It is rare to hear a discussion of "land superiority" or even "control of the land domain." Instead, land theorists have historically focused on winning battles and wars, which usually also gave control of the land or "land superiority." Since combat in the land domain came first, there is also a tendency, especially acute in earlier authors, to consider land combat as the totality, or at least the principal point of warfare. This narrow view is very natural given the geography of the land domain.

Land domain combatants have a very specific view of control circumscribed by their geography. Naval officer and strategist J.C. Wylie noted that, "Where the sailor or airman think in terms of an entire world, the soldier at work thinks in terms of theaters, in terms of campaigns, or in terms of battles."[5] The boundaries of a soldier's world are the physical realities of his environment. Mountains, rivers, hills, and forests shape his world and dramatically affect the struggle for superiority on land. In addition, these features greatly influence which forces have the greatest efficacy.

The geographical features in the land domain determine which forces are most effective in a specific area. For example, in classical Greek warfare, heavy infantry hoplites ruled supreme on flat unbroken terrain, but hoplites could not compete with missile troops in mountainous or heavily wooded terrain such as on the island of Sphacteria where a large number of Spartan hoplites were unexpectedly defeated.[6] This advantage of light over heavy forces when they are in mountainous or urban terrain is still true today where light infantry has significant advantages over armored forces. Conversely, in the open, the advantage goes to the heavy armor force. The geographical features in the land domain also influence how land forces look at achieving objectives.

Land forces are reliant on protecting their lines of communication and supply, which normally forces them to take a sequential approach to achieving objectives. For example, if a combatant wanted to occupy the enemy capital, he would have to deal with each of the obstacles in front of him sequentially. The attacker has to cross the river in front of him, defeat the army defending the capital, then seize the city. A combatant must complete each of those steps in order; attempting to jump straight to laying siege to the city without defeating the enemy army would open the attacker up to an assault from the rear and the loss of his supply lines. These characteristics of the land domain also affect whether the offense or defense has primacy within the domain.

Offensive or Defensive Primacy in the Land Domain

As noted by Gray, the advantage for offense or defense in a domain is dependent upon the "tactical–technical logic" of that domain.[7] As technology and tactics change over time, the advantage for the offense or defense can also change over time in a given domain. The advantage can shift due to technological developments such as when the invention of rapid firing breech loading rifles shifted the advantage in land warfare toward the defensive. Sometimes, tactical innovations are required before the technical innovations have major impact. For example, the invention of the tank did not completely change warfare until the Germans connected it to the tactical innovations of *Blitzkrieg*.[8] The current state of the tactical–technical logic of the land domain gives the advantage to the defender.

In the modern era of land warfare, it has normally been the case that the defender has had the advantage if the forces were roughly comparable. Thus, it has become almost a military truism that attackers should have a three-to-one advantage over defenders if they are to be successful. Gray explains the advantage of the defensive in land warfare by noting that on land, the attacking side has to expose itself to move forward and attack, while the defender can remain hidden or under cover while firing on the attacking force.[9] Although it is possible that the general ability of a defending force to hide more effectively than an attacking force could change with improved sensors, given the current state of technology it seems unlikely.[10] With present technology and tactics, the defense has an advantage in land combat that an attacker has to overcome before gaining superiority.

Method of Gaining Land Superiority

Physical presence with forces in a local area of the domain is the key to establishing superiority in the land domain. Wylie gave one of the simplest and most compelling concepts of land control or superiority when he said, "*The ultimate determinant in war is the man on the scene with a gun*. This man is the final power in war. He is control."[11] Infantry or police forces, which have heavier firepower on call as needed, have most often established this control. The larger and more important issue is how an attacker can get possession of the contested terrain in the first place.

The most common way of establishing control over terrain throughout history has been to defeat the enemy army in battle. Strategic theorist Carl von Clausewitz expected that defeating the enemy army would normally be a prerequisite for control and saw control of terrain as a consequence of that victory. Only in unusual cases did he expect that a force should occupy land before defeating the enemy army.[12] Most campaigns from antiquity to Operation IRAQI FREEDOM follow this model where a combatant neutralizes enemy ground forces first, then occupies and controls territory. One of the reasons this pattern seems to hold is the advantage a concentrated force has over a dispersed force. A concentrated force can bring all of its combat power to focus on a single point, whereas a dispersed force can only utilize a fraction of its power at any one location. However, a force cannot always remain concentrated because to control terrain effectively, the force must usually disperse. Therefore, land forces normally stay concentrated until the enemy army has been defeated, then disperse to control terrain. In addition, defeat of the enemy army will not always be required as an undefeated enemy army may withdraw and cede land superiority over an area.

Another way to gain control over terrain is for the enemy to choose to give you that control through some sort of settlement. Clausewitz did not state that battle was the only possible way to gain your objectives; he identified that occupying a "lightly held or undefended province," or changing the political environment by gaining new allies or disrupting the enemy's alliances can serve as a "short cut on the road to peace."[13] If the objective of the war was to gain territory, there is still need for Wylie's "man on the scene with a gun," but that man may be a police officer instead of an infantryman if the enemy agrees to surrender the territory without a major battle. Wylie summed it up well when he said,

> As we have noted before, it may well be necessary to defeat the enemy army. It may even be necessary to defeat it to the last remnant. But if we always saddle ourselves with the self-imposed restriction that we must, no matter what, defeat the enemy army in combat, then we have indeed denied to ourselves consideration of a vast span of actions that might more readily and easily achieve the needed measure of control.[14]

Even if a combatant has won the battle or achieved a settlement, there may be a second step to achieve the "needed measure of control."

A signed peace treaty or a battle won may not be sufficient to establish meaningful control over territory if the population does not accept that control. If a combatant intends to establish land domain superiority in an area that previously belonged to the enemy, destroying or disrupting the enemy army, or forcing a settlement is often only the first step. Step one of destroying the enemy army gives a combatant physical access to the terrain where he can start step two of gaining population acceptance of that control. Lonsdale has highlighted the importance in land superiority of getting the "man on the scene with a gun" in place to start the struggle for the population. The criticality of the soldier or police officer is that only he can "provide prolonged, durable presence and exert control over the key issue, whether that be a population or some other resource."[15] The recent wars in Iraq and Afghanistan have once again clarified that physical access to the terrain is only the precondition for the fight to gain the acceptance of the population, and does not represent "mission accomplished." These concepts require some modification to the generic model of how to gain superiority.

In the land domain, there is not a clear difference between offensive and defensive forces as there is in the air or cyberspace domains. As a result, the universal forces under offensive and defensive collapse together, as they are generally the same forces whether a combatant assigns them offensive or defensive missions. The offensive and defensive split is still evident in local superiority as local forces are a smaller subset of the universal pool of forces that are not simultaneously attacking and defending in a local area. Losses at the local level feedback into the overall universal force whether the local force was on the defensive or offensive. One area where the land domain superiority model aligns with the generic model is in the equal weighting of local and universal superiority.

In the land domain, both the universal and local levels of superiority are important and receive equal weight in the model. This equivalence partially results because a combatant can use the same forces for offense and defense, which increases the importance of the universal level. However, strategic mobility can be slow in the land domain and it can take a long time to move ground forces from one

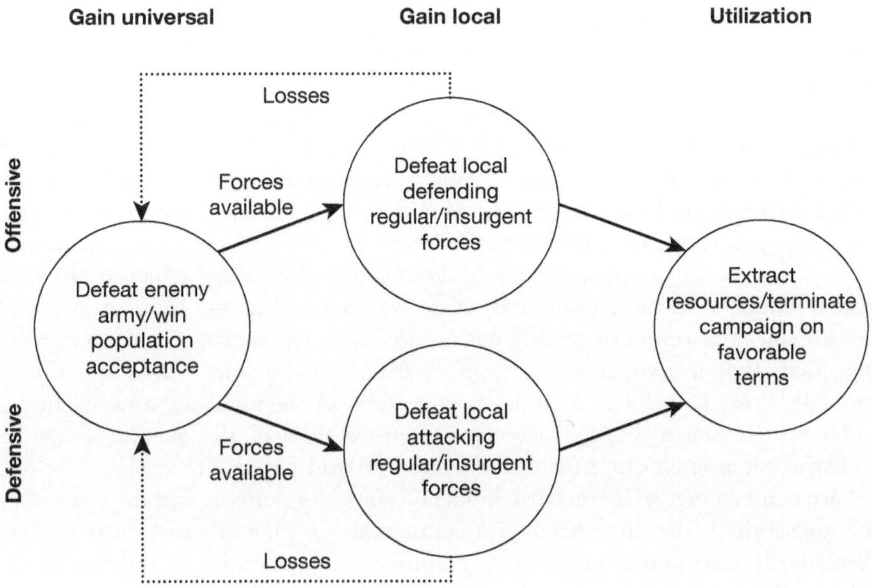

Figure 2.3 Model of Gaining and Utilizing Land Superiority

Source: *Author's original work*

local area to another, which increases the importance of the local level. In addition, land forces tend to be equally vulnerable at the local and universal levels as a combatant can more easily disperse and hide forces than in the other domains. Finally, a nation generally has far more tanks and artillery pieces than ships and aircraft so the loss of a few systems in the land domain normally does not have the same impact of losing the same number of ships or aircraft. The equal balance between the universal and local levels in the land domain is very unlike the cyberspace domain where the local level is dominant in cyberspace superiority. Figure 2.3 shows the modified model of gaining and utilizing land domain superiority.

Gaining land superiority will be very different from gaining cyberspace superiority. At the universal and local level of land superiority, defeat of conventional forces is a prerequisite for land superiority, but a combatant will not be able firmly to establish superiority or control over an area until the local population accepts it. There is no equivalent to population acceptance in cyberspace. In the land domain, universal and local superiority are important; in the cyberspace domain, the local level is dominant. When a combatant in the land domain has achieved defeat of enemy forces and the acquiescence of the population, they can exploit that victory.

Use of Land Domain Superiority

Once a combatant establishes superiority in the land domain to include the acceptance of the situation by the population, he can normally dictate terms to the enemy or, if the overall conflict continues in other theaters, a combatant can utilize the local area where the combatant has superiority to produce additional resources. These resources can include raw materials, finished goods or weapons, or even soldiers. A combatant can use the resources from the land domain to generate power in the other domains. Unlike other domains, such as maritime or air, where control of the domain is principally of value as a way to influence the other domains, on the land, control is about affecting the enemy center of gravity. According to Wylie, the primary aim of the strategist is to exert some degree of control over the enemy, which a combatant normally achieves through manipulation of the center of gravity of the war to the advantage of the strategist.[16] Historically, this center of gravity has most often been control of territory or the resources that a combatant can extract from that territory. Land superiority provides both. Control of territory is important for the attacking and defending sides, which causes the defensive and offensive sides of the generic model to collapse into a single circle for the utilization of land superiority.

A second change to the generic model of land superiority is that the utilization of superiority is the same whether a combatant is on the offensive or defensive. Both the attacker and defender are attempting to extract resources and control the terrain. The situation is quite different in the cyberspace domain where both sides are trying to accomplish different objectives in an attack. When a land force is contesting an area, such as the Germans and Soviets contesting for Ukraine in World War II, they are normally both seeking similar things. In the Ukraine case, both sides wanted the grain and other extractable resources from Ukraine, and the opportunities for further offensives offered by the geographic position of Ukraine. In cyberspace, the attacker is normally trying to disrupt while the defender is trying to protect. However, nation A's success in attacking does not imply any success in defending; both combatants could be equally, or differently, successful or unsuccessful. Thus, in cyberspace, I separate the utilization of superiority into offensive and defensive aspects, unlike the land domain where I combined them in the model. That said, once a combatant has established land superiority, it will tend to be more persistent than is common in the other domains.

Persistence of Land Domain Superiority

Land domain superiority tends to be persistent due to greater influence of the universal level of superiority as well as the sequential tendencies of land combat, the inertia of populations whose support changes slowly, and the current primacy of the defensive.

The larger influence of the universal level of superiority in the land domain is the first factor producing greater persistence for land superiority. The combination of the ability of most land forces to perform offensive and defensive missions, as well as to shift rapidly from one local area to another through modern transportation, normally means that combatants cannot just overcome a small subset of enemy forces to establish land superiority in a local area. A combatant in the land domain who is attempting to wrest superiority in an area from the enemy must not only defeat the enemy defensive forces there before the attack, but also block the transfer of the reinforcements the enemy rushes to the scene who may have been performing offensive or defensive missions elsewhere. This ability to reinforce is not common in the cyberspace domain. If an attacker in cyberspace overcomes the defenses on one system, the defender cannot simply move defenses from a different system, and cannot utilize offensive weapons as defenses on the system under attack. The importance of the universal level of superiority is one reason the persistence of superiority in the land domain tends to be much longer than in the cyberspace domain.

The second factor is the sequential characteristic of land combat, which has tended to slow the pace of change of who has superiority in a given area. The geographic bounding of the land domain normally restricts changes in superiority to small areas. Taking a fortress only yields superiority in the area formerly controlled by that fortress and crossing one river opens up only the land area to the next geographic feature or defensive position. It is also difficult for a combatant who experiences a string of defeats to reverse the trend. The sequential characteristic of land combat does not only apply to geography, but also to time. The defeated side normally loses more resources than the winning side, although there are exceptions. Therefore, the side that was defeated last time is more likely to be defeated next time. The sequential characteristic of land combat contributes to the persistence of land superiority, which the inertia of populations further reinforces.

Populations link their political loyalty to language, culture, and identity, and this loyalty is extremely difficult to change, which is the third factor increasing the persistence of land superiority. Conquerors are often surprised at how difficult it is to substantially change the loyalty of a population. For example, after 70 years of varying levels of ruthless subjugation, non-Russian Soviet states immediately reasserted their national identities and loyalties. Even after generations of heavy-handed attempts to eradicate their languages and change their cultures, the Soviets had still failed to subordinate their population's national consciousness and loyalties to the model of the Soviet "new man." As Americans, we, of course, thought we could do it much better and faster; we attempted to remake Afghan tribal society and loyalties in a few years while failing just as spectacularly as previous invaders. Populations' resistance to change contributes to the persistence of long-term land superiority, and the advantage of the defense affects short-term land superiority.

The current primacy of the defensive is the final factor contributing to the persistence of land superiority, as two equally-matched forces will be able to hold what they have, but will generally be unable to successfully defeat the other force. As I discussed previously in the section on offensive and defensive primacy, the fact that an advancing attacker is normally far more vulnerable than a hidden or entrenched defender creates the primacy of defense in the land domain with current tactics and technology. This factor also contributes to the greater persistence of land superiority as attacking forces will normally have to establish clear superiority before their attacks can be successful and even start the process of changing land superiority in a local area. If an analyst only considers the major wars in the last few decades, this superiority of the defensive may not be immediately obvious as the defenders in Iraq and Afghanistan were quickly defeated. However, the United States had overwhelming superiority in technology, tactics, and even numbers in most battles; and these factors overcame the advantages of the defensive. Measuring how persistent land superiority is will require measuring land superiority in general, and I will turn next to this difficult problem.

Measurement Concepts of Land Domain Superiority

Land superiority consists of territorial control and population acceptance of that control; territorial control by itself is necessary but insufficient without population acceptance. Measuring whose soldiers are standing on a particular piece of terrain is by far the easier task and is how combatants have historically measured land superiority. According to James Clancy and Chuck Crossett, "In the grand movement of military forces, the gaining and control of territory is considered success."[17] From the Napoleonic wars to modern times, staff officers have drawn lines on maps that clearly delineated what areas friendly forces controlled and what areas were enemy controlled. The second part of the equation that planners examine is how many soldiers each side has available to occupy the terrain.

As the universal level of superiority is so important in the land domain, another way to measure land superiority is to examine how many forces each side has on the universal level that a combatant can use to contest superiority at the local level. Clancy and Crossett refer to this traditional metric of success as the order of battle.[18] It is important not just to look at numbers and weapons but tactics and training as well in order to develop a comparison of combat power. A combatant should use the measurement of terrain controlled as well as combat power expressed as an order of battle to develop a sense not only of the current state of land superiority, but also the potential for the future. An example of this principle happened in the early stages of the Korean War when United Nations forces gained dominant land control over the enemy after the Incheon landings. In this case, land superiority was not secure as the Chinese had a large and capable army on the border ready to intervene. Measurements of the territory controlled and forces available are an appropriate way of measuring control during the first stage of the fight to control terrain, but planners need to use a significantly different approach to measure the level of population control.

The precise metrics used to determine population support will vary with the conflict. Clancy and Crossett broadly categorize them as measures of sustainability, legitimacy, and stability.[19] The first area to focus on is the sustainability of the enemy force, which can include the supply of material such as weapons to the enemy. It is important that measurements focus on how much material is getting to the enemy, rather than the amount of material seized by friendly forces, which is far easier to measure. Sustainability metrics also look at the financial backing supporters provide to an insurgent enemy and how that support changes over time, as well as the estimated number of active enemy fighters and supporters. These are very difficult things to measure with accuracy, and analysts have to apply measures appropriate to each specific situation very carefully. It is easy for a combatant to focus too much on sustainability measurements, because the second area of legitimacy is much harder to measure.

The population determines the legitimacy of a government, which can be determined using measures of legitimacy and the effectiveness of those measures. Election results, surveys of the population, and measures of government efficiency and corruption can be helpful here. These metrics will be harder to assign numbers to, as legitimacy is primarily in the eyes of the local population. The United Nations may view a government as being legitimate, but that will matter little to the population if that government is unable to provide basic services, or if it appears to them that a hostile outside power is actually in control. Government legitimacy is important, but without the final category of stability, measures of sustainability or legitimacy may not matter.

The final stability metric attempts to measure the level of security and ability to function of a local society. The security aspect is somewhat easier to measure as most insurgent attacks leave a clear signature that analysts can track over time. Unfortunately, merely counting attacks may not yield a complete picture. If there were 100 attacks last week and only 50 this week, does that represent progress? What if each attack was four times as deadly as the previous week's attacks? What if the reason there were fewer minor attacks is that the enemy is preparing for a major attack? Analysts will have to carefully comb reports for the relevant messy details and not get lulled into presenting simple metrics that look good on a PowerPoint chart. The ability of a society to function can be more difficult to measure and requires developing an understanding of the daily lives of the local people and what types of markets, institutions, and infrastructure they require. Analysts will need to combine security and societal functioning metrics with legitimacy and sustainability metrics to determine who has superiority in the land domain. However, both land domain measures have limited utility in the cyberspace domain.

Order of battle information and metrics on population support do not apply very well to the cyberspace domain. Forces in the cyberspace domain are much harder to compare, as they tend to be unique, as well as extremely difficult to find. In addition, as population support is not an important determinant of cyberspace superiority, sustainability, legitimacy, and security metrics have little applicability. Cyberspace can potentially help to measure population support for the land domain, but these measurement concepts will not apply to the cyberspace domain as readily as will those from the maritime and air domains. Next, we turn from the land domain to the maritime domain, which has very different characteristics.

Maritime Domain

Geography and Characteristics of the Maritime Domain

The maritime domain consists of a bounded maneuver space accessed by technology that is principally important due to the sea lines of communication that carry most of the world's cargo.

The air and land domains bound the maritime domain at its edges. This bounding produces an uneven, normally un-commanded domain with multiple strategic chokepoints as well as large open areas. This complex topography is the first major characteristic of the maritime domain.

The maritime domain started out as a two-dimensional surface, bounded by landmasses, which combatants in the twentieth century expanded to a third dimension with the inclusion of undersea warfare. Technology is required to access the maritime domain much as is the case in the newer air, space, and cyberspace domains. The boundaries between the maritime domain and other domains define the edges of the domain.

The maritime domain, like the land domain, has distinct edges with the other domains; unlike land, the maritime domain produces its most significant effects in the other domains. The defeat and destruction of the Spanish Armada by a storm was most significant because it prevented Imperial Spain from conquering England on the land. The Battle for the Atlantic in World War II was important because it determined whether the United States could keep Great Britain supplied with vital resources required by those living on the land. A nation can deter or compel its enemies by threats to enemy seaborne commerce as the Royal Navy effectively did for many years; however, maritime power has had its greatest impact in projecting power ashore. Since World War II, maritime power, in the form of aircraft carriers, has also been able to project significant power into the air domain. Maritime combatants have projected this power from an area that became the first recognized global common.

Modern international law considers significant portions of the maritime domain as a global common to which all nations have free access.[20] The United Nations Convention on the Law of the Sea (UNCLOS) considers the high seas far from land as a global common, as opposed to territorial waters and economic exclusion zones closer to land. According to Article 87 of the UNCLOS, nations have freedom of navigation as well as other rights on the high seas.[21] This right of non-interference on the high seas is of critical importance to marine commerce, and now many policymakers are attempting to establish the same expectations and norms in cyberspace. However, the movement of information through cyberspace is not completely analogous to the movement of maritime shipping. Individual actors that reside within international borders own all the computing devices and network connections that create cyberspace, unlike the international high seas. Despite the differences in the domains, there is a significant effort underway in international circles to create the structures and norms to treat cyberspace as a global common. Even though lawyers label it a global common, the maritime domain still has numerous chokepoints that constrain maritime lines of communication.

The interaction of the land domain with the maritime domain produces a large number of chokepoints that become important strategic terrain. These chokepoints funnel movement and are a key characteristic of the maritime domain, as they become strategic areas for a combatant to control.[22] We will see a similar dynamic in the cyberspace domain where limited undersea cables or portals into a particular nation can become equivalent strategic chokepoints. The two most prominent theorists of the maritime domain, Mahan and Corbett, focused their work on the importance of controlling lines of communication in the maritime environment. I will weave their differing theories of maritime domain control throughout this section, but first I will discuss Corbett's idea that normally no one has maritime superiority.

Because the seas are so vast, and there are so few ships on them, Corbett maintained that normally no one has maritime superiority.[23] Writing in 1907, a French admiral, Gabriel Darrieus, agreed with Corbett and thought it was "megalomania" to think that real "mastery of the sea" was even possible.[24] The concept that the sea is normally un-commanded by either side will translate well into the cyberspace domain, where private individuals normally own domain elements and domain architecture allows transit virtually at will. This open architecture results in a situation similar to the high seas, where the vast majority of traffic flows without any interference by either side of a conflict. The openness of the maritime domain also has significant impact on whether the offense or defense has superiority.

Offensive or Defensive Primacy in the Maritime Domain

In the maritime domain, neither the offensive or defensive has clear primacy, it depends on the specifics of the engagement. In most land combat, an approaching enemy has to "unmask" and come out into the open to attack. The defending soldiers can continue to hide undercover and can fire effectively on the advancing enemy, which provides much of the defensive advantage. In the maritime domain, however, surface ships are generally "unmasked" whether they are on the offensive or defensive so there is no clear advantage to being on the defensive. Lord Nelson believed in aggressive attack, not because attacking made his ships relatively more powerful, but because he thought that his better-trained and aggressive crews would win in the confused melee after breaking apart the enemy formation. At Jutland, the British fleet was on the strategic defensive and the German fleet was on the strategic offensive, but that meant little at the tactical level. Both fleets could see and fire on one another at roughly the same time, so being on the attack or defense gave no advantage one way or the other. There are other types of maritime combat other than fleet action where there is an advantage for the defense.

In undersea combat, the advantage goes to the one who stays hidden, which gives a benefit to the defense, as it is easier to stay silent and hidden. This situation is analogous to that of an infantry unit who can wait quietly in hidden positions until the enemy advances and becomes vulnerable. Another type of maritime combat that gives an advantage to the defender occurs when the defender can call upon land-based combat power and defenses.

A fleet operating within range of friendly land-based defenses gains a significant advantage. This factor has normally helped the fleet defending its home territory although with aircraft it is possible that the attacking and defending fleets will be within range of each other's airfields. Some of the naval conflict in the English Channel between Germany and Britain during the early stages of World War II illustrates a case where both sides could send land-based aircraft into a disputed maritime area. Historically, the more common situation has been where a defensive fleet sheltered behind minefields, coastal guns, or aircraft in a port. The French fleet in the Napoleonic wars and the German fleet in World War I are two of the most famous examples. A fleet in such a defended position can be very difficult to attack although there are cases such as Taranto and Pearl Harbor where attackers accomplished it successfully using the element of surprise. The case of a fleet in port has interesting parallels in the cyberspace domain.

Cyberspace "fleets" shelter behind cyberspace defenses that cannot take part in offensive operations akin to a maritime fleet defended by port defenses. Mahan saw maritime defenses, such as coastal guns, as protecting and providing a secure base for the maritime offense in the form of the fleet.[25] Cyberspace defenses serve to protect the systems used to develop and field offensive weapons. Cyberspace defenses also protect the "ports" where commerce flows, but the analogy breaks down when it comes to how a combatant gains maritime rather than cyberspace superiority. Maritime weapons, such as ships, can generally engage each other out on the high seas wherever they meet; cyberspace weapons cannot, which makes the gaining of maritime superiority very different from cyberspace superiority.

Method of Gaining Maritime Superiority

Theorists have disagreed on the relative importance of the local or universal level in gaining maritime superiority. For Mahan, the only way to gain maritime superiority was to destroy the enemy's fleet, while Corbett saw other possibilities. According to McCarthy, the central idea of Mahan's thesis was that ensuring access to maritime lines of communication was only possible through the neutralization of the enemy's fleet by your own fleet action.[26]

Corbett had a more complex view and saw additional possibilities. He believed that a combatant could achieve maritime superiority by either destroying the enemy's fleet or by blockading it in port. Corbett also thought that a navy could contest the command of the sea by maintaining a fleet in active service that only gave battle on favorable terms and launched small counter-attacks whenever possible.[27] He thought this strategy was possible because a fleet was nearly impossible to destroy in a well-defended harbor absent a land invasion to seize the port. As we examine Mahan and Corbett's ideas in relation to cyberspace, Corbett's ideas seem more pertinent.

Corbett's methodology for gaining maritime superiority has more applicability to cyberspace superiority than Mahan's concept, as cyberspace "fleets" cannot meet and do battle. Offensive cyberspace weapons are as difficult to attack "in port" as a well-defended fleet, and simple force-on-force battle is impractical in cyberspace, because the weapons cannot normally sense and react to each other as ships at sea can. As a result, cyberspace weapons will go right past each other if they cross in cyberspace, more like cruise missiles en route to targets than ships or fighter aircraft that can fight each other when they meet. This difference between cyberspace and the other domains will be crucial to understanding how to gain superiority in the cyberspace domain. To understand further gaining maritime superiority, it is helpful to break it down into its universal and local components.

In the maritime domain, combatants can more easily contest superiority at the universal level by attacking the enemy's fleet than in the other domains. Destroying the enemy's fleet will significantly affect the resources available to contest superiority at the local level, but normally only if the enemy is willing to cooperate and fight a major fleet battle. Mahan's theory focuses on a major fleet battle and if the enemy fleet is willing to sail out and be defeated, then the winning combatant can disperse his victorious fleet to attack enemy shipping and defend friendly shipping with confidence. What Corbett saw was that the weaker party will often not be willing to sail out to be defeated. Instead, the weaker force can avoid major battle but remain as a threatening "fleet in being" that can retreat to a fortified port if pressed too closely. This action puts the stronger combatant on the horns of a dilemma because if he disperses to attack and defend commerce, the enemy can sally forth and defeat elements of his fleet before he can concentrate. However, if a combatant stays concentrated, he cannot use his maritime superiority to accomplish his other objectives. A weaker combatant can also avoid a universal fleet battle and instead fight a series of small local actions.

A combatant can send out cruisers to attack enemy shipping while avoiding the enemy's stronger battle fleet. This strategy can rob the stronger navy of most of his ability to control the sea lanes and project power because his fleet has to remain constantly ready to fight the weaker navy. Mahan focused on the destruction of the enemy fleet and expected that "command of the sea" would go to the victor of the fleet battle. However, the experience of World War I showed the importance of Corbett's "fleet in being" concept as the mere presence of the German fleet in port forced the British to keep their fleet concentrated in case the German fleet sailed out. In the one case where the German fleet did sail forth, the ensuing battle proved indecisive. However, because the British fleet was still concentrated, it could not focus all its resources on protecting the sea lines of communication under attack by German U-boats, which in this case took the place of Corbett's "cruisers." Despite the utility of a weaker combatant contesting superiority at the local level, the universal level of maritime superiority carries more weight.

In determining superiority in the maritime domain, the universal level is of greater importance than the local level due to a number of factors. First, maritime forces can normally perform offensive or defensive missions, which allow a combatant to use universal forces either way. A destroyer, submarine, or even carrier battle group can attack enemy targets or defend friendly ones with a similar level of efficacy. Second, maritime forces tend to have better strategic mobility than the land or air domains, and can move from one local area to another with greater speed and over longer distances than land forces, while not needing the elaborate, and slow to build, airfields of the air domain. Third, ships are expensive and nations tend only to have a few of them so they represent a more concentrated form of national power than is typical in the land or even air domain. Therefore, destroying or degrading even a handful of ships will more greatly affect the forces a combatant has available to contest local superiority in other areas. All these

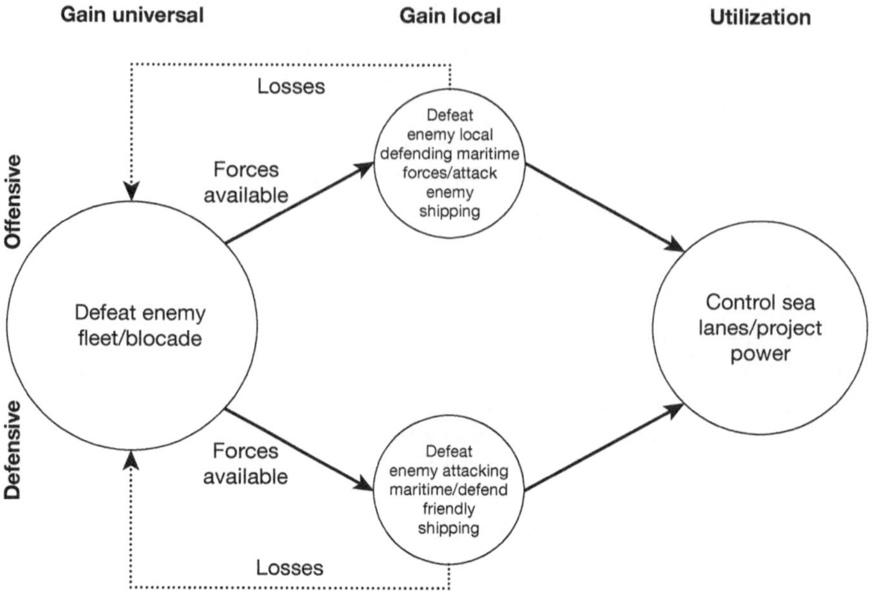

Figure 2.4 Model of Gaining and Utilizing Maritime Superiority
Source: *Author's original work*

factors, combined with the vulnerability of maritime forces at the universal level to attack, contribute to the relatively greater level of importance for universal or local maritime superiority. The modified model of gaining and utilizing maritime superiority is shown in Figure 2.4.

Although the universal level is more significant, it is still possible for a combatant to achieve maritime superiority by focusing on the local level. If defeating the enemy fleet is not an option, there is also a longer and harder road of attritional "war of a thousand cuts." Eventually this strategy can produce a level of universal maritime superiority as the resources available to the enemy continue to shrink if the losses from combat at the local level accumulate faster than the enemy can acquire more forces. Mahan was dismissive of commerce, or local warfare.[28] Corbett, on the other hand, thought a combatant could exercise domain control by using cruisers optimized to seize enemy shipping while avoiding the enemy's main battle fleet and saw utility in blockades.

Corbett also proposed a different way for a combatant to attain some level of universal superiority through blockading the enemy's fleet in port. If a combatant successfully blockades the enemy fleet, then at least some of his lighter units can engage in attacking enemy commerce and protecting friendly shipping. Although Corbett's commerce warfare has parallels in cyberspace, his "fleet in being" as well as Mahan's fleet battles and blockades do not have direct equivalents in cyberspace.

Much of the current combat in cyberspace looks analogous to Corbett's commerce warfare. In Corbett's commerce warfare, attackers would attempt to interfere directly with an enemy's commercial maritime activity, while defenders would attempt to protect their commerce. In cyberspace, most current conflict involves disruption of commerce, theft of information, or attempts by defenders to prevent successful attacks. Just as the principal utility of the maritime domain is moving goods, the principal utility of the cyberspace domain is moving information, which sets up some similar dynamics. One of Corbett's concepts with less applicability to cyberspace is the fleet in being.

Although cyberspace forces are very difficult to attack "in port," they cannot act as a fleet in being, as they cannot force the enemy to divert resources in order to prevent them from sallying forth. In the maritime domain, a fleet in being principally acts to keep the enemy force concentrated so that it cannot engage in commerce warfare. As neither combatant can easily attack the other's cyberspace "fleet," there is no need for forces to remain concentrated and both sides can engage freely in cyberspace warfare in various local areas. Cyberspace forces can potentially act as a deterrent as combatants cannot easily attack them; in this they are no different from any other domain force. What cyberspace forces cannot do is force the enemy to divert resources and remain concentrated to fight a fleet action if the fleet in being sorties out. Combatants also cannot easily blockade cyberspace forces.

The inability of combatants to directly attack or block enemy cyberspace forces also prevents the maritime concept of a blockade from transferring to cyberspace. Cyberspace weapons are stealthy and a combatant can launch them from almost anywhere, so it is extremely difficult to "blockade" them. Even severing an enemy nation's connections to the Internet would not be a sure defense as enemy agents could still easily insert weapons from other locations. In maritime surface warfare and cyberspace, there are some parallels with commerce warfare, however, there are better parallels to cyberspace in undersea warfare.

The situation in cyberspace is analogous to a struggle for maritime superiority undertaken by fleets composed entirely of super-stealthy submarines. One of Mahan's key assumptions was that each fleet could effectively find and attack the other. If each combatant had a fleet consisting of only super-stealthy submarines then they could not effectively find or attack each other's offensive forces, but only attack surface shipping. Then, attacking the enemy fleet or conducting a blockade becomes meaningless and there is no conceivable fleet action to deliver maritime superiority. Both combatants would have to mitigate the damage caused by enemy submarines while attempting to maximize the damage done by their own.

This circumstance parallels the situation in cyberspace where cyberspace offensive weapons cannot find or engage each other. Some attempts to reduce the enemy's offensive capability, such as attacking submarine pens in the maritime realm or bombing a cyberspace operation center, may be worthwhile, but effective opportunities to do damage will be rare. The next question after successfully gaining maritime superiority is what to do with it.

Use of Maritime Superiority

Once a combatant gains maritime superiority, they can protect friendly sea lines of communication and attack those of the enemy while enabling friendly power projection ashore and preventing enemy power projection. Corbett identified the same categories, although he broke it up slightly differently into defense against invasion, attack and defense of commerce, and attack, defense, and support of military expeditions.[29] Maritime superiority enables a combatant to control the sea lanes, which enables friendly shipping while interfering with enemy shipping.[30] Maritime superiority also affects enemy power projection, which Corbett identified as defense against invasion. Power projection ashore is a critical element of maritime superiority.

Although Mahan viewed sea power as being critical to a nation in its own right, Corbett saw the greater importance in the maritime domain as lying in what it could do to influence the land domain.[31] For Corbett, the reason sea lines of communication were so vital was that they enabled the projection of power ashore. Superiority at sea principally mattered because it could provide superiority on the land. Cyberspace is similar to the maritime domain in this respect.

A combatant will feel the most important effects of cyberspace superiority, not in cyberspace, but in the other domains. Disrupting enemy communications matters most if a combatant can use that disruption to attack in other domains. Defending friendly systems enhances the ability of a combatant to generate and utilize power to establish superiority in other domains. As an example, consider the cyberspace systems that support a Combined Air Operations Center (CAOC). The most important effect of disrupting those systems may not be in the cyberspace domain, or even in the air domain. If an enemy disrupted command and control systems in the middle of a major land offensive, the loss of the cyberspace systems could result in the reduction of coordinated close air support over the battle and lead to the loss of the battle in the land domain. All the domains have connections, but cyberspace is the most interconnected as combatants have embedded cyberspace in all the other domains through modern information systems. Turning back to maritime superiority, the next question is how persistent maritime superiority will be once a combatant has attained it.

Persistence of Maritime Domain Superiority

Whether the maritime superiority gained by a combatant is local or universal will greatly affect the persistence of it. If a combatant gains only local superiority, then the enemy can transfer forces from the universal level by moving them into the local area and fighting for superiority again. If a combatant gains a significant level of superiority on the universal level, the enemy has to build, purchase, or get new forces from allies, which will normally take much longer than merely moving forces from one area to another. This ability to reinforce from other areas is especially important in the maritime domain, where strategic mobility is usually very good. However, just because a combatant loses overall universal domain superiority, it does not follow that he will lose local superiority in every local area. The losing combatant may concentrate his remaining forces in a different area than his adversary and still attain superiority in that local area. In the maritime domain, Mahan and Corbett disagreed on whether maritime superiority tended to be persistent or not, largely because they differed on how universal or local it was.

According to Mahan, who focused on universal maritime superiority, superiority should be persistent, based on major fleet actions that would affect universal superiority. Much like the battle of armies on the land, if a combatant fights and wins a major fleet action it will provide some measure of persistent superiority, as it is hard for the enemy to win the next battle with diminished resources. Corbett questioned Mahan's idea of stable overall command of the seas and asked about an enemy who chooses not to fight a fleet action.

If the enemy refuses to fight a major fleet action for universal control, then control will not only be localized, but also fleeting, as the enemy can dash out of port to raid convoys and establish local control in an area, then retreat back into port when threatened by the main adversary fleet. The French fleet used this strategy during much of the Napoleonic wars. The British attempted to blockade the French fleet in port, but they could not stop a steady stream of French cruisers from slipping through the blockade to raid British merchant shipping, as the French established local maritime superiority in their operating areas. Also, the British had not established universal superiority as the French fleet was still formidable, and the French could contest local superiority in the area of the blockade at any time by sailing out. The British were unable to establish stable maritime superiority until they had largely destroyed the French fleet at Trafalgar. Unfortunately for cyberspace operators, the inability of cyberspace forces to fight the equivalent of a fleet battle suggests that the persistence of superiority will be limited in the cyberspace domain.

Because cyberspace forces cannot engage each other in fleet actions and normally have to contest superiority at only the local level, the linkage in the maritime domain between persistence and universal superiority suggests that cyberspace superiority will have a short duration. The speeds at which combatants can develop weapons in the maritime and cyberspace domains also suggest a short duration for cyberspace superiority. In the maritime domain, where producing a major combatant takes years, universal domain superiority can be persistent. However, in the cyberspace domain, even if a combatant achieves a high level of domain superiority, the enemy could develop, or purchase from an ally, an entirely new set of weapons or defenses within weeks or months. This difference between the maritime and cyberspace domains further suggests that cyberspace superiority will be fleeting. The final area of maritime superiority to examine is how analysts have measured it over time to determine whether there are elements of measurement that may be applicable to cyberspace.

Measurement Concepts of Maritime Superiority

Traditional measures of maritime superiority include the balance of forces between the two fleets, metrics to measure the openness of sea lines of communication, and the ability of combatants to project power from the maritime environment into other domains.[32] The balance of forces can include the total number of ships, the type of ships, and tonnage or combined weight of ships. Analysts should use these numbers with care, as the material aspects of a navy are only part of the story. During the Napoleonic wars, the British routinely outfought opponents who had heavier, faster, and better armed ships because the British had better morale and training. As noted earlier, the balance of forces is only theoretical until a combatant induces the enemy to come out and fight.

The balance of forces will only produce equivalent maritime superiority if combatants are both fully utilizing their forces. If one fleet stays in port, the one out on the high seas will have the greater measure of maritime superiority in that local area. That local superiority may be transitory and persist only until the enemy fleet comes out of port to contest it. Mahan focused his measurement of maritime superiority on the balance of forces between the two fleets. If the combatant had fought and won the fleet battle, then he had established maritime superiority, although Mahan did recognize maritime superiority did not imply that enemy ships could not operate at all.[33] Comparing maritime forces is only part of measuring maritime superiority; analysts must also consider the health of sea lines of communication.

There are numerous ways to measure the health of sea lines of communication, including percentages of friendly shipping that make it safely into port, the tonnage of enemy shipping seized, etc. There are two parts to the analysis of sea lines of communication: are friendly forces able to ship material, and is the enemy able to ship material? They are both elements of a related question of who is able to use the maritime domain effectively. An analyst needs to make sure that they examine both sides and much like in the land domain, the analyst will need to choose the metrics with care. For example, the amount of enemy tonnage getting to the enemy will likely be more important than the amount of tonnage that a combatant has sunk although it is harder to measure. A final area of measurement in the maritime domain is power projection from the domain.

If combatants can project power from the maritime domain into other domains, it implies a significant level of maritime superiority. Amphibious landings or raids and projecting power into the air or space domains all imply a level of maritime superiority that analysts can observe and measure. Potential power in the maritime domain can affect the other domains even if a combatant does not choose to utilize it. One example of this principle in action was during the first Gulf War, where the Iraqis dedicated a significant amount of resources to defend against an amphibious assault that the United States never launched. Some of these types of measurements will also be useful in the cyberspace domain.

Comparing the balance of forces in the cyberspace domain is more problematic than in the maritime domain, however, measuring the health of lines of communications and power projection into other domains has utility for the cyberspace domain. In the cyberspace domain, it is much harder to compare forces than in the maritime domain. Battleships and cruisers are much easier to compare than cyberspace weapons, which are easier to hide and more difficult to compare. Measurement of the openness of cyberspace lines of communication is a more promising approach from the maritime domain. Also, measuring how well a combatant can project power from cyberspace into the other domains is a method that will have utility in cyberspace. There are a number of concepts useful for cyberspace superiority that we can pull out of the maritime domain; the same is also true of the air domain where we turn next.

Air Domain

Geography and Characteristics of the Air Domain

The geography of the air domain is very different from that of land or sea and gives the domain its unique characteristics, including that the air domain is mostly open and less constrained. Although the air domain has boundaries below on the surface, and above in the limits of the atmosphere, there are no natural chokepoints such as mountain ranges and swamps, or reefs and straits in the horizontal dimension. According to McCarthy, "The air domain is free of geographic boundaries that define chokepoints and lines of communications on the land and within the maritime commons."[34] Early airpower theorist, Giulio Douhet, put it even more strongly when he said that the airplane had complete freedom of action and could fly anywhere without the possibility of interference by surface forces.[35] Douhet overstated the case, and while there are not natural constraints, there can be man-made ones.

The air domain is not completely unconstrained; there can be man-made constraints in the air domain, such as effective surface to air missiles. Ground-based defenses set up by a combatant can form artificial chokepoints that are roughly analogous to land or maritime chokepoints. One major difference is that these chokepoints are very mutable and can be destroyed or moved much more easily than a mountain range or strait. The cyberspace domain has even greater tendencies toward mutability, as the entire cyberspace domain is artificial and constructed, whereas in the air domain only the ground-based defenses move or change quickly.[36] The open terrain of the air domain also allows air forces to bypass most defenses and attack deep into enemy territory.

A characteristic of airpower that is different from the land and maritime domains is that air domain forces can more easily bypass defenses to directly target civilians and infrastructure. According to Douhet, the battlefield would not be limited to only soldiers, but all citizens would become combatants. [37] The German Zeppelin raids over London during World War I represented the start of this trend and presaged the wholesale destruction of German and Japanese cities using nuclear and conventional bombs during World War II. The cyberspace domain is similar to the air domain in this respect, as cyberspace attacks can bypass fielded military forces to directly affect civilian life and infrastructure, whether by design or as collateral damage. Both strategic cyberspace attacks on infrastructure, and attacks that get out "in the wild" and do things their designers did not intend exhibit this ability to directly affect civilians. Douhet identified that airpower had independence of surface limitations allowing direct attack on civilians, and also had the next key characteristic of speed.[38]

Another characteristic of the air domain is great speed of action compared to the land and maritime domains. This great speed results from the physical characteristics of modern aircraft that can move from place to place much faster than land or maritime forces. A second component to the speed of action of air domain forces is their ability to move unpredictably. Space vehicles, such as satellites, are far faster than aircraft in terms of velocity, but they are greatly constrained by the laws of orbital mechanics and so are also very predictable. Aircraft, on the other hand, can easily feint in one direction before attacking in another. Clausewitz stated that the two basic principles underlying strategic planning were concentration and speed.[39] Airpower provides great speed, as well as the ability to concentrate quickly.

The great speed, long range, and flexibility of modern aircraft make it very easy for air domain forces to concentrate rapidly on a mission or location. The multi-role capabilities of many modern aircraft contribute greatly to this characteristic. A multi-role fighter could launch from Al Udeid airbase in Qatar on Monday to do intelligence and surveillance in Iraq, fly close air support in Afghanistan on Tuesday for ground forces, then provide a defensive combat air patrol over shipping in the Persian Gulf on Wednesday. Land and surface forces generally take much longer to re-orient to different missions or to move physically to the area where they need to execute the new mission. Cyberspace shares many of these characteristics with the air domain.

Cyberspace is more like the air domain than the land and maritime domains in its speed of action and flexibility. Although specific cyberspace weapons tend to be very tailored and unique to a single mission, the units performing those missions are not, and can rapidly shift from one mission set to another. The weapons of cyberspace can move even faster than aircraft and they often arrive at their destination in microseconds. Thus, cyberspace can also achieve great speed of action. Air domain forces rely on technology for speed of action, and for access to the domain.

Combatants access the air domain through technology much as combatants access the maritime, space, and cyberspace domains. Douhet identified that war in the air domain was heavily dependent upon the technical means available and would change rapidly over time. Douhet stated that, "The form of any war—and it is the form which is of primary interest to men of war—depends upon the technical means of war available."[40] In World War I, the rapidly changing technology had a major impact on who had air superiority. The Germans had interruption gear that let them fire through their propeller arcs, but the French and British did not, so the Germans had air superiority.[41] Once the French and British copied the technology, the fight was nearly equal, at least until the next technological innovation, as the combatants were improving their aircraft at a rapid rate. The pace of innovation in World War II was slower than World War I because the technology was more mature, but a similar dynamic was at work as technological innovation had a significant impact on who had air superiority.

Despite the importance of technology in the air domain, technological advantage is not sufficient to determine air superiority. The Iran–Iraq war is one case where a lower technology combatant was still able to achieve air superiority despite technological disadvantages. Larger numbers, training, and tactics can all offset a combatant's superior technology. The technological edge of U.S. Air Force in North Vietnam was often offset by the better North Vietnamese tactics and training. The United States lost a number of expensive and high technology F-4s to lower technology MiG-17s and MiG-19s.[42] That these losses were driven by tactics and training rather than technological shortcomings is illustrated by the very different levels of success achieved by the U.S. Navy and U.S. Air Force, who were flying the exact same aircraft against the same enemy with different training and tactics.[43]

Technology is also tremendously important in the cyberspace domain, because combatants create cyberspace using technology. It is harder for cyberspace combatants to offset deficiencies in technology with tactics and training, as there is less real-time human interaction in cyberspace than in the air domain. One area where the air and cyberspace domains are quite different is in the cost of technological access to the domain.

Access to the air domain is expensive and requires costly high technology aircraft and infrastructure in the form of airfields. Modern aircraft of all classes, from fighters to transports, are very expensive and involve long design and production lead times. The technology required for a functional airfield is not as advanced, but airbases are massively costly infrastructure projects that normally take many years to plan and build. The United States has been fortunate to fight recent wars in areas where abundant oil money has built numerous large modern bases. Trying to carve a functioning fighter base and transport hub out of a remote location in sub-Saharan Africa would be much more challenging.

Fortunately for cyberspace operators, they do not require extensive infrastructure. In the cyberspace domain, the cost of entry is much lower; a cheap laptop and network connection may be all that is required to deliver a weapon, although developing the weapon will take more resources. The final characteristic of the air domain is one that the cyberspace and air domains share: success in the domain is neither necessary nor sufficient for attainment of military objectives.

The last characteristic of air superiority applicable to cyberspace superiority is that its importance is highly contentious. Some airmen have unfortunately felt the need to claim that airpower was all that a nation needed for success in warfare due to the long and bruising fights for organizational independence.[44] When these overenthusiastic predictions turned out not to be true, and the Germans did not surrender after the Allies destroyed German cities, analysts sometimes shifted to the other extreme of claiming that airpower accomplished nothing of significance. Both sides are wrong, air superiority is an important factor in modern warfare, but does not guarantee victory.

Air superiority is normally not sufficient to produce a successful outcome for a combatant by itself, however, it can certainly help a nation win a conflict. The wars in Korea and Vietnam, among many others, have shown that air superiority alone is not enough to guarantee victory. At the same time, no sane army officer would want to fight a war without air superiority if it were at all possible. Air superiority provides tremendous advantages to the side that has it. The never-ending debates over whether airpower or land power was "decisive" in the Gulf War provide little more than organizational cheerleading, and not good analysis. It is much like arguing over which side of a pair of scissors was decisive in cutting a piece of paper. The scissors work because of the interaction between the two sides, and each is required to produce the effect. The same dynamics that have produced contention about the importance of air superiority also exist in cyberspace.

Cyberspace superiority is even less likely than air superiority to prove sufficient to win wars by itself despite its great potential to help achieve objectives. Cyberspace is a new domain whose support is immensely important to operators in the other domains. At the same time, cyberspace operators often feel that leaders downplay their ability to provide direct action through cyberspace to ensure that they stay organizationally under the thumb of officers who are more familiar with the other domains. Cyberspace superiority has an important role to play in its own domain, and in supporting the other domains. In this way, it is similar to air superiority. Another area where there is some similarity between the air and cyberspace domains is that the technology of cyberspace drives the advantage for the offense or defense.

Offensive or Defensive Primacy in the Air Domain

Although earlier air domain theorists favored the offensive, whether the defensive or offensive has primacy in the air domain has shifted over time with technological change. Douhet stated that the airplane was inherently offensive and completely unsuited for the defensive based on World War I air combat.[45] Colonel Billy Mitchell, who had far more experience in actual combat in World War I, understood that aircraft could mount a successful defense through air combat. [46] In the interwar period, airpower theorists generally agreed with Douhet that the offensive had a significant advantage; Stanley Baldwin famously stated that, "the bomber will always get through."[47] This theory was reasonable given the facts of the time, but it did not turn out to be correct.[48]

Several technological changes during and after World War II shifted air domain effectiveness to the defense. Fighter aircraft became more capable, radar allowed for early warning, and improved command and control schemes enhanced the effectiveness of the defense. Overwhelming numbers of aircraft on the side of the Allies proved decisive in the battle for air superiority in the European theater.

After World War II, the development of effective surface to air missiles gave an entirely new category of tools to the defense that shifted the balance further toward the defense. Stealth technologies provided new avenues for the offense, which defenders have partially countered with new types of detection systems and improved SAMs. These changes have brought the offense and defense in the air domain into rough balance.

Right now, there is no clear primacy to the offense or defense in the air domain; the more effective operational and tactical force is likely to defeat its foe on either the offense or defense. The various conflicts fought by Israel demonstrate that the more effective Israeli Air Force was able to defeat its foes when Israel started on the defensive in the Yom Kippur War, and on the offensive in the Six Day War and Bekaa Valley campaign. According to McCarthy,

> Today, with the benefit of extensive airpower history and an understanding of the maturity of air defense weapons, we know that air domain power is not inherently offensive in nature. Air defense assets can deny an enemy access to vital points and can wear down an attacking force, effectively eliminating an adversary's airpower through defensive action.[49]

A healthy understanding of the importance of the offensive and defensive sides of combat in the air domain is critical to a proper understanding of how to gain superiority in the air domain.

Method of Gaining Air Superiority

Early airpower theorists focused on universal air superiority but they thought combatants could achieve it in different ways. For Douhet, the most efficient way of achieving air superiority was to attack the enemy aircraft on the ground.[50] Airpower theorist Alexander De Seversky agreed with Douhet that a combatant would win air superiority by attacking offensively, however, Seversky focused on shattering enemy industry, not just attacking airfields.[51] Mitchell thought that the best way to destroy the enemy air force was to fight them in the air after forcing them up by bombing targets the enemy would have to defend.[52] RAF officer and airpower theorist, J.C. Slessor, agreed with Mitchell, but put more emphasis on forcing the enemy to defend his vital centers while also attacking the enemy air force directly.[53] The common thread through all of these airpower theorists was offensive attack, either at the enemy air force directly, or at the industry and infrastructure that created and supported it. This correlates closely to land and maritime superiority concepts that involve defeating the enemy army or fleet respectively. A common concept with all these theorists is the idea that to gain universal air superiority, a combatant needs to attack enemy universal air domain forces.

As the earlier theorists identified, to gain air superiority at the universal level a combatant needs to attack the enemy's offensive and defensive air domain forces. On the offensive side a combatant should degrade the enemy strategic Integrated Air Defense Systems (IADS) as much as possible. These are the forces with a long enough reach to see and target attacking air domain platforms. Attacking the enemy strategic IADS has normally been the first step in any offensive air campaign as it enables the follow-on portions of the campaign. On the universal defensive side, a combatant should degrade the enemy's offensive airpower as much as possible whether that is through strikes on airfields, missile launching and storage facilities, or other infrastructure. These are the first two elements of the model of gaining and utilizing air superiority shown in Figure 2.5.

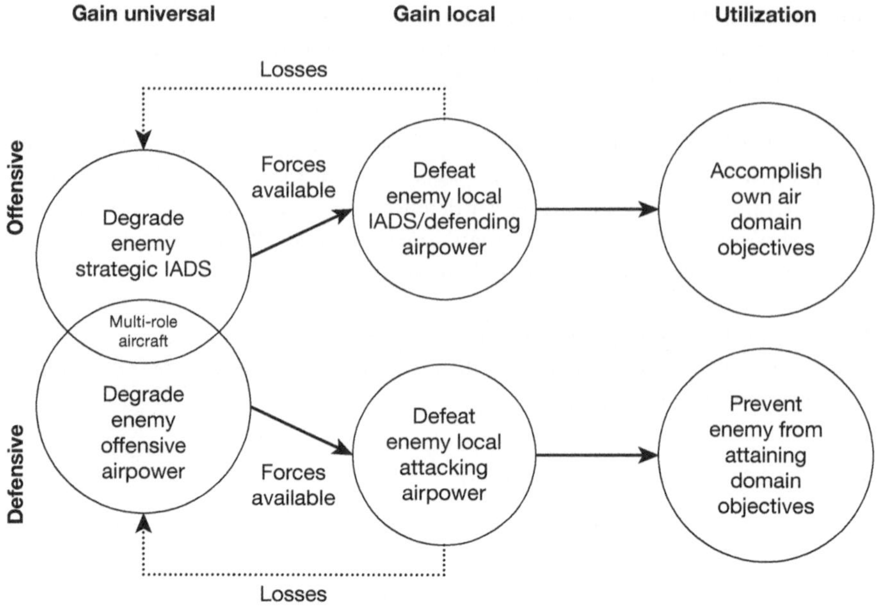

Figure 2.5 Model of Gaining and Utilizing Air Superiority
Source: *Author's original work*

Note that there is some overlap between the offensive and defensive sides in the form of multi-role airpower. Multi-role aircraft can perform either defensive or offensive roles and so can swing between offensive missions and participating as part of the friendly IADS. The size of the overlap will vary depending on the forces available to a specific combatant. The next elements of the model relate local air superiority and universal air superiority.

The universal level of air superiority is more significant than the local level due to the excellent mobility of airpower, the concentrated nature of the airpower instrument and the vulnerability of universal airpower to attack. These factors are more important than the different offensive and defensive forces, which increase the importance of the local level of air superiority. Airpower's long range and great speed expands what constitutes a local area. Even short-range fighters can easily perform missions hundreds of miles from their airbases; with air refueling, they can go much further. At the logical extreme, if all aircraft could range the entire theater at great speed, there would be no local level as any air domain combatant could engage in any local combat.[54] The constraints of range and speed do not allow this collapse of the local level over large theaters, but the air domain comes much closer to this ideal than the land and maritime domains. The concentrated character of airpower also increases the significance of the universal level of air superiority.

The small numbers of air domain forces, combined with their vulnerability to attack further increases the importance of the universal over the local level of air superiority. Aircraft are generally much more expensive than tanks or artillery pieces so nations tend to have fewer of them. Aircraft are also fragile and easy to destroy, particularly if they are on the ground. Even the best shelters Saddam could buy provided minimal protection for the Iraqi Air Force during both Gulf Wars. The Israelis also demonstrated how the concentration and vulnerability of an air force could lead to universal air superiority when they destroyed the bulk of the Egyptian Air Force on the ground during the Six Day War. Although the universal level is more important, the local level still matters in the air domain.

Local air superiority involves defeating only those enemy forces required to attain a specific objective in a local area whether that be offensive or defensive. The forces available to contest local superiority come from the universal level and losses taken in the fight for local superiority affect what forces are available for the next fight at the local level, as was discussed earlier. On the local offensive side, a combatant has to defeat the enemy local IADS to be able to operate and accomplish objectives in the local area. Destruction of the entire IADS is not required; deception, disruption and denial are all options; an attacker can consider any of them as defeat of the IADS if the enemy IADS is unable to accomplish its mission of prohibitively interfering with the attacker. On the local defensive, the defensive side does not need to destroy the enemy's offensive airpower; it is sufficient for a defender to keep the enemy from attaining his offensive objectives. Of course, destruction is preferred, as those aircraft then cannot come back and attack again tomorrow. A combatant does not have to defeat enemy offensive airpower strictly with air domain forces, other domain forces can have key elements of that fight from ground or maritime-based SAMs to cyberspace weapons implanted in enemy aircraft. Once air superiority is gained, the next question for a combatant is how best to utilize it.

Use of Air Superiority

There are three major ways that airpower analysts have suggested a combatant can use airpower to achieve his campaign objectives. The first is to attack some portion of the enemy population to get them to bring pressure on enemy decision-makers, to terminate the conflict on terms favorable to the attacker. The second is to attack infrastructure or industry to prevent the enemy from constructing weapons. The third is to use airpower to support surface forces. There is often some blurring of the categories. For example, if the Allies knocked out a railway yard in Germany prior to the Normandy invasion, it could conceivably have been putting pressure on the population, disrupting weapons production, and hitting troops headed to the front at the same time. Each of these mechanisms has a cyberspace equivalent and I will look at all three starting with direct attacks on the population.

The first proposed theory by which airpower could bring victory was direct attacks on the population, but this theory was largely discredited by the experiences of World War II. The earliest proponent of attacking enemy cities was Douhet, who considered attacking enemy vital centers the proper role of air domain forces.[55] Prior to World War II, many airpower advocates, including Douhet, thought that bombing would result in the collapse of enemy morale and end the conflict. Seversky disagreed with Douhet on this point even before World War II. During the war, and despite the utter devastation wrought by Allied bombers on many German cities, the Germans still did not surrender until their military had completely collapsed. In the Japanese case, even greater destruction did not bring surrender until after two nuclear weapons were used and the entry of the Soviet Union into the war. After World War II, Seversky stated that, "The morale of a nation determined to defend itself cannot easily be broken, especially in a national life or death struggle. Ideologically inspired people can withstand great amounts of punishment. It is never fear, horror, or misery which makes a people at war collapse but the actual elimination of the physical industrial means to make war."[56] This focus on industry leads to the next proposed mechanism for airpower of disrupting the industrial web of a nation.

A second theory for the proper use of airpower was that instead of destroying enemy cities and populations, bombers should destroy carefully selected "bottlenecks" in enemy industry, which would prevent the enemy from continuing to fight. A number of U.S. Army Air Corps officers in the faculty of the Air Corps Tactical School developed this theory during the interwar period.[57] The industrial web theory led to the U.S. Army Air Corps pursuing daylight precision bombing during World War II, but it was not as effective as its proponents had hoped due to a combination of the bombers being more vulnerable as well as less accurate, and the enemy more resilient than they expected. The shortcomings of daylight precision bombing led some analysts to conclude that the principal utility of air superiority was in support to surface forces.

A final concept for the proper use of air superiority was to utilize it to provide support for friendly surface forces. Some early airpower theorists such as Douhet and Seversky disagreed with this approach.[58] John Warden, a more modern airpower theorist, agreed with Douhet and Seversky and placed fielded military forces in the outside ring of his model.[59] On the other hand, among early airpower theorists, Mitchell recognized the importance of what happens on the ground and Slessor agreed that who won on the ground determined who won the war.[60] Robert Pape, a modern airpower theorist, postulated that the way for a combatant to coerce an enemy into submitting was by defeating their strategy, but often the enemy strategy depended on the enemy's fielded military forces so attacking fielded forces could be the best way to defeat the enemy's strategy.[61] Airpower can have beneficial effects by destroying targets deep behind enemy lines, as well as by attacking enemy forces directly on the front lines. Early airpower advocates were unnecessarily dismissive of attacks on fielded military forces because they were focused on "strategic" targets, but there are cases where the army is the most important "strategic" target because it is the force that the leaders rely on to keep themselves in power or accomplish their strategy. Each of these three approaches has some utility in cyberspace.

Cyberspace superiority aligns closely with air superiority in how combatants can use it; cyberspace analysts should carefully consider the historical lessons from the air domain. Cyberspace strategists who propose approaches intended to pressure populations should seriously consider whether turning off power and water will put more pressure on a population than high explosive bombs and incendiaries did during World War II. It is possible that pressure strategies could work if the issue is of relatively low importance to the enemy, but the historical record of accomplishment from the air domain is not encouraging regarding such punishment strategies. Strategists should also be cautious when assuming they can successfully interfere with enemy industry and infrastructure based on airpower's experience with the industrial web theory. Cyberspace weapons may not be as effective as expected, and the enemy may be able to react in creative ways to mitigate the weapon's effects. Finally, the importance of using air superiority to support the other domains also applies to cyberspace where, at the current time, cyberspace is likely to have the most impact. The utility to a combatant of achieving cyberspace or air superiority will also vary with how long he can expect to maintain that superiority.

Persistence of Air Domain Superiority

Because of the high mobility of air domain forces to move from one local area to another, a combatant will be able to achieve persistence of superiority in the air domain only if he is able to achieve universal rather than local air superiority. The theorists who believed air superiority was persistent also tended to assume it was universal. Seversky was the most clear in his claim that there was no such thing as local air superiority when he said that, "Any attempt to conquer a small part of it—to protect a base underneath or for some other purpose—will rapidly resolve into a showdown battle for dominance in the air. Because of the enlarged ranges, mastery of the skies has come to mean *all* the skies."[62] Seversky reached this conclusion because he thought that all combat aircraft would be capable of ranging the entire theater of operations. If Seversky had been correct that all air superiority was going to be universal, his expectations about its long persistence would likely have also been correct. However, most aircraft did not achieve domain-wide range, which increased the importance of the local level of air superiority while decreasing persistence. In addition to the limited range of most aircraft, the creation of effective land based defenses also increased the relative importance of local superiority.

Modern IADS can break down a theater of operations into separate local areas in which different combatants have air superiority. If two nations went to war with less capable fighters and modern SAMs such as Patriots, SA-10s or SA-20s, it is reasonable to expect that both nations would be able to control the airspace above their own territory, while not being able successfully to penetrate that of the enemy without taking prohibitive losses. It is even conceivable that if the theater of operations were small, and both sides possessed effective long range SAMs such as the SA-12, neither side might be able to effectively utilize aircraft at all, even over their own territory. A much more common scenario is that a nation might have local air superiority in the areas where the most capable components of its IADS reach, but might not have air superiority in the areas outside their reach. Because aircraft can move so quickly from one zone into another, local air superiority also tends to be transient.

Airpower theorists, who saw that air superiority could be local, also recognized that local superiority would tend to be transient. Soviet General P.P. Ionov believed that the air superiority that mattered would be both temporary and local. In addition, Ionov argued that he would be willing to trade universal air superiority for local superiority in a critical area.[63] Slessor, with a similar focus on land campaigns as Ionov, thought that air superiority was not a "condition to be achieved once for all."[64]

Seversky and Douhet treated air superiority as persistent. Once a combatant achieved air superiority, the enemy would not have an opportunity to get it back because the victorious side would have destroyed the enemy's air force. Even Douhet had to admit that localized air superiority was the best that either side achieved during World War I, although he attributed this shortcoming to the inefficiency of air-to-air combat as a method of gaining air superiority.[65] Douhet and Seversky were wrong because most combat aircraft did not have the range to affect the entire theater of operations, and air forces proved far more resilient and able to spring back from battlefield defeats. In World War II, the British and the Russians regained air superiority despite tremendous early losses and air superiority was certainly not domain-wide for any combatant until the final months of the war. French Admiral Raoul Castex thought that the concept of permanent air superiority was absurd, as aircraft could only stay airborne for a short period.[66] Given the short endurance and high mobility of most current combat aircraft, the only way to generate persistent air superiority is at the universal level.

Air superiority will tend to be local and transient unless one side has such an overwhelming abundance of superiority that they can achieve it across the entire theater of operations as the Coalition did in the Gulf War. The primary reason for this situation is that a combatant can quickly move aircraft from one local area to another. Achieving dominance in a local area by destroying local air domain forces will only last until the enemy can move replacements into the threatened area and once again contest for superiority. An attacker could achieve slightly longer superiority persistence by attacking airfields or support equipment, but the enemy can also rebuild these in days or weeks through repair and reconstitution; or the enemy could still contest the local area using longer-range aircraft or air refueling. A more promising approach for a combatant is to utilize effective long range SAMs to establish local air superiority. However, if a combatant bases air superiority purely on these systems, the enemy will respond by focusing on them and air superiority will only last as long as those systems remain effective. As strategic theorist Edward Luttwak has observed, the more effective a system is, the shorter its utility tends to be as the enemy focuses on finding ways to defeat it.[67]

The tendency in the air domain for local superiority to be transitory has important implications for cyberspace superiority. Because universal superiority will be extremely difficult to achieve, as will be discussed in Chapter 3, the evidence from the air domain suggests that persistence of domain superiority will also be short in cyberspace. To understand how much air superiority a combatant has, I will next turn to how analysts have measured it over time.

Measurement Concepts of Air Superiority

If we accept Mitchell's definition of airpower or air superiority as, "the ability to do something in the air," then measuring it is a question of measuring how effectively an attacker or defender is accomplishing their objectives.[68] Common measurements include how often strike aircraft have to jettison their bombs before getting to their targets, how often targets are struck successfully, how many enemy sorties get into friendly territory and what was their effectiveness. A combatant can also utilize an estimated balance of forces, but those measurements need careful scrutiny as nations produce airpower through a system, not from a single component. For example, a nation may have the best fighter aircraft on the planet, but if their pilots are substandard, they may not be very effective at projecting airpower. We can say the same thing about logistical systems, integration, munitions, etc. A combatant can utilize relative measurements, such as the fact that the enemy has lost 50% of his aircraft while you have only lost 10% of your own, to determine which direction air superiority is going. Finally, actions by the enemy that demonstrate he has given up seriously contesting the air such as burying his planes in the sand, or flying them to a neutral country can be strong indicators that a significant level of air superiority or even supremacy has been achieved. Not all of these measurement concepts will transfer well to the cyberspace domain.

The core of assessing cyberspace supremacy will be measuring the accomplishment of a combatant's objectives similar to the air domain, however, measuring the balance of forces will be less useful. Estimating the balance of forces in the cyberspace domain is much more difficult than in the air domain. Air domain analysts can examine the number and types of aircraft available to each combatant, consider logistical and sortie generation capabilities, and examine infrastructure such as airfields relatively easily. In the cyberspace domain, a combatant cannot examine the enemy's weapons and infrastructure on satellite photos; they are much more difficult to find. In addition, comparing the capabilities of an F-16 and an MiG-29 is relatively simple compared to determining the relative effectiveness of various cyberspace weapons. Cyberspace weapons are very different from each other; how can an analyst compare a worm and an intrusion detection system? I will carry forward the focus on measuring objectives from the air domain to construct a measurement concept in Chapter 3 for cyberspace. Now we can summarize the findings from the land, sea, and air domains.

Conclusion

I can apply a number of different elements from the land, maritime, and air domains to the cyberspace domain. The geography and characteristics of each domain determine whether the offense or defense has primacy, how a combatant gains and uses superiority, the persistence of superiority, and appropriate measurement concepts for superiority. In each of these categories, there were major differences across the domains. Although the land domain is the one least like cyberspace, there are still key elements I can bring forward into the cyberspace domain.

The principal elements of land superiority applicable to cyberspace include the interaction between universal and local superiority and how that interaction affects the persistence of superiority in the domain. In the land domain, a combatant can achieve universal superiority by defeating the enemy army, which can produce persistent superiority. If a combatant can only achieve local superiority, then the persistence he can achieve tends to be much more fleeting. This point suggests that domain superiority in the cyberspace domain will be very short, as it is very difficult to achieve anything other than local cyberspace superiority, as will be discussed in Chapter 3. A second critical element is that forces at the universal level of superiority provide the forces that a combatant can move into a local area to contest local superiority, and the losses at the local level feed back into what is available at the universal level. Of all the domains examined, land domain superiority is the most different from cyberspace superiority. The maritime domain has more areas of similarity to the cyberspace domain.

The maritime domain is similar to the cyberspace domain in that the primary purpose of the domain is to serve as a communication pathway. In the maritime domain, goods transit the sea lines of communications; in the cyberspace domain, information transits cyberspace. The maritime domain chokepoints such as straits and ports are analogous to cyberspace's chokepoints of undersea cables and server farms. Cyberspace will also likely be similar to the maritime domain in that the domain will normally be un-commanded as there will be so few domain forces to cover large areas in both domains. There is also potential utility in examining cyberspace conflict in terms of maritime commerce warfare. The maritime concepts of a fleet in being, fleet battles, and blockades do not have similar resonance in cyberspace. There is even more similarity between the cyberspace and air domains than the maritime domain.

The air domain is closer to the cyberspace domain than the maritime domain in its separation into mostly distinct offensive and defensive forces, its speed of action, reliance on technology, and the continuing debate on whether the most effective use of the domain is to target the enemy directly or support friendly action in other domains. The air domain differs from cyberspace in the cost of access and the importance of the universal level of superiority. Whereas the universal level is very significant in the air domain as combatants can easily attack universal air domain forces, in cyberspace it is much more difficult to attack enemy cyberspace forces. This circumstance results in far greater importance for the local level of domain superiority in cyberspace compared with the air domain. In the air domain, a combatant can only achieve persistent domain superiority at the universal level, which again implies that combatants will be unable to achieve persistence easily in cyberspace as it functions primarily at the local level. Finally, the measurement concepts from the air domain of focusing on the achievement of friendly objectives, while preventing the enemy from achieving his objectives will provide a starting point from which to develop a cyberspace measurement system. A summary of the findings for domain superiority across the land, maritime, and air domains is shown in Table 2.1.

Table 2.1 Summary of Domain Superiority for Land, Maritime, and Air Domains

Geography / Characteristics	
Land	• Physical terrain such as mountains, rivers, and swamps dictate lines of communication and which forces are most effective where combat tends to be sequential, with forces excluding each other from areas of their control while protecting their own lines of communication.
Maritime	• Maneuver space is bounded by land masses and ports which form chokepoints. • Sea lines of communication are the key element worth fighting over. • Accessed via expensive technology (ships) and expensive entry points (ports).
Air	• Open and relatively unbounded without natural chokepoints. • No clear front line; involves civilians directly in combat operations. • Characterized by great speed of action. • Dependent upon technology for access. • Accessed via expensive technology (aircraft) and expensive entry points (airfields). • Dominance in this domain is not sufficient for victory, however, it enables the land and maritime domains.
Offensive or Defensive Primacy	
Land	• With modern weapons the defensive has primacy as the defender can stay under cover while the offender must unmask to advance.
Maritime	• There is no clear offensive or defensive primacy in the maritime domain. ◦ Normally both offensive and defensive forces can see each other at the same distance • Exceptions include submarine warfare which favors the offender and a fleet in a defended port which favors the defense.
Air	• Older theorists favored the offensive, but the advantage has shifted back and forth over time depending on technology.
Method of Gaining Superiority	
Land	• Universal: defeat enemy army to allow physical access to the terrain, then gain control and support of the population. • Local: defeat local regular or insurgent forces.
Maritime	• Universal: defeat enemy fleet or blockade them in port; weaker combatant can contest by keeping a "fleet in being" and executing small counter attacks. • Local: disrupt enemy shipping while protecting your own.
Air	• Offensive universal: degrade enemy strategic IADS. • Defensive universal: degrade enemy offensive airpower. • Offensive local: defeat enemy local IADS. • Defensive local: defeat enemy local offensive airpower.

(Continued)

Table 2.1 (Continued)

Use of Superiority	
Land	• Often control of the land domain will terminate the conflict; if not, combatants can extract resources for continued combat in other areas and domains.
Maritime	• Enable shipment of military and commercial goods. • Project power into the land domain while preventing the enemy from doing the same.
Air	• Offensive: directly striking enemy centers of gravity to either affect enemy capabilities or change enemy decisions; support other domain forces. • Defensive: prevent enemy from striking friendly centers of gravity.
Persistence	
Land	• Land domain superiority tends to be persistent due to greater influence of the universal level of superiority as well as the sequential tendencies of land combat, the inertia of populations whose support changes slowly, and the current primacy of the defensive.
Maritime	• Whether the maritime superiority gained is local or universal will greatly affect the persistence of maritime superiority. ◦ If a combatant can achieve universal maritime superiority through defeating the enemy fleet, then persistence can be high. • If the enemy refuses to fight a major fleet action for universal control, then control will not only be localized, but also fleeting as the enemy can dash out of port to raid convoys and establish local control in an area, but then retreat back into port when threatened by the main adversary fleet.
Air	• Because of the high mobility of air domain forces to move from one local area to another, a combatant will be able to achieve persistence of superiority in the air domain only if he is able to achieve universal or local air superiority.
Measurement Concept	
Land	• Whose soldiers are in possession of the terrain. • Metrics to determine the level of support of the population.
Maritime	• Universal: remaining capability of enemy fleet. • Local: metrics to measure friendly and enemy utilization of sea lines of communication; ability to project power into other domains.
Air	• Ability to achieve objectives in the air. • Relative measurement and trends of resources.

Cyberspace shares more characteristics with the maritime and air domains because both are domains accessed by technology. Accordingly, more of the characteristics of maritime and air superiority will be applicable to cyberspace. Examining the characteristics of the cyberspace domain in detail will be required to determine which characteristics cyberspace superiority and the other domains share. This analysis will then permit the addition of the cyberspace domain to Table 2.1, which I will present at the end of the next chapter.

Notes

1 The definitions are from The Merriam-Webster online dictionary, quoted in Thomas David McCarthy, "Traveling Domain Theory: A Comparative Approach for Cyberspace Theory Development" (PhD diss., Fletcher School of Law and Diplomacy, 2012), 47.
2 R.G. Grant, *Battle at Sea: 3,000 Years of Naval Warfare* (London: Dorling Kindersley, 2008) 24.
3 McCarthy, "Traveling Domain Theory," 187.
4 SAMs are generally defensive weapons, but one exception to this tendency is if their range is so great that their effective range extends well into enemy territory. If a combatant could shoot down any aircraft flying in enemy territory with long-range SAMs that would constitute an offensive use of SAMs no different from shooting down enemy aircraft with offensive fighter patrols. Although theoretically possible, at the current time this situation is uncommon.
5 J.C. Wylie, *Military Strategy: A General Theory of Power Control* (New Brunswick, N.J.: Rutgers University Press, 1967), 49.
6 Robert B. Strassler ed., *The Landmark Thucydides: A Comprehensive Guide to the Peloponnesian War*, (New York: Touchstone, 1996), 240.
7 Colin S. Gray, *Modern Strategy* (Oxford: Oxford University Press, 1999), 110.
8 The French *Mitrailleuse* provides another example of poor tactical doctrine hampering technical innovation. The French *Mitrailleuse* was a primitive form of machine gun that had minimal impact on the Franco-Prussian War of 1870 because it was treated as artillery by officers who had no idea how to use it effectively. The *Mitrailleuse* could have shifted the balance toward the defensive, much as later machine guns did, but it did not change the balance in 1870 due to poor tactical doctrine.
9 Gray, *Modern Strategy*, 214.
10 The revolution in military affairs or RMA promised to change the ability of a defending force to hide through a combination of ubiquitous sensors and networked communications and thus largely dispense of Clausewitz's famous fog of war. The results in actual combat have been disappointing; it is possible that future technological innovations will produce complete awareness for an attacker, but it seems unlikely in the near term.
11 Wylie, *Military Strategy*, 85.
12 Carl von Clausewitz, *On War*, ed. and trans. by Michael Howard and Peter Paret (Princeton, NJ: Princeton University Press, 1976), 92.
13 Clausewitz, *On War*, 92.
14 Wylie, *Military Strategy*, 85.
15 David J. Lonsdale, *The Nature of War in the Information Age* (London: Frank Cass, 2004), 211.
16 Wylie, *Military Strategy*, 91.
17 James Clancy and Chuck Crossett, "Measuring Effectiveness in Irregular Warfare," *Parameters*, Summer 2007, 90.
18 Clancy and Crossett, "Measuring Effectiveness in Irregular Warfare," 90.
19 Clancy and Crossett, "Measuring Effectiveness in Irregular Warfare," 96.
20 Major General Mark Barrett, Dick Bedford, Elizabeth Skinner, and Eva Vergles. "Assured Access to the Global Commons." ed. by Supreme Allied Command Transformation. (Norfolk, VA: North Atlantic Treaty Organization, 2011), 5.
21 United Nations, *United Nations Convention on the Law of the Sea* 1994, 57. www.un.org/depts/los/convention_agreements/texts/unclos/unclos_e.pdf
22 McCarthy, "Traveling Domain Theory," 74–75.

23 Sir Julian Stafford Corbett, *Some Principles of Maritime Strategy, Classics of Sea Power,* (Annapolis, MD: Naval Institute Press, 1988), 91.
24 Admiral Gabriel Darrieus, quoted in Beatrice Heuser, *The Evolution of Strategy: Thinking War from Antiquity to the Present* (Cambridge: Cambridge University Press, 2010), 244.
25 Alfred T. Mahan, *Mahan on Naval Strategy: Selections from the Writings of Rear Admiral Alfred Thayer Mahan*, Edited by Allan Westcott (Boston: Little, Brown, and Company, 1918) 129.
26 McCarthy, "Traveling Domain Theory," 81.
27 Corbett, *Some Principles of Maritime Strategy*, 165.
28 McCarthy, "Traveling Domain Theory," 81.
29 Corbett, *Some Principles of Maritime Strategy*, 165.
30 Alfred T. Mahan, *The Influence of Sea Power Upon History, 1660–1783* (New York, NY: Dover Publications, 1987), 26, and Corbett, *Some Principles of Maritime Strategy*, 93.
31 Corbett, *Some Principles of Maritime Strategy*, 16.
32 Clancy and Crossett, "Measuring Effectiveness in Irregular Warfare," 90.
33 Mahan, *Influence of Sea Power Upon History*, 14.
34 McCarthy, "Traveling Domain Theory," 114.
35 Giulio Douhet, *The Command of the Air* (1921; new imprint, Mechanicsburg, PA: Stackpole Books, 1999), 283.
36 Gregory J. Rattray, *Strategic Warfare in Cyberspace* (Amazon: MIT Press, 2001), Kindle Location 76.
37 Douhet, *The Command of the Air*, 283.
38 Douhet, *The Command of the Air*, 289.
39 Clausewitz, *On War*, 617.
40 Douhet, *The Command of the Air*, 279.
41 In 1915, a Frenchman, Roland Garros developed deflectors that enabled him to fire a forward-facing machine gun through the propeller arc of his aircraft to deflect the 10% of bullets that would have hit the propeller. The system enabled him to shoot down three German aircraft before it disabled his aircraft and forced him to land behind German lines. When the Germans turned over the deflector to a Dutch engineer, Anthony Fokker, he developed a more sophisticated device that prevented the gun from firing when the propeller was in front of the machine gun. This technological innovation led to a period of German dominance of the skies over Europe called the "Fokker Scourge" until the French and British developed their own interruption gear about six months later. John H. Morrow Jr. *The Great War in the Air: Military Aviation from 1909 to 1921* (Washington: Smithsonian Institute Press, 1993), 92.
42 For a detailed discussion of how poor tactics and training by the U.S. Air Force gave the North Vietnamese the edge in air combat, see Marshall L. Mitchell III, *Clashes: Air Combat over North Vietnam 1965–1972* (Annapolis, MD: Naval Institute Press, 1997).
43 Mitchell, *Clashes: Air Combat over North Vietnam 1965–1972*, 4.
44 Gray, *Modern Strategy*, 228.
45 Douhet, *The Command of the Air*, 355.
46 William Mitchell, *Winged Defense: The Development and Possibilities of Modern Air Power, Economic and Military* (1925; new imprint, Mechanicsburg, PA: Stackpole Books, 1999), 502.
47 Stanley Baldwin, "A Fear for the Future," Speech given in Parliament 10 November 1932. http://en.wikisource.org/wiki/A_Fear_For_The_Future
48 Analysts based the idea that bombers would always get through to their targets on several factors. One was that pursuit aircraft only had a slight speed advantage over bomber aircraft and took so long to get to altitude that the bombers would be gone before pursuit aircraft could engage them. A second was that bomber aircraft would be able to defend themselves with their own defensive firepower. Both concepts turned out to be wrong. Fighter aircraft developed a significant speed advantage over contemporary bomber aircraft, and radar as well as better command and control greatly enhanced their capability to intercept bombers and get to altitude before the bombers arrived.

Additionally, the bombers were much less able to defend themselves than expected because defensive gunners turned out to be less effective than analysts had predicted.

49 McCarthy, "Traveling Domain Theory," 185.

50 Douhet, *The Command of the Air*, 307.

51 Alexander P. De Seversky, *Air Power: Key to Survival* (New York, NY: Simon and Schuster, 1950), 193.

52 Mitchell, *Winged Defense*, 436.

53 J.C. Slessor, *Air Power and Armies* (1936; new imprint, Tuscaloosa, AL, Alabama University Press, 2009), 15.

54 The projection that all aircraft would be able to range the entire theater is why Alexander P. De Seversky confidently predicted that local air superiority could not exist. Seversky was incorrect in this prediction, and very few aircraft possess the range today that he predicted they would have by the 1950s and 1960s.

55 Douhet, *The Command of the Air*, 338.

56 Seversky, *Air Power: Key to Survival*, 58.

57 David MacIsaac, "Voices from the Central Blue: The Air Power Theorists," in *Makers of Modern Strategy: From Machiavelli to the Nuclear Age*, ed. Peter Paret (Princeton: Princeton University Press, 1986) 634.

58 Douhet went so far as to state that, "For the rest, anyone who read Part I with attention must have understood perfectly that I considered auxiliary aviation *worthless, superfluous, harmful.*" Douhet, *The Command of the Air*, 338. Seversky agreed with Douhet that action in support of the other services was a secondary function of airpower; the primary function was to strike directly at the enemy. Alexander P. De Seversky, *Victory Through Air Power* (New York, NY: Simon and Schuster, 1942), 264.

59 John Warden, "The Enemy as a System," *Air and Space Power Journal* (1995), 46.

60 Slessor, *Air Power and Armies*, 1.

61 Robert Pape, *Bombing to Win: Air Power and Coercion in War* (London: Cornell University Press, 1996), 17.

62 Seversky, *Air Power: Key to Survival*, 58.

63 Heuser, *The Evolution of Strategy*, 301.

64 Slessor, *Air Power and Armies*, 10.

65 Douhet, *The Command of the Air*, 317.

66 Heuser, *The Evolution of Strategy*, 302.

67 Edward N. Luttwak, *Strategy: The Logic of War and Peace* (Cambridge, MA: Belknap Press, 2003), 28–29.

68 Mitchell, *Winged Defense*, 425.

Bibliography

Baldwin, Stanley. "A Fear for the Future." Speech given in Parliament 10 November 1932. http://en.wikisource.org/wiki/A_Fear_For_The_Future

Barrett, Major General Mark, Dick Bedford, Elizabeth Skinner, and Eva Vergles. "Assured Access to the Global Commons." Edited by Supreme Allied Command Transformation. Norfolk, VA: North Atlantic Treaty Organization, 2011.

Clancy, James and Chuck Crossett. "Measuring Effectiveness in Irregular Warfare." *Parameters*, Summer 2007, 88–100.

Clausewitz, Carl von. *On War.* Edited and Translated by Michael Howard and Peter Paret. Princeton, NJ: Princeton University Press, 1976.

Corbett, Sir Julian Stafford. *Some Principles of Maritime Strategy, Classics of Sea Power.* Annapolis, MD: Naval Institute Press, 1988.

De Seversky, Alexander P. *Victory Through Air Power.* New York, NY: Simon and Schuster, 1942.

De Seversky, Alexander P. *Air Power: Key to Survival.* New York, NY: Simon and Schuster, 1950.

Douhet, Giulio. *The Command of the Air.* Mechanicsburg, PA: Stackpole Books, 1921. Reprint, 1999.

Grant, R.G. *Battle at Sea: 3,000 Years of Naval Warfare.* London: Dorling Kindersley, 2008.

Gray, Colin S. *Modern Strategy.* Oxford: Oxford University Press, 1999.

Heuser, Beatrice. *The Evolution of Strategy: Thinking War from Antiquity to the Present.* Cambridge: Cambridge University Press, 2010,

Lonsdale, David J. *The Nature of War in the Information Age.* London: Frank Cass, 2004.

Luttwak, Edward, N. *Strategy: The Logic of War and Peace.* Cambridge, MA: Belknap Press, 2003.

MacIsaac, David. "Voices from the Central Blue: The Air Power Theorists," in *Makers of Modern Strategy: From Machiavelli to the Nuclear Age*, ed. Peter Paret, 634, Princeton: Princeton University Press, 1986.

Mahan, Alfred T. *Mahan on Naval Strategy: Selections from the Writings of Rear Admiral Alfred Thayer Mahan.* Edited by Allan Westcott. Boston: Little, Brown, and Company, 1918.

Mahan, Alfred T. *The Influence of Sea Power Upon History, 1660–1783.* New York, NY: Dover Publications, 1987.

McCarthy, Thomas David. "Traveling Domain Theory: A Comparative Approach for Cyberspace Theory Development." PhD Dissertation, Fletcher School of Law and Diplomacy, 2012.

Mitchell, Marshall L., III. *Clashes: Air Combat over North Vietnam 1965–1972.* Annapolis, MD: Naval Institute Press, 1997.

Mitchell, William. *Winged Defense: The Development and Possibilities of Modern Air Power, Economic and Military.* Mechanicsburg, PA: Stackpole Books 1925. Reprint, 1999.

Morrow, John H., Jr. *The Great War in the Air: Military Aviation from 1909 to 1921.* Washington: Smithsonian Institute Press, 1993.

Pape, Robert. *Bombing to Win: Air Power and Coercion in War.* London: Cornell University Press, 1996.

Rattray, Gregory J. *Strategic Warfare in Cyberspace.* Amazon: MIT Press, 2001. Kindle edition.

Slessor, J.C., *Air Power and Armies.* 1936; new imprint, Tuscaloosa, AL, Alabama University Press, 2009.

Strassler, Robert B. ed. *The Landmark Thucydides: A Comprehensive Guide to the Peloponnesian War.* New York: Touchstone, 1996.

United Nations. *United Nations Convention on the Law of the Sea.* 1994. www.un.org/depts/los/convention_agreements/texts/unclos/unclos_e.pdf

Warden, John. "The Enemy as a System." *Air and Space Power Journal*, 1995, 41–55.

Wylie, J. C. *Military Strategy: A General Theory of Power Control.* New Brunswick, N.J.: Rutgers University Press, 1967.

3 Cyberspace Domain Characteristics

In this chapter I will examine the characteristics of cyberspace that are necessary to understand cyberspace superiority. Cyberspace is immensely complex and I will not attempt to explain all its characteristics, but instead I will focus only on those concepts necessary to understand how to gain cyberspace superiority and what a combatant can do with cyberspace superiority once gained. Chapter 2 laid out the characteristics of superiority in the land, maritime, and air domains, while this chapter will lay the foundation for an understanding of cyberspace superiority, enabling Chapter 4 to build on that foundation and provide the details of how cyberspace superiority operates at the local level. I will analyze cyberspace superiority by utilizing the same categories examined in Chapter 2 for the land, maritime, and air domains. I will examine the geography and characteristics of cyberspace, offensive or defensive primacy in cyberspace, methods of gaining cyberspace superiority, the use of cyberspace superiority, the persistence of cyberspace superiority, and measurement concepts of cyberspace superiority. A connecting strand throughout these categories will be the interaction between the universal and local levels of domain superiority.

In Chapter 2, I showed that we could analyze domain superiority at universal and local levels; while there is a universal level of superiority in cyberspace, the local level will be dominant. This dominance is due to a number of factors, which I will explore in this chapter, including the uniqueness of offensive and defensive cyberspace forces, the difficulty of attacking cyberspace forces at the universal level, and the dispersed character of cyberspace forces. To build this argument, I will first examine a few of the characteristics of cyberspace as a domain.

Geography and Characteristics of Cyberspace

Cyberspace is composed of information and connections in a virtual space, but it is grounded in the physical world.[1] According to cyberspace analyst Paul Rosenzweig, "we should never forget that though the cyber domain is an artificial one created by man, it exists only in the context of the fundamental natural domain of the world."[2] Events in the physical world affect cyberspace. If the heart of cyberspace is the connection between computing devices, then anything that affects those devices or their connections affects cyberspace. A failed air conditioning unit at a server farm, a backhoe cutting a fiber cable, or an anchor dragging across an undersea cable can all have a tremendous impact on cyberspace. These links and connections to the physical world can provide attackers seeking cyberspace superiority important levers to utilize. Before delving into methods of gaining cyberspace superiority, it is helpful to consider a model of cyberspace that illuminates why cyberspace superiority operates the way it does.

Models of Cyberspace

There are numerous models of cyberspace, and many of the models share common characteristics. The earliest layered model that analysts have applied to cyberspace is the well-known Open Systems Interconnection (OSI) seven-layer model of a communication system. The OSI model starts with the physical then moves through data link, network, transport, session, presentation, and application layers. I find it less useful in analyzing cyberspace superiority than other models as it focuses only on the communication system and does not adequately separate the information from the information carrying system. How one accounts for information and the system on which it travels, is a critical concept in cyberspace superiority.

The U.S. Army Training and Doctrine Command (TRADOC) proposes that analysts can best understand cyberspace in three layers with five components. The layers are the physical, logical, and social. The physical layer includes the geographic and physical network components, while the logical layer includes only the logical network component. The social layer has two components: the persona and cyber persona components.[3] The persona component is composed of actual people, while the cyber persona is composed of cyberspace identities. Thus, a single person can have multiple cyber personas (such as multiple e-mail accounts) and a single cyber persona can be made up of multiple people (such as an organizational e-mail account).

I find that the social layer of the TRADOC model is problematic from a cyberspace superiority perspective. The social layer consists of real people in the form of persona components, and virtual people in the form of cyber persona components. Cyberspace superiority is about achieving objectives through the cyberspace domain. If people are included in the model, then the distinctiveness of the domain starts to break down. Influencing people through cyberspace is something you do with cyberspace superiority; it is not cyberspace superiority itself. People drive cyberspace superiority, but from the outside, not the inside. In this way cyberspace is more like the space domain than the land or maritime domains. In the land domain, people live and interact with the tools that they use in that domain. In the space domain, with the exception of a few astronauts, the people driving the satellites are not in the space domain, they are in the land domain. As there are no cyberspace equivalents to astronauts, including people conflates the land and cyberspace domains in unhelpful ways, and there are several other problems with the TRADOC model as well.

Like the OSI model, I also find TRADOC's model lacking in not separating information from the information system. Another issue with the model is that

TRADOC defines the logical layer to consist of network devices such as routers and so this layer conflates with the physical layer, which I also do not find helpful.

David Clark from MIT has offered a model with four layers. The bottom layer consists of the physical foundations, next is logical building blocks, then information, and finally, people.[4] Clark views cyberspace as hierarchical with people at the top connecting through information to logic to the physical foundations of cyberspace. Clark also states that cyberspace can be thought of as a "think veneer" drawn over the real world, rather than a separate world or space.[5]

I find Clark's model to have several helpful elements, especially in the distinction made between logical building blocks and information as separate layers. However, the people layer brings elements of the land domain into cyberspace, which, as discussed earlier, is not helpful. All of these models include a physical and some sort of network or logical layer, although they differ in the higher layers. However, there is a model more applicable to understanding cyberspace superiority.

Libicki's description of cyberspace is the most helpful, especially in the context of cyberspace superiority. Libicki builds his model using an analogy from linguistics and breaks cyberspace into the physical, the syntactic, and the semantic.[6] The physical layer consists of the wires, routers, and computers that create cyberspace and is the foundation of the model. The syntactic layer consists of the rules by which cyberspace actors move and process information in cyberspace. The software of cyberspace, both operating systems and applications, normally represents this layer. The final layer is the semantic layer. The semantic layer is the information itself. All three layers must work together for cyberspace to function.

As a simple example of how the three layers interact, consider a user opening a web browser to view "cnn.com." The initial input will come into the system at the physical level through a mouse and keyboard. At the syntactic level, the computer will interpret the input by utilizing the rules in the operating system. The operating system then uses the physical level to send the request through the network card to a router whose syntactic rules seek out the information and return it to the computer. The computer then displays the semantic information through a syntactic web browser on a physical monitor. The three-layer model can be viewed as a pyramid (see Figure 3.1).

Each higher layer of the model is dependent on the lower layers: if the lower layers fail, the higher layers also fail. The syntactic layer is dependent on the physical layer and the semantic layer depends on the syntactic. Elimination of the physical layer would cause the syntactic and semantic layers to dissolve, but the converse is not true. If a completely effective semantic attack deleted all the information in a database, it would not affect the syntactic and physical layers. If a backup of the information exists, which is increasingly common due to reduced storage costs, then a combatant could rapidly reconstruct the semantic layer using the still intact syntactic and physical layers. The same is true of the syntactic layer. If a syntactic attack completely erases the operating system, but leaves the physical hardware untouched, it is much easier to reconstitute than if an attacker destroyed the hardware itself. Although the layers interact, their different characters require different approaches for combatants seeking cyberspace superiority.

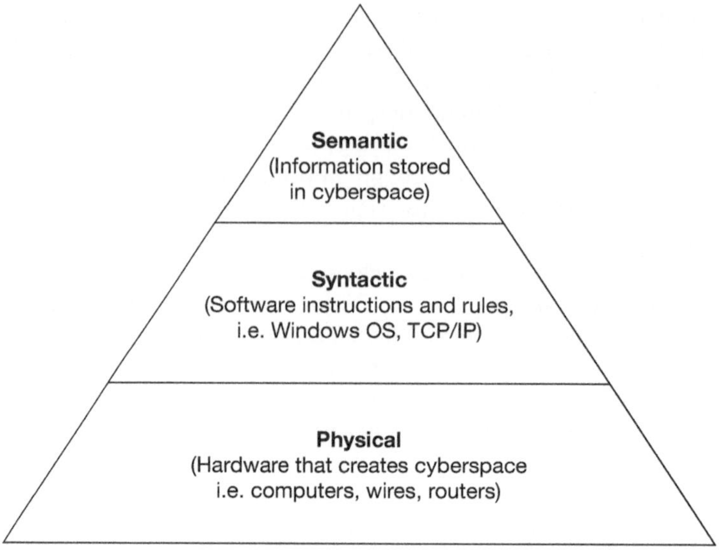

Figure 3.1 Libicki's Model of Cyberspace

Source: *Adapted from* Martin C. Libicki, *Conquest in Cyberspace: National Security and Information Warfare* (Cambridge: Cambridge University Press, 2007), 236–237

Each of the three layers is part of the struggle for cyberspace superiority, however, as identified by Libicki, combatants attack and defend them in very different ways. [7] If a combatant can cut communication links or destroy cyberspace components in the physical realm, that does not imply any ability to manipulate the operating system, or the information stored on the system. Likewise, a combatant who can manipulate the data flowing into, or stored in, a system has not automatically gained the ability to change the rules by which data is stored and managed. A combatant must attack or defend cyberspace in ways that are unique at each level with the physical layer being the most obvious one.

Within the physical layer, an attacker can attack the hardware of cyberspace, such as cable repeaters, fiber optic cables, or servers. Physical attacks can come through any of the physical domains or the cyberspace domain itself. As engineers demonstrated in the Aurora test, a cyberspace attack can physically destroy a generator.[8] There are also ways that a cyberspace attacker can target computing devices on the physical level. One technique is to rewrite the cooling protocols to generate a physical failure of the processor. The defender will respond to these types of attacks utilizing whatever domain forces are available and appropriate. Physical security of installations, air defenses, and isolating systems through an "air gap" provide some of the common defenses on this level.[9] Moving from the physical to the syntactic level is where an attacker enters the realm of software and physical hardware.

Software and operating systems reside at the syntactic level and offenders normally attack them through errors in the code that allow an attacker to trick a computer system into executing a set of instructions sent by the attacker. The syntactic level is what most people think of when discussing cyberspace attack. This layer is the home of protocols such as TCP/IP, operating systems, and applications. Attacks on this level include software Trojans, utilizing software flaws, and denial of service attacks.[10] Defenses include firewalls, intrusion detection systems, and patching vulnerabilities. It is important to note that this level deals with the rules and processes by which computing devices handle information, not the information itself. This distinction is critical to understanding cyberspace attacks and defense. Libicki draws a clear line, "between *attacks on information* and *attacks on information systems*."[11] He also notes that,

> those who would attack the mind of the enemy by attacking information systems may succeed in making much of what the enemy knows inaccessible, but not necessarily by changing the content of the information itself. It is akin to claiming that one has successfully messed with someone's mind by giving him or her a headache.[12]

If an attacker is trying to change the information itself, they have moved onto the semantic level.

The semantic level is where the actual information lies and combatants attack on this level by manipulating, destroying, or even adding information. The semantic level is where most information operations take place.[13] An attacker can destroy or manipulate information at rest by attacking information storage; he can also attack information in motion by disrupting communication systems.[14] Examples abound of ways to implement this type of attack at the semantic level.

There are many ways for a combatant to attack information and several avenues of defense at the semantic level. Examples include altering intelligence to mislead, corrupting logistical databases, changing manufacturing processes to induce flaws in equipment, etc. The possibilities are endless and limited only by the imagination of the attacker. Defenders have several avenues of defense to these attacks; they can boost the signal-to noise ratio, strengthen the signal through redundancy, or weaken the noise through filtering.[15] Examples of these defenses include keeping backups of databases and comparing them, utilizing multiple sources of intelligence with crosschecking, as well as data checking and verification processes. The key to a successful attack at the semantic level is that, "it relies more on the victim's predisposition to believe something than on the technical power to simulate that something convincingly."[16] One of the more famous examples of deception is the successful Allied campaign of World War II to convince Hitler that the European landings would be at Calais, not Normandy. The plan succeeded because the Allies were providing false evidence to reinforce what Hitler was inclined to believe already. This sort of information warfare is extremely difficult and requires an understanding of enemy leaders and their decision-making processes that will normally be hard to acquire, although the equipment used to execute the attacks may be relatively inexpensive.

Cost of Entry into Cyberspace

An entry-level capability for a nation-state in cyberspace can be very economical, however, significant capability is still expensive. Combatants access the physical domains of maritime, air, and space by technology and do so as well in cyberspace. Although the cost of ports, ships, airfields, aircraft, and spacecraft are very high, all a combatant needs to connect to cyberspace is an inexpensive computing device that they have connected to an Internet Service Provider (ISP). The entry costs into cyberspace are so low that collectives of civilians, such as Anonymous, or even individuals, can become significant actors.[17] Libicki notes that although armored warfare is normally beyond the reach of private individuals, and that rogue tank units are easy to spot, the tools of cyberspace warfare are available to anyone and easily hidden.[18] When acting on their own, non-state actors are more of an irritant than a significant threat to nation-states, however, they can be more threatening when used as part of a broader nation-state cyberspace conflict.

Several nations have utilized so-called "patriotic hackers" as proxy forces, which made them important in interstate conflict. As I will discuss in the case studies, there is good evidence that Russia used "patriotic hackers" in support of state objectives in the conflicts in Georgia and Estonia. Chinese "patriotic hackers" have also been very active, and while the evidence of links to the government is not as clear as in the Russian case, it is reasonable to assume that there is some level of connection between the government and the hackers. China has exceptionally robust control of cyberspace inside the country, and they have, at a minimum, chosen not to interfere with groups who were executing attacks aligned with Chinese objectives. Although these groups represent a low cost entry into cyberspace conflict for a nation-state, their capabilities are limited. To develop and field cyberspace capabilities that could challenge a technically-advanced nation-state for cyberspace superiority is very expensive.

Although cost of entry is low, significant capability in cyberspace is not cheap and requires substantial expenditure of resources. Despite the romantic Hollywood appeal of a brilliant hacker in a basement taking on and beating the CIA or NSA, it is not likely to happen. An analysis of Stuxnet, for example, has shown that it would have taken approximately ten man-years to write and develop.[19] Stuxnet was not written by a single individual or even a small team. Actually, the ten man-year estimate is low because it does not include the immense amount of detailed intelligence work that must have occurred prior to writing Stuxnet, or the extensive testing alleged to have occurred at various sites.[20] A cheap laptop and an Internet café will get you into cyberspace, but a substantial offensive or defensive capability is still something that is principally only accessible to nation-states due to the resources required. The expensive resources for success in cyberspace warfare require the abilities of many skilled people.

It seems counter intuitive for a domain that derives its very existence from technology, but well trained and capable people are more important in the battle for cyberspace superiority than equipment. A cheap laptop, sold for less than $500, almost as a commodity, has more computing power than the "supercomputers" that used to fill entire rooms and cost millions of dollars only a few decades ago. In certain areas, such as cryptography, technology and computing power can be significant, but in many areas of cyberspace superiority technology is not the most important component. What brings success is people, and not just any people. According to Libicki, "Success at hacking requires daring, initiative, and the rapid identification and seizure of fleeting opportunities."[21] These cyberspace warriors are operating in a domain with a networked structure, which has implications for cyberspace superiority.

Additional Cyberspace Characteristics Relevant to Cyberspace Superiority

The network structure of cyberspace gives it a high level of built-in resilience to attacks that focus on interfering with communication between nodes. When a computer sends information from point to point in cyberspace, the sending computer splits it into small pieces called packets that the computer sends separately for the receiving computer to reassemble into the complete message. These packets flow along the quickest logical, not physical, pathway between the two computers. An e-mail sent to your next-door neighbor, may flow geographically a very long way before ending up in his inbox, especially if he uses a different ISP. The routers that manage Internet traffic exchange information about how quickly they are transmitting traffic based on data load and environment. The routers then use that information to determine the fastest pathway for a packet of data, which can send a packet from Los Angeles to Denver through Miami. If an attacker were to interrupt a pathway from point to point, it is likely that no one would even notice, as packets would simply flow around the disabled communications node. If packets are lost when an attacker takes down a node, the receiving computer can automatically request the missing packets from the sending computer, which will flow through different channels and the complete message will still get through.[22] This network character of cyberspace gives it substantial built-in resilience, which makes it much harder for attackers to interrupt or modify information in transit. Although cyberspace is a network, it is not evenly distributed and there are places where multiple communication pathways converge.

There are chokepoints in cyberspace that we can consider as roughly analogous to mountain ranges or other geographic features. Rattray likens cyberspace nodes such as undersea fiber optic cables or communications satellites to mountain passes in the land domain or straits in the maritime domain.[23] If an attacker disrupted these chokepoints, it could have a major impact on cyberspace superiority. As a result, these chokepoints may become the focus of battles for cyberspace superiority. If a combatant can control them, they are well on their way to gaining cyberspace superiority. An example of a constructed chokepoint is China's "great firewall." China has deliberately set up their Internet infrastructure so that there are only three major entry points.[24] An analogy from the land domain might be a nation surrounded by an impassible mountain range that has only three passes connecting it to the outside world. It is much easier for the Chinese to control traffic through the three cyberspace "mountain passes" than it would be if there were hundreds or thousands of connections to other countries. China has created these limited entryways in an attempt to control communication in China, but there is also a down side as there are only three major connections into or out of China that an adversary needs to attack to cut China off from the rest of cyberspace. These chokepoints are not as static as mountain passes; combatants build them, and can change them far more quickly than in the other domains.

There are two facets to cyberspace's changing geography over time. First, combatants can connect, disconnect, or change the linkages between the components that create cyberspace. Every computer, router, or device attached, or removed, from cyberspace changes the cyberspace domain as a whole. We can think of an individual computer coming online as another grain of sand on the beach, one more or less grain of sand is not going to make much of a difference in the overall environment. However, much more significant changes are also possible. Rattray states that while mountains and oceans cannot be moved by combatants, in cyberspace a combatant can move or even turn off the equivalent geographic features quickly.[25] Someone does not even have to throw the switch deliberately; communications officers often joke that the most effective cyberspace weapon is a backhoe in the hands of someone who does not know where the utility company buried the cables. As an example, in 2008, a ship anchoring in the wrong spot severed 75% of the communications between Europe and the Middle East, and that incident was not nearly as significant as the 2006 earthquake that damaged seven undersea cables near Taiwan.[26] The chokepoints discussed previously represent nodes where physical disruption can produces major degradation and represent particularly vulnerable targets for combatants to attack and defend.

The second facet of cyberspace's changing geography is that designers rapidly continue to make the individual hardware more capable. Not only is cyberspace expanding as engineers connect more components, each new upgraded component can process faster, handle more connections, and store more data than the older ones. Computing power has risen at an exponential rate while storage costs have plummeted even faster.[27] Computers can process, move, and store amounts of data that were nearly inconceivable a few years ago. This fact has significant implication in the fight for cyberspace superiority as it makes it much more realistic to have multiple redundant computer systems that a defender can substitute for systems an attacker has disabled. Hardware redundancy has become far less cost prohibitive than in the past. As hardware becomes more capable and cyberspace expands, no nation will have superiority over the majority of cyberspace.

Because of the small number of cyberspace forces in relation to the vast amount of cyberspace, normally no nation-state will have superiority in a given area. Most of cyberspace is open and not directly controlled or regulated by any nation-state. There are also no border guards and customs posts as cyberspace communications cross borders. Lonsdale believes that because of its open nature with few forces similar to the maritime domain, Corbett's concept of no-one having superiority in the majority of cases will also apply to cyberspace.[28] This concept also implies that cyberspace superiority will trend toward neutral in the absence of significant effort by one side or the other, which will also limit the amount of superiority that a combatant can gain and how long a combatant can hold it.

Like the maritime, air, and space domains, analysts increasingly see cyberspace as a global common. According to NATO, "The Global Commons comprise four domains: maritime, air, space and cyber."[29] McCarthy concurs that "almost all modern scholarly analysis" includes the cyberspace domain as a global common and further illustrates the key element of a global common as, "that these areas are unowned and that no one nation is capable of exercising sovereignty over them in a manner that denies global access to the domain."[30] Despite the attempts to define cyberspace as a global common, it is not a settled question.

The argument that cyberspace is a global common seems to run counter to the fact that someone owns every piece of equipment that creates cyberspace, and every component physically exists in some country under a set of local laws.[31] The argument in favor of cyberspace as a global common is that the cyberspace that emanates from these devices is not "owned." It is not my intention to settle this debate, but the growing concept of cyberspace as a global common can restrain what attackers choose to do in cyberspace.

Combatants may restrain themselves in cyberspace to avoid crossing perceived global norms of cyberspace as a global common. For example, a cyberspace defender may want to disable computers that are attacking his systems. However, the attacker does not likely own those computers, but unaware, neutral third parties own them. If the defender disables them, is that akin to a naval combatant sinking neutral shipping on the high seas? Attackers may choose not to take actions that will move international public opinion against them. Another factor that cyberspace operators must consider is the inability of cyberspace weapons flexibly to engage enemy cyberspace forces.

Offensive cyberspace weapons have no ability to detect enemy offensive cyberspace weapons and so they cannot destroy them in opportune "meeting engagements."[32] If cyberspace weapons happen to cross paths in cyberspace, each will go right past one another with each heading on to its destination.[33] Cyberspace weapons do not have the ability to adapt to changing circumstances; they are more like an artillery shell fired by a cannon than a manned aircraft or ship that can choose to engage any enemy they find. This characteristic of cyberspace weapons makes the idea of offensive counter cyberspace from cyberspace unlikely to be useful.[34] Attacking an enemy's offensive cyberspace capability from one of the other domains is much more promising if you can cause physical destruction. A Joint Direct Attack Munition (JDAM) dropped on the building housing the enemy's cyberspace warfare center is an example of one possibility. This inability of cyberspace weapons to target each other as they cross in cyberspace is one of several reasons the offense currently has the advantage in cyberspace.

Offensive or Defensive Primacy in the Cyberspace Domain

In the land domain, attackers are normally out in the open and susceptible to attack, however, in the cyberspace domain it is the defenders who are visible and open to attack. This situation is the fundamental reason the offensive has the advantage in the cyberspace domain. However, as I will discuss later in the persistence section, this predominance tends to be short-lived and only lasts until the defender feels the effects of the weapon and detects the offender. The differences between offensive and defensive tools in cyberspace also heavily influence cyberspace superiority.

Attackers and defenders in cyberspace rely on fundamentally different weapons and tools for offense and defense, similar to the air domain. In modern air combat there is a difference between offensive air power and ground-based defenses. A modern Integrated Air Defense System (IADS) utilizes ground-based Surface to Air Missiles (SAMs) and Anti-Aircraft Artillery (AAA), surveillance assets integrated with Command and Control (C2), and airborne fighters. With the exception of multi-role fighters, these ground-based defenses cannot perform offensive missions into enemy territory; they can only target incoming aircraft. There is a similar difference between the defense and offense in cyberspace where offensive and defensive systems are neither similar nor interchangeable.

In the cyberspace domain, offensive and defensive weapons are not exchangeable, unlike the weapons of the maritime and land domains. At sea, a surface combatant such as a destroyer can perform either offensive or defensive missions. Even though there are specialized platforms such as submarines and anti-submarine aircraft, they can normally perform offensive or defensive missions. This flexibility in the use of forces also exists in the land domain as tanks and infantrymen can be used for offensive and defensive roles. However, in the cyberspace domain, a firewall and a worm are fundamentally different and while both are important, they are no more interchangeable than a Patriot and a B-52. Another way that cyberspace weapons are different from weapons in the maritime and land domains is that designers intend many of them to attack the target from the inside.

Cyberspace weapons can be thought of in two broad categories: those that attack from outside enemy systems, and those that attack from inside. Outside attacks focus on disrupting an enemy system's communication or access. The most common form of these attacks today are Distributed Denial of Service (DDoS) attacks where an attacker gains control of numerous neutral systems, then utilizes them to flood an enemy system with requests that prevent the enemy system from operating effectively. Other types of cyberspace-based external attacks are attacks on supporting infrastructure for the targeted system, such as attacking power or cooling. These attacks might be internal to the power control system, but they are external to the actual target. For example, consider a cyberspace attack that causes the cooling system for a server farm to heat up the server room to the point that the servers fail. It was an internal attack to the cooling system, but an external attack to the server farm. Less sophisticated and capable attackers generally utilize DDoS attacks; an attacker can achieve greater effectiveness by getting inside enemy systems.

Offensive cyberspace weapons striking the inside of an enemy system attack in a two-stage process: first they gain access, then they execute the mission. There are several ways that an aggressor can achieve access into an enemy system. The most common is through deception, where an attacker tricks a user into providing access. The most common method of accomplishing this is through an e-mail with an innocent looking attachment or link that opens the door for the attacker to get into and establish control of a system. Other potential avenues of access for an aggressor include software flaws, supply chain attacks, or software Trojans.[35] This first stage of the strike will look the same whether the attacker intends to take down a national power grid, or quietly look for intelligence. Thus, it is hard for defenders to know what type of attack they are under until the, "cyber payload 'explodes' and the effects are felt."[36] In both stages of an internal attack, an offensive weapon tries to hide from the defender.

Most cyberspace weapons rely on deception to get in, and stealth to persist and accomplish their missions. Deception involves pretending to be something you are not; stealth involves attempting to keep defenders from seeing you at all. Cyberspace wolves may wear sheep's clothing to get into a system; but once there, they attempt to disappear completely. It is normally easy for a cyberspace weapon to hide within the millions of lines of code resident in a typical computer. Until a weapon does something that draws attention to itself, system administrators rarely find it. Attackers can design their weapons carefully to remain hidden. Stuxnet is a famous example of a weapon that went out of its way to hide its presence by making the failures of the Iranian centrifuges look like mechanical and design failures instead of the result of a cyberspace attack.[37] This reliance of cyberspace weapons on hiding has several consequences.

Because most offensive cyberspace weapons rely on stealth and deception, defenders will generally be unable to see them coming, which gives an advantage to the offense. Unlike an infantry assault across an open field or an airborne strike package identified by radar, the first indication for a defender that an attack is underway may be the cyberspace weapon "going off." To remain hidden, attackers can utilize vulnerabilities that are unknown for new attacks. Analysts refer to cyberspace attacks that utilize unknown exploitable flaws as "zero day" attacks, because the timer on the vulnerability starts at zero when the defender discovers the attack, then increments up as software engineers scramble to develop a patch. Defenders who are unaware of the specific vulnerability will be unable to patch their system to eliminate the vulnerability. That is why zero day exploits are so important and guarded so carefully when discovered. Hackers often consider them the "crown jewels" and they can get prices of $60,000 to $120,000 on the black market for an exploitable Window's vulnerability.[38] Cyberspace defenders are unable to see attacks coming before they arrive, and they are often unable to determine where an attack came from after the defender discovers it.

The difficulty of attribution in cyberspace makes it challenging for defenders to understand where an attack is coming from and makes defensive responses more difficult. At the current time, it is fairly simple for actors in cyberspace to remain anonymous with widely available tools. The designers of the Internet built it to be open and they emphasized communication over security and attribution. As a result, although covert operations are difficult and rare in the physical world, they are the norm in cyberspace.[39] Fortunately for defenders, difficult does not equate to impossible, and defenders have some ability to eventually attribute attacks.

The anonymity of cyberspace is not absolute, even if the attackers are well resourced and competent. In the "Gh0stnet" attacks, an investigative team was able to determine that the attack on the Dalai Lama's network originated in China, but it took a year of effort.[40] In the battle for cyberspace superiority, knowing who did it a year after an attack may not be very useful, however, sometimes attribution is apparent from the context of the attack.[41] For example, in 2007 the Syrian air defense network went down due to a cyberspace attack. The fact that the cyberspace attack happened at the exact same time that Israeli fighter aircraft crossed the border to strike a suspected nuclear facility produces a reasonable level of confidence that the Israelis were behind the attack.[42] Sometimes attribution may be good enough for a nation to choose to respond, even if the evidence is not strong enough to convince the international community. However, if an attack is serious enough, attribution may become less problematic.

As combatants go up the cyberspace escalation ladder, attribution is likely to become easier.[43] For example, if someone breaks into DoD computers and steals some information, everyone expects the Chinese to be unhelpful whether or not they did it. However, if someone were to bring down large sections of the United States' power grid causing widespread chaos, destruction, and loss of life and that attack came from a Chinese IP address, the Chinese would have a choice. If they really were innocent of the attack, would they simply deny it while continuing to be unhelpful? Or is it more likely that they would not want to get into a confrontation with a wounded and angry superpower and would choose to cooperate with the United States in the investigation? Why would the Chinese consent to being framed, when they have a choice in the matter and can cooperate instead?[44] Of course, whoever attempted something as bold as framing the Chinese for an attack on the United States would be taking a terrible risk; if they got caught, they would have to face the wrath of both nations at the same time.

The difficulties with attribution suggest that combatants need to be cautious in assuming from where an attack is coming. This hesitancy to act can provide further advantage to the attacker in cyberspace. The advantage in the cyberspace domain goes to the attacker who can be proactive, as he can remain hidden and anonymous, while the defender is out in the open and reactive. The ability of attackers to hide their origin increases this advantage, but does not make it absolute. Both the offense and defense will have a role to play in gaining cyberspace superiority.

Method of Gaining Cyberspace Superiority

In this section, I will analyze various concepts of how to gain cyberspace superiority from different authors, then build a model using elements of several authors as well as the insights gained from the other domains in Chapter 2. Before moving on to theories of gaining cyberspace superiority, I will first analyze some of the arguments analysts have made that cyberspace superiority does not exist or is not useful. I will start with those authors that are most critical of the usefulness of cyberspace superiority before moving on to those who see greater utility in the concept.

Libicki is a well-known cyberspace author who does not see much utility to cyberspace superiority, and writes that the entire question of cyberspace superiority is meaningless and not a proper goal for cyberspace operators.[45] He believes that cyberspace superiority is impossible because combatants can simultaneously keep each other off their networks and he believes that it is not useful to state that a hacker "controls" a system when the defender still has physical control.[46]

There are two reasons I think Libicki is mistaken and there is utility to cyberspace superiority. First, the fact that combatants can simultaneously keep each other off their networks is a reflection of the different weapons and tools utilized by the defense and offense in cyberspace. This observation does not invalidate the concept of cyberspace superiority, it merely means that an analyst needs to examine two dyads instead of just one. An analyst needs to consider nation A's attack on nation B alongside nation B's attacks on nation A. This examination becomes most important when developing a measurement construct.

Second, I do not find Libicki's argument about physical control to be compelling. If a combatant "owns" his cell phone by right of physical possession, then does he still "own" it if it is working for the enemy? That cell phone could be reporting every private conversation, every e-mail or text, and providing the coordinates for the guided bomb about to land on the cell phone's owner. The physical owner may "own" the cell phone but if someone else controls and exploits it, the attacker would have meaningful cyberspace superiority according to the Joint Staff definition.

A second author who is skeptical of cyberspace superiority is Sean Butler. Butler has written that cyberspace superiority is not a useful doctrinal term as planners do not design campaigns to achieve it, and cyberspace superiority then ends up as merely a "shallow descriptor" of the quality of the engaged forces.[47] Butler thinks that a measurement of cyberspace superiority would simply be a comparison of how capable the opposing forces are, as he does not think there is any ability to maneuver in cyberspace.

I think Butler misses two points in his analysis. First, I think he is incorrect in his assertion that planners do not design campaigns to attain cyberspace superiority. The Georgian case study from 2008, the details of which are in Chapter 6, is a prime example. Just as in the air domain, well-designed campaigns will plan to get enough cyberspace domain superiority to accomplish their overall objectives.

Second, superiority in the other domains is not a "shallow descriptor;" we can see that the relative strengths of the combatants do not directly determine who has domain superiority. The entity with the better-equipped, trained, and larger force does not always achieve land, maritime, or air superiority, why should cyberspace be any different? There is ample opportunity for an agile combatant to "maneuver" in cyberspace by creatively applying the cyberspace power they have against appropriate enemy weak points. Although Butler and Libicki do not see much utility to cyberspace superiority, some authors see value to the concept without proposing a detailed theory of how to gain it.

Several authors support cyberspace superiority as a concept without providing a detailed map to gaining and maintaining it. Daniel Kuehl defines cyberspace superiority as, "the degree to which one can gain advantage from the use of cyberspace while if necessary preventing one's adversaries from gaining advantage from it."[48] This explanation is very close to the Air Force doctrinal definition and includes offensive and defensive elements of cyberspace superiority.

Merna Hsu also supports cyberspace superiority as a concept when she states that, "cyberspace superiority may be gained and maintained in a manner that exploits aspects significant to controlling the other mediums."[49] She is unfortunately vague about how a combatant can precisely gain and maintain cyberspace superiority.

Charles Eassa identifies cyberspace superiority as mirroring air and maritime superiorities although he does not think it is measurable and his proposed method of gaining it is too general to be helpful.[50] As for how to gain cyberspace superiority he says,

> To gain superiority, the CCDR [Combatant Commander] must have unfettered access in a constantly evolving and always contested environment. This requires a greater degree of integration of actions and capabilities and at lower echelons than ever before to achieve this effect. Actions at all levels focus on ensuring required information flows through the cyber domain while maintaining access or control of the infrastructure necessary to gain cyber superiority.[51]

"Unfettered access" sounds like a great thing, but Eassa tells you to achieve it by "integration of actions" and "maintaining access or control." It is hard to disagree, but these concepts are too broad and not actionable. "Maintaining access and control" is a way to define what cyberspace superiority is, but it does not tell you what to do to get it. Integration will be important to gaining cyberspace superiority but advocating "a greater degree of integration" without providing specific organizational recommendations is not useful. One author provides a more in-depth view of how to achieve cyberspace superiority.

McCarthy provides a more comprehensive analysis of gaining and maintaining cyberspace superiority. He states that combatants seeking cyberspace superiority should focus on controlling the flow of traffic in the cyberspace domain to degrade the enemy's ability to use cyberspace.[52] He goes on to identify the control of chokepoints as the most efficient means of creating cyberspace superiority.[53] Here there is a solid concept that I will use to produce a more fully developed theory of how a combatant can gain cyberspace superiority. McCarthy came to this conclusion after studying domain control theory from maritime domain chokepoints where combatants could deny transit to enemy traffic while retaining it for friendly forces. If control of chokepoints were currently technically and politically feasible in cyberspace, this method would be the most efficient.

Unfortunately, at the current time, policy and technical limitations make controlling chokepoints in cyberspace challenging and not a practical way of achieving cyberspace superiority. The network design of cyberspace enables most traffic to seamlessly and rapidly divert around attempted blocks with no active intervention by the user. In addition, because of the problems with attribution, it will not be clear to a combatant that streams of information belong to the enemy. Also, the enormous amount of data passing across chokepoints, such as major undersea cables, makes filtering it very difficult with current technology. Trying to filter out enemy communications would likely slow friendly communication to a crawl, as the defender would need to inspect each packet to determine whether he will allow it to pass or block it. The Chinese are the closest to being able to control traffic using chokepoints as they have limited portals into China and do not have any legal issues with intrusive scanning that would be illegal in most Western nations. Even so, they have great difficulty controlling information into and out of China. Despite our inability to copy the Chinese methods directly, there are other ways that Western nations can pursue cyberspace superiority.

Because controlling chokepoints is not practical with the current technology and structure of cyberspace, combatants should pursue whatever universal superiority is attainable, while focusing on the fight for local cyberspace superiority. In Chapter 2, I built a generic model of domain control that was broken into offensive and defensive segments before I applied it to the land, maritime and air domains. Applying the same methodology to the cyberspace domain yields the model of gaining and utilizing cyberspace control shown in Figure 3.2.

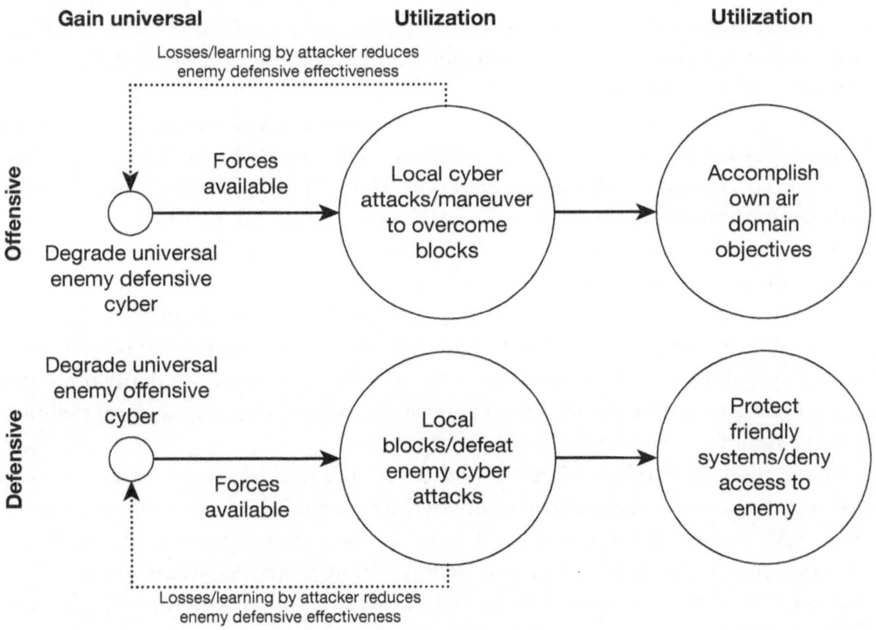

Figure 3.2 Model of Gaining and Utilizing Cyberspace Superiority

Source: *Author's original work*

In cyberspace, the local level of superiority is far more important than the universal when compared to the other domains. First, it is difficult to move cyberspace weapons from one local area to another. Despite the fact that cyberspace weapons and tools are easy to copy, they do not transfer easily to other local areas. On the offensive side, the problem is that designers carefully tailor weapons to a precise target. Stuxnet, for example, would only function if it were on a system with one of two types of Siemens controllers, and only if the weapon detected a specific configuration of the controllers. On the defensive side, moving upgraded defenses from system to system is somewhat easier, but still challenging because many systems are incompatible or run different operating systems. Many users and even IT professionals are slow to patch their systems, which slows the transfer of defensive upgrades to different local areas. For example, one month after an important Java security update, only 7% of users had downloaded the patch.[54]

Second, offensive and defensive forces in cyberspace are very different, which prevents combatants from moving between offensive and defensive missions. In contrast, the infantry, armor, and artillery of the land domain can all act on the offense or defense; the same is true of ships or multi-role fighter aircraft. In cyberspace, offensive weapons have no utility as defenses, and vice versa. This limitation removes the flexibility available in the other domains when combatants are moving forces and allocating them from the universal level to various local areas.

A third reason combatants normally fight for cyberspace superiority at the local level is the highly specialized, single system characteristic of cyberspace weapons. Attackers have to design offensive weapons to attack a specific system. In the air domain, a 500-pound general-purpose bomb from an aircraft can destroy a bridge, tank, ship, or building. In the cyberspace domain, attackers have to design most offensive weapons for a specific system configured to work in distinctive ways, with particular patches and connections. Designers have to create very specific weapons because they normally rely on vulnerabilities that are dissimilar in different systems. As a simple example, a Windows virus sent to an Apple machine normally does nothing interesting at all because it is speaking the wrong language.

A fourth reason cyberspace superiority tends to be local is that it is extremely difficult for combatants to find and attack enemy cyberspace "fleets" and "armies." Cyberspace weapons are more difficult to find than tanks, artillery, ships, and aircraft. The key resource in a cyberspace weapons system on offense or defense is the highly trained people, who are very hard to find and target. A combatant can hide a cyberspace lab or operations center in just about any non-descript building with no identifying smokestacks or cooling towers.

In addition, the relative unimportance of physical distance in cyberspace makes it very easy for cyberspace forces to disperse widely across multiple installations. Cyberspace operators do not have to be concentrated to be effective. Cyberspace defenses are broken into multiple systems and locations so even if an attacker takes down the systems in one local area, the rest are not directly affected. This fragmentation does not mean there may not be opportunities to degrade overall enemy cyberspace capability, but these opportunities will not be routine and will often require support from other domain forces.

On the rare occasions it is possible, directly targeting cyberspace forces will require the utilization of physical domain forces. For example, if a cyberspace facility is located, a combatant could attack it directly with land, maritime, or air-based kinetic forces. The loss of the equipment, and more importantly personnel, could have a significant impact on the enemy's universal cyberspace superiority and could affect multiple local areas as those resources are not available, but a smart adversary can prevent devastating physical attacks by keeping his cyberspace forces hidden and dispersed. A bomb on a building is not the only possibility for degrading an enemy's cyberspace capability at the universal level, but it is one of the most straightforward.

Although a combatant can probably not destroy the enemy's cyberspace weapons from cyberspace due to backups, an attacker could render the enemy's offensive weapons ineffective if he analyzed them before the enemy launches them. It is conceivable that a clever cyberspace attacker might be able to locate, or use, a spy to access an enemy's stock of cyberspace weapons. Even if the weapons themselves were untouched, if the attacker could determine what vulnerabilities they utilized, then patch those vulnerabilities, it would significantly degrade the enemy's offensive cyberspace potential. If the enemy has limited access to cyberspace, an attacker has another option.

In a fight with a nation having limited cyberspace portals, an attacker could take those portals down through cyberspace or physical attack. This approach would correlate well to McCarthy's suggested strategy of focusing on chokepoints. For example, if an attacker disrupted all three of China's portals to the Internet, it could reduce the number of attacks China could launch in return. However, taking down portals might not do very much to reduce potential enemy attacks, as there are multiple ways for the Chinese to access cyberspace through other communications pathways, such as satellite communications, agents outside the chokepoints, or hidden additional pathways. It would also be very difficult to take down enough portals in a well-connected nation such as the United States to have much of an impact. The enemy will react to the down portals, but these attacks may still be worthwhile even if they only reduce his effectiveness slightly. In cyberspace, physical destruction such as a bomb onto an Internet portal will be the exception; much more common will be countering enemy cyberspace weapons through learning.

Cyberspace weapons can sometimes have physical effects, and non-cyberspace weapons from the other domains can create physical losses that affect cyberspace assets, but in the vast majority of cases, what causes a weapon or tool to lose its effectiveness in cyberspace is learning by the enemy. For cyberspace attackers, enemy learning is the principal threat, as once the enemy learns how the attack functions, the defenders can normally inoculate their systems against that particular attack, as I discussed earlier. The weapon itself has not been touched, but it has lost its ability to produce effects, as the enemy system is now immune to its attacks.

Although their problem is less acute, cyberspace defenders face a similar dynamic. As an attacker probes a set of defenses and learns where the weak points and gaps are, the system's defenses become less effective. Stuxnet is an example where the creators of a weapon made adjustments based on learning to reach their objectives more effectively.[55] This learning is much faster for defenders than attackers, so offensive weapons lose their effectiveness more quickly. These losses will have their most pronounced impact on the local rather than the universal level of cyberspace superiority.

The local level of cyberspace superiority is more important because of the very different offensive and defensive forces, the difficulty of attacking universal cyberspace forces, and the dispersed character of cyberspace resources. The method of gaining local cyberspace superiority will be different for the attacker and defender.

An attacker will gain local cyberspace superiority by successfully accessing enemy systems to accomplish desired objectives. Doctrine has defined cyberspace superiority as the ability to conduct operations without prohibitive interference. Therefore, if an attacker is attaining his objectives in cyberspace, he is also gaining cyberspace superiority. Conflicts for cyberspace superiority are dynamic; the defender will be attempting to stop the attacker at the same time.

A defender will gain local cyberspace superiority by successfully blocking the enemy from achieving his offensive objectives, and protecting friendly access to cyberspace systems. A defender's objectives in cyberspace are both positive and negative. On the negative side, the defender is attempting to prevent the attacker from accomplishing his objectives whether they are overt or covert. On the positive side, the defender is attempting to keep their friendly systems up and running effectively. Keeping friendly systems up and running does not assume success for the defender. The attacker may not be trying to disable the defender's systems, but may have more subtle objectives. An attacker could be attempting to manipulate data inside a defender's systems to produce bad decisions by the defender's leadership. Just because the system appears to be functioning does not mean the defender has successfully maintained cyberspace superiority if the system has become secretly corrupted. Once a combatant gains local superiority, he can then utilize it to achieve his objectives through several mechanisms.

Use of Cyberspace Superiority

A combatant pursues various uses for superiority in the offensive and defensive realms of cyberspace. On the offensive side, an attacker will use superiority to accomplish his objectives or ways. These normally include Strategic Information Warfare (SIW), intelligence collection, reducing enemy logistics, disrupting enemy actions, misdirecting enemy actions, and support to other domain forces. Detailed descriptions of these ways and how they operate can be found in Chapter 4 as part of the local cyberspace superiority model. Defenders will attempt to use their cyberspace superiority to protect their systems and prevent the enemy from achieving their objectives.

Although it often receives less attention, protecting friendly systems and denying access to the enemy is likely the most important result of cyberspace superiority for a highly connected nation such as the United States. The more connected and cyberspace reliant a nation is, the more devastating it is if an attacker can disrupt those systems.

U.S. military forces have become increasingly reliant upon cyberspace-enabled tools and connectivity such as data links and friendly tracking systems. Connectivity can greatly increase effectiveness. For example, the installation of data link systems into fighter aircraft makes them far more capable. The down side is that pilots can become so dependent upon the new systems that they are unable to accomplish their missions without them.[56] The same is true across other types of domain forces. Beyond degradation of fielded military forces, a nation's infrastructure can come under assault if cyberspace superiority is lost.

On the home front, the loss of cyberspace superiority will open up a nation's infrastructure to potential long-range attack. The electrical grid, water, transportation, and communications infrastructure are critical to modern life. Their loss would be far more important today than 100 years ago when much of the population still lived in rural settings and were either involved in, or at least close to food production. If an attacker could disrupt these systems, they could exert tremendous pressure on decision makers to concede issues not involving the survival of the nation. The amount of pressure that an attacker can bring to bear will vary depending on the targeted nation's level of dependency on cyberspace.

Taking down the electrical grid in North Korea is unlikely to cause them to surrender in a perceived fight for national survival; taking down the electrical grid in the United States may have a greater impact. The importance of the issues under discussion to the nation under attack is a critical variable. In Vietnam, the United States did not suffer a military defeat, but the nation determined that the cost of continuing the war was not worth the potential gain. If the Chinese were invading the West coast while demanding unconditional surrender, it is unlikely that the United States would capitulate because the power grid went down. If the Chinese were demanding that the U.S. stay out of a fight over Taiwan, the response from U.S. decision makers to the loss of the power grid might be different. One of the key inputs into a decision maker's calculus will be how persistent they expect cyberspace effects to be.

Persistence of Cyberspace Superiority

Cyberspace superiority is measured relatively between two combatants and so only has significance in a contested portion of cyberspace. It is true, but not particularly illuminating, to state that a defender has cyberspace superiority when they are not under attack. When I analyze the persistence of cyberspace superiority, it is from the perspective of an attacker. If a defender maintains superiority, they will still keep it after an attack stops. However, if an attacker is successful at seizing cyberspace superiority during an attack, how long are they likely to be able to keep it?

The persistence of cyberspace superiority for an attacker will be very short due to the replicability of cyberspace, its great speed of action, and the rapid degradation of offensive cyberspace weapons. The primacy of the local over the universal level in cyberspace superiority discussed earlier is also an important driver in offensive cyberspace superiority's lack of persistence. The characteristic of cyberspace affecting persistence that is most unlike the other domains is its replicability.

Software and data in cyberspace are replicable, which makes software- and data-based attacks easier to recover from. One way for a defender to reduce the effects of an attack is if he keeps several complete up-to-date copies of software and data in locations inaccessible to an attacker. If an information system is "destroyed," then is back up and running a few hours later from a clean backup copy, the window of effect from even a successful attack is very short. If a defender can copy the software and data of a system, he could easily repair damage done by non-hardware attacks.[57] The increasingly inexpensive replicability of cyberspace systems also makes attacks based on manipulating data harder to execute. A defender can crosscheck multiple copies of information and see whether an attacker has modified the data. This replicability of cyberspace contributes to the short timescale of most attacks because recovery tends to be very fast. In addition to its replicability, cyberspace's lack of distance also decreases persistence.

Physical distance is less important in cyberspace than in the other domains. According to journalist Robert O'Harrow, "It almost doesn't matter where hackers work. In the physics governing cyberspace, hackers, terrorists and cyberwarriors can operate virtually next door. . ."[58] Push a button in Kabul and a power grid in Nebraska goes down; cyberspace warriors do not have to gain physical access or even be on the same continent as the target. Where physical distance and location still matter is if an attacker is going to use the other domains to attack cyberspace assets such as with an air delivered bomb on the enemy cyber operations center. The lack of virtual distance in cyberspace also contributes to its great speed of action, which reduces the persistence of cyberspace superiority.

The short timescales of cyberspace produce great speed of action and rapidly changing dominance. Robert Belk and Matthew Noyes state that the millisecond timescale of cyberspace communications makes cyberspace warfare more rapid than any of the other domains.[59] The release of a single weapon in cyberspace that travels to its target and has catastrophic effects in seconds can change the entire battlespace. This speed, and lack of distance, means that a battle, or even a campaign, can turn in an instant from success to failure and back again. Another characteristic of cyberspace discussed earlier that affects persistence is the importance of the local over the universal level.

The greater importance of local or universal cyberspace superiority reduces persistence significantly. If a combatant achieves a high level of universal superiority in a domain, it can be hard for the enemy to recover, as he has to build up an entirely new set of forces to contest domain superiority again. Thus, if combatants fight for domain superiority at the universal level, as has often been the case in the maritime domain, superiority can be very stable. If, as in cyberspace, the domain superiority achieved is only local, then the enemy does not have to build new forces, he only has to shift them from another local area and he can rapidly contest domain superiority again. As has been discussed, cyberspace tools may not shift easily from one local area to another if they are different systems, but combatants can move the people writing and using the tools effectively and quickly.

Another reason offensive cyberspace superiority will not tend to be persistent is the rapid degradation in the effectiveness of attacking cyberspace weapons once defenders discover them. Defenders can easily access the hardware and software on their systems and can normally eliminate the weapons quickly once discovered. If the weapon is too hard to eliminate in a system, administrators can erase everything and completely reload systems from clean backup copies. In the attacks on ARAMCO, or the 2011 and 2013 North Korean attacks on South Korea, administrators were able to clean the systems and get them back running in days once the attacks started and the weapons could no longer hide. Cyberspace weapons are akin to glass swords: they can be very sharp and lethal, but they tend to break on the first swing. Because offensive cyberspace weapons lose their effectiveness so quickly, attackers can normally only use them once.

Once a defender finds an enemy weapon, he will be able to inoculate his other systems and the weapon will lose most of its utility for future attacks. The following medical analogy is apt.[60] A vaccine protects the body by "teaching" the immune system what to look for. In the same way, once an administrator teaches an anti-virus system what to look for, that anti-virus system will be very effective at keeping out a particular attack. As a result, offensive cyberspace weapons tend to be single use. In other domains, weapons can keep their relative effectiveness after an attacker has used them, but not so in cyberspace. Designers of cyberspace weapons can use several approaches to mitigate this rapid loss of effectiveness.

One approach is to co-opt the defender's tools. North Korea used this concept when they utilized the update mechanism of a popular South Korean anti-virus program to propagate their 2013 attack.[61] However, taking over the anti-virus program still did not produce long-term cyberspace superiority as one can see in the case studies.

A second approach is to propagate widely an aggressive weapon so that it can re-infect machines that defenders clear; it appears that Stuxnet used this strategy.[62] This approach was part of the success of Stuxnet and attackers could use aggressive infection protocols for other cyberspace weapons. The drawback to this approach is that the more aggressive the weapon is, the more likely it is to trigger alarms, even though it is attempting to stay hidden. It appears that the aggressive nature of the upgraded Stuxnet is what caused it to get out "in the wild."[63]

A third approach by cyberspace attackers is to produce different versions of the weapon that are just different enough to escape notice by anti-virus programs relying on signatures of previous versions. Polymorphic viruses do this automatically every time they jump to another machine. Defenders who utilize heuristic scanning to look for characteristics of malicious software instead of just specific signatures, can mitigate this technique.

A fourth approach is to focus on chokepoints and expensive, difficult to replace, infrastructure components. Attacking software will not yield much effect if the defender can reload from clean copies. Destroying racks full of servers will also not accomplish much if the enemy has warehouses full of replacements or an easy way to route information around the disabled node. However, there are hardware components that are more expensive and difficult to replace than generic routers and computers. Some of these targets may not be cyberspace components at all, but instead support the cyberspace components such as power generation. For significant, persistent effects, cyberspace attackers should look to attack difficult to replace hardware in support of a chokepoint that carries multiple communication pathways.

A final approach to achieve longer persistence of cyberspace superiority is for the weapon to stay hidden and work in the background. Defenders can only reconstitute damaged systems and inoculate against attacks they know have occurred. Certain types of attacks lend themselves to this technique. If an attacker is attempting to manipulate databases, collect information, or create physical effects that look like they have another source, the weapon can stay hidden. Stuxnet and various espionage attempts are examples of this sort of attack.

These strategies can help extend offensive cyberspace superiority, but the examples of nation-state cyberspace attacks currently known show a short duration for offensive cyberspace superiority. In the eight cases studied in Chapter 6, seven of them persisted less than two weeks and the one case that lasted longer was because Stuxnet was able to hide successfully its activity from the Iranian defenders for an extended period of time. In some cases, such as ARAMCO and Stuxnet, defenders brought in outside resources, which are available to any nation-state. A broad exception to the short-lived characteristic of cyberspace attacks is espionage; I excluded them from the case studies for reasons I discuss in Chapter 6. If an attacker is able to stay hidden, the attack can continue, but this tactic is only possible if there is no external manifestation of the attack detected by the defender. To be able to analyze properly the persistence of cyberspace superiority in the case studies, it will first be necessary to develop a measurement system capable of measuring the level of cyberspace superiority in a given conflict.

Measurement Concepts of Cyberspace Superiority

Measuring cyberspace superiority will be challenging due to the characteristics of the domain. The anonymity and secrecy that surrounds cyberspace operations makes it difficult to determine what is actually going on in any given conflict. This uncertainty can even include who the combatants are, as attacking nations may attempt to cast the blame on someone else. Comparing force capabilities in cyberspace is also very challenging, which limits the utility of order of battle comparisons as a measurement tool. Finally, developing a numerically-based cyberspace superiority measurement system will at some point require quantifying qualitative data, which is often a difficult and error prone process. Fortunately, there are elements of domain superiority from the other domains that we can utilize.

In the land domain, analysts measure superiority by whose soldiers are in possession of the terrain and who has the acquiescence or support of the population. These metrics have limited utility to cyberspace superiority other than the general principle that superiority is a relative measurement based on a dyad in conflict, not an absolute measurement. Measuring superiority in the maritime domain is more applicable to cyberspace.

In the maritime domain, analysts measure universal superiority by the strength of the opposing fleets, and local superiority by who is able effectively to utilize sea lines of communication. Although comparing cyberspace "fleets" is not a promising approach, the parallels between moving goods on the seas and moving information in cyberspace implies utility to measuring the health of lines of communication in cyberspace. For cyberspace combatants, this utility will most often be on the defensive side and will involve effectively measuring the health of defended cyberspace systems. Analysts should couple this measurement of the functionality of defensive systems gleaned from the maritime domain with offensive measurement from the air domain.

Measuring air domain superiority principally revolves around measuring combatants' ability to achieve their objectives in the air. This concept has direct applicability to cyberspace where two of the principal measurements will be the accomplishment of objectives by cyberspace attackers, and the prevention of the completion of enemy objectives by cyberspace defenders. These measurement concepts will lie at the heart of cyberspace superiority measurement.

Cyberspace domain superiority is fundamentally about a combatant being able to achieve their objectives in cyberspace while preventing the enemy from achieving his, thus objectives will be key to measurement. A cyberspace superiority measurement method should account for the offensive and defensive sides of a conflict. It must also include measurement of the success of both combatants, as superiority is a relative measurement. We need to develop a method that allows for the incorporation of multiple measurement factors into a single system.

A weighted preference measurement construct will provide the analytical rigor and flexibility needed for cyberspace superiority measurement. I will further develop this approach in Chapter 5 and the measurement system will provide the ability to combine multiple inputs and weight them for their relative importance. Before turning to the details of local cyberspace superiority in the next chapter, I will review what we have determined so far about cyberspace superiority.

Conclusion

Cyberspace is a unique domain with distinctive characteristics, many of which have a significant impact on cyberspace superiority. It is a man-made domain that an analyst can usefully model using Libicki's linguistic model. Utilizing Libicki's three layers of the physical, syntactic, and semantic is helpful as cyberspace superiority operates very differently in each category. In the physical layer, the fight is over the hardware of cyberspace, whether using bombs from the air domain or cyberspace weapons that attack hardware components. The syntactic layer is composed of software and it is here that worms, Trojans, and viruses operate in an attempt to manipulate the instructions and rules of cyberspace systems. Finally, it is at the semantic level that one stores information in cyberspace; this level is the arena of information operations and changing enemy decision-making by manipulation of data and information. Cyberspace superiority operates on all of these layers in different ways, however, cyberspace superiority first requires access.

Contesting cyberspace superiority has a low cost of entry, but significant capability will still require a substantial investment. Although a laptop and an Internet connection are very cheap, developing modern and effective cyberspace weapons such as Stuxnet or Flame is not. The low cost of entry means there are many more players in the struggle for cyberspace superiority than is the case in the air or maritime domains where the cost of entry is high. There are not only nation-states, but also private individuals and collectives such as Anonymous or "patriotic hackers" that can weigh in and influence cyberspace superiority, for example, in conflicts between nation-states such as Russia and Georgia or Russia and Estonia where Russian "patriotic hackers" played a major role. These hackers had some initial advantage over their opponents as the offense currently has the advantage in cyberspace.

The offense has the advantage in cyberspace, as it is the attacker who remains hidden, while the defender is visible and vulnerable. This is the opposite of the land domain, where attacking soldiers generally have to move out in the open while defenders can remain hidden until they choose to engage. This circumstance provides an initial advantage to the offense over the defense in cyberspace superiority. This advantage will normally play out at the local instead of the universal level of cyberspace superiority.

Although universal cyberspace superiority is theoretically possible, in the majority of cases, superiority will be determined at the local level. The local level of cyberspace superiority is usually predominant in part because designers tailor cyberspace weapons to the local area and the system within which they designed them to operate. This specialization makes it much harder for a combatant to shift resources from one local area to another and decreases the importance of universal cyberspace superiority. The differences between offensive and defensive weapons in cyberspace further intensify the relative importance of the local level.

Another factor that drives the importance of local superiority is the inability of combatants to target the enemy's cyberspace "fleets" and "armies." On the universal level, cyberspace superiority assets are very easy to hide and extremely difficult to target and destroy. When the opportunity presents itself, a combatant should target any universal cyberspace targets, such as a cyberspace operations center, that present themselves. However, combatants should expect these opportunities to be rare. Once a combatant has gained superiority, he can utilize it for several purposes.

Combatants can utilize cyberspace superiority to accomplish offensive objectives, or to defend their cyberspace systems. Generally, cyberspace combatants will be trying to do both at the same time. Strategic information warfare is where a combatant attempts to achieve some effect directly through cyberspace. However, at the current time cyberspace is actually more important as an integrator and enabler of other domain forces. A modern cyberspace dependent force such as the U.S. military can be extremely effective when everything is working, but also effectively hamstrung by an opponent who successfully attacks their cyberspace systems. Finally, any combatant with cyberspace infrastructure will want to defend their systems to prevent the enemy from achieving his objectives. The rapid degradation of cyberspace attacks once launched significantly helps the defender.

Once an attacker is unmasked, physical ownership, replicability, and the frangibility of offensive weapons will enable defenders to recover rapidly and thus the persistence of offensive cyberspace superiority will be very short. Although attackers have an initial advantage, this advantage rapidly deteriorates once the defender realizes they are under attack. Historically, defenders have been able to rebuild their systems very quickly by either restoring from backups or rebuilding systems. Some defenders, such as the less capable Saudis and Georgians, brought in outside help in order to defend their cyberspace systems. These factors have resulted in a very short persistence for offensive cyberspace superiority.

The best way for an attacker to maintain greater persistence of cyberspace superiority is through remaining masked and hidden, which is a tactic only available in certain situations. Stuxnet took this approach by masking its effects to make the Iranians think the failures of their systems were due to manufacturing errors or poor design. As a result, Stuxnet was able to maintain cyberspace superiority much longer than has been observed with other cyberspace weapons. If an attacker is attempting to completely collapse the enemy's power grid, it is unlikely that the defender will not notice what is going on. To properly analyze the persistence of cyberspace superiority, we need to develop a measurement tool.

By utilizing a weighted preference model, cyberspace combatants can usefully determine what level of cyberspace superiority they have achieved compared to an opponent. The critical inputs into the measurement system are the objectives of the attacker and his level of success as well as the importance of various systems to the defender and his level of success in defending them. This information is difficult to obtain, but a weighted preference model will still allow for analysis.

The unique characteristics of the cyberspace domain produce three major elements of cyberspace superiority. First, offensive and defensive tools in cyberspace operate differently, with the offense having an initial, but short-lived advantage. Second, local cyberspace superiority will be far more important than universal cyberspace superiority, which will normally be unachievable and not worth pursuing. Third, cyberspace superiority will not normally be very persistent as the initial advantage for the offender will evaporate quickly once the defender realizes they are under attack. Combining the characteristics discussed previously with the domain superiority components from Chapter 2 produces Table 3.1.

Now that we have gathered the elements of domain control from the other domains in Chapter 2, as well as the unique characteristics of the cyberspace domain as they apply to cyberspace superiority, we can move forward to dive into the details of what cyberspace superiority actually looks like and how it operates. Because cyberspace superiority is principally a local phenomenon, that means developing a detailed model of how all the weapons and defenses such as worms, viruses, Trojans, firewalls, and everything else, interact and create local cyberspace superiority for the successful combatant.

Table 3.1 Summary of Domain Superiority Characteristics

Geography and Characteristics	
Land	• Physical terrain such as mountains, rivers, and swamps dictate lines of communication and which forces are most effective where combat tends to be sequential, with forces excluding each other from areas of their control while protecting their own lines of communication.
Maritime	• Maneuver space is bounded by land masses and ports which form chokepoints. • Sea lines of communication are the key element worth fighting over. • Accessed via expensive technology (ships) and expensive entry points (ports).
Air	• Open and relatively unbounded without natural chokepoints. • No clear front line; involves civilians directly in combat operations. • Characterized by great speed of action. • Dependent upon technology for access. • Accessed via expensive technology (aircraft) and expensive entry points (airfields). • Dominance in this domain is not sufficient for victory, however, it enables the land and maritime domains.
Cyberspace	• Man-made but connected to the physical world. • Can usefully be modeled by Libicki's three layers of physical, syntactic, and semantic. • An entry-level capability for a nation-state in cyberspace can be very economical, however, significant capability is still expensive. • The network structure of cyberspace gives it a high level of built-in resilience to attacks that focus on interfering with communication between nodes. • There are chokepoints in cyberspace that we can consider as roughly analogous to mountain ranges or other features in the land domain. • Combatants can connect, disconnect, or change the linkages between the components that create cyberspace. • Designers continue rapidly to make the individual hardware more capable. • Because of the small number of military cyberspace forces in relation to the vast amount of civilian cyberspace, normally no nation-state will have superiority in most areas of cyberspace. • Combatants may restrain themselves in cyberspace to avoid crossing perceived global norms of cyberspace as a global common. • Offensive cyberspace weapons have no ability to "see" and react to each other, thus, there is no analog to a meeting engagement in cyberspace.
Offensive or Defensive Primacy	
Land	• With modern weapons the defensive has primacy as the defender can stay undercover, while the offender must unmask to advance.

Maritime	• There is no clear offensive or defensive primacy in the maritime domain.
	  ○ Normally both offensive and defensive forces can see each other at the same distance.
	  ○ Exceptions include submarine warfare, which favors the offender and a fleet in a defended port, which favors the defense.

Offensive or Defensive Primacy

Air
- Older theorists favored the offensive, but the advantage has shifted back and forth over time depending on technology.

Cyberspace
- The advantage in the cyberspace domain goes to the attacker, who can be proactive as he can remain hidden and anonymous, while the defender is out in the open and reactive.

Method of Gaining Superiority

Land
- Universal: defeat enemy army to allow physical access to the terrain and then gain control and support of the population.
- Local: defeat local regular or insurgent forces.

Maritime
- Universal: defeat enemy fleet or blockade them in port; weaker combatant can contest by keeping a "fleet in being" and executing small counter attacks.
- Local: disrupt enemy shipping while protecting your own.

Air
- Offensive universal: degrade enemy strategic IADS.
- Defensive universal: degrade enemy offensive airpower.
- Offensive local: defeat enemy local IADS.
- Defensive local: defeat enemy local offensive airpower.

Cyberspace
- Controlling chokepoints is one way of establishing universal cyberspace superiority, however, it will not normally be possible.
- There are a number of reasons local cyberspace superiority will normally be all that is achievable:
  - It is difficult to move cyberspace weapons from one local area to another.
  - Offensive and defensive forces in cyberspace are very different and are not interchangeable.
  - The specialization of cyberspace weapons that attackers design for a single system.
  - It is extremely difficult for combatants to find and attack enemy cyberspace "fleets" and "armies".
- An attacker will gain local cyberspace superiority by successfully accessing enemy systems to accomplish desired objectives.
- A defender will gain local cyberspace superiority by successfully blocking the enemy from achieving his offensive objectives, and protecting friendly access to cyberspace systems.

Use of Superiority

Land
- Often control of the land domain will terminate the conflict; if not, combatants can extract resources for continued combat in other areas and domains.

Maritime
- Enable shipment of military and commercial goods.
- Project power into the land domain while preventing the enemy from doing the same.

Air
- Offensive: directly striking enemy centers of gravity to either affect enemy capabilities or change enemy decisions; support other domain forces.
- Defensive: prevent enemy from striking friendly centers of gravity.

Cyberspace
- Offensive: accomplish operational objectives through strategic information warfare, intelligence collection, reducing enemy logistics, disrupting enemy actions, misdirecting enemy actions, and support to other domain forces.
- Defensive: prevent enemy from accomplishing their offensive objectives while protecting friendly systems and maintaining their effectiveness.

(Continued)

Table 3.1 (Continued)

Persistence	
Land	• Land domain superiority tends to be persistent due to greater influence of the universal level of superiority, as well as the sequential tendencies of land combat, the inertia of populations whose support changes slowly, and the current primacy of the defensive.
Maritime	• Whether the maritime superiority gained is local or universal will greatly affect the persistence of maritime superiority. ◦ If a combatant can achieve universal maritime superiority through defeating the enemy fleet, then persistence can be high. ◦ If the enemy refuses to fight a major fleet action for universal control, then control will not only be localized, but also fleeting, as the enemy can dash out of port to raid convoys and establish local control in an area, then retreat back into port when threatened by the main adversary fleet.
Air	• Because of the high mobility of air domain forces to move from one local area to another, a combatant will be able to achieve persistence of superiority in the air domain only if he is able to achieve universal versus local air superiority.
Cyberspace	• The persistence of cyberspace superiority will be very short due to the replicability of cyberspace, its great speed of action, and the rapid degradation of offensive cyberspace weapons once defenders discover them.
Measurement Concept	
Land	• Whose soldiers are in possession of the terrain? • Metrics to determine the level of support of the population.
Maritime	• Universal: remaining capability of enemy fleet. • Local: metrics to measure friendly and enemy utilization of sea lines of communication; ability to project power into other domains.
Air	• Ability to achieve objectives in the air. • Relative measurement and trends of resources.
Cyberspace	• On the offensive side, key inputs of cyberspace superiority include the offenders objectives and level of success. • On the defensive side, key inputs of cyberspace superiority include the level of functionality of defended systems and their importance.

Notes

1 Gregory J. Rattray, *Strategic Warfare in Cyberspace* (Amazon: MIT Press, 2001), Kindle Location 28.

2 Paul Rosenzweig, *Cyber Warfare: How Conflicts in Cyberspace are Challenging America and Changing the World* (Santa Barbara, CA: Praeger, 2013), Kindle Location 488, chap. 2.

3 TRADOC Pamphlet 535-7-8, *The United States Army's Cyberspace Operations Concept Capability Plan 2016–2028*, 22 February 2010, 8.

4 David Clark, "Characterizing cyberspace: past, present and future" MIT CSAIL, Version 1.2. 12 March 2010, 1.

5 Clark, "Characterizing cyberspace: past, present and future," 5.

6 Martin C. Libicki, *Conquest in Cyberspace: National Security and Information Warfare* (Cambridge: Cambridge University Press, 2007), 8–9.

7 Libicki, *Conquest in Cyberspace*, 9.
8 Paulo Shakarian, Jana Shakarian and Andrew Ruef, *Introduction to Cyber-Warfare: A Multidisciplinary Approach* (Amsterdam: Syngress, 2013), Kindle Location 6561, chap. 12.
9 Air gaps are networks that designers have not physically connected to the Internet or other networks as there is a "gap of air" between them. This is a common way of protecting important systems, but it does have some limitations and weaknesses, as I will discuss in Chapter 4.
10 For a description of these types of attacks and others, see Chapter 4.
11 Libicki, *Conquest in Cyberspace*, 23.
12 Libicki, *Conquest in Cyberspace*, 24.
13 According to Joint Pub 1-02 information operations is, "The integrated deployment, during military operations, of information-related capabilities in concert with other lines of operation to influence, disrupt, corrupt, or usurp the decision-making of adversaries and potential adversaries while protecting our own." Department of Defense, *Joint Publication 1-02*, 15 December 2012, 140. Operations in the cyberspace domain will often contribute to information operations, but operations that have physical effects such as taking down a power grid will not. Some information operations will not be in the cyberspace domain, such as dropping pamphlets from aircraft. There is overlap between information operations and cyberspace operations, but there are exclusive areas as well.
14 Libicki has identified that there are many other ways to attack information as well. An attacker can attack the credibility of enemy information by injecting false information that will call into question the veracity of the rest of the information the enemy has. More subtly, given the difficulties most organizations and decision-makers have in successfully filtering information, an attacker could inject large quantities of factually correct but low-grade information into the enemy system to bury important information under an avalanche of trivia. An attacker who cannot directly manipulate the information possessed by an adversary may be able to raise the level of noise in the system and thus still degrade enemy decision-making. Libicki, *Conquest in Cyberspace*, 124.
15 Libicki, *Conquest in Cyberspace*, 55.
16 Libicki, *Conquest in Cyberspace*, 55.
17 Anonymous is a well-known international "hacktivist" group associated with numerous cyberspace attacks.
18 Libicki, *Conquest in Cyberspace*, 257.
19 Sean Sullivan, "Stuxnet Redux: Questions and Answers," *F-Secure*, 23 November 2010. www.f-secure.com/weblog/archives/00002066.html
20 David E. Sanger, *Confront and Conceal: Obama's Secret Wars and Surprising Use of American Power* (New York: Broadway Books, 2013), 192.
21 Libicki, *Conquest in Cyberspace*, 257.
22 Whether this actually occurs depends on the protocols being used. Some protocols such as the User Datagram Protocol (UDP) commonly used for streaming content, do not check for missed packets.
23 Gregory J. Rattray, "An Environmental Approach to Understanding Cyberpower," in *Cyberpower and National Security*, ed. Franklin D. Kramer, Stuart H. Starr and Larry K. Wentz (Washington, DC: Potomac Books, 2009), 268.
24 Chris C. Demchak and Peter Dombrowski, "Rise of a Cybered Westphalian Age," *Strategic Studies Quarterly*, Spring 2011, 42.
25 Rattray, "An Environmental Approach to Understanding Cyberpower," 256.
26 Elham Nakhlawi, Mustafa Al Arab, Caroline Faraj, Tess Eastment, Aneesh Raman and Brad Lendon. "Third undersea Internet cable cut in Mideast." *Cable News Network*, 1 February 2008. www.cnn.com/2008/WORLD/meast/02/01/internet.outage
27 Rosenzweig, *Cyber Warfare*, Kindle Location 2248, chap 12.
28 David J. Lonsdale, *The Nature of War in the Information Age* (London: Frank Cass, 2004), 185.

29 Major General Mark Barrett, Dick Bedford, Elizabeth Skinner, and Eva Vergles. "Assured Access to the Global Commons." ed. by Supreme Allied Command Transformation. (Norfolk, VA: North Atlantic Treaty Organization, 2011), 5.
30 Thomas David McCarthy, "Traveling Domain Theory: A Comparative Approach for Cyberspace Theory Development" (PhD diss., Fletcher School of Law and Diplomacy, 2012), 61.
31 Patrick W. Franzese laid out five components of a global common and found all of them problematic in cyberspace. Patrick W. Franzese, Lt Col, USAF. "Sovereignty in Cyberspace: Can it Exist?" Air Force Law Review 64, (2009): 17.
32 In a meeting engagement, both forces are moving forward and engage each other as soon as one side detects the other. These engagements are common in the land, maritime, and air domains. An example would be two opposing fighter aircraft that detect one another and engage despite the fact that they are both on bombing missions.
33 Sean C. Butler, "Refocusing Cyber Warfare Thought," *Air Space Power Journal* Volume 27, no. 1 (January–February 2013): 51.
34 Offensive counter cyberspace is a USAF doctrinal concept where cyberspace forces go out, find, and destroy opposing cyberspace forces. It is drawn directly from offensive counter air, which makes much more sense in the air domain. An attack on an enemy airfield is an example of offensive counter air; it is difficult to find realistic equivalent missions in cyberspace that only involve cyberspace forces.
35 For full descriptions of these types of attacks, see Chapter 4.
36 Rosenzweig, *Cyber Warfare*, Kindle Location 511, chap. 2.
37 Barrett, et al., "Assured Access to the Global Commons," 41.
38 Andy Greenberg, "Shopping for Zero-Days: A Price List for Hackers' Secret Software Exploits," Forbes, 23 March 2012. www.forbes.com/sites/andygreenberg/2012/03/23/shopping-for-zero-days-an-price-list-for-hackers-secret-software-exploits
39 Robert Belk and Matthew Noyes, "On the Use of Offensive Cyber Capabilities" (Master's Thesis, Harvard Kennedy School, 2012), 16.
40 Rosenzweig, *Cyber Warfare*, Kindle Location 4630, chap. 21.
41 Richard L. Kugler, "Deterrence of Cyber Attacks." In *Cyberpower and National Security*, edited by Franklin D. Kramer, Stuart H. Starr and Larry K. Wentz, 309–340. (Washington, DC: Potomac Books, 2009) 320. See also Jason Healey, *A Fierce Domain: Conflict in Cyberspace 1986 to 2012*, (Amazon: Cyber Conflict Studies Association, 2013) Kindle Location 3529.
42 Aki J. Peritz, and Michael Sechrist, "Protecting Cyberspace and the US National Interest" (Harvard Kennedy School Belfer Center for Science and International Affairs, 2010), 5.
43 Thomas Rid correctly identifies the heart of attribution as a political problem that can and will be solved when the political stakes are high enough. Thomas Rid, *Cyber War Will Not Take Place* (Amazon: Oxford University Press, 2013), Kindle Location 2781.
44 Rid, *Cyber War Will Not Take Place*, Kindle Location 3181.
45 Martin C. Libicki, *Cyberdeterrence and Cyberwar* (Santa Monica: RAND Corporation, 2009), 141.
46 Libicki, *Cyberdeterrence and Cyberwar*, 141.
47 Butler, "Refocusing Cyber Warfare Thought," 52.
48 Daniel T. Kuehl, "From Cyberspace to Cyberpower: Defining the Problem." in *Cyberpower and National Security*, ed. Franklin D. Kramer, Stuart H. Starr and Larry K. Wentz (Washington, DC: Potomac Books, 2009), 37.
49 Merna H., H. Hsu, "Gaining and Maintaining Cyberspace Superiority: Quest for a Holy Grail?" (Master's Thesis, The School of Advanced Air and Space Studies, 2009), 45.
50 Charles N. Eassa, "Enabling Combatant Commander's Ability to Conduct Operations in the Cyber Domain" (Master's Thesis, U.S. Army War College, 2012), 14.
51 Eassa, "Enabling Combatant Commander's Ability to Conduct Operations in the Cyber Domain," 15.

52 McCarthy, "Traveling Domain Theory," 235–236.
53 McCarthy, "Traveling Domain Theory," 288.
54 Dan Kaplan, "One month after recent Java update, 7 percent of users patched," *SC Magazine for IT Security Professionals*, 5 June 2013. www.scmagazine.com/one-month-after-recent-java-update-7-percent-of-users-patched/article/296431
55 Sanger, *Confront and Conceal*, 203.
56 The impact is even greater when a new generation of personnel has never operated the system without data links. Older personnel may be able to adapt and utilize the system at a lower level of efficiency using old techniques not reliant upon data links; new personnel will have more difficulty.
57 Libicki, *Conquest in Cyberspace*, 5.
58 Robert O'Harrow, *Zero Day: The Threat in Cyberspace* (New York: Diversion Books, 2013), Kindle Location 135, part 1.
59 Belk and Noyes, "On the Use of Offensive Cyber Capabilities," 16.
60 Paul Rosenzweig suggests that the medical world presents a very useful template for looking at cyberspace. Rosenzweig, *Cyber Warfare*, Kindle Location 752, chap. 34.
61 Economist. "North Korean cyber-rattling." *The Economist*, 17 May 2013. www.economist.com/blogs/babbage/2013/05/digital-warfare
62 Shakarian, et al., *Introduction to Cyber-Warfare*, Kindle Location 7003, chap. 13.
63 For more information, see the Stuxnet section of the case studies in Chapter 6. In short, it appears that Stuxnet got out in the wild when an Iranian scientist inadvertently interrupted the more aggressive version of Stuxnet in the middle of a process. The scientist then plugged an infected computer into the Internet, and despite not being on the right system, Stuxnet had already completed the protocols to check for a specific system and started to propagate. This circumstance resulted in it spreading beyond the nuclear system the designers intended to infect. Sanger, *Confront and Conceal*, 204.

Bibliography

Barrett, Major General Mark, Dick Bedford, Elizabeth Skinner, and Eva Vergles. "Assured Access to the Global Commons." Edited by Supreme Allied Command Transformation. Norfolk, VA: North Atlantic Treaty Organization, 2011.

Belk, Robert and Matthew Noyes. "On the Use of Offensive Cyber Capabilities." Master's Thesis, Harvard Kennedy School, 2012.

Butler, Sean C. "Refocusing Cyber Warfare Thought." *Air Space Power Journal*, Volume 27, no. 1 (2013): 44–57.

Clark, David. "Characterizing cyberspace: past, present and future." MIT CSAIL, Version 1.2. 12 March 2010.

Demchak, Chris C. and Peter Dombrowski. "Rise of a Cybered Westphalian Age." *Strategic Studies Quarterly*, Spring 2011: 32–61.

Eassa, Charles N. "Enabling Combatant Commander's Ability to Conduct Operations in the Cyber Domain." Master's Thesis, U.S. Army War College, 2012.

Economist. "North Korean cyber-rattling." *The Economist*, 17 May 2013. www.economist.com/blogs/babbage/2013/05/digital-warfare

Franzese, Patrick W., Lt Col, USAF. "Sovereignty in Cyberspace: Can it Exist?" Air Force Law Review 64, (2009): 1–42.

Greenberg, Andy. "Shopping for Zero-Days: A Price List for Hackers' Secret Software Exploits." *Forbes*, 23 March 2012. www.forbes.com/sites/andygreenberg/2012/03/23/shopping-for-zero-days-an-price-list-for-hackers-secret-software-exploits

Healey, Jason. *A Fierce Domain: Conflict in Cyberspace 1986 to 2012*. Amazon: Cyber Conflict Studies Association, 2013. Kindle edition.

Hsu, Merna H., H. "Gaining and Maintaining Cyberspace Superiority: Quest for a Holy Grail?" Master's Thesis, School of Advanced Air and Space Studies, 2009.

Kaplan Dan, "One month after recent Java update, 7 percent of users patched." *SC Magazine for IT Security Professionals*, 5 June 2013. www.scmagazine.com/one-month-after-recent-java-update-7-percent-of-users-patched/article/296431

Kuehl, Daniel T. "From Cyberspace to Cyberpower: Defining the Problem." In *Cyberpower and National Security*, edited by Franklin D. Kramer, Stuart H. Starr and Larry K. Wentz, 24–42. Washington, DC: Potomac Books, 2009.

Kugler, Richard L. "Deterrence of Cyber Attacks." In *Cyberpower and National Security*, edited by Franklin D. Kramer, Stuart H. Starr and Larry K. Wentz, 309–340. Washington, DC: Potomac Books, 2009.

Libicki, Martin C. *Conquest in Cyberspace: National Security and Information Warfare.* Cambridge: Cambridge University Press, 2007.

Libicki, Martin C. *Cyberdeterrence and Cyberwar.* Santa Monica: RAND Corporation, 2009.

Lonsdale, David J. *The Nature of War in the Information Age.* London: Frank Cass, 2004.

McCarthy, Thomas David. "Traveling Domain Theory: A Comparative Approach for Cyberspace Theory Development." PhD Dissertation, Fletcher School of Law and Diplomacy, 2012.

Nakhlawi, Elham, Mustafa Al Arab, Caroline Faraj, Tess Eastment, Aneesh Raman and Brad Lendon. "Third undersea Internet cable cut in Mideast." *Cable News Network*, 1 February 2008. www.cnn.com/2008/WORLD/meast/02/01/internet.outage

O'Harrow, Robert. *Zero Day: The Threat in Cyberspace.* New York: Diversion Books, 2013. Kindle edition.

Peritz, Aki J. and Michael Sechrist. "Protecting Cyberspace and the US National Interest." Harvard Kennedy School Belfer Center for Science and International Affairs, 2010.

Rattray, Gregory J. *Strategic Warfare in Cyberspace.* Amazon: MIT Press, 2001. Kindle edition.

Rattray, Gregory J. "An Environmental Approach to Understanding Cyberpower." In *Cyberpower and National Security*, edited by Franklin D. Kramer, Stuart H. Starr and Larry K. Wentz, 253–274. Washington, DC: Potomac Books, 2009.

Rid, Thomas. *Cyber War Will Not Take Place.* Amazon: Oxford University Press, 2013. Kindle edition.

Rosenzweig, Paul. *Cyber Warfare: How Conflicts in Cyberspace are Challenging America and Changing the World.* Santa Barbara, CA: Praeger, 2013. Kindle edition.

Sanger, David E. *Confront and Conceal: Obama's Secret Wars and Surprising Use of American Power.* New York: Broadway Books, 2013. Kindle edition.

Shakarian, Paulo, Jana Shakarian and Andrew Ruef. *Introduction to Cyber-Warfare: A Multidisciplinary Approach.* Amsterdam: Syngress, 2013. Kindle edition.

Sullivan, Sean. "Stuxnet Redux: Questions and Answers." *F-Secure*, 23 November 2010. www.f-secure.com/weblog/archives/00002066.html

TRADOC Pamphlet 535-7-8. *The United States Army's Cyberspace Operations Concept Capability Plan 2016–2028*, 22 February 2010.

U.S. Department of Defense, Joint Chiefs of Staff. "Department of Defense Dictionary of Military Associated Terms Joint Publication 1–02." Washington DC: Government Printing Office, 2010, as amended through 15 December 2012.

4 Local Cyberspace Superiority

Because universal cyberspace superiority will be rare and difficult to obtain, the heart of the struggle for cyberspace superiority will be at the local level and in this chapter I will develop a detailed model of local cyberspace superiority. As was discussed in Chapter 3, universal cyberspace superiority will generally not be attainable due to the localized nature of cyberspace systems, the specialization of cyberspace weapons that are normally designed to attack a single system, the ability to rapidly shift defensive resources, and the difficulty for combatants to find and attack enemy cyberspace "fleets" and "armies." Although a combatant will always want to seize any opportunity to increase their level of universal cyberspace supremacy, these opportunities will be rare. The difficulty in obtaining universal cyberspace superiority is what has caused some analysts such as Martin Libicki to decide that the concept is not useful.[1]

Instead of giving up entirely on cyberspace superiority, the focus should shift to the local level, where superiority is routinely possible for a determined and capable combatant. The learning that occurs out of each local engagement does have an effect on universal cyberspace superiority, but this influence is minimal as was also discussed in Chapter 3. As a result, in most cases, combatants will have to fight a continuing series of localized engagements for cyberspace superiority. Although the overall level of cyberspace superiority can be determined by summing up the results of these engagements, their linkages will normally be weak. This makes it difficult for a combatant to dominate all of cyberspace, but they do not have to dominate cyberspace to achieve a useful level of overall cyberspace superiority that can contribute in meaningful ways to the accomplishment of campaign and national objectives.

Although a combatant will generally be unable to achieve universal cyberspace superiority, a combatant can achieve a useful level of cyberspace superiority across selected systems. A combatant does not have to control all of cyberspace to have an impact. Stuxnet is a good example of this; the designers of Stuxnet focused it on the single objective of delaying the Iranian nuclear enrichment program. Stuxnet's success met some of the attacker's objectives while avoiding another kinetic war in the Middle East, but it never achieved anything close to universal cyberspace superiority, nor did the designers intend it to. Stuxnet achieved local cyberspace superiority while it remained hidden, and that was sufficient for the attacker to achieve his objectives. An analyst can add up the level of success or failure in separate local cyberspace combats to get a useful overall measurement of cyberspace superiority in a conflict, but that does not imply cyberspace superiority in all of cyberspace. When the designers of Stuxnet attacked Iranian nuclear enrichment, they left banking, telecommunication, power generation, and everything else untouched because they did not need to attack those systems to achieve their objectives. Accordingly, when I develop a measurement construct for cyberspace superiority in Chapter 5, it will only examine those local cyberspace systems that come under attack. It is easy to talk about the level of cyberspace superiority as a concept; the difficulty comes in connecting that overarching concept to concrete actions that combatants can take in the real world.

Modeling Domain Superiority

To build a model of cyberspace superiority, I will start with the foundational concept of means, ways, and ends. At its most basic, an attacker attacks, because they want to accomplish something. They should connect that something to an end they are seeking. Thus, you have the classic means, ways and ends. The means are the resources an attacker has available, while the ways represent the things the attacker is going to do with those means in pursuit of his ends. A simple diagram of the relationships between means, ways and ends is shown in Figure 4.1.

Means connect to ways through operations and ways connect to ends through strategy. As an example, in Kosovo, the United States' desired end state was the cessation of ethnic cleansing in Kosovo. After diplomatic efforts failed, the U.S. strategy became to utilize airpower to apply military pressure on Serbia until they agreed to end the ethnic cleansing. The things the U.S. could do with airpower such as strategic attack against infrastructure, or attack of enemy armed forces were the ways. The aircraft and support infrastructure were the means, which connected to the ways through operations in the air domain. This example helps to illustrate a key point, which is where superiority is active in Figure 4.1.

Domain superiority is about enabling operations without prohibitive interference, thus the focus of the model I will present is the connection between domain means and ways though operations. The box labeled "Area of Domain Superiority Influence" identifies the part of the diagram where domain superiority plays a significant role. The model I develop will not address the ends or the strategy to accomplish those ends. One reason for this focus is that the strategy and ends will normally incorporate means and ways from all of the physical domains plus more elements such as diplomatic and economic power. A combatant can accomplish ends through different domains depending on the strategy and most often, an effective strategy requires deliberately creating and utilizing interactions between the domains. Colin Gray's strategic bridge connecting military means and ways to desired ends is not the focus of this book.[2] The focus of this book is the role that cyberspace superiority plays in the interaction between cyberspace means and ways, where the enemy always gets a vote.

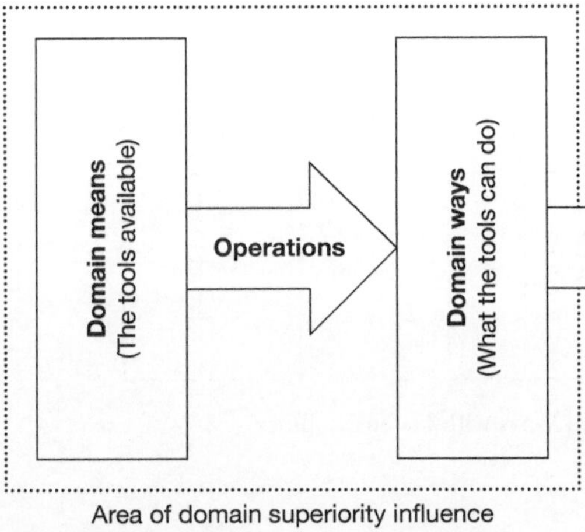

Figure 4.1 Domain Means, Ways, and Ends
Source: *Author's original work*

Conflict in any domain is interactive; a defender will attempt to interfere with an attacker to prevent him from accomplishing his objectives in cyberspace. Any proposed model must account for the dynamic nature of conflict where both sides make decisions in response to each other. Clausewitz captured this interaction with the analogy of two wrestlers struggling together, each attempting to throw the other, and anyone building a model of conflict must capture this vigorous interaction in the model.[3] Figure 4.2 illustrates the operations arrow connecting means and ways, but now the defender is attempting to prevent the attacker from achieving his objectives. This action by the defender is not the end of the story as the offender gets to react to the defender as well.

In each domain, there are numerous actions that an attacker can take to evade, circumvent, or punch straight through defensive blocks. Martin Libicki has observed that, "Unfortunately, next to failure to learn, the second most fundamental mistake in warfare is failure to anticipate that the other side also learns."[4] The attacker does not have to accept passively that the defender has blocked him, but can instead come up with a set of actions to remove or mitigate the defender's blocks as is illustrated in Figure 4.3.

There are reactions to the reactions and so on *ad infinitum* but going only two levels up is sufficient to make the dynamic nature of the contest apparent without making the model too complex to be useful. This model shows not only the dynamic nature of conflict in a domain, but also provides the toolkit to understand the nature of domain superiority in a specific domain or case.

In the domain superiority model given in Figure 4.3, an effective connection of means and ways through operations represents offensive domain superiority while severing that connection represents defensive superiority. The linking of the presence of offensive domain superiority to the connection between means and

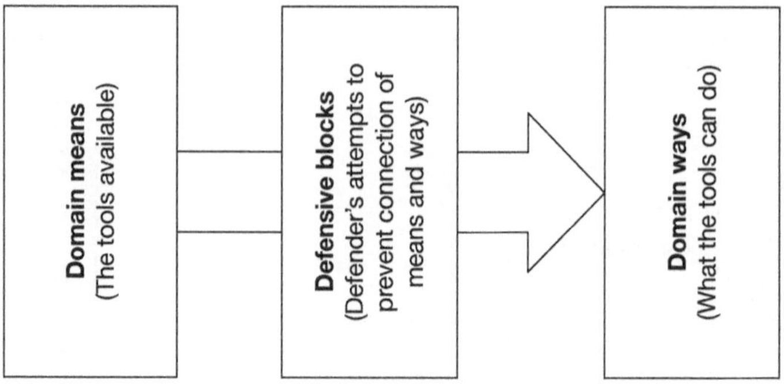

Figure 4.2 Domain Means and Ways with Defensive Block
Source: *Author's original work*

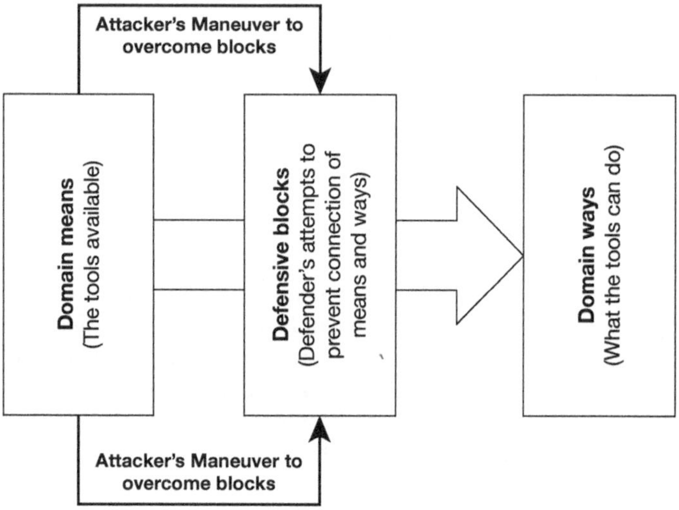

Figure 4.3 Domain Superiority Model
Source: *Author's original work*

ways flows logically from the definition of superiority, which is to be able to accomplish objectives in the domain without prohibitive interference. At an operational level, objectives are often associated with domain ways. For example, in Operation ROLLING THUNDER in Vietnam, the U.S. desired end was that North Vietnam stop supporting the insurgency in the south. The means largely utilized was tactical airpower and the way was strategic attack on targets of importance to the North Vietnamese. Effectively attacking the targets selected was an operational objective. Whether accomplishing that objective would result in the end desired was in the domain of strategy and is outside of this model. Analysts could roughly measure the level of U.S. air domain superiority by examining how effectively the U.S. was accomplishing its operational objectives. One complication in this approach is that planners often identify domain superiority itself as an operational objective, which would seem to set up circular reasoning.

The fact that domain superiority can sometimes be an operational objective or way does not invalidate modeling offensive domain superiority as an effective connection of means and ways. It may not seem intuitive that superiority can be the effective connection between means and ways and a way at the same time, but consider air superiority as an example. In most campaigns, air superiority is an objective and a way, which can lead to desired ends. The mechanism or strategy by which air superiority could lead to desired ends is that an enemy decides to agree to desired terms in fear of what the attacker can do with air superiority. If air superiority is an objective, then achieving air superiority requires air superiority. Although this is confusing, a special case does not invalidate the broader principle that the connection between means and ways shows the presence of an offender's domain superiority, and the lack of connection between the attacker's means and ways shows the presence of the defender's superiority. Next, I will turn to filling in the details of this model for cyberspace superiority starting with looking at means available in cyberspace.

Cyberspace Means

Cyberspace means are the tools that a combatant can use in cyberspace to accomplish their objectives. Some of the tools have evolved rapidly, but the categories of tools have not. For example, Distributed Denial of Service (DDoS) attacks evolved from simpler Denial of Service (DoS) attacks, but what they are attempting to do to the targeted system remains the same. There is a continuous refinement of the tools, but only rarely does an entirely new category appear.

The means available to an attacker in cyberspace are not completely separate and distinct. At times they can blend together and one tool may be required for the action of another. For example, scanning may reveal an opening that an attacker can utilize through a discovered software flaw to implant a software Trojan. All three means were required to make the overall attack happen. In a normal cyberspace attack, an attacker collects intelligence on the target to identify an opening, then the attacker exploits the opening to insert a payload and accomplish some action.

Social Engineering

The first important cyberspace means is social engineering or the use of psychological manipulation to trick a user into providing access into a system for an attacker. This manipulation is usually the most effective method of gaining access into an enemy system. A famous hacker, Kevin Mitnick has said,

> A company can spend hundreds of thousands of dollars on firewalls, intrusion detection systems and encryption and other security technologies, but if an

> attacker can call one trusted person within the company, and that person complies, and if the attacker gets in, then all that money spent on technology is essentially wasted.[5]

Social engineering is probably the most utilized and effective method of attacking computer systems and networks today, and it is very hard to defend against because if one person says no, the attacker can keep going down the phone list until they find someone more gullible.

There is no "patch" for social engineering according to O'Harrow, "Social engineering works because it targets a vulnerable part of cyberspace that cannot be patched with technical fixes: human beings."[6] As the most common means utilized by cyberspace attackers, social engineering plays an important role in cyberspace superiority and sometimes opens the door for the second means of attack in cyberspace, software Trojans.

Software Trojan

A second means used in cyberspace superiority is software Trojans that rely on inserting secret "back doors" into software to provide an attacker access into a defended system. According to Homer, the Greeks attacking Troy could not get into the city, so cunning Ulysses hatched a plan to sneak soldiers into the city inside a large wooden horse that the Trojans would think was a statue honoring the Greek gods. Once the Trojans brought the horse into the city, the Greeks snuck out, opened the gates to their forces outside and took the city. This story is an excellent analogy of how a "software Trojan" works. Although social engineering relies on tricking a human into opening a door, software Trojans accomplish the same thing through malicious code inserted into trusted software.

The complexity of modern software makes it easier for attackers to insert back doors. Software has become increasingly complex and some operating systems such as Windows Vista have in excess of 50 million lines of code. When you include the fact that the industry average for errors per 1,000 lines of code is 5–15, there are a tremendous number of mistakes in every piece of software running on any computer.[7] Software Trojans rely on hiding inside the massive number of lines in modern code and the difficulty in debugging them. Attackers can emplace these access points when the authors write the code, or attackers can plant them in the code through access provided by social engineering or other techniques, then utilize them to access systems running the modified software. Most modern systems utilize firewalls, which automatically block incoming access requests but allow computers inside the firewall to establish connections outside. A simple software Trojan will "phone home" and open an access point through the defenses, which gives the attacker a way in. Software Trojans are widely used by nation states with significant cyberspace resources and are important elements of cyberspace superiority. Software Trojans are like a traitor inside a castle under siege who opens a back door to the enemy. Unfortunately for defenders, software Trojans are not the only potential traitors inside the walls.

Supply Chain Attacks

Another major means of implanting access ports into a combatant's systems to gain cyberspace superiority is through supply chain attacks, or implanting tools into the hardware itself. According to the Comprehensive National Cybersecurity Initiative ordered by President Obama, "Globalization of the commercial information and communications technology marketplace provides increased opportunities for those intent on harming the United States by penetrating the supply chain to gain unauthorized access to data, alter data, or interrupt communications."[8] This threat may have already manifested itself in kinetic combat, there has been speculation that the Israelis caused the Syrian radar system's mysterious failure, precisely timed to coincide with an Israeli airstrike on the Syrian nuclear facility, through this type of hardware supply chain attack.[9] The United States is attempting to find reliable methods of discovering hardware "trap doors" but the complexity of modern digital electronics makes this goal very challenging.[10] A new Xbox One video game has the equivalent of five billion transistors; a complex defense related network will have far more. The government purchases the majority of its equipment as Commercial off the Shelf (COTS) components that could have made under less than stringent control of suppliers or even by an adversarial country. This avenue is most open to combatants seeking cyberspace superiority who have significant electronics design or manufacturing sectors such as the U.S. and China. If an attacker is not able to implant a trap door on the inside, there is the opportunity to find a chink in the armor on the outside through scanning.

Scanning

Although supply chain attacks require a high level of technical sophistication, port scanning is available to cyberspace attackers at all levels. Port scanning is largely responsible for the gigantic number of "cyberspace attacks" reported in the media.[11] To use the airpower domain as an analogy, these "attacks" are not blowing up factories, they are attempted penetrations of airspace to see whether the adversary notices, to figure out how good his defenses are, and where there are gaps. Every network has thousands of "ports" or openings to the outside. Normally, firewalls keep the vast majority closed unless they are in use by a legitimate program. The problem is that given the complexity of modern networks, often the defender accidentally leaves a door open that they should have closed. An attacker can "scan" across all the possible ports to see whether there are any open that he can exploit. This scanning is extremely easy to do and there is free software on the web that will accomplish port scans, which is one of the reasons there are so many "attacks." Finding an open port is only the first step; an attacker who intends to achieve a useful level of cyberspace superiority has to do more. Exploiting an open port requires a greater level of skill and the ability to utilize a service behind that port on the target computer system to accomplish the attacker's objectives.

Denial of Service

Cyberspace attackers without the skill or resources required to break into systems can still attempt to damage an enemy by attempting to deny the ability of his systems to communicate. These types of attacks are much easier to execute than actually breaking into an enemy system and modifying information. A denial of service attack is a method of blocking access to some Internet enabled service or database, such as a web page. One simple method is to request the page to supply information over, and over, and over at such a volume that the attacked system cannot keep up, which blocks access to the real users. There are also many more sophisticated methods that normally exploit flaws in networking protocols. If the attack is coming from one address or one region, it is relatively simple to block by instructing the defending computer to ignore requests from those addresses.

To get around IP address exclusion defenses, the most common method of executing a denial of service attack today is a Distributed Denial of Service attack (DDoS) where the attacker does not use their own system, but instead uses a network of computers under their control. These are normally computers owned by private individuals, who through poor computer security practices have had their computers turned into "zombies" or "bots", which are secretly controlled by a "bot-herder". To the owner of the computer, there is nothing to indicate they are no longer in control of their machine as it still seems to work normally, if perhaps a bit slower. Behind the scenes, the "bot-herder" can use the compromised computer to target a combatant's network as part of a DDoS. These botnets are part of organized cyberspace crime's basic business model and anyone can rent them for a small fee; as of 2010, the average price was $9 an hour.[12] During the attack on Estonia in 2007, "The 10 largest assaults blasted streams of 90 megabits of data a second at Estonia's networks, lasting up to 10 hours each. That is a data load equivalent to downloading the entire Windows XP operating system every six seconds for 10 hours."[13] It is important to note that these attacks can go well beyond not being able to access a website. There is no technical reason an attacker could not use DDoS against any system connected to the Internet such as a logistical database that would have far more serious operational impact. One of the reasons DDoS attacks are so difficult for defenders to handle is due to the "innocent" character of the attacking computers.

DDoS attacks have proven difficult for nation states to deal with as disabling the attacking computers involves disabling neutral "civilian" computers whose owners are unaware they are being used in cyberspace warfare. Several of the attacks I examined in the case studies involved these types of attacks where governments had to decide whether to disable the attacking computers. If the attacking computers are located in neutral countries, the political costs of doing so will normally be high, and the computers selected for attacks will normally be in nations that have better Internet connectivity. In at least one case, the South Korean government did decide to disable attacking computers, but that decision only applied to the machines within South Korea.[14] A more insidious type of attack misdirects instead of blocks the user.

DNS Poisoning

DNS Poisoning is another method attackers can use to redirect users to sites that may look legitimate, but actually are under the control of the attacker.[15] In the context of cyberspace conflict, this technique could be used to trick a user into downloading a weapon into the defender's network. That weapon could then execute an attack on the defender's network. DNS poisoning works because the Internet operates on trust and when you type in "www.safenewssite.com" that is not the real address. The real address is a string of numbers such as 157.166.226.25 and your computer requests the actual IP address from a Domain Name Server or DNS. If an attacker has altered the data in the DNS, typing in "www.safenewssite.com" might actually take you to "www.evilhackersrus.com" and the user may be fooled into downloading a weapon. Attackers can utilize DNS poisoning in concert with "drive-by downloads" to deliver their weapons.

Drive-by Downloads

Attackers can often exploit vulnerabilities in web browsers to download and execute software on a defender's system.[16] Attackers can seize control of a poorly defended "watering hole" where they expect the defender's users might stop. For example, if an adversary was trying to get into U.S. Army networks, they might get control of a website offering information on the upcoming Army-Navy football game. Then malicious script is inserted that automatically downloads and executes when the site is visited. User interaction by clicking on a link may, or may not be required depending on the details of the attack and vulnerability. If attacks through cyberspace are not getting the results desired by an attacker, he can shift to attacking cyberspace targets through the physical domains.

Support from Kinetic Forces

Because the assets that produce cyberspace exist in the physical world, physical attacks against these assets with kinetic forces are an important means that nation states can utilize in seeking local cyberspace superiority. In the midst of a kinetic conflict, the most effective cyberspace weapon may be a 2000lb bomb dropped on a telecommunications hub or control center. Physical destruction is much harder to repair than simply reloading software from a backup and an attack does not have to be as blatant as a bomb from above. Communications officers already live in fear of innocent backhoes; not-so-innocent targeted backhoes can do even more damage if an attacker severs the right cables. The only limit on the number of ways to disrupt networks through attacking their physical components is the imagination and resources of the attacker.

The linkage between cyberspace and the physical world provides an attacker's best opportunity to attack an enemy's offensive cyberspace capabilities through offensive counter cyberspace. Some authors, such as Butler, do not think that offensive counter cyberspace is a useful concept but is instead a doctrinal bleed over from the air domain where it does have applicability.[17] I agree that offensive counter cyberspace is most likely not a useful concept if you restrict the discussion to cyberspace weapons. However, if you broaden the scope to include the other physical domains, there is more potential utility. If a combatant is able to identify the main operations center from which the adversary is launching attacks and physically destroy it, killing many of the personnel; that could be a tremendously effective offensive counter cyberspace attack akin to destroying an enemy fighter airfield in an offensive counter air attack. This type of physical attack can affect not only local, but also universal cyberspace superiority if an attacker can find and attack the enemy's universal cyberspace assets.

Discovered Software Flaws

A critical means through which cyberspace attackers pursue their objective in cyberspace is discovered software flaws. As noted previously, software flaws are extremely common given the large numbers of lines of code and attackers can often easily exploit these flaws due to the characteristics of computers. Libicki helps explain why these flaws create vulnerabilities when he says, "What helps slip attackers past guards is that the control systems of cyberspace are complex, arcane, generally opaque, and brittle. They do not react well to the unexpected—which is to say, conditions for which they are not specifically programmed."[18] One example is a "buffer overflow." Essentially, an attacker deliberately writes information past what is legitimate in response to a query and if the defending computer does not catch it, the attack writes that information directly into memory. Then the attacked system interprets the overflow as legitimate code and executes it. Software companies attempt to patch vulnerabilities that they know about, but they can do nothing to deal with the ones that they do not know about.

Software flaws known only to the attacker are the "crown jewels" of a cyberspace attacker's arsenal. These vulnerabilities are referred to as zero-day attacks, because the timer on the vulnerability starts at zero when the first attack is made, then increments up day by day as software engineers scramble to develop a patch. Defenders who are unaware of the specific vulnerability rely on scanners looking for generic signatures that often have only moderate success. That is why zero-day exploits are so important and guarded so carefully when discovered. There is even a market in zero-day vulnerabilities with a Window's vulnerability selling for $60,000 to $120,000 and an iOS vulnerability going for $100,000 to $250,000.[19] According to Carr, targeted zero day attacks are the most powerful weapons available to offensive cyberspace operators.[20] It is important to note that just because the defender knows about a vulnerability, it does not automatically follow that the defender has properly patched the particular system under attack. A system administrator can inadvertently leave a vulnerability open well after a patch has been developed and issued if they do not keep the entire network up to date, which can be an overwhelming task on a large network. If zero-day discovered software flaws are the crown jewels, Industrial Control System (ICS) attacks represent the cyberspace version of heavy artillery that can do the most damage.

Industrial Control System (ICS) Attacks

The cyberspace means with the greatest current potential to alter a nation state's decision-making is attacks on Industrial Control Systems. These systems control industrial processes and are sometimes discussed as Supervisory Control and Data Acquisition (SCADA) systems. SCADA systems cover a large geographic area and are a subset of the broader category of ICS. Attacking utilizing this means can have the greatest strategic payoff for an attacker. ICS are the unseen heroes of our modern industrial society and operate infrastructure such as power plants, dams, water treatment facilities, etc., but have important vulnerabilities. The largest problem is that when most of these systems were developed, there was no need for security and so developers did not design it in. Most ICS were "stand alone" and not connected to the Internet so to implant malicious code would have required an attacker to access a physically secured facility and directly connect to the control system. However, in the interest of efficiency, many utility companies connected their ICS to the Internet to allow for better monitoring and updating so now anyone can access all those connected systems worldwide. Many of these ICS still have no substantial security and companies and governments are scrambling to catch up and put better security on the vulnerable systems. To make things easier for attackers, there is a "Google for hackers" that provides a search engine for vulnerable ICS.[21] Attackers have shown that even systems that are "air gapped" and in high security areas are still vulnerable.

There are numerous examples of attackers getting into an ICS. The core of Stuxnet was a SCADA attack used by an attacker to cause the physical destruction of centrifuges while reporting that all was well to the system's engineers.[22] There have also been successful SCADA attacks against power grids, water plants, gas pipelines and many other types of infrastructure.[23] According to Robert Miller and Daniel Kuehl, the four types of infrastructure most vulnerable include systems that deal with electricity, communications, money and transportation. Disruption of those systems would quickly cause societal confusion and disorder.[24]

Recovering from an ICS attack may not be as simple as resetting a system and turning back on the things that an attacker turned off. The Aurora test demonstrated that an attacker could physically destroy a generator through cyberspace by sending malicious commands.[25] Generators are not the only physical devices that attackers could theoretically damage through ICS attacks; an attacker could damage almost any computer-controlled item. Attackers can order chips to do work incorrectly, disable cooling systems to produce hardware failure, order actuators past their physical stops burning out motors, and the designers of Stuxnet ordered nuclear centrifuges to spin erratically causing failure.

Although many ICS are vulnerable, access into the system does not automatically translate into the ability to destroy it. Generating physical damage requires deep understanding of how a designer has configured a system. Fortunately, most hackers have proven unable to accomplish more than nuisance ICS attacks, such as dumping some sewage. Unfortunately, nation states do have the knowledge and resources required to translate ICS access into more significant physical effects.

ICS attacks represent what may be the most important means to cyberspace attackers, and also the area most in need of aggressive defense from cyberspace defenders. In a significant nation state conflict, ICS will be a key battleground of cyberspace superiority. Although the fight over ICS enabled infrastructure will be out in the open, behind the scenes another cyberspace means will be quietly at work.

Code and Password Cracking

An important cyberspace means that will allow an attacker to execute many of the other types of attacks is the ability to break passwords and codes. Many systems now utilize encrypted data and while it is easier to get someone to give you their password through social engineering and pretending to be tech support, code and password cracking will sometimes be required. In general, those who properly encrypt their data have the advantage right now, and barring significant changes in the computing environment such as the development of quantum computing, they are likely to maintain that advantage. Fortunately for attackers, humans run the encryption schemes and often make mistakes. Even "unbreakable" encryption can be broken through exploiting human errors. Common errors include weak passwords such as "password," using the same password on multiple systems, and poor physical control of written down passwords. Lifting up the keyboards in most any large office environment will likely still produce a good number of written down passwords, even today when people should know better. Breaking access codes can also facilitate attacking systems through wireless networks.

Wireless Networks

Wireless networks represent a way for an attacker to break into a defended system that bypasses many of the defenses. Wireless networks have become almost ubiquitous from coffee shops to corporate boardrooms but come with significant security vulnerabilities that some defenders do not fully appreciate. To a network, someone who has connected with wireless often looks like someone who is "inside" and thus they are already inside the first lines of defense of firewalls and intrusion detection systems. According to O'Harrow, anyone who comes into a facility with a wireless device can often connect to the network through "osmosis" and bypass most of the defenses.[26] However, with the proper equipment, a combatant may not have to send anyone into the facility.

Attackers can use larger, more focused antennas to achieve a connection despite being well outside of what defenders would normally expect. The wireless antennas most people use in cellular phones and laptops are miniscule and the physics of antennas limits their range. Commercially available antennas can produce ranges of several miles with a clear line of sight. The current record for a Wi-Fi connection is 238 miles, although that was with very large, specialized equipment.[27] Now that I have examined the most common means utilized by attackers in cyberspace, it remains to turn next to the things that an attacker can do with those means in pursuit of cyberspace superiority.

Cyberspace Ways

An attacker is able to achieve offensive cyberspace superiority when he can connect his cyberspace means and his cyberspace ways to achieve his operational objectives in cyberspace. A defender achieves defensive cyberspace when he is able to protect his systems and block the attacker from achieving his objectives.

Dominance of cyberspace is useless if a combatant cannot translate that dominance into concrete gains that enable the combatant's strategists to connect successfully means, ways, and ends. According to Libicki, "If control, influence, or competence in the medium has little to do with the delivery of military power in the more conventional realms, then no one would need it except perhaps for bragging rights."[28] Fortunately for cyberspace operators, cyberspace superiority does deliver military power in the conventional realms through the ways we will next explore.

Strategic Information Warfare

The first way that an attacker can utilize in cyberspace to deliver military power is through strategic information warfare, which is an unfortunate name for several reasons. First, although there are many definitions of strategic, its use in "strategic information warfare" tends to obscure rather than illuminate. If strategy is connecting domain ways and policy ends, what is "strategic" about strategic information warfare? It is a tool used by attackers to execute a strategy, not a strategy itself. In some ways, the confusion in the term is similar to the confusion over "strategic bombing" which once again is a tool, not a strategy. If strategic information warfare is not strategic, then what is it?

Analysts have given many definitions of strategic information warfare. Roger Molander, Andrew Riddile, and Peter Wilson are largely responsible for the widespread use of the term strategic information warfare from a 1996 RAND study they authored and I will start with their definition. Strategic information warfare is, "wherein nations utilize cyberspace to affect strategic military operations and inflict damage on national information infrastructures."[29] One limitation of this definition stems from its 1996 date, when analysts did not yet consider the concept of striking anything in the physical domains through cyberspace so the Molander, Riddile and Wilson definition is not as complete as the definitions of some later analysts.

Lonsdale offers that strategic information warfare bypasses enemy surface forces to affect directly an enemy center of gravity.[30] Lonsdale's definition is more useful because it focuses more broadly on affecting a center of gravity directly through cyberspace. Lonsdale's definition is similar to that of Eric Trias who said that, "The goal of strategic attack is to apply force systematically against enemy centers of gravity in order to produce the greatest effect for the least cost in dollars and lives."[31]

Lonsdale and Trias' definitions are helpful, but I find it more useful to bound strategic information warfare not only by the domain, but also by its objectives.

I define strategic information warfare as actions by an attacker through cyberspace to produce an effect that changes the defender's decision-making calculus in a way favorable to the attacker. This definition deliberately excludes brute force methods and relies on military coercion to bring the enemy to choose to submit to an attacker's demands.

Cyberspace attackers should focus strategic information warfare on coercion instead of attempting brute force attacks, which are unlikely to be effective in the cyberspace domain. There are two basic paths to success for attackers in any domain, the enemy can choose to accept the attacker's demands, or the attacker can deprive the enemy of any means to resist. Genocide and the capture of the enemy's territory without surrender are examples of brute force methods. When the Ottoman Turks captured Constantinople in 1453, there was no surrender, and while numerous individual Byzantines survived, they had lost any organized ability to resist. Because people live in the land domain, it is extremely unlikely that any conceivable attack based in cyberspace could completely remove a nation's ability to resist. If the United States destroyed every computing device in North Korea, while simultaneously disrupting all North Korean infrastructure, the North Koreans could still resist, albeit with less effectiveness. Because a nation will still have options and choices available to them, strategic information warfare will have to rely on coercion. Because of the similarities between strategic information warfare and strategic bombing, the air domain provides a good template to look at strategic information warfare.

In *Bombing to Win*, Robert Pape develops three strategies of military coercion that an attacker can use to attempt to change the decisions made by a defender.[32] The first of these strategies is punishment, which attempts to raise the societal cost to the defender, normally through inflicting suffering. The second strategy is risk, which is a modulated form of punishment that threatens further suffering if the defender does not comply with the attacker's demands. The third strategy is denial, in which the attacker targets the defender's military ability to achieve his objectives.[33] An attacker could execute each of these strategies from cyberspace with cyberspace superiority. For example, an attacker could utilize a punishment strategy and shut down the enemy's power grid. That same attacker could instead use a risk strategy and shut down one small section of the enemy power grid as a demonstration that he can shut down the rest if the defender does not comply with his demands. Finally, the Stuxnet attack is an example of denial, where the attacker attempted to prevent the defender from achieving the defender's objectives, in this case through destroying the centrifuges Iran was utilizing to make the material for nuclear weapons. Pape's analysis of these three strategies in the airpower domain also has utility when looking at the cyberspace domain.

In the air domain Pape found that coercion could work, but only if the concessions sought by the attacker are relatively unimportant to the defender.[34] After looking at 40 cases of attempted coercion in the air domain, Pape found that denial strategies had the best chance of success.[35] Punishment strategies had a low probability of success, and risk strategies fared even worse as a weaker form of punishment. It is reasonable to assume that these same findings are likely to apply in cyberspace conflict as well. The mechanism of weapon delivery is different, but the heart of coercion lies in the decision-making processes and psychology of the defender, not in the specifics of how pressure is applied. This analysis suggests that cyberspace operators would do well to be cautious when predicting how likely strategic information warfare is to cause the enemy to concede on important issues.

Because physical destruction of targets and infrastructure by high explosives was normally insufficient to induce nations to surrender their war aims, it seems unlikely that cyberspace attacks will prove more effective. Lonsdale captures this circumstance well when he says that, "The notion that a population, or state, would surrender as a result of its electricity or banking system going down in the face of SIW [Strategic Information Warfare] is difficult to accept in light of the experience of strategic bombing."[36] One of the key reasons punishment has often been disappointing is that the enemy gets to decide when he has had enough, and historically that "enough" has often been higher than the attacker thought it would be.[37] Strategic information warfare can provide an important tool in the toolkit, but attackers should not expect it to be a shortcut to easy victory any more than strategic bombing was.

For coercion by strategic information warfare to succeed, the cyberspace attacks must be more unpleasant than the sacrifice the attacker is asking the defender to make, and it needs to appear that things are going to get worse for him, not better. Clausewitz clearly laid out both of these conditions in his discussion on forcing the enemy to do your will.[38] Unfortunately for strategic information warfare, the characteristics of cyberspace as discussed in Chapter 3 most often result in cyberspace attacks that get less severe over time. Airpower tends to succeed when societies are convinced that matters will only get worse. With cyberattacks, the opposite is more likely."[39] Although strategic information warfare is no more panacea than strategic bombing, it has a role to play in cyberspace conflict and attackers can use it successfully given the right conditions. Once again from Lonsdale, strategic information warfare and airpower, "should not be dismissed as failures simply on the basis that they have failed to achieve the dizzy heights set by their most ardent enthusiasts."[40] Although strategic information warfare will likely not provide a short-cut to an easy victory, it will have an important role to play in future conflict.

Intelligence Collection

A second way that nation states can connect cyberspace means to policy ends is through intelligence gathering and cyberspace espionage. Breaking into an enemy's system to read his war plans, or check on the readiness of his forces or his capabilities are all examples of this type of operation. The importance of cyberspace intelligence in support of other cyberspace operations cannot be overstated. One of the reasons that the United States did not use cyberspace attack in Libya is that there was not time to do the necessary intelligence preparation.[41] There are also several more issues beyond just time.

One issue with cyberspace intelligence is that doing intelligence work can cause the enemy to react in negative ways even if you do not actually intend to attack. Libicki calls cyberspace intelligence gathering "Heisenberg country" because the act of gathering intelligence can change enemy actions much like the observer alters quantum states in physics.[42] Scanning and intelligence work can generate a similar effect to the security dilemma in realist international relations theory. Nation A scans nation B because nation A thinks nation B might be hostile. Nation B was not actually intending to attack but takes nation A's scan as evidence that A is intending to attack so builds weapons to attack nation A. Nation A has generated the very outcome it was trying to avoid. A cyberspace attacker also has to decide whether to use the intelligence collected, or to stay quiet and try to gather more.

The second major issue with cyberspace and intelligence work is that there is often a tradeoff between a successful attack and continuing intelligence. If an attacker has developed a successful intrusion into an enemy computer system, he can often use that intrusion to produce a cyberspace attack, or keep quiet and use the intrusion for intelligence gathering. There is an obvious and automatic tension between operations and intelligence staffs, as the operators will tend to value action and the intelligence professionals continuing intelligence. There is no easy and obvious answer to the dilemma, so an attacker will have to deal with each situation as priorities and senior leaders determine.[43] Despite these tensions, intelligence gathering will remain one of the key ways that cyberspace attackers utilize.

For an attacker to move beyond brute force attacks such as distributed denial of service attacks into more effective types of attacks will require significant cyberspace intelligence collection. As Carr wrote, "A sophisticated attacker aided with intelligence gathered from reconnaissance can execute a devastating attack, whereas an unsophisticated attacker without any intelligence on its targets will be relegated to simple brute-force attacks."[44] An attacker's success in gathering intelligence can make all the difference in cyberspace conflict.

Reduce Enemy Logistics

The third way that cyberspace attackers can connect cyberspace means and ends is through attacking enemy logistical systems. Modern militaries rely on their information systems for logistical support and as multiple users need to access them in various locations, these systems are often on unclassified networks and more open to attack. Misdirection that sends supplies to the wrong places, changes inventory information, or alters timetables could have tremendous impact on a campaign, particularly if the enemy is heavily reliant upon moving large numbers of forces in a short period of time a great distance. There is a long history of cyberspace attacks on logistic systems going all the way back to the early 1990s. During Operation Desert Shield, a group of hackers attacked U.S. logistics networks and databases. These attacks delayed the deployment of some elements because logisticians had to re-verify information from the affected databases.[45] This attack will likely not be the last time that cyberspace attackers focus on U.S. logistics.

These types of attacks on logistics are of particular interest to potential foes of the United States. Any nation relying on long or fragile logistical lines of communication is vulnerable to logistics based attacks, even if those lines of communication are internal. However, the United States has historically relied on massive and complex logistical systems to project power. Not surprisingly, the Chinese have shown a special interest in this type of attack and analysts expect them to attempt to attack American transportation, logistics, and command and control networks if a conflict were to occur.[46] Although the attacker accomplished the effects with airpower, not cyberspace attack, analysts can see what is possible from the first Gulf War when a lack of supplies completely immobilized Iraqi units.[47] Accomplishing the same immobilization from cyberspace would be more difficult as cyberspace weapons are more likely to be disruptive rather than destructive.

Although attacking enemy logistics through cyberspace can have utility, disrupting logistical systems will only provide a temporary effect when compared with destroying the supplies themselves. In the first case, the supplies will still exist; the attacker may only have managed to have them shipped to the wrong place or categorized incorrectly. If a cyberspace attacker breaks into the database for a critical warehouse and scrambles it, the parts and equipment are still physically there on the shelves and accessible once the database is rebuilt. Therefore, attacking logistics only through cyberspace will likely not have long term effects, it should be integrated into other forms of attack where it can play an important, albeit normally supporting, role. Disruption certainly has its place, and not only in the realm of logistics.

Disrupt Enemy Actions

The fourth way that cyberspace attackers can utilize to connect their cyber means to policy ends is disrupting enemy actions, which may be one of the key contributions of cyberspace attack. Chris Demchak sees disruption as the key element behind all of successful warfare, "Conflict between human societies has always been about successfully disrupting the opponent, whether that opponent was a raiding party, an army, a city, or a whole nation, to get some desired outcome."[48] Demchak overreaches somewhat in claiming that warfare has always been about disruption, but clearly disruption of an enemy can make success much easier. Demchak also thinks that disruption is easier now than it was before as the advent of cyberspace has enabled distant and small-scale opponents to utilize societal disruptions that were previously only available to neighbors or superpowers.[49] Here I think she is on firmer ground and it is certainly true that global cyberspace has opened up the possibility of tremendous societal disruption at a distance. However, societal level disruption is not the only thing a cyberspace attacker can aim for.

Attempts to disrupt the enemy's decision-making process are as old as warfare, but cyberspace opens new possibilities, particularly with an enemy that is heavily reliant upon cyberspace systems such as the United States. Even if all an attacker can manage is to introduce some doubt about the veracity of some of the data, it can radically slow decision-making. If a defender discovers that an attacker corrupted a single database, it calls into question if the attacker has also corrupted other databases or systems.[50] According to Libicki, it is not even necessary actually to get into the database and insert false information. An attacker can attack with "noise" or false information fed in from the outside through false reports, intelligence feeds, etc.

> Noise has its place in the arsenal. It can help paralyze or at least inhibit command and control. Under attack, decision makers are not sure that what they know is true, and neither are those who are supposed to carry out their decisions; so, commanders cannot exercise control over their forces or instruments. Even if all a prioris are accurate, the victim's sense that all information flows are fraught with error makes almost every resulting decision tentative. Nothing can be done boldly, cleanly, or decisively. Fall-backs must always be in place.[51]

Disruption through cyberspace attack can produce significant benefits for the attacker, but deliberate misdirection can do even more damage.

Misdirect Enemy Actions

The fifth cyberspace way is deception, which can be an even more effective way to utilize cyberspace superiority than disruption. Disruption attacks the enemy's information gathering abilities and attempts to make it difficult for him to communicate and make decisions, while deception attempts to shape the information environment in such a way that the enemy makes decisions favorable to the attacker. An attacker taking down a communications system would be disruption, while the same attacker inserting false information into the system would be deception. Sun Tzu saw deception as the heart of successful warfare and suggested always making efforts to mislead the enemy as to your capabilities and intentions.[52] Although Clausewitz did not have as high a view of deception as Sun Tzu did, he saw some use for it and stated that deception was useful as it could encourage the enemy to make mistakes.[53] For an attacker to successfully deceive a defender is actually much harder to do in practice than is commonly understood because it requires understanding the targeted individual's decision-making process at a very deep level.

Deception involves attacking an enemy's mind, and it is most successful when the deception aligns with something the enemy is already inclined to believe. According to Gray, "To deceive, one must first penetrate the cultural veil to comprehend an adversary's world-view so that one can feed his expectations. Because people tend to believe what they want to believe, deception requires an empathy with their adversary's expectations."[54] The most famous example of this approach is Operation Fortitude where Hitler was convinced that the Allied landing would be at Calais instead of Normandy.[55] Hitler's reluctance to utilize his central reserve because he feared a second landing at Calais gave the Allies critical time to build up their beachhead. More recently, the United States has used deception to great effect in Iraq and against Al-Qaeda.[56] If tying the enemy's decision makers into knots and melting their cyberspace infrastructure does not make the enemy quit, you may have to go and dig him out of his foxhole. Although labeled as mere "support," cyberspace attack can significantly affect the struggle for domain superiority in the other domains.

Support to Other Domain Forces

The final way that cyberspace operators can connect their means with policy ends is through support to the other warfighting domains.[57] Sometimes a combatant will have to fight and defeat the enemy on a physical battlefield. Some analysts such as Libicki believe that cyberspace's greatest contributions will be in support of warfighters in other domains instead of in strategic information warfare.[58] A modern military like that of the U.S. is heavily dependent on cyberspace. For example, consider a small U.S. Army patrol in Afghanistan. On the surface, it might appear that cyberspace forces are not providing anything of importance to the patrol, but as you look deeper, there are numerous cyberspace connections. The patrol likely knows where it is principally through space based GPS, which is highly dependent upon cyberspace for command and control. The military has also linked those GPS systems into a "blue force tracking" system that provides information to headquarters on the location of the patrol, and information on other friendly forces to the patrol. A logistical system completely dependent upon cyberspace brought the vehicles the patrol is riding in, as well as the people, their weapons, ammunition, and food into country. An Air Tasking Order (ATO) built and disseminated in cyberspace put the fighter aircraft overhead providing top cover and the weapons on board the aircraft were mission planned on a network of computers vulnerable to cyberspace attack. Digging further reveals more and more links to cyberspace for modern military forces, but there are some limitations in attacking those links.

Offensive cyberspace support to other domain forces has some limitations due to the difficulty in receiving accurate and timely assessment of its effects. It will often be unclear if the attacker has really disrupted the enemy system or if the enemy is merely making it look like the attacker was successful. Consider an attacker that disables an enemy IADS to allow an airborne strike package to hit its targets. The cyberspace operators can verify that they sent the command to shut down the IADS and the radars have all gone offline, but is that because the attack was successful or because the enemy is waiting to ambush the strike package? Because of this uncertainty, warfighters will often still prefer to put a bomb on the radar, as physical destruction is more certain. Libicki has identified that while using offensive cyberspace operations in support of an attack may be prudent, betting the entire operation on the success of that cyberspace attack may not be.[59] Support to other domain forces is the last of the cyberspace ways we will cover and so we are ready to look at their connection through cyberspace superiority.

Connecting Cyberspace Means and Ways

An attacker successfully achieves cyberspace superiority when he can successfully connect cyberspace means and ways. Now that I have discussed the various means and ways in cyberspace, I can fill in the details of cyberspace means and ways in Figure 4.4.

The enemy is not likely to let you do all these things to him in cyberspace without some response and so Figure 4.4 represents only the halfway point in the journey to an understanding of cyberspace superiority. Cyberspace defenders are not going to sit idly by while attackers connect their cyberspace ways and means; instead, they are going to try actively to block them.

Cyberspace Defensive Blocks

Cyberspace attackers do not have such an overwhelming advantage that cyberspace defenders cannot effectively contest cyberspace superiority. Although machines are brittle and do not react well to change or conditions that they do not expect, cyberspace is a domain in which people operate, not just machines. Humans excel at adapting and responding to changes in their environment. Some authors have put so much emphasis on offensive cyberspace capabilities that they have been dismissive of the capabilities of cyberspace defense. This situation parallels the early days of airpower when Stanley Baldwin overstated the power of the offensive in the air and famously stated that, "the bomber will always get through."[60] Stanley Baldwin was wrong, and so are his equivalents in the cyberspace domain today. There are some potential changes in cyberspace that may favor the defender.

Several developments could swing the advantage in cyberspace toward the defense. One development is that engineers are working on new protocols that might make some of the issues with attribution less difficult. It is possible that some of these ideas will result in separate "trusted" Internets that are easier to defend, as actors have to give up anonymity to enter. Other defensive technologies such as firewalls and intrusion systems continue to improve and there are policy changes that Congress could implement that would significantly change the playing field as well. Right now, most attacks come through zombies and botnets. Often Internet Service Providers (ISPs) or security agencies can readily identify these machines, but they cannot do anything about them under current law, because private third parties own them. If cyberspace attacks became more disruptive, Congress could change the law to enable authorities to remove these computers from the Internet until their owners had cleaned them. There are also other policy changes that politicians could make, for example, to require industry to meet some minimum standards for the defense of their networks. Right now, there is not sufficient political will to implement these policy changes. However, it is not hard to imagine how a major cyberspace attack could dramatically change that environment.

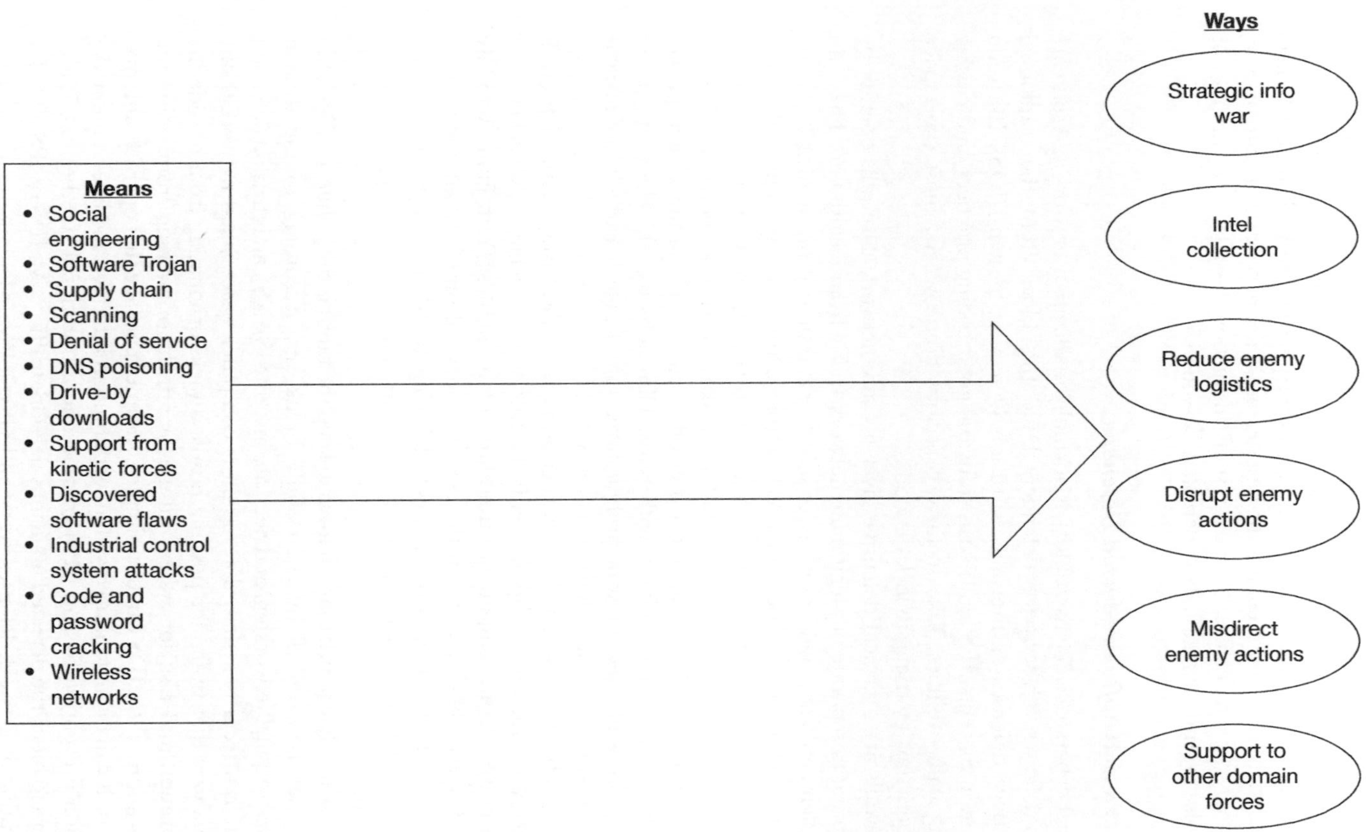

Figure 4.4 Cyberspace Means and Ways

Source: *Author's original work*

Cyberspace defenders are not completely without tools even today that they can use to sever the connection between an attacker's means and ways to gain cyberspace superiority. Defenders stop the vast majority of cyberspace attacks now with simple defenses. After examining cyberspace offense and defense, Libicki concluded that, "in this medium, the best defense is not necessarily a good offense; it is usually a good defense."[61] In the rest of this section, I will lay out a number of the tools currently available to cyberspace defenders.

Network and Software-based Defenses

The first cyberspace defensive block is normally made up of network and software based defenses. Cyberspace defenders build this block from the traditional cyberspace defenses of firewalls, Intrusion Detection Systems (IDS), Intrusion Prevention Systems (IPS), anti-virus software, good coding practices, and closing existing vulnerabilities. Like security conscious homeowners, most cyberspace defenders start by trying to lock the door.

Firewalls are a critical defensive layer for any network. Firewalls operate by attempting to separate out legitimate network traffic from illegitimate. They can be implemented in either hardware or software and sit at a communications node where they control network traffic. As a simple example, a typical firewall would allow an outbound connection from a user to connect to www.microsoft.com, then would let the information sent back from www.microsoft.com through the port. On the other hand, most firewalls would block an unsolicited packet from the IP address associated with www.evilhackersrus.net. There are many types of firewalls and firewall architectures that range greatly in sophistication from simple packet filtering based on addressing information to complex screened subnets using stateful or kernel proxy firewalls.[62] Some type of firewall is a necessity for any computer with an Internet connection as hackers will compromise a clean computer with no firewall in minutes. From January to July of 2013, researchers found that the average "survival time" for an unprotected computer was less than two minutes.[63] Locking the door is a good start, but a determined attacker will often find a way through so another layer of defense is needed.

A firewall is like a lock that attempts to keep the burglar out, while an IDS is the alarm that goes off if he successfully breaks in. According to the System Administration, Networking, and Security institute (SANS), an intrusion detection system "is a security system that monitors computer systems and network traffic and analyzes that traffic for possible hostile attacks originating from outside the organization and also for system misuse or attacks originating from inside the organization."[64] An IDS can be a simple consumer package that operates automatically, or it can be a monitored system with human interface and intervention. An Intrusion Prevention System (IPS) goes beyond a traditional IDS because it also attempts to block the detected malicious network traffic.[65] An IDS or IPS looks for penetration of network defenses, while anti-virus software looks for malicious logic inside defended computer systems.

Anti-virus software is a key component of any computer defense. There are uncountable numbers of viruses out "in the wild" because many of the nastiest ones are polymorphic, which means they change constantly as they infect new machines.[66] This has made it very difficult for traditional signature based anti-virus software as it is based on looking for specific viruses. Modern anti-virus software now normally includes heuristic detection, where the anti-virus package attempts to look for software that exhibits the characteristics of known viruses, even if it does not match a specific signature.[67] Heuristic software does not always detect new viruses and the constant battle between the writers of viruses and the writers of anti-virus software continues unabated. Because the writers of viruses rely on software coding mistakes, defenders can improve their defenses by reducing those mistakes.

Almost every exploit relies on a vulnerability in a piece of software and the number of vulnerabilities in software can be greatly reduced during its development through good coding practices. There are dozens of software development models that have been used by industry.[68] Different models are appropriate for different types of applications and developmental environments and there is no one most correct method. Many of them have proven to be effective when implemented correctly with good configuration and change control. There are also various automated methods that search code for known errors or vulnerabilities although the insider threat is still always present. A code scanner will not find a properly coded and secured back-door inserted by a programmer for malicious use. Although it is certainly better to eliminate vulnerabilities as a piece of code is written, the reality is that many organizations are forced to operate using poorly written code full of vulnerabilities. This is why it is also important that cyberspace defenders do whatever they can to reduce those vulnerabilities.

Cyberspace defenders need to do everything they can to close and reduce vulnerabilities in their software. Unfortunately, even professional system administrators often do not keep their systems fully patched. According to a 2013 survey, 17% of security professionals admitted that they have not fully patched the enterprise operating systems under their care.[69] The CERT coordination center estimates that keeping up to date with appropriate patches could avoid 95% of all network intrusions across enterprise and private computers.[70] Closing known vulnerabilities is the minimum bar for cyberspace defenders; they can go further and aggressively seek out unknown vulnerabilities. It is also critical for system administrators to disable unused services, as that will close off entire sections of potential vulnerabilities. Owens and Dam have noted that an unneeded capability brings unnecessary additional vulnerability, so every "nice-to-have" feature increases risk for the entire system.[71] Network and software based defenses are the first block, but defenders must also mitigate the weaknesses of the human element of the system.

Hardening Users Through Training

The second block that a cyberspace defender can utilize to contest cyberspace superiority is to increase the capability of the humans using the system. Users are the bane of system administrators the world over and many attacks rely on finding a user who can be tricked into doing something to compromise the system. Most users have only a rudimentary knowledge of computer security, so spending time and money training them can produce a significant payoff. Mandatory training programs are a start, but not all users will pay attention to training or be convinced that it is important to them. System administrators need to convince the users that there is significant benefit to following good security practices whether it is monetary rewards for best practices or reprimands for those who do not follow procedures. An active and aggressive "red team" program is essential to have, not just for the network, but also to have the users probed on a regular basis to see where security practices are weak and whom an attacker can trick into providing access. Performance ratings and rewards need to be explicitly tied to following security practices and those who cannot follow proper protocols may need to be fired to emphasize that the organization is taking security seriously.

Without aggressive action to provide training, and incentivize good security practices, organizations will still remain vulnerable to social engineering, which is one of the most common ways that a cyberspace attacker can utilize to connect their means and ways. As an example, in a recent study, security testers left USB thumb drives on the ground in a parking lot outside of a federal office building. All federal employees receive regular training on the dangers of plugging in unknown USB devices, but 60% of these highly trained employees plugged them in anyway. The addition of an official looking logo on the drive increased the percentage of USB drives employees plugged in to 90%.[72] Clearly simple training is not enough, so system administrators are also turning to increasing restrictions and controls on users.

Increasing Restriction and Controls on Users

A third way for a defender to block a cyberspace attacker from achieving cyberspace superiority is through increasing restrictions and controls on users. According to Libicki, "It is only a modest exaggeration to say that organizations are vulnerable to cyberattack only to the extent they want to be. In no other domain of warfare can such a statement be made."[73] At the extreme end, network administrators could disconnect every wire in the network and power off every device. The network would be "safe" but also useless. The purpose of information systems is to process and share information; if overzealous system administrators can be convinced to shut systems off from the outside world that may actually hand the attacker cyberspace superiority. A cyberspace defender who shuts down and "protects" his system is doing the same thing the Iraqi Air Force did in the air domain by flying their aircraft to Iran during the Gulf War. The assets were "protected," but also completely useless in the conflict at hand. It is critical to find the right balance between access and security so that defenders can avoid doing the attacker's work for him.[74] Marjory Blumenthal and David Clark have identified "the key paradox of securing the Internet: it is the act of communication that is risky, but communication is the whole goal of the Internet."[75] In situations where security is more critical than communication, cyberspace defenders can turn to the next block of "air gapping" their systems.

Air Gap Critical Systems

A fourth way that a defender can attempt to deny an attacker cyberspace superiority is through air gapping. Air gapping refers to disconnecting a system from the rest of the Internet. Early on, most industrial control systems were physically air gapped and they performed their control tasks without any access or communication to the outside world. Often classified systems are air gapped and built as a separate stand-alone network. It is not always the case that air gapped systems are physically air gapped. Systems can be logically air gapped and it is possible to separate a system from the Internet by encrypting it although the data travels over the Internet. A combatant might still use major transoceanic cables to move the data, but encrypt the data to prevent attackers from accessing the network information, but that is no guarantee of security.

Just as there are multiple ways of setting up an air gap, there are also many ways to cross it for an attacker.[76] An attacker can use physical media such as USB flash drives or CDs inserted by spies or unwitting accessories such as the federal employees discussed earlier. Air gapped systems must still be maintained and often engineers connect to air gapped systems to accomplish maintenance using systems that can carry attacks. Air gapped systems can be accessed using modems, which in some cases were never installed securely. There is also the avenue of wireless network attack, which was discussed in the cyberspace means section earlier. It only takes one computer on the network that an administrator forgot to disable the wireless modem to give an attacker a back door into the entire network. Finally, if an attacker can physically access the cables carrying encrypted information from an air gapped system, it could disrupt the network by interfering with the traffic even if the encryption could not be broken.

Cryptography, Passwords, and Biometrics

The fifth defensive block that defenders can use to stop attackers from gaining cyberspace superiority is by utilizing cryptography, passwords, and biometrics. Cryptography makes it more difficult for attackers to access information and manipulate cyberspace systems. There are many types and strengths of encryption.[77] A cryptographic system is composed of the algorithm, or the mathematical process of encryption, and the key.[78] Private key systems rely on a shared secret between two users, while public key systems require the sender and receiver to utilize different keys, allowing more options for key distribution. In general, a longer key length is stronger than a shorter one if they are both utilizing the same algorithm, but a long key length is no guarantee of security as many algorithms have weaknesses that can be exploited. Encrypting data does not guarantee security, but it provides an important part of a defender's toolkit.

Passwords are a basic defense much like firewalls or an IDS, and there are few significant systems that do not require a password for access. However, passwords can often be broken rather easily if users do not build strong ones, but strong passwords are hard to remember and users will often choose weaker passwords. Hackers can easily break weaker passwords by utilizing dictionaries of commonly used passwords. Believe it or not, the most common password in the world is still "password."[79] In the constant war between system administrators and users, the system administrators set up more difficult password rules and the users figure out ways to circumvent them to generate passwords they can actually remember. No one can remember 27 random 15-character passwords without either writing them down, or utilizing the same one or variations, but fortunately, there are other solutions.

One way out of the dilemma of secure passwords being too difficult to remember is to use a physical token such as a Department of Defense Common Access Card (CAC) coupled with a single password. This token system makes it more difficult for a hacker and easier for the user as long as they physically have the card. Another approach is to utilize biometrics where the user themself is the physical token. In the past, cyberspace defenders have used fingerprint and retina scans as biometric access control measures. These techniques are not unbreakable if a defender does not implement them properly. A defender can leave holes by not implementing biometrics correctly, but they can also be a step forward. Every technique is going to have some weakness and defenders do well to plan for failure and have a plan to quickly recover and reconstitute.

Increasing Resilience

The sixth way that a defender can use to deny an attacker cyberspace superiority is through increasing resilience. The Department of Homeland Security Risk Steering Committee has defined resiliency as, "The ability to adapt to changing conditions and prepare for, withstand, and rapidly recover from disruption."[80] There is an ancient Japanese proverb that highlights that resilient bamboo bends and springs back during a storm, but the strong and rigid oak falls. Resilience in cyberspace entails the same concept that instead of relying only on strength, a flexible system that can be attacked and continue to function will be more successful. The key to resilience in cyberspace conflict will be a combination of flexibility and maneuver.

Flexibility, or the ability to accept deformation without failure in cyberspace conflict will largely stem from creating flexible people, although good network design that allows flexible cyberspace operators more options will also help. People are the ones who react, not machines. The machines will simply do what their instructions tell them to do, even if those instructions are complex and allow for some ability to respond to stimuli. Cyberspace operators need to move beyond asking "how can I best secure this system against attack?" to "how do I design my system to still work after my defenses fail?" This requires a significant mindset shift for military cyberspace operators to include focusing on response capabilities such as emergency and incident response teams and plans.[81] One of the best ways to accomplish this shift is through aggressive and thorough red teaming. A red team is a group of friendly attackers who attempt to attack systems to find their vulnerabilities and weaknesses. They use the same techniques as real attackers and provide an invaluable service in not only finding vulnerabilities, but giving defenders practice in how to respond to attacks and keep their systems functioning. Red teams should also be used in large scale exercises that are unscripted and prepare defenders to deal with high level maneuvering adversaries. Resilient cyberspace defenders can be more effective if they also have systems that give them room to maneuver.

Efficiency can be an enemy of resilience as if you are 100% efficient, the smallest perturbation can lead to catastrophic failure. Cyberspace defenders should be careful to ensure that they do not build homogenous, easy to maintain systems that utilize the same hardware and software. An entire network that runs a single operating system is efficient and easy to administer; and also just as easy to take down through a single vulnerability. Edward Luttwak noted that in the strategic realm with a thinking enemy, "homogeneity can easily become a potential vulnerability."[82] Efficiency experts have also been collapsing multiple small networks into larger ones. Cyberspace defenders should buck the trend toward ever-larger and homogenous networks and deliberately build in heterogeneous enclaves based on a small number of carefully selected hardware and software configurations. These types of systems will enhance the maneuver options available to defenders, but they have to use their options smartly.

Cyberspace defenders must maneuver dynamically in response to attack. Cyberspace operators need to develop better situational awareness of their own networks and develop intelligence capabilities to understand what the enemy is planning. Attackers and defenders on the same side also should lower the walls between them and share more information to enable cyberspace defenders to be better able to defend their networks, while protecting offensive capabilities. Effective cyberspace command and control that treats cyberspace operators as maneuvering forces to be commanded, compared to an IT management problem with an engineering solution is also important.

Despite protestations by some that there is no maneuver in cyberspace, conflict in the cyberspace domain remains driven by humans who make decisions and react to their adversaries in ways that would still be familiar to Clausewitz and other military thinkers.[83] Attempting to reduce military conflict to an engineering problem was a bad idea in the physical domains, why would we expect it to be a good idea in cyberspace? Accordingly, structuring cyberspace forces as maneuver units that are expected to react and maneuver to defeat a thinking and reacting adversary is a good start. Building systems with multiple backups will also help give cyberspace defenders options and room to maneuver.

Backups enable a defender to rapidly reconstitute damaged systems and data, and therefore limit the amount of cyberspace superiority an attacker can achieve. An attacker who breaks into a logistics system and erases all the data can cause significant problems for a defender. If the defender has a backup and can have the system restored and operating in a day, the defender can minimize the attack's long-term effects. One of the hopeful trends for cyberspace defenders is the decreasing cost of electronic data storage. This decreasing cost makes it far easier for defenders to keep one, two, or ten copies of the data needed to restore a system. Defenders need to keep the copies in a manner that prevents an attacker from getting to the backups and the primary system at the same time. Automatic backup systems may be convenient, but they are automatic and will copy a cyberspace weapon just as easily as valid data. Backups are part of resilience, but defenders should also structure their systems to maximize resilience.

Cyberspace defenders should not assume success when designing their systems, but instead should plan for failure. Rosenzweig has identified that there are other systems, such as the electric grid, where designers plan for failure and build in significant resiliency and redundancy.[84] As much as possible, defenders need to build networks so that the disruption of a single node does not prevent the entire system from functioning. There is promise in cloud computing although there are some new dangers as well. Cyberspace defenders need to practice against large-scale disruptions, which is hard to do without being in a cyberspace training range. The local base commander will likely not want their network to go down for a week so that the cyberspace warriors can build it up again. This tension between training and operations is only one of the cultural tensions engendered by a resiliency based defense.

Shifting to a resiliency focused defense involves a paradigm shift that is difficult for many military officers. Antoine Bousquet has highlighted the U.S. military's tendency to strive for "100% relevant content, 100% accuracy, and zero time delay" to allow, "the perfect operation of a frictionless cybernetic war machine."[85] Resilience instead calls for embracing uncertainty and designing for failure and the unforeseen. The supposed revolution in military affairs that was going to dissipate the Clausewitzian "fog" through perfect information has largely been discredited, but it still echoes in U.S. military cultural preferences to pursue perfect information. It is not just the cyberspace warriors who need to adapt, operators and support personnel who focus on the other domains also need to practice operating effectively in an environment where not everything works. Although this training is easiest for defenders to accomplish in difficult exercise scenarios, the defenders in the United States military do not often practice against difficult scenarios due to a cultural fear of failure. When is the last time a U.S. military unit fought an exercise "war" with none of their computers working? It is possible, previous generations did it for years before the construction of computers, but without practicing it, the capability will not be there when needed. Combatants need to prepare for failure and be able to continue fighting, even if they temporarily lose cyberspace superiority in certain systems. One way to mitigate some attacks is to divert them somewhere that they will not do any damage.

Honey Nets

The seventh defensive block that a defender can utilize to keep an attacker from attaining cyberspace superiority is a honey net. A honey net diverts attackers into a false network full of whatever the defender wants the attacker to see. If a cyberspace attacker is attempting to break into a system and the defenders know it, they can divert him into a false network. If you block the attacker, there is nothing preventing him from trying again using a different access that the defender might miss. If the defender instead diverts the attacker but provides him with false information, that can be far more effective. Something similar to this allegedly happened in the early 1980s when a spy provided information that the Soviet Union was planning secretly to acquire gas pipeline technology. Instead of blocking the sale, the U.S. quietly altered the computer code that eventually led to, "the most monumental non-nuclear explosion and fire ever seen from space."[86] Defenders can do much the same thing in cyberspace. Once a defender captures an attacker in a honey net, the defender can keep the attacker busy with false information, examine attack patterns and techniques, or whatever is most useful. One of the most useful techniques for a defender is instilling doubt in the mind of the attacker.

Introducing doubt into the mind of an attacker through a honey net can affect the attacker's connection of cyberspace means and ways in other cyberspace attacks as well. A defender does not have to falsify everything; successfully falsifying one piece of information can make the attacker doubt everything else he got as well. One way of accomplishing this increased doubt is through a defender falsifying Battle Damage Assessment (BDA.) It is normally difficult for an attacker to understand how effective his attacks have been; a honey net can make it even worse. A defender can use a honey net to make it look like an attack has been successful, but then suddenly turn the system back on to ambush the attacker's forces at the most opportune time.[87] Tricking the enemy this way once, will also have the effect of making the enemy very reluctant to trust any future cyberspace BDA. This potential for false BDA is why airmen are generally not very enthusiastic when a cyberspace warrior tells them they are "pretty sure" the surface to air missile system they are going to fly over has been disabled. The tendency of warfighters is to put a bomb on it anyway, "just in case," which diminishes the utility of the cyberspace attack. Honey nets are powerful tools for defenders in cyberspace, but there are some even more powerful techniques taken from the attackers themselves.

Active Defenses and Hackbacks

The final way that a defender can contest cyberspace superiority is through active defense and hackbacks. According to Clausewitz, defenders should not simply wait passively, "the defensive form of war is not a simple shield, but a shield made up of well-directed blows."[88] Active defenses and hackbacks are a critical part of the defender's arsenal, and if they are not used, significantly constrain the defender's effectiveness. Owens, Dam, and Lin identified that with only a passive defense the defenders have to succeed every time, and as there are no penalties for the attacker, he can continue attacking until he is successful.[89] This difference places, "a heavy and asymmetric burden on a defensive posture that employs only passive defense."[90] A defender can be attempting to accomplish several things when utilizing active defenses. A defender can disable the computers executing the attack. A defender can also attempt to trace an attack back to its source. Attackers will normally bounce attacks through multiple servers to attempt to hide themselves, but a persistent defender can sometimes work back through the servers to the source. If a defender makes it all the way back to the originator of the attack, there are now a number of unpleasant things they could theoretically do to the attacker's networks in retaliation. Unfortunately, most of those things are currently illegal for defenders to do under U.S. law.

Because active defense normally involves breaking into a number of privately owned computers along the way, it is illegal under the Computer Fraud and Abuse Act (CFAA.) According to Rosenzweig, any active defense that reaches outside of the defender's computer system is "almost certainly a crime in and of itself."[91] This legal issue opens cyberspace defenders up to prosecution and lawsuits whether they are military or civilian. That is just if the attacking computers are only in the United States, which is normally not going to be the case. Breaking into computers in foreign countries brings on an entirely new set of legal and political problems. The difficulty in attributing attacks might work in the defender's favor, as it can be hard to attribute hackbacks if the defender chooses to use the same techniques to mask where he is coming from, but that does not deal with the legal and ethical issues.

There is also an additional practical issue with a combatant using hackbacks. A third party might have actually made the attack, but then made it look like someone else did it. Without clear attribution, a combatant might start a war with the wrong country and play right into their real enemy's hands. Hackbacks quickly devolve into a legal and political Gordian knot. Active defenses are required for effective defense, but they are problematic, clearly illegal, and just as clearly even private organizations are now using them.[92] Hopefully, policy and legal authorities will catch up in this important area. Now that we have discussed each of the defensive blocks, I can add them to the model.

Adding Defensive Blocks to the Model

The blocks that a defender can use to contest cyberspace superiority are shown in Figure 4.5.

These defensive blocks will provide the most cyberspace superiority for a defender when combined in a layered defense. This "defense in depth" is critical to success as there will always be a way around any particular defense. Jeffrey Carr identifies that layered defenses are more effective than a single outer wall, no matter how solid.[93] Defense in depth can refer to multiple types of defenses or multiples of the same type. An example of multiple layers of the same defense would be a defender with firewalls on the outside of a network, and also on each individual machine. An example of multiple defenses would be a defender who has firewalls, an aggressive training program to make users less vulnerable, and restricted accesses for most users. A defender should combine as many of the

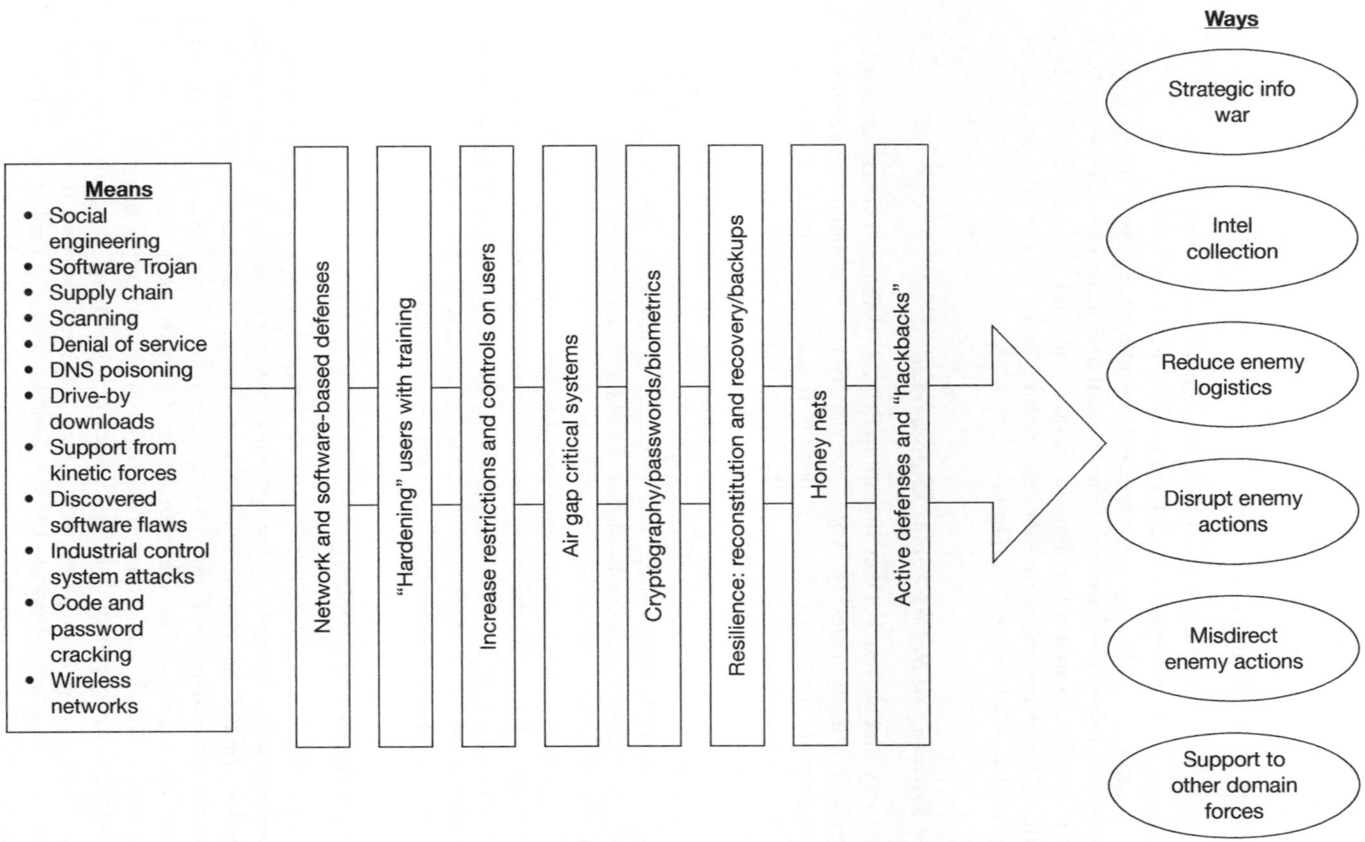

Figure 4.5 Model of Local Cyberspace Superiority with Defensive Blocks

Source: *Author's original work*

blocks as are feasible to give the best chance of maintaining cyberspace superiority. Attackers though, are just as capable of reacting as defenders, and have some tools and techniques they can use to overcome these defensive blocks.

Counters to Defensive Blocks

Cyberspace forces can and do "maneuver" against each other in cyberspace. Some analysts have been too deterministic and have argued that cyberspace weapons do not have the capability to maneuver. As I noted earlier, cyberspace is a blending of brittle technology and flexible people. The technology may not be able to maneuver, but the people can and will. We just finished examining how defenders can react to attackers, however, the attacker gets to react as well and "maneuver" in response.

Utilize Training to Refine Social Engineering

The first way that an attacker can attempt to degrade defensive cyberspace blocks preventing him from achieving cyberspace superiority is through refinement of social engineering based on the defender's own training program. If there is a means of social networking that the defender has not covered in the training that may be a good avenue of attack to pursue. Another possibility would be for an attacker to look at any examples given in training as to what is acceptable and what is not, then design attacks that look like the acceptable examples as much as possible but actually compromise the system. Depending on the quality of the training, there may be significant mistakes or old information that an attacker can exploit. Even if the training is extremely thorough, knowing how a defender trained employees can provide insights useful to the attacker. "Dumpster diving" for unclassified, but useful information can provide a gold mine of information that can also allow attackers to focus their social engineering attacks. If social engineering is not providing access, an attacker can always switch to machine or human-based attacks through code and password cracking.

Code and Password Cracking

A second method attackers can utilize to overcome defensive blocks is code and password cracking. As noted in the defensive block section, properly encrypted information should be almost impossible to break with current technology, however the same was true of the German Enigma machine in World War II and it was broken anyway.[94] The Allies broke the German codes through a suite of techniques that mostly relied on human errors in implementing the code system, not in breaking the system itself using "brute force" methods. Humans are no less likely to make mistakes in procedures today than they were in the 1940s and so there are still many opportunities for code-breakers to exploit, even if the codes themselves are "impossible" to break. Any code can be broken if a "trusted agent" is actually passing information to the other side, and sometimes a single weak password can be used by an attacker to leverage access to other passwords and systems.

If an attacker cannot trick someone into giving up their password through social engineering, a weak password may fall to brute force password cracking methods. In addition, an individual may use the same password on more than one system and if an attacker can break into a less secured system, he may now have the keys to the more secure system. Understanding the training that users get can also help refine attacks on passwords. If the defender trained users to utilize geometric patterns to generate passwords, then those can be included in the attacker's password dictionary. In cryptography, persistence is often the key to success as it is in some other types of cyberspace attacks.

Simultaneous and Persistent Attacks

A third way for attackers to outmaneuver defenders and gain cyberspace superiority is through simultaneous and persistent attacks. Persistence is an important avenue of attack to overcome various defensive blocks, not just in cryptography. Libicki highlights the difficulty of permanently damaging systems through cyberspace and notes that system administrators can generally restore network performance within 48 hours while preventing further attacks using the same weapon.[95] Accordingly, for an attacker to be persistent will normally require a timed cascade of different attacks instead of sending more of the same attack. Owens, Dam and Lin highlight that it is actually easier for an attacker to be successful in the first attack rather than follow-up attacks because the defenders learn from the attack and close down access avenues.[96] The requirement for persistence is not unique to the cyberspace domain, air planners know that just because an enemy airfield has been "destroyed" it does not mean it is going to stay destroyed. There are several elements of persistence in the cyberspace domain that attackers should consider.

It is important to note two caveats to persistence by an attacker. First, doubling of effort does not necessarily correspond to doubling of effect. From Libicki, "Alas, it is too easy to react to insufficient BDA information by attacking repeatedly, but doubling the effort may reduce the effect."[97] Second, a cyberspace attacker does not need mulish persistency. Persistence must be flexible, creative and not simply be more of the same attack. This need for flexibility is true of the other physical domains as well and Luttwak captures this concept when he states that, "Sheer persistence is the key to success in all things, except in war, when only those who persist flexibly can hope to prevail."[98] One way for an attacker to introduce flexibility is not to metaphorically charge straight up the same hill; instead an attacker should charge the hill from multiple directions.

Simultaneous attack is a critical tool in the cyberspace attacker's toolkit to mitigate defensive blocks. Distributed Denial of Service (DDoS) attacks rely on this simultaneity as a defender can shrug off an attack from a single computer easily. A 10,000-computer botnet is much harder to ignore as the attacks come from all directions. It is also important that an attacker attempt to build as many points of access as possible so that if the defender finds and seals one access point the attacks can still continue. Another form of simultaneous attack is to go after more than one component of a system. For example, instead of just attacking on the software side, there are ways to attack hardware as well.

Attacking the hardware and software components of a system is a way for attackers to utilize simultaneous attack to seek cyberspace superiority. Although the regular Internet hoaxes about viruses that have the ability to melt your computer into a puddle of goo overstate the threat, it is possible to damage hardware using techniques such as shutting down cooling systems and deliberately causing hardware to overheat. Damaged hardware can greatly increase the persistence of attacks, as it takes much longer for a defender to recover functionality. It is also important for a cyberspace attacker to go after backup systems at the same time whenever possible to prevent easy recovery by the defender. Simultaneous attacks will also often be required when an attacker is attempting to breach a highly secured system protected by an air gap.

Non-Internet-Based Attacks

The final method that cyberspace attackers can utilize to evade defensive blocks is non-Internet based attacks. These attacks are particularly important in accessing air gapped systems. Air gapped systems are difficult, but not impossible to access and often the access point will be provided through mistakes made by humans operating the system. A wireless modem that was inadvertently left or turned on, a hardware or software based attack through inserting malicious code in the defender's supply chain, and physical access to the system through espionage or special operations are all possibilities. There are air gaps that attackers have successfully crossed in the past; Stuxnet is the best-known example where a cyberspace weapon penetrated into a highly secured nuclear site in Iran. One of the problems with keeping security on an air gapped system is that engineers need to maintain and update it. To accomplish updates, they normally do not rewrite code on the air gapped computer terminal, but insert updates from another machine that an engineer has temporarily connected to the secured system. However, if an attacker has secretly compromised the maintenance computer, it presents an opportunity for a weapon to access the secured system every time a computer or storage device is connected.

Conclusion

In this chapter I set out to develop a more detailed model of how cyberspace superiority works that would capture the dynamic maneuvering between attackers and defenders. I started with the classic definitions of ends, means, and ways and determined that the attempted connection between an attacker's means and ways through operations was the realm where cyberspace superiority operated. The defender will attempt to block this connection using the tools at their disposal in the form of defensive blocks. The attacker then reacts to the defender's blocks and

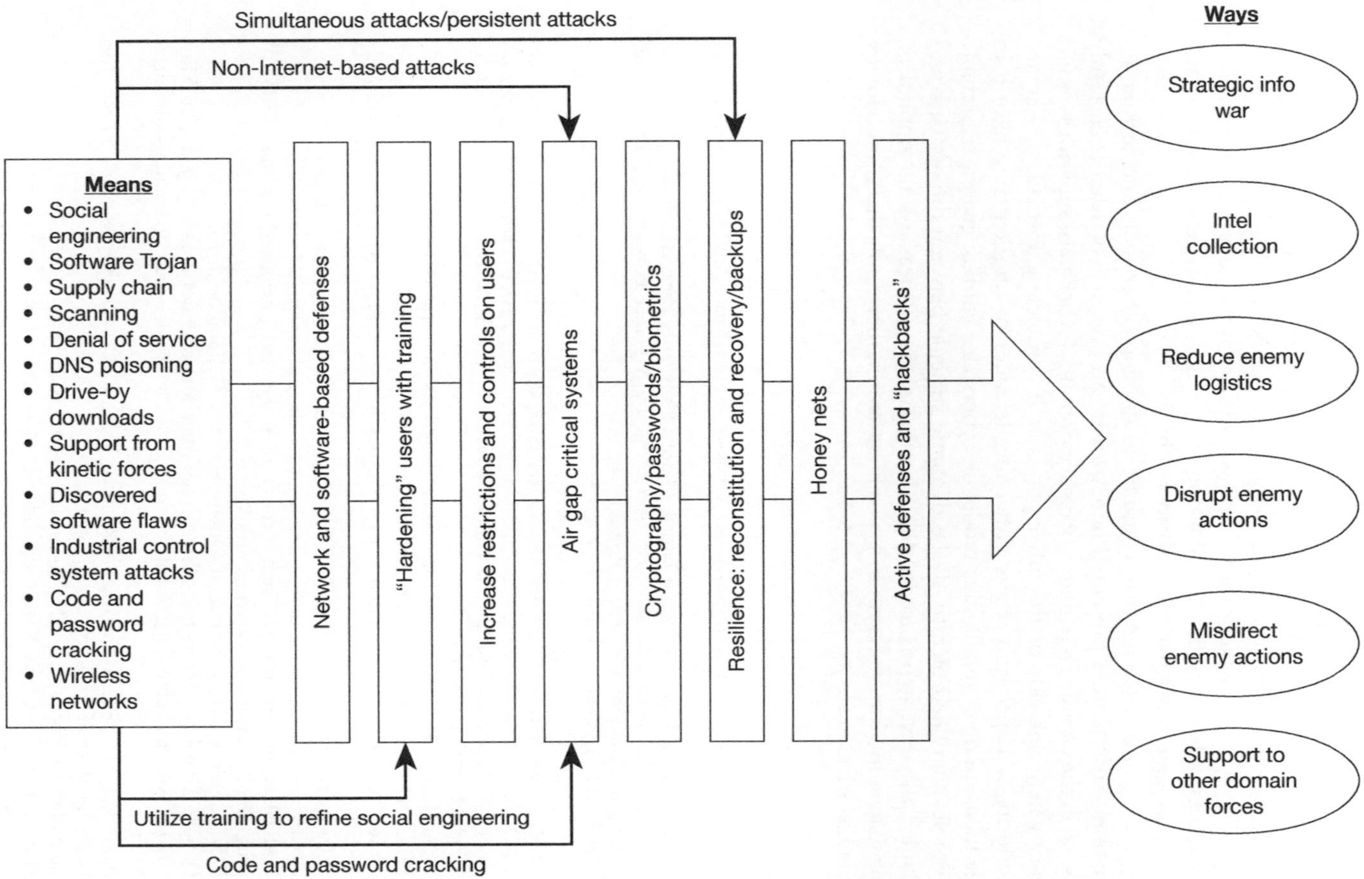

Figure 4.6 Complete Model of Local Cyberspace Superiority

Source: *Author's original work*

attempts to circumvent them. The defender reacts again and the cycle continues until the end of the conflict, although illustrating this through too many levels would make the model too complex to be useful. The complete model of local cyberspace superiority. including the attacker's responses, is shown in Figure 4.6.

Figure 4.6 represents cyberspace superiority for the attacker by the successful connection of the attacker's means and ways through the large operations arrow traveling from left to right. The blocking of that connection between means and ways represents cyberspace superiority by the defense.

Attackers and defenders will continue to develop other tools and techniques over time, but the ones presented here provide an overview of what is currently possible in the rapidly changing cyberspace domain. Cyberspace superiority is not binary where one side or the other possesses it completely. Instead, cyberspace superiority is a spectrum where either the defender or attacker may have it in large measure or in small. This model of cyberspace conflict gives a reasonably accessible, simplified picture of the dynamic struggle between the attacker and defender, the next step is to develop a methodology to measure the amount of cyberspace superiority present in a specific situation, then apply that methodology to the historical evidence.

Notes

1 Martin C. Libicki, *Cyberdeterrence and Cyberwar* (Santa Monica: RAND Corporation, 2009), 141.
2 Colin S. Gray, *Modern Strategy* (Oxford: Oxford University Press, 1999), 17.
3 Carl von Clausewitz, *On War*, ed. and trans. by Michael Howard and Peter Paret (Amazon: Princeton University Press, 1976), 75.
4 Martin C. Libicki, *Conquest in Cyberspace: National Security and Information Warfare* (Cambridge: Cambridge University Press, 2007), 114.
5 Cable News Network. "A convicted hacker debunks some myths," *Cable News Network*, 13 October 2005. www.cnn.com/2005/TECH/internet/10/07/kevin.mitnick.cnna
6 Robert O'Harrow, *Zero Day: The Threat in Cyberspace* (New York: Diversion Books, 2013), Kindle Location 600, part 4.
7 Shon Harris, *All in One CISSP Exam Guide*, 6th ed. (New York: McGraw Hill, 2013), 409.
8 White House, "The Comprehensive National Cybersecurity Initiative," Accessed on 30 August 2013. www.whitehouse.gov/issues/foreign-policy/cybersecurity/national-initiative
9 Sally Adee, "The Hunt for the Kill Switch," *IEEE Spectrum*, 2008. http://spectrum.ieee.org/semiconductors/design/the-hunt-for-the-kill-switch/0
10 DARPA is studying this problem through their Trusted Integrated Circuits (TRUST) program but has not released any results.
11 Belk and Noyes, "On the Use of Offensive Cyber Capabilities," 19.
12 Dancho Danchev, "Study finds the average price for renting a botnet," *ZDNet*, 26 May 2010. www.zdnet.com/blog/security/study-finds-the-average-price-for-renting-a-botnet/6528
13 Andrew P. Hansen, "Cyberflag: A Realistic Training Construct," (Master's Thesis, Air Force Institute of Technology, 2008), 12.
14 Jane Han, "Cyber Attack Hits Korea for Third Day."
15 Harris, *All in One CISSP Exam Guide*, 6th ed., 272–273.
16 Peter W. Singer and Allan Friedman, *Cybersecurity and Cyberwar: What Everyone Needs to Know* (Amazon: Oxford University Press, 2013), 43.

17 Sean C. Butler, "Refocusing Cyber Warfare Thought," *Air Space Power Journal* Volume 27, no. 1 (January–February 2013): 52.
18 Libicki, *Conquest in Cyberspace*, 33.
19 Andy Greenberg, "Shopping for Zero-Days: A Price List for Hackers' Secret Software Exploits," Forbes, 23 March 2012. www.forbes.com/sites/andygreenberg/2012/03/23/shopping-for-zero-days-an-price-list-for-hackers-secret-software-exploits
20 Jeffrey Carr, *Inside Cyber Warfare: Mapping the Cyber Underworld* (Beijing: O'Reilly Media, 2011), Kindle location 3562, chap. 10.
21 Naraine, Ryan, "Shodan search engine exposes insecure SCADA systems," *ZDNet*, 2 November 2010. www.zdnet.com/blog/security/shodan-search-exposes-insecure-scada-systems/7611
22 Belk and Noyes, "On the Use of Offensive Cyber Capabilities," 8–9.
23 Peritz, and Sechrist, "Protecting Cyberspace and the US National Interest," 8.
24 Robert A. Miller and Daniel T. Kuehl, "Cyberspace and the 'First Battle' in 21st century War," *Defense Horizons* 68, (2009): 2.
25 Paulo Shakarian, Jana Shakarian and Andrew Ruef, *Introduction to Cyber-Warfare: A Multidisciplinary Approach* (Amsterdam: Syngress, 2013), Kindle Location 6561, chap. 12.
26 O'Harrow, *Zero Day*, Kindle Location 304, part 2.
27 Michael Kanellos, "New Wi-Fi distance record: 382 kilometers," *CNet*, 18 June 2007. http://news.cnet.com/8301-10784_3-9730708-7.html
28 Martin C. Libicki, "Military Cyberpower." in *Cyberpower and National Security*, ed. Franklin D. Kramer, Stuart H. Starr and Larry K. Wentz (Washington, DC: Potomac Books, 2009), 275.
29 Roger C. Molander, Andrew S. Riddile and Peter A. Wilson, *Strategic Information Warfare: A New Face of War* (Santa Monica, CA: RAND, 1996), 1.
30 David J. Lonsdale, *The Nature of War in the Information Age* (London: Frank Cass, 2004), 135.
31 Eric D. Trias and Brian M. Bell, "Cyber This, Cyber That. . .So What?" *Air Space Power Journal* Volume 24, no. 1 (2010): 91.
32 Robert Pape, *Bombing to Win: Air Power and Coercion in War* (London: Cornell University Press, 1996), 19.
33 Pape, *Bombing to Win*, 19.
34 Pape, *Bombing to Win*, 20.
35 Pape, *Bombing to Win*, 20.
36 Lonsdale, *The Nature of War in the Information Age*, 165.
37 Lonsdale, *The Nature of War in the Information Age*, 163.
38 Clausewitz, *On War*, 77.
39 Libicki, *Cyberdeterrence and Cyberwar*, xv.
40 Lonsdale, The Nature of War in the Information Age, 169.
41 Paul Rosenzweig, *Cyber Warfare: How Conflicts in Cyberspace are Challenging America and Changing the World* (Santa Barbara, CA: Praeger, 2013), Kindle Location 805, chap. 3.
42 Libicki, *Conquest in Cyberspace*, 91.
43 William A. Owens, Kenneth W. Dam, and Herbert S. Lin, eds. *Technology, Policy, Law, and Ethics Regarding U.S. Acquisition and Use of Cyberattack Capabilities* (Washington, DC: National Academies Press, 2009), 156.
44 Carr, *Inside Cyber Warfare*, Kindle location 4189, chap. 12.
45 Miller, et al., "Cyberspace and the 'First Battle' in 21st century War," 3.
46 Carr, *Inside Cyber Warfare*, Kindle location 4015, chap 11.
47 Edward N. Luttwak, *Strategy: The Logic of War and Peace* (Cambridge, MA: Belknap Press, 2003), 196.
48 Chris C. Demchak and Peter Dombrowski, "Rise of a Cybered Westphalian Age," *Strategic Studies Quarterly*, Spring 2011, 1.
49 Chris C. Demchak, *Wars of Disruption and Resilience* (Athens: The University of Georgia Press, 2011), 2.

50 Owens, et al., *Technology, Policy, Law, and Ethics Regarding U.S. Acquisition and Use of Cyberattack Capabilities*, 113.
51 Libicki, *Conquest in Cyberspace*, 71.
52 Sun Tzu, *The Art of War*, trans. Samuel B. Griffith with forward by B. H. Liddell Hart, (London: Oxford University Press, 1971), Kindle Location 1166, chap. 1.
53 Clausewitz, *On War*, 202.
54 Gray, *Modern Strategy*, 35.
55 John Keegan, *The Second World War* (New York, Penguin, 1989), 373.
56 Rosenzweig, *Cyber Warfare*, Kindle Location 1023, chap. 3.
57 Shawn Brimley, "Promoting Security in Common Domains." *Washington Quarterly* 33, no. 3 (2010): 122.
58 Libicki, *Cyberdeterrence and Cyberwar*, 6.
59 Libicki, *Cyberdeterrence and Cyberwar*, xv.
60 Stanley Baldwin, "A Fear for the Future," Speech given in Parliament 10 November 1932. http://en.wikisource.org/wiki/A_Fear_For_The_Future
61 Libicki, *Cyberdeterrence and Cyberwar*, 176.
62 For an excellent brief discussion of firewall types and architectures see Harris, *All in One CISSP Exam Guide*, 6th ed., 628–653.
63 SANS Technology Institute, "Survival Time," *Internet Storm Center*, Graph generated from 1 Jan 2013 to 30 July 2013 on 31 August 2013. http://isc.sans.edu/survivaltime.html
64 SANS, "Intrusion Detection Systems: Definition, Need and Challenges," *SANS*, 2001. www.sans.org/reading-room/whitepapers/detection/intrusion-detection-systems-definition-challenges-343
65 Harris, *All in One CISSP Exam Guide*, 266.
66 Ed Bott, "The malware numbers game: how many viruses are out there?" *ZDNet*, 15 April 2012. www.zdnet.com/article/the-malware-numbers-game-how-many-viruses-are-out-there
67 Stephen Hernandez, ed., *Official (ISC)2 Guide to the CISSP CBK*, 3rd ed. (Amazon: Auerbach Publications, 2012), Kindle Location 13783.
68 For a brief discussion of some of the current models see Harris, *All in One CISSP Exam Guide*, 1111–1122.
69 Kelly Jackson Higgins, "Nearly One-Fifth of Enterprise Operating Systems not Fully Patched," *Security Dark Reading*, 23 August 2013. www.darkreading.com/vulnerability/nearly-one-fifth-of-enterprise-operating/240160403
70 USDA, "Patch Management and Systems Updates," Accessed 31 August 2013. www.ocio.usda.gov/sites/default/files/docs/2012/DM3535-002.htm
71 Owens, et al., *Technology, Policy, Law, and Ethics Regarding U.S. Acquisition and Use of Cyberattack Capabilities*, 84.
72 Rosenzweig, *Cyber Warfare*, Kindle Location 815, chap. 3.
73 Libicki, *Cyberdeterrence and Cyberwar*, xiv.
74 Gregory J. Rattray, *Strategic Warfare in Cyberspace* (Amazon: MIT Press, 2001), Kindle Location 133.
75 Marjory S. Blumenthal and David D. Clark, "The Future of the Internet and Cyberpower," in *Cyberpower and National Security*, ed. Franklin D. Kramer, Stuart H. Starr and Larry K. Wentz (Washington, DC: Potomac Books, 2009), 229.
76 Singer and Friedman note that after hundreds of air gap vulnerability assessments of private businesses, the National Cybersecurity and Communications Integration Center has not discovered one they could not find a way around. Singer and Friedman, *Cybersecurity and Cyberwar*, 63.
77 For a chapter length discussion of cryptography see Harris, *All in One CISSP Exam Guide*, 759–870.
78 The exception to this is one-way hashing, which utilizes an algorithm but no key.

79 + Chenda Ngak, "The 25 most common passwords of 2012," *CBS News*, 24 October 2012. www.cbsnews.com/8301-205_162-57539366/the-25-most-common-passwords-of-2012
80 Risk Steering Committee, *DHS Risk Lexicon: 2010 Edition,* September 2010. Accessed 17 January 2015, www.dhs.gov/xlibrary/assets/dhs-risk-lexicon-2010.pdf, 26
81 Rattray, *Strategic Warfare in Cyberspace*, Kindle Location 220.
82 Luttwak, *Strategy*, 39–40.
83 Clausewitz, *On War,* 75.
84 Rosenzweig, *Cyber Warfare*, Kindle Location 3727, chap. 16.
85 Antoine Bousquet, *The Scientific Way of Warfare* (New York: Columbia University Press, 2009), 156.
86 Thomas C. Reed, *At the Abyss: An Insider's History of the Cold War* (New York: Ballantine Books, 2004), 269. Other authors such as Thomas Rid have questioned whether the explosion actually occurred, Reed, given his various government positions to include Secretary of the Air Force, was in a good position to know of the events if they occurred as alleged. See Thomas Rid, *Cyber War Will Not Take Place* (Amazon: Oxford University Press, 2013), Kindle Location 275.
87 Owens, et al., *Technology, Policy, Law, and Ethics Regarding U.S. Acquisition and Use of Cyberattack Capabilities*, 125.
88 Clausewitz, *On War*, 357.
89 Owens, et al., *Technology, Policy, Law, and Ethics Regarding U.S. Acquisition and Use of Cyberattack Capabilities*, 13.
90 Owens, et al., *Technology, Policy, Law, and Ethics Regarding U.S. Acquisition and Use of Cyberattack Capabilities*, 13.
91 Rosenzweig, *Cyber Warfare*, Kindle Location 2024, chap. 7.
92 Kelly Jackson Higgins, "Free 'Active Defense' Tools Emerge," *Security Dark Reading*, 11 July 2013. www.darkreading.com/intrusion-prevention/free-active-defense-tools-emerge/240158160
93 Carr, *Inside Cyber Warfare*, Kindle location 3674.
94 R. A. Ratcliff, *Delusions of Intelligence: Enigma, Ultra, and the End of Secure Ciphers* (Cambridge: Cambridge University Press, 2006), 2.
95 Libicki, *Conquest in Cyberspace*, 37.
96 Owens, et al., *Technology, Policy, Law, and Ethics Regarding U.S. Acquisition and Use of Cyberattack Capabilities*, 112–113.
97 Libicki, *Conquest in Cyberspace*, 87.
98 Luttwak, *Strategy: The Logic of War and Peace*, 200.

Bibliography

Adee, Sally. "The Hunt for the Kill Switch." *IEEE Spectrum*, 2008. http://spectrum.ieee.org/semiconductors/design/the-hunt-for-the-kill-switch/0

Baldwin, Stanley, "A Fear for the Future," Speech given in Parliament 10 November 1932. http://en.wikisource.org/wiki/A_Fear_For_The_Future

Belk, Robert and Matthew Noyes. "On the Use of Offensive Cyber Capabilities." Master's Thesis, Harvard Kennedy School, 2012.

Blumenthal, Marjory S., and David D. Clark. "The Future of the Internet and Cyberpower." In *Cyberpower and National Security*, edited by Franklin D. Kramer, Stuart H. Starr and Larry K. Wentz, 206–240. Washington, DC: Potomac Books, 2009.

Bott, Ed. "The malware numbers game: how many viruses are out there?" *ZDNet*, 15 April 2012. www.zdnet.com/article/the-malware-numbers-game-how-many-viruses-are-out-there

Bousquet, Antoine. *The Scientific Way of Warfare.* New York: Columbia University Press, 2009.

Brimley, Shawn. "Promoting Security in Common Domains." *Washington Quarterly* 33, no. 3 (2010): 119–132.

Butler, Sean C. "Refocusing Cyber Warfare Thought." *Air Space Power Journal*, Volume 27, no. 1 (2013): 44–57.

Cable News Network. "A convicted hacker debunks some myths." *Cable News Network*, 13 October 2005. www.cnn.com/2005/TECH/internet/10/07/kevin.mitnick.cnna

Carr, Jeffrey. *Inside Cyber Warfare: Mapping the Cyber Underworld.* Beijing: O'Reilly Media, 2011. Kindle edition.

Clausewitz, Carl von. *On War.* Edited and Translated by Michael Howard and Peter Paret. Princeton, NJ: Princeton University Press, 1976.

Danchev, Dancho. "Study finds the average price for renting a botnet." *ZDNet*, 26 May 2010. www.zdnet.com/blog/security/study-finds-the-average-price-for-renting-a-botnet/6528

Demchak, Chris C. *Wars of Disruption and Resilience.* Athens: The University of Georgia Press, 2011.

Demchak, Chris C. and Peter Dombrowski. "Rise of a Cybered Westphalian Age." *Strategic Studies Quarterly*, Spring 2011: 32–61.

Gray, Colin S. *Modern Strategy*. Oxford: Oxford University Press, 1999.

Greenberg, Andy. "Shopping for Zero-Days: A Price List for Hackers' Secret Software Exploits." *Forbes*, 23 March 2012. www.forbes.com/sites/andygreenberg/2012/03/23/shopping-for-zero-days-an-price-list-for-hackers-secret-software-exploits

Han, Jane. "Cyber Attack Hits Korea for Third Day." *Korea Times*, 9 July 2009. www.koreatimes.co.kr/www/news/biz/2009/09/123_48203.html

Hansen, Andrew P. "Cyberflag: A Realistic Training Construct." Master's Thesis, Air Force Institute of Technology, 2008.

Harris, Shon. *All in One CISSP Exam Guide.* 6th ed. New York: McGraw Hill, 2013.

Hernandez, Stephen, ed. *Official (ISC)2 Guide to the CISSP CBK,* 3rd ed. Amazon: Auerbach Publications, 2012.

Higgins, Kelly Jackson. "Free 'Active Defense' Tools Emerge." *Security Dark Reading*, 11 July 2013. www.darkreading.com/intrusion-prevention/free-active-defense-tools-emerge/240158160

Higgins, Kelly Jackson. "Nearly One-Fifth of Enterprise Operating Systems not Fully Patched." *Security Dark Reading*, 23 August 2013. www.darkreading.com/vulnerability/nearly-one-fifth-of-enterprise-operating/240160403

Kanellos, Michael. "New Wi-Fi distance record: 382 kilometers." *CNet*, 18 June 2007. http://news.cnet.com/8301-10784_3-9730708-7.html

Keegan, John. *The Second World War.* New York: Penguin, 1989.

Libicki, Martin C. *Conquest in Cyberspace: National Security and Information Warfare.* Cambridge: Cambridge University Press, 2007.

Libicki, Martin C. *Cyberdeterrence and Cyberwar.* Santa Monica: RAND Corporation, 2009.

Libicki, Martin C. "Military Cyberpower." In *Cyberpower and National Security*, edited by Franklin D. Kramer, Stuart H. Starr and Larry K. Wentz, 275–284. Washington, DC: Potomac Books, 2009.

Lonsdale, David J. *The Nature of War in the Information Age.* London: Frank Cass, 2004.

Luttwak, Edward, N. *Strategy: The Logic of War and Peace.* Cambridge, MA: Belknap Press, 2003.

Miller, Robert A., and Daniel T. Kuehl. "Cyberspace and the 'First Battle' in 21st century War." *Defense Horizons* 68, 2009: 6.

Molander, Roger C., Andrew S. Riddile and Peter A. Wilson. *Strategic Information Warfare: A New Face of War*. Santa Monica, CA: RAND, 1996.

Naraine, Ryan. "Shodan search engine exposes insecure SCADA systems." *ZDNet*, 2 November 2010. www.zdnet.com/blog/security/shodan-search-exposes-insecure-scada-systems/7611

Ngak, Chenda. "The 25 most common passwords of 2012." *CBS News*, 24 October 2012. www.cbsnews.com/8301-205_162-57539366/the-25-most-common-passwords-of-2012

O'Harrow, Robert. *Zero Day: The Threat in Cyberspace*. New York: Diversion Books, 2013. Kindle edition.

Owens, William A., Kenneth W. Dam, and Herbert S. Lin, eds. Technology, *Policy, Law, and Ethics Regarding U.S. Acquisition and Use of Cyberattack Capabilities*. Edited by National Research Council. Washington, DC: National Academies Press, 2009.

Pape, Robert. *Bombing to Win: Air Power and Coercion in War*. London: Cornell University Press, 1996.

Peritz, Aki J. and Michael Sechrist. "Protecting Cyberspace and the US National Interest." Harvard Kennedy School Belfer Center for Science and International Affairs, 2010.

Ratcliff, R., A. *Delusions of Intelligence: Enigma, Ultra, and the End of Secure Ciphers*. Cambridge: Cambridge University Press, 2006.

Rattray, Gregory J. *Strategic Warfare in Cyberspace*. Amazon: MIT Press, 2001. Kindle edition.

Reed, Thomas C. *At the Abyss: An Insider's History of the Cold War*. New York: Ballantine Books, 2004.

Rid, Thomas. *Cyber War Will Not Take Place*. Amazon: Oxford University Press, 2013. Kindle edition.

Risk Steering Committee. *DHS Risk Lexicon: 2010 Edition*. September 2010. Accessed 17 January 2015. www.dhs.gov/xlibrary/assets/dhs-risk-lexicon-2010.pdf

Rosenzweig, Paul. *Cyber Warfare: How Conflicts in Cyberspace are Challenging America and Changing the World*. Santa Barbara, CA: Praeger, 2013. Kindle edition.

SANS. "Intrusion Detection Systems: Definition, Need and Challenges." *SANS*, 2001. www.sans.org/reading-room/whitepapers/detection/intrusion-detection-systems-definition-challenges-343

SANS Technology Institute, "Survival Time." *Internet Storm Center*. Graph generated from 1 Jan 2013 to 30 July 2013 on 31 August 2013. http://isc.sans.edu/survivaltime.html.

Shakarian, Paulo, Jana Shakarian and Andrew Ruef. *Introduction to Cyber-Warfare: A Multidisciplinary Approach*. Amsterdam: Syngress, 2013. Kindle edition.

Singer, Peter W. and Allan Friedman. *Cybersecurity and Cyberwar: What Everyone Needs to Know*. Amazon: Oxford University Press, 2013. Kindle edition.

Sun Tzu. *The Art of War*. Trans by Samuel B. Griffith with Forward by B. H. Liddell Hart. Oxford University Press: Oxford, 1971.

Trias, Eric D. and Brian M. Bell. "Cyber This, Cyber That. . .So What?" *Air Space Power Journal*, Volume 24, no. 1 (2010): 90–100.

USDA. "Patch Management and Systems Updates." Accessed 31 August 2013. www.ocio.usda.gov/sites/default/files/docs/2012/DM3535-002.htm

White House. "The Comprehensive National Cybersecurity Initiative." Accessed on 30 August 2013. www.whitehouse.gov/issues/foreign-policy/cybersecurity/national-initiative

5 Measuring Cyberspace Superiority

Thus far, we have explored the elements of domain superiority and applied them to cyberspace superiority. Before moving on to the case studies, we need a method of measuring cyberspace superiority. When we examined measurement concepts of cyberspace superiority in Chapter 3, we saw that the two most significant components of a cyberspace superiority measurement system should be the combatant's objectives in cyberspace and their ability to defend their systems. As we will need to balance several factors, we need to utilize a methodology that weights multiple factors.

Although there are challenges with measuring cyberspace superiority, a weighted preference analytical model can provide a powerful instrument that will provide a methodology to minimize the challenges of a sparse and qualitatively-based data set. Quantifying the qualitative inputs is an important element that I discuss more fully in Appendix A, the model allows the incorporation of multiple inputs from whatever relevant sources are available in a particular case. I use this model to focus measurements on areas of greatest importance to characterize cyberspace superiority and to analyze the case studies.

The cyberspace superiority measurement system I develop here will balance the offensive and defensive sides of cyberspace superiority, while accounting for the varying levels of reliance upon cyberspace in different nations. The system will need to account for two dyads: nation A's attack on nation B's defense, and nation B's attack on nation A's defense. On the offensive side, I will consider an attacker's success against cyberspace objectives with the importance of those objectives to determine a level of offensive cyberspace superiority. On the defensive side, I will utilize the defender's success in maintaining the functionality of defended systems and include the importance of those systems to the defender to measure defensive cyberspace superiority. I will round out the model with a variable to account for the different reliance upon cyberspace in different nations. Before building the cyberspace superiority measurement model, I will first look at a few of the challenges to building a successful measurement system in cyberspace.

Challenges of Cyberspace Superiority Measurement

Measuring cyberspace superiority is difficult for several reasons, starting with the difficulty of getting accurate information on a cyberspace conflict. Any measurement system can only be accurate if an analyst can feed correct information into the system. In cyberspace, that information is often difficult to obtain due to classification issues, attribution uncertainty, and structural incentives on all sides to falsify data. Cyberspace combatants classify their capabilities and efforts at high levels to protect them. Most cyberspace attackers cloak their activities in cyberspace and rarely admit to attacks, and so provide no information on how effective they thought they were. Depending on their objectives, defenders may also choose either to deliberately exaggerate, or downplay the scale and impact of a particular attack. Some attacks are blocked so effectively that analysts have no idea that an attempted, unsuccessful attack has taken place. Even if an analyst can find good information, converting qualitative data into quantitative inputs remains a concern.

Quantification and coding of the data is a major issue for developing a cyberspace superiority measurement system. If a targeted system is "partially disrupted," does that represent 20% capability or 80% capability? If an analyst does not code the inputs into the system in a systematic and repeatable manner, then the outputs lose analytical significance, no matter how elegant the measurement system. Accordingly, I developed coding methodology for the major inputs into the system and detail this coding in Appendix A. For the measurement system to be useful for analysis, different researchers should decide on similar inputs given the same data set and coding rules. With a method of quantifying the inputs, we can start developing the measurement system by examining the definition of cyberspace superiority.

Elements of the Definition of Cyberspace Superiority Needed for Measurement

The definition of cyberspace superiority given in AFDD 3–12 is, "The operational advantage in, through, and from cyberspace to conduct operations at a given time and in a given domain without prohibitive interference."[1] Pulling this definition apart yields several crucial phrases that help build the structure of the measurement tool.

The first key phrase of the definition is "operational advantage." The first definition of operation in JP 1–02 is, "A series of tactical actions with a common purpose or unifying theme."[2] Cyberspace superiority is about more than measuring the success of aggregated tactical actions. If those actions are not moving a combatant any closer to their objectives, then they are not relevant. Objectives are the way an attacker will normally spell out the desired common purposes or unifying themes that they are seeking in cyberspace, and those objectives must be a key component of any measurement system. The word "advantage" in the definition illustrates that cyberspace superiority is relative, as advantage has no meaning without being in relation to something or someone else.

The second key phrase of the definition is "to conduct operations." Cyberspace superiority is not meaningful unless it allows you to do something. This phrase also gives the key to measuring cyberspace superiority. Any measurement system should illustrate how easily a combatant can conduct operations, as that is what cyberspace superiority allows you to do, quite literally by definition. Note that operations do not have to be offensive. Feeding the troops can be "conducting operations" just as much as sending out a patrol. A measurement of cyberspace superiority will need to account for both offensive and defensive components.

The third key phrase of the definition is "given time." Cyberspace superiority will be limited temporally. As the level of cyberspace superiority will change with time, it also follows that the advantage can, and will, swing back and forth between combatants. A measurement of cyberspace superiority may be just a snapshot in time, not a final answer.

The fourth key phrase of the definition is that cyberspace superiority takes place in a "given domain." The language here is unfortunate as what the U.S. Air Force meant by a "given domain" is not the whole of the cyberspace domain. Instead, they are referring to a given domain as a smaller sub-set, or slice, of cyberspace that is of particular interest to a combatant. This meaning is clear from the next sentence in AFDD 3–12, which states that cyberspace superiority can be localized. Just because a combatant has superiority in one slice of cyberspace, it does not follow that they will be dominant across all of cyberspace. This fragmentation means that cyberspace superiority is highly localized and the measurement system must account for multiple levels of superiority across different slices, or systems, in cyberspace.

The final key phrase in the definition for developing a method of measurement is that an attacker needs to accomplish all of the elements mentioned "without prohibitive interference." This statement again highlights the relational aspect of cyberspace superiority. As one combatant is attacking enemy systems, the enemy is not just defending his systems; he is actively attacking the first combatant's systems, who is trying to overcome the second combatant's defenses, etc. This dynamic is the heart of the wrestling analogy used by Clausewitz and we must keep it in mind while developing the measurement scheme.[3] I will start by considering the easiest possible case of measurement.

Measurement in the Trivial Case

To illustrate the measurement system, consider first a "trivial case" where there are only two actors, combatant A and combatant B, only one system in cyberspace, and a single attack from A to B to accomplish a simple objective that is either completely met, or completely fails. In this case, cyberspace superiority would be a binary measurement: if combatant A is successful, A's cyberspace superiority would be 1.00. If the attack were unsuccessful or blocked, then A's cyberspace superiority would be 0.00. The next step is to examine how to measure objectives in warfare when they are not simple binary measurements.

Measurement of Objectives as an Input to Measuring Cyberspace Superiority

As the level of success an attacker has in achieving objectives in cyberspace is a key element of cyberspace superiority, it will be necessary to look at how to measure

Definitions and relationships

- Objective ***Goals to be achieved***
  - Objective: A stable and secure environment is established
  - Effect ***Behaviors/capabilities to be created***
    - Effect: Host nation Government provides basic human services
    - Measure of Effectiveness ***Progress toward/away***
      - MOE: Increase/decrease in the availability of electricity in key urban areas
      - Indicators ***What is measured***
        - Indicator: Average daily hours of electricity in key urban areas
        - Criteria ***The metric***
          - Criteria: Green = 16 Hrs – 16 Hrs+; Amber = 8–15 Hrs; Red = <8 Hrs

Figure 5.1 Effects Component Summary

Source: *Figure I-3*, U.S. Department of Defense, U.S. Joint Forces Command. "Joint, Techniques, and Procedures: Assessment of Joint Operations." 10, March 2008, I-6

success against objectives in general. Fortunately, Joint Forces Command (JFCOM) has done a great deal of work already in this area. JFCOM developed one of the more detailed systems, shown in Figure 5.1.

The lower levels in Figure 5.1 feed into the higher levels and it is important to note that there can be multiple indicators for each Measure of Effectiveness (MOE), multiple MOEs for each effect, and multiple effects for each objective. Depending on the situation, there can also only be one effect per objective, etc.

As an example of how this method of measurement can work in a physical domain, an attacker's objective might be to reduce enemy logistical capability. The effect would be that an attacker has immobilized enemy armored forces due to a lack of supply. The corresponding MOE could be an increase/decrease in the supply status of enemy armored divisions. An indicator would be the level of supply possessed by specific divisions in the regular categories of supply. For example, the defender's metric might be that for a specific adversary division, green is 24 hours or less of fuel reserves, amber is 24–72 hours, and red is more than 72 hours of fuel reserves.

If, in the previous example, an attacker sought the same objective through the cyberspace domain, then nothing changes in the measurement. The tools would change from kinetic forces to cyberspace forces but the objective of reducing enemy logistical activity, the effect desired, the MOE's and metrics could be similar or the same. When measuring the success of a combatant in achieving their objectives, it is not the medium or domain used, but the effects that matter. Planners already understand this system of objective measurement across the Department of Defense (DoD), and operators use similar systems today in USAF

Combined Air Operations Centers (CAOCs) to measure success. A system of measuring success against objectives is only the first step and helps develop one of the inputs for measuring offensive cyberspace superiority.

Measuring Offensive Cyberspace Superiority

On the offensive side, the first independent variable is S, the level of success an attacker has achieved against a particular cyberspace objective. S can range from 1.0 if an attacker has completely met their objective to 0.0 if the attacker has not met any part of his objective. You can then utilize the effects, MOEs, indicators, and criteria to determine an S for each objective. For example, if one of the commander's objectives was to shut down an enemy power grid to put pressure on enemy decision makers, the effect might be that the enemy's power control system was non-functional. The measures of effectiveness might include how well the control system was running the power grid. An indicator would be whether the enemy was providing power to the population. The criteria might be what amount of the enemy's population still had effective power. S would come out of the calculation as a percentage, for example, if the enemy power grid was providing 50% of its normal power, then S = 0.50.

An attacker needs to calculate S for each objective, then multiply it by a weighting factor, W. The weighting factor captures the level of importance that the commander has assigned to each objective and all the weighting factors have to add up to 1. For example, if there were three objectives and the commander assigned 50% weight to the first one, 30% to the second and 20% to the third, then $W_1 = 0.50$, $W_2 = 0.30$ and $W_3 = 0.20$.

Once the success levels and weighting factors have been determined, the overall Offensive Cyberspace Superiority Index (OCSI) can be determined by summing up the multiples of all the objectives and their weights.

$$OCSI = \sum_{1}^{n} ((S_1 \times W_1) + (S_2 \times W_2) + (S_3 \times W_3) + \ldots (S_n \times W_n))$$

Or

$$OCSI = \sum_{k=1}^{n} S_k \times W_k$$

OCSI will range from 0.0 to 1.0 with 1.0 equaling complete offensive dominance and 0.0 representing total failure in the offensive arena.

Measuring Defensive Cyberspace Superiority

The critical factor in measuring your defensive cyberspace superiority is the level of functionality (L) in critical systems. This measurement, L, is the defensive equivalent of S and I express it from 0.0 to 1.0 like S. If a system was considered 50% functional, then L = 0.50.

Next, L is multiplied by C, which is a measure of the system's criticality. C, like W, must add up to 1.0 so if the first system was considered twice as important as the second and third systems then $C_1 = 0.50$, $C_2 = 0.25$ and $C_3 = 0.25$.

This construct yields a measurement similar to OSCI but on the defensive side named Defensive Cyberspace Superiority Index (DCSI). Like OSCI, DCSI will range from 0.0 to 1.0 and I calculate it using the following formula:

$$DCSI = \sum_{1}^{n} ((L_1 \times C_1) + (L_2 \times C_2) + (L_3 \times C_3) + \ldots (L_n \times C_n))$$

Or

$$DCSI = \sum_{k=1}^{n} L_k \times C_k$$

Note that the critical systems are only those in the local area that combatants are contesting. Recall that in cyberspace superiority, the local level is the one that has the greatest impact and the one I focus on in these calculations.

In some cases, such as Russia's attack on Estonia, there is only one attacker and one defender. Because Estonia was not attacking Russia at all, the Estonian OCSI would be 0.0. In addition, as the only critical systems included in DCSI are those in a contested local area, the Russian DCSI was 0.0.

Reliance on Cyberspace

Before I can combine the offensive and defensive indices into the overall local Cyberspace Superiority Index (CSI), I need to address another issue. Not every nation is equally dependent upon the cyberspace domain. For example, in a conflict of the United States versus North Korea, North Korea would happily eliminate cyberspace capability for everyone. The elimination of the cyberspace domain would significantly increase North Korea's combat power relative to the US because North Korea does not rely on cyberspace as much as the United States does to generate combat power. To account for this factor, I have used an independent variable, R, in the calculation, which accounts for how reliant a nation is on its cyberspace systems. There will be two R, one for each combatant in the pair and the value of the two R has to add up to 1.0. For example, if nation A and B were equally reliant upon cyberspace, then $R_A = 0.50$ and $R_B = 0.50$. However, in a pairing such as the United States and North Korea where there is a significant disparity, $R_{\text{United States}}$ might equal 0.95 and $R_{\text{North Korea}}$ might equal 0.05.

A high level of reliance on cyberspace does not automatically imply a high level of vulnerability to cyberspace attack; the more important cyberspace is to a nation, the harder it will work to defend it. I will capture this factor in the lower levels of success that attackers will have against more effectively defended targets and the greater resources required to affect the same percentage of assets. For example, a moderate amount of resources might be sufficient to disable 50% of the telecommunications infrastructure in a small underdeveloped nation. However, disabling 50% of the U.S. telecommunications infrastructure would require an immense expenditure of resources and overcoming significant cyberspace defenses. Now we are ready to put the defensive and offensive sides together.

Cyberspace Superiority Index

The Cyberspace Superiority Index (CSI) combines a nation's offensive and defensive success while accounting for varying levels of cyberspace importance for different combatants. It is imperative to capture the importance of the cyberspace domain to each combatant because complete dominance of an area that is of little importance to the enemy is less valuable than dominance of an area upon which he is reliant. This element also acts as a multiplier to ensure that the final CSI is between 0.0 and 1.0, despite adding the two indices together. I calculate Nation A's CSI by:

$$CSI_A = ((OCSI_A \times R_B) + (DCSI_A \times R_A))$$

Note that I multiplied the offensive index by the defender's reliance on the cyberspace domain, while I multiplied the defensive index by the offender's reliance. This cross multiplication is because the importance of success in the offensive domain depends on how reliant the defender is on cyberspace, while the importance of success at achieving cyberspace superiority in the defensive domain also depends on how reliant the defender is on cyberspace. To return to the North Korean example, the U.S. establishing high offensive cyberspace superiority is less important than North Korea establishing high offensive cyberspace superiority and R accounts for that fact. I calculate the CSI for nation B the same way:

$$CSI_B = ((OCSI_B \times R_A) + (DCSI_B \times R_B))$$

Relative Cyberspace Superiority Index

The final dependent variable is the Relative Cyberspace Superiority Index (RCSI), which is a measurement of which side has superiority. I calculate it per nation and simply determine it by:

$$RCSI_A = CSI_A - CSI_B$$

As CSI_A and CSI_B range from 0.0 to 1.0, $RCSI_A$ can range from -1.0 to +1.0. At -1.0, nation B completely dominates nation A and at +1.0, nation A dominates nation B. Nation B's RCSI is the opposite and I calculate it by:

$$RCSI_B = CSI_B - CSI_A$$

If you substitute in the equations for OCSI and DCSI, you get the complete equation of:

$$RCSI_A = \left(\left(\left[\sum_{k=1}^{n} S_k \times W_k\right]_A \times R_B\right) + \left(\left[\sum_{k=1}^{n} L_k \times C_k\right]_A \times R_A\right)\right) - \left(\left(\left[\sum_{k=1}^{n} S_k \times W_k\right]_B \times R_A\right) + \left(\left[\sum_{k=1}^{n} L_k \times C_k\right]_B \times R_B\right)\right)$$

Initial Testing of the Cyberspace Superiority Index

To perform an initial test on whether RCSI provides a useful measurement of cyberspace superiority, I tested a number of simple hypothetical cases. I started at an extreme where combatant A had complete command of cyberspace. Nation A met all of their cyberspace offensive objectives and all of their cyberspace critical systems were 100% operational. Conversely, combatant B had achieved none of their cyberspace objectives and none of their systems were functional. This scenario gave the following inputs and outputs:

$OCSI_A = 1.00$
$DCSI_A = 1.00$
$R_A = 0.50$
$OCSI_B = 0.00$
$DCSI_B = 0.00$
$R_B = 0.50$

$CSI_A = 1.00$ and $CSI_B = 0.00$, which yields:

$RCSI_A = 1.00$
$RCSI_B = -1.00$

As expected, combatant A has complete "command of the cyber" with an RCSI of 1.0 while combatant B is achieving nothing in the cyberspace domain with an RCSI of -1.0.

At the middle, if the sides have equivalent capabilities then:

$OCSI_A = 0.50$
$DCSI_A = 0.50$
$R_A = 0.50$
$OCSI_B = 0.50$
$DCSI_B = 0.50$
$R_B = 0.50$

$CSI_A = 0.50$ and $CSI_B = 0.50$, which yields:

$RCSI_A = 0.00$
$RCSI_B = 0.00$

Neither side has cyberspace superiority. Both A's and B's efforts exactly balance each other out and give an RCSI of 0.0. However, if side A gains an advantage then:

$OCSI_A = 0.75$
$DCSI_A = 0.50$
$R_A = 0.50$
$OCSI_B = 0.50$
$DCSI_B = 0.25$
$R_B = 0.50$

$CSI_A = 0.63$ and $CSI_B = 0.38$, which yields:

$RCSI_A = 0.25$
$RCSI_B = -0.25$

Note that as the importance of the cyberspace domain for side B diminishes, A's relative advantage shrinks as well.

$OCSI_A = 0.75$
$DCSI_A = 0.50$
$R_A = 0.75$
$OCSI_B = 0.50$
$DCSI_B = 0.25$
$R_B = 0.25$

$CSI_A = 0.56$ and $CSI_B = 0.44$, which yields:

$RCSI_A = 0.13$
$RCSI_B = -0.13$

The importance of the reliance factor can also be seen in a case where each side is equally successful at offense, but unsuccessful at defense. If the reliance factor is balanced then you get:

$OCSI_A = 0.75$
$DCSI_A = 0.25$
$R_A = 0.50$
$OCSI_B = 0.75$
$DCSI_B = 0.25$
$R_B = 0.50$

$CSI_A = 0.50$ and $CSI_B = 0.50$, which yields:

$RCSI_A = 0.00$
$RCSI_B = 0.00$

Each side has the same RCSI as you would expect. However, if the cyberspace domain is more important for combatant A than combatant B, then you no longer have parity:

$OCSI_A = 0.75$
$DCSI_A = 0.25$
$R_A = 0.75$
$OCSI_B = 0.75$
$DCSI_B = 0.25$
$R_B = 0.25$

$CSI_A = 0.38$ and $CSI_B = 0.63$, which yields:

$RCSI_A = -0.25$
$RCSI_B = 0.25$

This example might occur if a high technology nation is fighting one that does not utilize information systems as much to generate combat power. These results suggest that the weighted preference methodology is sound and this approach should yield a useful measurement of cyberspace superiority for a given moment if the inputs are correct. The model also has some other uses.

Other Applications of the Measurement Tool

In addition to measuring cyberspace superiority, this weighted preference analytical model has a potential utility for training. Combatants could utilize this measurement system in training exercises. Instructors could incorporate this measurement concept into computerized scoring systems to project the trainee's effectiveness.

Another area where combatants could utilize this measurement system is in planning for cyberspace operations. This measurement system could provide a method to quantify the expected success of various courses of action to improve planning. This system will also provide the ability to look at tradeoffs within courses of action. This measurement system will provide an analytical framework that planners can use to examine branches and sequels to their plans. Wishful thinking as an input will still result in bad output, but a more rigorous analytical approach can be helpful.

This measurement methodology also has tremendous potential for combatants to utilize in cyberspace domain wargaming as a scoring mechanism. It could provide a clear quantitative index of how each side is doing in an exercise compared with a purely qualitative approach. If trainers or simulators are used, referees could build this scoring mechanism into the wargaming system. If a combatant ran the same scenario multiple times with different cyberspace domain units, it could help identify best practices as well as encourage higher levels of performance as each unit attempted to beat the "high score." Like any measurement system, this one can be "gamed" once the participants understand the weighting of the factors. Referees will have to ensure that the wargaming stays grounded in valid intelligence and commander's expectations on the importance of various objectives. This system provides a flexible tool that can be adapted to various scenarios and situations.

Conclusion

Combatants in cyberspace can utilize the weighted preference analytical model presented here to analyze which of two combatants has superiority in cyberspace. The model also quantifies the amount of cyberspace superiority for a combatant at a given time and in a local area. Combatants can use the measurement system for planning, wargaming, and training, and it balances offensive and defensive achievement in cyberspace.

The weighted preference measurement system developed in this chapter includes the offensive and defensive elements for both combatants. The measurement system starts by defining an attacker's objectives, then weighting those objectives. It balances the measurement of success on the offensive for both combatants with their level of success in defending their systems weighted toward the systems that are more critical to each combatant. Finally, I incorporate a variable to allow for the varying levels of reliance that different nation-states have on cyberspace. This system also needs valid inputs.

While the measurement system here is methodologically solid, it is dependent upon accurate inputs, which may be difficult to obtain. There are three major issues with inputs. First, cyberspace combatants often obscure everything they do in cyberspace conflict behind walls of anonymity and high levels of classification. Second, cyberspace combatants on the offense or defense often have numerous incentives, not just to hide, but also to actively mislead and lie about the outcomes of a cyberspace conflict. Finally, analysts must translate fundamentally qualitative data into quantitative inputs. Analysts mitigate the first two issues by seeking as much data from as broad a set of sources as possible. Analysts can alleviate the third issue with a detailed coding system.

Analysts need to code inputs into the measurement system in a repeatable manner, such that different analysts would give similar inputs from the same data. To accomplish this repeatable coding, I provide a detailed breakdown and definitions of the various inputs in Appendix A. I will use this coding methodology in the next chapter to analyze the cyberspace superiority case studies.

Notes

1 Air Force Doctrine Document (AFDD) 3–12, *Cyberspace Operations. Change 1*, 15 July 2010, 2.
2 Department of Defense, *Joint Publication* 1–02, 15 December 2012, 216.
3 Carl von Clausewitz, *On War*, ed. and trans. by Michael Howard and Peter Paret (Princeton, NJ: Princeton University Press, 1976), 75.

Bibliography

Air Force Doctrine Document (AFDD) 3–12, *Cyberspace Operations,* Change 1. 30 November 2011.

Clausewitz, Carl von. *On War.* Edited and Translated by Michael Howard and Peter Paret. Princeton, NJ: Princeton University Press, 1976.

Department of Defense, *Joint Publication* 1–02, 15 December 2012.

6 Cyberspace Superiority Case Studies

Although it would certainly be preferable to have a large number of case studies with detailed information on cyberspace operations and their effects, such cases and data do not exist, as the conflicts have not happened yet. To draw an analogy from airpower, cyberspace today is in a similar place to where airpower was before World War I. Before World War I, a few nations in conflicts, such as the Italians in Ethiopia, had taken airplanes to war, but they had not been very effective. Cyberspace warfare today is in an analogous position, as nations have made cyberspace attacks in support of national objectives, but there have been no worldwide cyberspace wars and attackers have barely scratched the surface of the potential of cyberspace conflict. This lack of historical record does not mean it is not worth trying to figure out how cyberspace superiority could work in a future conflict. We can look at the evidence available and extrapolate concepts from warfare in other domains as was done in Chapter 2. One of the issues with the cyberspace evidence is the difficulty in finding out what happened in the few case studies available.

During a conflict, a combatant will have some idea of their progress toward their objectives based on Battle Damage Assessment (BDA) and intelligence work, but there will always be uncertainty because the enemy will be actively trying to deceive and mislead. The attacks that you think have been so successful may have been diverted into "honey nets" and the Integrated Air Defense System (IADS) you thought your cyberspace warriors took down may actually be completely operational and just waiting for your aircraft to get within range before the enemy turns it back on. Even absent active attempts by an enemy to mislead, other structural issues will make accurate data elusive.

After a conflict has terminated it will normally be hard to acquire appropriate data to determine who achieved what level of cyberspace superiority during a conflict for several reasons. Most information related to the specifics of attacks and defense in cyberspace is highly classified. Even if a researcher has full access to the classified information on one side, it is unlikely that they would have access to the classified information on the other side. Actually, the situation is worse than that because most cyberspace information is not only classified, it is so highly compartmentalized so that not only does the left hand frequently not know what the right hand is doing, often the left hand does not know the right hand exists.

According to the Vice Chairman of the Joint Chiefs of Staff, General Cartwright, "We make sure the recce teams don't tell the defenders what they found, or the attacker, and the attackers go out and attack and don't tell anybody they did. It's a complete secret to everybody in the loop and it's dysfunctional."[1] This problem is much more challenging for the analyst who is working at the unclassified level where information is abundant, but of low quality.

There is a fair amount of data out in the unclassified realm, but it is mostly journalistic or analytical in character. A researcher has to sort through the data available to establish the objectives of the attacker and what level of success an attacker achieved. In many cases, the identity of the attacker is even in doubt because most attackers, so far, have chosen to claim innocence. This uncertainty does not mean that it is impossible to analyze superiority in the cyberspace domain, but there will always be a level of uncertainty about the calculation of superiority in any particular case. Often, as in the case of Stuxnet or the Aramco attack, there is consensus in the open source press as to who did it and why, but there will not be certainty. Accordingly, it will be important to cast the net as broadly as possible to ensure that outlying data will not too easily skew the results of this study.

Although I attempted to capture as wide a range of cases as possible, the struggle for cyberspace superiority under examination here is the one between nation states. As a result, the possible range of case studies is limited despite the multiple types of groups operating in the cyberspace domain.

Cyberspace Superiority Actors

There are four main types of actors in cyberspace. The first is what I term "cyberspace vandals"; these are the same people who used to spray paint the front of rival schools with scatological references, but they now can do the same thing through cyberspace. Often, this attacker really is the stereotypical bored teenager with a computer in their parents' basement, in accordance with popular culture's idea of a hacker. Generally, this group has low skills and resources and relies on pre-packaged attack programs downloaded off the Internet. These scripts are the origin of the derogatory term "script kiddies" and this category of hacker is normally not a serious threat in cyberspace. The next three groups, hacktivists, cyberspace criminals, and state actors, are more serious threats, as they possess the capability to create their own attack and spyware programs.[2]

As you move up the cyberspace threat ladder, analysts refer to the second group as "hacktivists." These actors focus on a political end and can have significant capabilities although their skills vary widely. There are large multi-national groups such as Anonymous as well as smaller more focused groups such as LulzSec. These groups intend to make some political statement, often about privacy, free speech, and governmental control of the Internet, however, their chosen causes are almost as numerous as the hacktivists themselves. These groups can have significant capability and cause difficulty for governments, but they are not part of the struggle between nation states and legal experts do not consider attacks by them as part of interstate warfare. The line between hacktivists and states can be blurred by so-called "patriotic hackers" when civilian activists are utilized by a government in pursuit of national ends. Examples of these types of attacks include the cyberspace attacks into Estonia in 2007 and Georgia in 2008. I will examine those attacks under the assumption that the attackers executed them, if not under the direction of, at least in coordination with a state government. I will discuss the details of the evidence tying those attacks to the Russian government in the appropriate cases. The next threat group in cyberspace presents a more focused threat than typical hacktivists.

The third group active in cyberspace consists of professional criminals. They use many of the same tactics as state actors and can have significant capability. However, their objectives are profit based as they are principally interested in making money. The easiest way to determine a state cyberspace attack from one undertaken by criminals is by examining the subject and characteristics of the attack. States can and do attack banking institutions in rival states, but they are usually trying to disrupt the banks, not steal money. Examples of these types of attacks include attacks on South Korean banks alleged to originate in North Korea and attacks on U.S. banks linked to Iran. A state actor is more likely to undertake a denial of service type of attack on a bank, as there is no theft, only disruption of the rival. A criminal organization is more interested in getting into the bank accounts and getting money out, or they rely on Internet fraud and spam e-mail. State actors can utilize criminal organizations just like hacktivists, and in one example, analysts traced many of the attacks on Georgia to the Russian Business Network (RBN), which was a Russian criminal organization.[3] I consider an attack to be state sponsored if a state was directing or coordinating an attack undertaken by criminal hackers in pursuit of state objectives. If criminal organizations are not reliable or capable enough, a state can also use its own military or governmental forces directly in cyberspace.

The final category consists of state actors, and the capabilities here range widely. Some nations have nascent cyberspace warfare programs and many are starting to build capable programs, but significant capability requires substantial expenditure of resources. Although the cost of entry into cyberspace is low, a capable program requires more "means." Currently, the most capable nations in cyberspace include Israel, the United States, the United Kingdom, China, and Russia.[4] It is difficult to establish an exact hierarchy because combatants do not openly display and discuss cyberspace assets. Other nations widely suspected to have capable cyberspace warfare programs include North Korea and Iran. This project focuses on cyberspace conflict between state actors, however, other issues make it difficult to select cases to study cyberspace superiority.

One of the most common types of cyberspace attacks between state actors attempts to steal information. These attacks are, in principle, similar to sending in a "James Bond" spy with a fancy car and watch, but they are lower risk, as there are no operatives to compromise or expose. These attacks are important and can generate an operational advantage from cyberspace, but by their design, they are very hard to pin down and analyze. States engaging in cyberspace espionage do not publicize what they are doing, and victims rarely publish it either unless they are trying for court convictions or to cast some blame on the attacker. If the attacker does his job correctly, the victim will never even know the attack took place. Consequently, it is not a useful category to examine, as any case study that we know about was a failure on some level because we know about it.

Other types of cyberspace attacks produce obvious results, and in some cases overt effects are the point of an attack, such as the Georgian attacks where official government websites were replaced by images comparing the Georgian president to Hitler.[5] Unfortunately for analysts, it is often difficult to figure out the source of even an overt cyberspace attack.

Nations often attempt to mask their actions in cyberspace, however, attribution is important, as understanding the attacker's objectives is a critical input into measuring cyberspace superiority. In the cyberspace domain, it is extremely difficult to prove who was behind an attack even if it is widely believed that a particular country was responsible.[6] For this study, I will identify the presumed attacker as the one most often cited as behind an attack. This attribution may be incorrect in a specific case. For example, it is possible, though not likely, that the Russian government really had no part in the cyberspace attacks on Estonia and Georgia. Complete proof is not required to proceed on the assumption that the Russian government was involved, as this analysis is not a criminal court. Even if I turn out to be incorrect in one case, it will not necessarily invalidate all of my conclusions.

Another difficulty in examining cyberspace superiority case studies is the narrow evidentiary base. There are a few unclassified studies available on specific cyberspace incidents such as the US Cyber Consequences Unit study on the Georgian conflict or Jeffrey Carr's "Gray Goose" project, however, most sources are narrow in focus and journalistic instead of analytical in character. The information is available, but an analyst has to sift it carefully.

Most nations involved in a conflict in cyberspace have significant incentive to be less than fully forthcoming about their activities. Attackers often claim innocence or that someone is trying to frame them. China resolutely maintains that it is a victim in cyberspace, not a perpetrator of cyberspace espionage and attacks, despite significant evidence to the contrary.[7] Defenders have incentives to deceive or misdirect as well. If an attack was successful, but the defender does not want anyone to know, there can be a significant incentive to lie. The Iranians have steadfastly maintained that Stuxnet was not significant and was caught and stopped before doing substantial damage. Most non-Iranian sources have suggested otherwise. Sometimes a defender even has incentive to maximize the apparent damage in an attempt to cast additional blame on the attacker. Given the sources available, there will always be some doubt and great care is called for when examining the data.

Case Study Selection

I selected cases to examine for the study that met two major criteria.[8] First, both sides in the conflict had to be, or were widely suspected to be, nation states. Second, the attacks had to have enough documentation in open source literature to allow me to examine them in sufficient detail to utilize the cyberspace superiority measurement tool to determine who achieved how much cyberspace superiority. The main elements of information included a reasonable level of confidence in the attacker's objectives, as well as the success of the attack and some information on the defender's actions.

An example of a case that I was unable to use was the alleged Iranian attack against U.S. banks in September of 2012. Unfortunately, there is nothing except suspicion to pin the attack on Iran and there is not enough information in the open press on what Iranian objectives were, or more importantly, what impact the attacks had. After a few banks discussed the attacks, the banks stopped talking to the press, leaving no way to determine what level of success the attacks actually had. Fortunately, there were enough cases left to investigate.

I was able to determine enough information for analysis in eight cases across a broad range of conditions and combatants. The cases range in time from 2007 to 2013 and are arranged in chronological order. There are simple brute force attacks such as the Russian attacks on Estonia, as well as the immensely complex Stuxnet attack. There are attacks that involve advanced and technologically reliant countries such as the United States and South Korea, as well as four attacks from the technologically backward North Korea. However, the world's first overt nation-state cyberspace conflict did not occur in Asia, but in the tiny Baltic nation of Estonia.

Russia versus Estonia 2007

There are several significant features of the Estonian cyberspace attacks of 2007 relevant to the study of cyberspace superiority. The Estonian attacks were the first case of overt nation-state versus nation-state cyberspace conflict. The conflict pitted a large and powerful country against a small, but technologically competent one. It was also the first use of "patriotic hackers" by a state to provide some level of plausible deniability to their actions. Finally, the defenses held and Estonia was able to maintain cyberspace superiority, while the Russians did not accomplish their most important objectives. To analyze these attacks, we have to first look at what those objectives were, which means we need to identify the attacker.

Although there was no concrete attribution to the Russian government, there is enough circumstantial evidence to find it likely that the Russian government encouraged the attacks even if they did not directly execute them with government forces. The Estonian Prime Minister Andrus Ansip stated that the attacks originated, "from the servers of Russian state authorities," although the Estonian government later admitted they did not have conclusive proof.[9] Several years after the attacks, a Russian official from the pro-Kremlin Unified Russia party, Sergei Markov, admitted that one of his assistants was responsible for the attacks but claimed that the attack was actually "cyber defense."[10] A leader of a Pro-Kremlin Russian youth organization "Nashi," Konstantin Goloskokov, who may have been the "assistant" also verified Nashi's involvement in an interview with the Financial

Times.[11] Although this evidence does not prove collusion, when you consider that Nashi was also heavily involved in the Georgian cyberspace attacks where there was clear evidence of collusion, it suggests official sponsorship and support. Accordingly, I analyzed this case as a cyberspace attack by Russia on Estonia. Because Russia did not claim responsibility, I had to infer their objectives.

The main Russian objective appeared to be to coerce Estonia into replacing a World War II Soviet memorial. The attacks occurred after the Estonian government moved the memorial and ethnic Russians in Estonia rioted. Russia attempted to force Estonia to replace the statue and apologize through a range of measures including mysterious "railroad maintenance" cutting off Estonia's commerce, slowing oil shipments, political pressure and the cyberspace attacks.[12] The statue was important to the Russians principally as a symbol of their continuing influence, not just as a physical object.

The second Russian objective was to use the conflict with Estonia to demonstrate to the other former Soviet republics that they should give in to Russian demands. This objective was always in the background of the conflict given that Estonia had recently joined the EU and NATO over Russian objections. The Russians saw this situation as an opportunity to flex their muscles and demonstrate that there would be a price to pay for going against their wishes. Unfortunately for the Russians, their attempted intimidation was not very successful.

Russia made little progress toward its objectives. The statue stayed where it was and the Estonian government refused to back down. The Russians were also only minimally successful in intimidating neighboring states. The Baltic States continued to move further out of the Russian orbit and Georgia continued refuse to bow to Russian pressure, which led to the Georgian conflict a year later. However, Russia was minimally successful in at least showing that there would be a price for going against her interests.

The second step in determining cyberspace superiority is to look at the defended systems and their functionality. Although there were a number of systems attacked across Estonia, the two that were most important were government and banking websites.

The attacks initially affected the Estonian systems significantly, however, the defenders were able rapidly to reconstitute and so mitigated much of the damage. The attacks were simple Distributed Denial of Service (DDoS) with some website vandalism and the attackers did not target critical information such as banking transactions. However, over the period of time that the attacks continued, the disruptions were initially very severe until Estonian defenses became more effective. Because Estonian defenders reconstituted their systems rapidly, the Estonians were still able to maintain a reasonably effective level of functionality.

The final major input into the model is how important cyberspace was to both nations. In 2007 Estonia was one of the most highly wired and connected countries in the world earning it the nickname "e-stonia." If Russia had experienced the same level of Internet attacks, it would have been less disruptive for most Russian citizens because their dependence on cyberspace was much less.

When all of these inputs were put into the model it showed slight cyberspace superiority for Estonia. The specific coding and inputs can be found in Appendix A and B. In this case $RCSI_{Russia} = -0.15$ and $RCSI_{Estonia} = +0.15$. When compared to the other eight cases, this is on the low end of cyberspace superiority achieved by a combatant.

To visualize what elements of cyberspace superiority were active in this conflict, I utilized the model of local cyberspace superiority generated in Chapter 4 and grayed out the elements not operating in the Estonian conflict of 2007. The result is Figure 6.1.

The Russians were attempting to utilize the means of denial of service through strategic information warfare to coerce the Estonians into replacing the statue and giving more weight to Russia's desires in the future. The Russians did not succeed, in large part due to Estonian recovery and resilience and also due to Estonian defenses that prevented the Russians from accomplishing more damaging attacks that could have gotten inside Estonian systems. The Russians did attempt to get around Estonian resilience and reconstitution efforts through simultaneous and persistent attack, but this effort was largely unsuccessful and therefore the arrow is dashed and the defensive block held. It is also fair to ask whether any level of cyberspace superiority would have been enough to convince the Estonians to bow to Russian pressure after decades of repression by the Soviet Union and hard won independence. This again highlights the limits of what a nation can hope to achieve through strategic information warfare.

The aggressive Estonian defenses and refusal to be intimidated resulted in a Russia not gaining enough cyberspace superiority to accomplish its objectives. The attacks were not a complete failure, however, Russia clearly showed its neighboring nations that there would be a price for going against Russian interests, which is a lesson that Georgia would have done well to heed.

Russia versus Georgia 2008

The Russian and Georgian conflict of 2008 is one of the first cases of cyberspace superiority having an effect on conventional military operations. On 7 August 2008, a five-day war started between Georgia and Russia over two breakaway provinces, South Ossetia and Abkhazia. The war started with a Georgian attack into a breakaway region within its borders to re-establish government control, which led to a massive Russian invasion and eventually to an EU brokered cease-fire.[13] Russian strategic objectives in the conflict included expelling Georgian troops and effectively annexing South Ossetia and Abkhazia, preventing Georgia from joining NATO, and increasing Russian influence.[14] What analysts did not fully appreciate at the time was that this incident was also the first clear case of a cyberspace warfare campaign used by an attacker in support of a conventional ground attack. The first cyberspace attacks were actually started by the Georgians who began hacking South Ossetian media sites earlier in the week before the Georgian attack into South Ossetia.[15] What the Georgians apparently did not expect was the massive cyberspace assault that came right as Russian troops

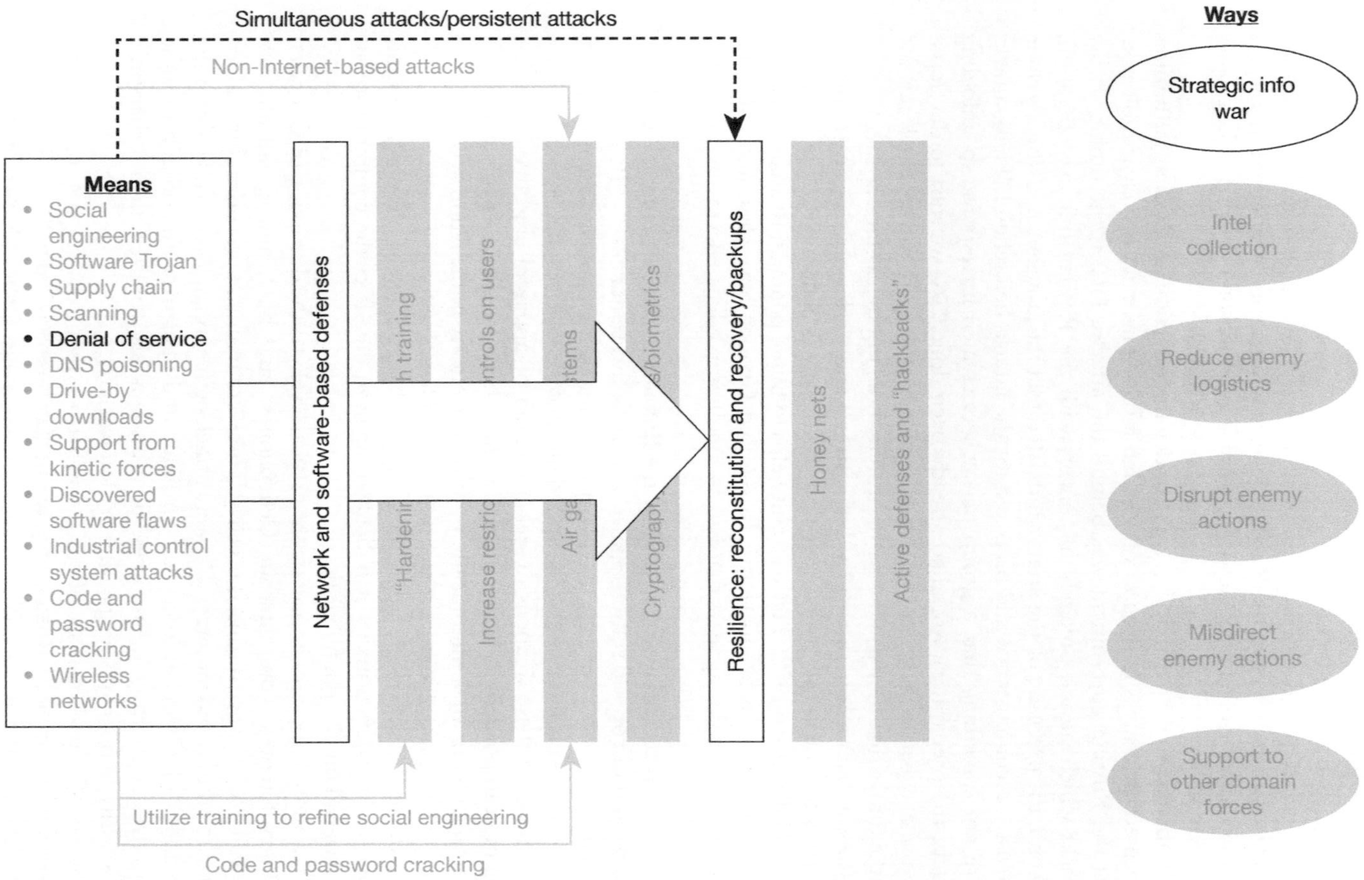

Figure 6.1 Russia versus Estonia 2007 Local Cyberspace Superiority Model

Source: *Author's original work*

invaded not only the breakaway provinces, but also Georgia itself. To analyze the cyberspace superiority achieved by the combatants and its effects, we need first to examine each side's attacks.

The first step in determining an offender's objectives is to determine who the attacker was. In this case, the Russian government has never admitted that it was behind the wave of attacks, however, there is good reason to attribute the attacks on Georgia to them anyway.

It appears that "patriotic hackers" under the direction of Russian authorities executed the attacks in support of Russian forces. There are two clear indicators that the Russian government was behind the attacks. First is the timing of the attacks which started precisely in concert with the Russian military operation. Second, the precision of the attacks indicated that the attackers had already done extensive reconnaissance and prepared for the attacks beforehand. These attacks were not something that a group of hackers created in response to unfolding events, the preparatory work had already been done.[16] As we start to develop a picture of what the Russians were seeking in cyberspace, we can also look at some of the things that they could have done, but chose not to, as clues.

Russian hackers did show a level of restraint and, "refrained from carrying out the sorts of attacks that would have done lasting physical damage to the Georgian critical infrastructure."[17] This restraint helps to frame potential Russian objectives leading to cyberspace superiority. Russia and Georgia have close and enduring economic ties and it appears that Russia sought immediate effect without causing lasting damage.

The two principal weapons used by the Russian hackers were denial of service attacks and discovered software flaws. For the software attacks, the Russians used Structured Query Language (SQL) injection attacks that enabled them to deface Georgian government websites and deny access to Georgian systems.[18] The Russians used these weapons to seek a number of apparent objectives. The first and most important objective appears to have been to disrupt enemy actions by attacking Georgian communications, to reduce enemy information access, and to disrupt Georgian actions, as it was difficult for Georgian forces to communicate.[19] This disruption also made it difficult to supply Georgian forces, although the short scale of this conflict makes it difficult to analyze the effect the communications attacks had on Georgian logistics.

The more important impact on the tactical level was the disruption of Georgian military forces to communicate. Cell phones, land lines, and e-mail all were unavailable at times during the war.[20] These communications disruptions aided Russian ground and air forces that were attacking Georgian forces while disrupting the ability of Georgian forces to coordinate and maneuver. In addition to these objectives supporting their forces, the Russians also utilized their cyberspace superiority to pursue strategic information warfare.

Some of the Russian's offensive objectives required the use of strategic information warfare.[21] Russia directly attacked Georgia's pipeline infrastructure through cyberspace. As argued by the United States Cyber Consequences Unit (US CCU), it actually appears that Russia may have been more interested in

Georgia's oil and gas pipelines than protecting ethnic Russian civilians.[22] The first areas Russian forces seized were not civilian areas but Georgian ports and facilities for handling oil and gas. The Russians also augmented these seizures with cyberspace attacks against Georgian pipelines coupled with a very conveniently timed attack on a Georgian pipeline in Turkey by local militants.[23]

In addition to pipeline attacks, there were further strategic information warfare attacks against the Georgian banking system, which took the entire system down for ten days.[24] According to Robert Pape's typology of coercion, I consider the banking attacks as part of a punishment strategy that the Russians intended to put pressure on the Georgian people and the Georgian elites.[25] The cyberspace elements of this strategy are strategic information warfare as they produced effects on physical systems directly from cyberspace.

There were four major Russian cyberspace objectives, the first of which was to cut Georgian internal communications. The attacks were extremely successful in achieving this objective as it, "was almost impossible for citizens and officials alike to communicate about what was happening on the ground during the military invasion."[26] Russia also successfully shut down Georgian cell phone and land line service, further reducing the capability of Georgians to communicate internally about what was happening.[27]

The next Russian objective was to sever Georgian communications with the international community, most likely in an attempt to get their overall campaign objectives achieved before the international community could bring much pressure to bear. Accordingly, they attacked the BBC and CNN with some success.[28] However, with the multiplicity of international communications, Russia was only minimally successful at cutting off information to the international community.

The third Russian objective was to shift customers from Georgian to Russian pipelines, I deduce this objective from the order in which the Russians attacked areas of Georgia coupled with the pressure brought on Georgian pipelines through mysterious insurgent attacks in addition to the cyberspace attacks. There was some damage to Georgian credibility and some oil and gas producers did look for alternate routes, but there was not long term impact and the Russians were minimally successful against this objective.[29]

I can infer the final Russian objective from the banking target set. Georgian banks were flooded with fraudulent transactions, which caused international banks to cut Georgia off from the international banking system.[30] This action had the effect of shutting down Georgia's banking system for 10 days, which produced hardship for regular Georgians, but special concern for the Georgian elites who were most affected by banking disruption, and also had the most voice with the government.[31] Although technically successful, this attack was only minimally successful in accomplishing the Russian objective, as there was no discernable pressure by either elites or regular Georgians on the Georgian government.

The Georgians were not completely idle on the offensive front, although they did not have nearly the success of the Russians. The Georgians launched two documented attacks of their own, the first was against South Ossetia in the week before the conflict. In the second, they attempted one known "counter-cyberspace" attack trying to make the Russian attack blowback on Russia by posting a counterfeit attack tool. This tool acted as if it was attacking Georgian sites while actually attacking Russian ones.[32] Unfortunately for the Georgians, both attacks had minimal impact against their targets and the Georgians had almost no success against their objectives.

On the defensive side of the conflict, the Russians appeared to have little difficulty dealing with Georgian attacks. Only two of their systems came under any Georgian attack at all: their conventional military command and control and their command and control of their cyberspace forces. There is no indication that the Georgians had any effect on Russian military command and control. As for the Russian command and control of their cyberspace forces, there was a counterfeit Georgian attack tool operative on some Russian bulletin boards used to control the Russian forces. Although there is no evidence that this counterfeit tool had any effect on Russian control of their cyber operators, it seems likely that the Georgians fooled at least a few.

The Georgians were very ineffective in defending their systems, which contributed to their lack of cyberspace superiority. Georgian cyberspace defenses fell into two broad categories, normal firewall type defenses, and system resilience. The Georgians had normal firewalls and intrusion detection systems in place. These systems were not adequate to stop even the initial wave of Russian attacks. The Georgians sought technical assistance from Estonia and other NATO countries to enhance their defenses but it soon became apparent that they were unable to defend successfully their systems. Georgia then shifted to a reconstitution and resilience mode where they moved their key websites to servers in Estonia and the United States. Although this attempt was marginally more successful, they still had great difficulty in keeping their websites accessible.[33] The Russian attackers overcame this attempted block through persistent and simultaneous attacks from multiple botnets, or groups of remotely controlled computers. At one point, the website of the Georgian president was under attack from 500 IP addresses simultaneously.[34]

Russia accomplished a very high level of cyberspace superiority and approached cyberspace supremacy; a condition where Georgia would have had no meaningful capability in cyberspace. $RCSI_{Russia} = 0.61$, which was the highest level of cyberspace superiority achieved in any of the case studies. Georgia was woefully unprepared for the conflict and apparently expected that Russia would not react as vigorously as it did. In addition, Georgia may have expected the United States or the EU to provide more forceful assistance, however, the Western nations had warned Georgia not to provoke a conflict, and so did not provide significant support. I combined the various elements used in this attack and they are shown in Figure 6.2.

The Russians were able to overcome Georgian defenses to establish a significant level of cyberspace superiority. The Russians principally relied upon denial of service and discovered software flaws to get through the first layer of Georgian defenses and persistent and simultaneous attacks to deal with Georgian attempts at resilience. This cyberspace superiority brought benefits to Russian forces.

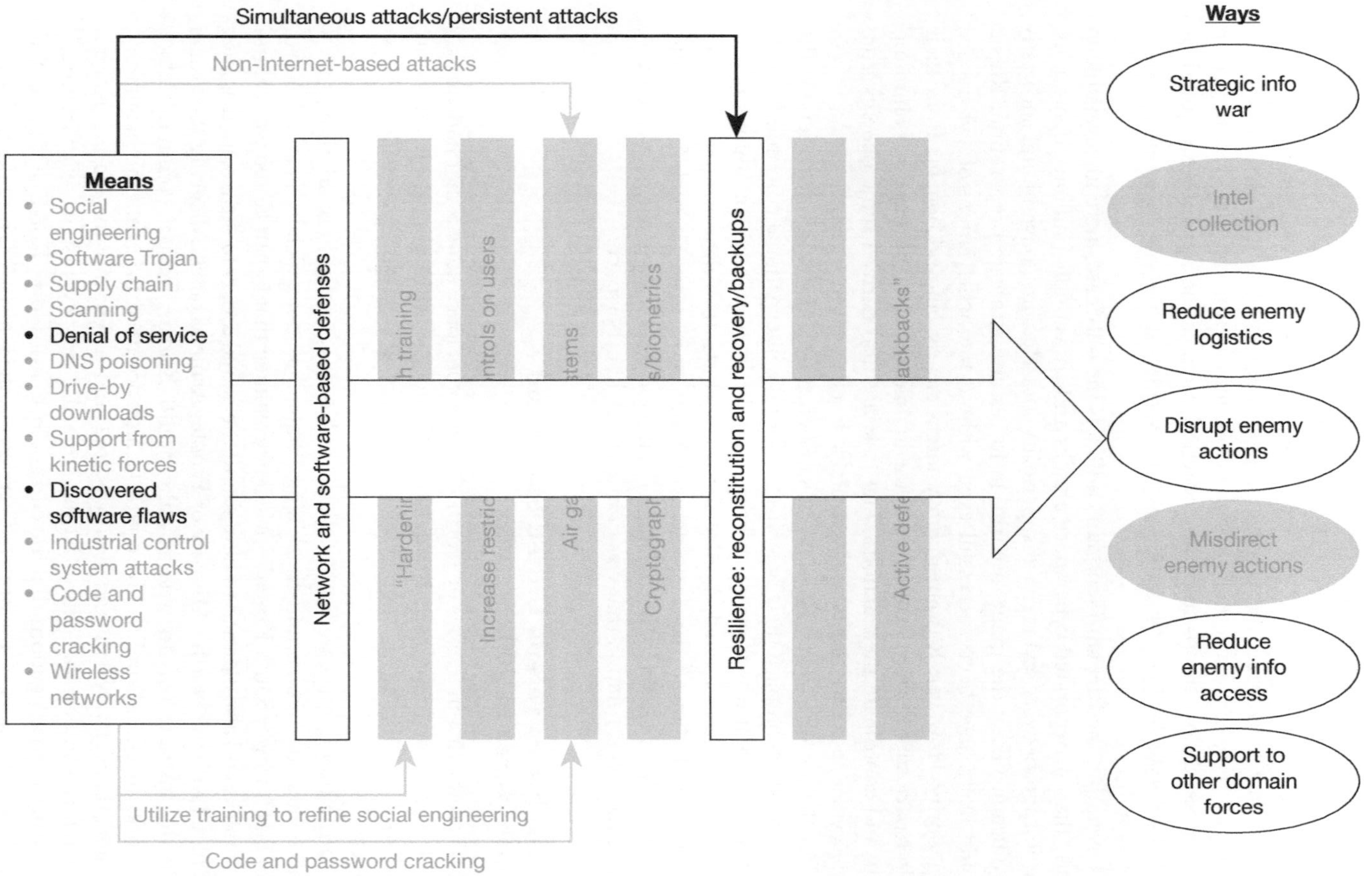

Figure 6.2 Russia versus Georgia 2008 Local Cyberspace Superiority Model

Source: *Author's original work*

Russian forces were able to capitalize on their opponent's lack of ability to communicate. Although Russian airborne forces performed creditably, their regular forces did not all perform well.[35] Had Georgian forces been able to communicate, it is conceivable that they could have been far more effective at the operational and tactical level. Had the Georgians been able to block the Roki tunnel for example, it would have had a significant impact on the speed with which Russia could flow troops into the contested area.[36] The advantage enjoyed by Russian forces because of their cyberspace superiority is of great importance to this study.

Given that the Russian-Georgian conflict is the only case currently available to study that incorporated cyberspace attacks and conventional military operations, the linkage between cyberspace superiority and Russian conventional success is significant. Given the great disparity in forces and strategic preparation, Russia would likely have been successful even without the achievement of cyberspace superiority. However, Russian military forces clearly enjoyed benefits from their cyberspace superiority, particularly in the inability of the Georgians to communicate and coordinate their actions. The Russians also derived some benefits from their cyberspace superiority at the strategic level.

On the strategic level, Russian cyberspace superiority made it easier for the Russians to accomplish their objectives before the international community really understood what was happening. Presenting the international community with a *fait accompli* made it much harder for other states to intervene to change the situation and allowed Russia to achieve many of its strategic goals in Georgia. Georgia played David to the Russian Goliath and lost badly, in the next case study, it was the weaker nation that was on the attack in cyberspace.

North Korea versus United States and South Korea in 2009

This was the first in a series of North Korean cyberspace attacks that had varying levels of success. In this case, North Korea did not establish cyberspace superiority and so did not gain any significant operational advantage as a result of these attacks.

Attribution in this case is not definite, as North Korea has not admitted that it was behind the attack and the United States has not officially accused North Korea. However, South Korea's spy agency claimed that North Korea was behind the attacks and also claimed to have found the actual orders to the research agency affiliated with the North's Ministry of Peoples Armed Forces. Allegedly, the orders said the institute was to, "destroy the South Korean puppet communications networks in an instant."[37] These attacks also occurred in a time of heightened tensions between North and South Korea and a few months after a Korean newspaper claimed that North Korea created a new cyberspace warfare unit.[38] There are even allegations that the current leader of North Korea, Kim Jong Un, was the commander of the unit that carried out the attacks.[39] Given the diplomatic realities in North East Asia, it is unsurprising that the United States is unwilling to identify publically North Korea as the attacker, but there is enough evidence to proceed with the case and identify the North Korean objectives.

As North Korea did not take responsibility for the attack, I have to infer their objectives from the target set. All of the attacks were Distributed Denial of Service (DDoS) attacks which attack access to Internet based websites or services, but do not access information on the targeted systems.[40] The targets included government sites in the United States and South Korea as well as the party website of the conservative party in South Korea, and finally what can best be characterized as economic targets in South Korea and the US such as South Korean banks and the NASDAQ stock exchange.[41] The objective of the attacker appeared to be to damage US and South Korean governmental and economic websites. Inferring what North Korea intended to gain from the attacks if they were successful is more challenging. Possibilities range from simply trying to damage adversaries, to continuing the normal cycle of escalation, to establishing Kim Jong Un as a military leader who could damage North Korea's enemies.

The attacks on US government websites were only marginally successful. Major targets such as the Pentagon and White House successfully defended themselves with no loss of capability. Some, less well-defended federal agencies such as the Department of Transportation and the FTC experienced some difficulty, but the overall effect on the US government was barely noticeable.[42]

The attacks on the South Korean government websites were more successful with the official Presidential website and the defense ministry paralyzed during the initial attacks.[43] However, the attack was not completely successful in South Korea and some of the websites under attack were able to continue functioning.

US economic sites experienced little disruption while some South Korean banking sites and an online auction system experienced difficulty.[44] The attackers had slightly more success against the South Korean economic sites and achieved minimal success against this objective.

On the defensive side, the United States and South Korea were both very active. Computer security firms bolstered the systems under attack, attacking IP addresses were cut off, and South Korea went so far as have the Korean Communications Commission (KCC) order service providers to deny access to 30,000 South Korean computers that were part of the attacking botnet.[45] Both South Korea and the United States responded quickly to the attacks and took aggressive measures to cut off attacking systems. Although there were stories in the press, there was little discussion of the attacks in the general media even shortly after the event and so North Korea failed to accomplish much other than to show that they were building capability in cyberspace. The local cyberspace superiority model is shown in Figure 6.3.

This model closely mirrors the Russia versus Estonia case in 2007. In both cases the attacker was attempting to utilize denial of service as the means and strategic information warfare as the way to achieve strategic goals, and in both cases the attacker was unsuccessful. This is partially due to aggressive defensive measures taken by the Estonian, South Koreans, and United States, but it is also due in part to the difficulties of coercion, particularly when attempting to utilize strategic

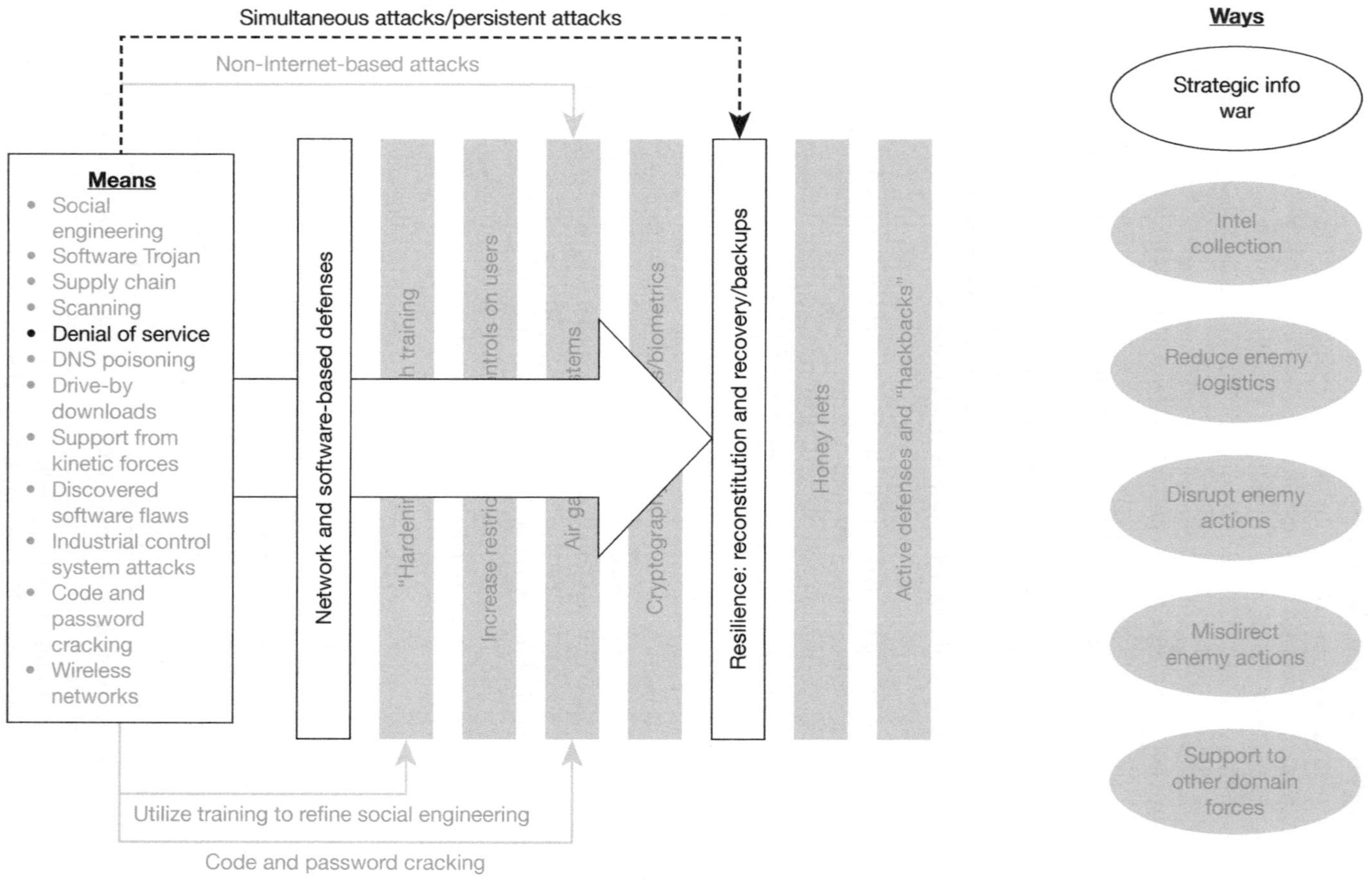

Figure 6.3 North Korea versus South Korea/U.S. 2009 Local Cyberspace Model
Source: *Author's original work*

information warfare. Strategic information warfare is a relatively weak tool compared to strategic bombing, and strategic bombing has often been unsuccessful in coercing combatants despite large scale physical destruction. The next case of Stuxnet relied on a much more subtle approach than coercion.

Stuxnet

Stuxnet is an important case to examine for this study, as it was the first known example of a cyberspace weapon that produced physical effects. On 17 June 2010, researchers at a small Belarusian computer security firm discovered a new piece of malicious software or malware infecting USB memory sticks.[46] That malware, which analysts eventually named Stuxnet based on a name found in the code, was the world's first precision cyberspace weapon designed to have effects outside of cyberspace in the other physical domains.

Stuxnet was not a normal piece of malware that hackers in a basement or even a criminal syndicate put together. Prior to Stuxnet, no piece of malware had utilized more than one, zero-day vulnerability.[47] The complicated "Aurora" malware, responsible for attacks on Google in late 2009, and every other known piece of malware prior to Stuxnet, had relied on, at most, one zero-day vulnerability.[48] Most attacks do not have a single zero-day vulnerability and are instead built around known vulnerabilities. Stuxnet utilized five separate zero-day vulnerabilities and was far more complex than anything that security experts had discovered before.[49] It also did not appear as if the designers of Stuxnet intended it for the traditional criminal activities such as spam or fraud. According to Paulo Shakarian, "other malware include standard code for a variety of criminal activities – including identity and password theft, launching denial-of-service attacks, and sending spam emails. Despite its high degree of technical sophistication, Stuxnet was not designed to perform any of these activities."[50]

What Stuxnet was designed to do was to alter the instructions that were sent to a Siemens S7-417 or S7-315 industrial controller, but only if the controller was attached to a very specific configuration of devices.[51] Given that security researchers discovered the majority of infections in Iran, and the fact that Iran had configured their nuclear centrifuges in exactly the manner specified in Stuxnet, a motive and likely suspects were easy to come by.

Analysts immediately suspected that the United States and Israel were behind Stuxnet in an attempt to slow the development of an Iranian nuclear weapon. Experts determined that two organizations wrote Stuxnet based on their analysis of the code. The New York Times published a story reporting this claim and its connections to the administration.[52] The United States and Israel have not directly admitted to creating and deploying Stuxnet, but for the purposes of this study, the attribution is likely enough to proceed. David Sanger, the New York Times reporter, has written a book, which provides extensive detail on the decisions behind the development and deployment of Stuxnet. The government has not confirmed Sanger's story, but they are trying to figure out who gave him the information so that the Justice Department can prosecute the leaker.[53] Accordingly, attributing the attack to the United States and Israel in accordance with Sanger's reporting seems reasonable. Now that the identity of the attackers has been determined, we turn next to what their objectives were.

Based on American and Israeli policy and messaging, it appears that the overall objective of Stuxnet was to slow the Iranian nuclear program to provide time for sanctions and negotiation to solve the problem. Thus, the first objective was to delay enrichment activities at Natanz as much as possible by sabotaging the enrichment system. It also appears the attackers wanted effects beyond temporary disruption.

The attackers did not just want to stop current enrichment activities; they wanted physically to destroy equipment to prevent future enrichment. As evidence of this, it appears that Stuxnet escaped "into the wild" because the attackers began to utilize a more aggressive attack method when they were not achieving a high enough level of destruction.[54] It seems that the more aggressive version of Stuxnet got out in the wild when an Iranian scientist inadvertently interrupted Stuxnet in the middle of a process. This interruption resulted in Stuxnet spreading beyond the nuclear system the designers intended it exclusively to infect.[55] This mistake resulted in the attacker's failure to accomplish their third objective of secrecy.

A third objective was clearly to remain undetected as long as possible. One of the most impressive aspects of Stuxnet was that it not only destroyed centrifuges, it made it look like the centrifuges were dying of "natural causes." Stuxnet periodically changed the speed of the centrifuges in a specific manner designed to produce eventual failure, but continued to report to the controller that everything was fine and the centrifuge was spinning exactly as it should.[56] Part of the objective of Stuxnet was not just to delay, but also to confuse and mystify the Iranians as to why their centrifuges were not working, which would produce even more delay.[57] This was only possible as long as the weapon itself remained hidden.

The attackers only had mixed success against these objectives. On the one hand, it appears that there was damage done to Iranian centrifuges. Iran decommissioned and replaced about 1,000 IR-1 centrifuges at the Natanz Fuel Enrichment Plan in late 2009 or early 2010.[58] Stuxnet could easily have been responsible for the destruction of these centrifuges. It is also verifiable that although the Iranians designed Natanz for 50,000 centrifuges, there were only about one fifth of that number running after ten years of work.[59] On the other hand, the Iranians apparently responded to the reduction in efficiency by significantly ramping up the number of centrifuges they were running. The Iranians managed to increase their daily production by 20%, although the Institute for Science and International Security (ISIS) report considered this a significant underperformance given the number of new centrifuges the Iranians added.[60]

The delay in the enrichment program was significant, but it also was not everything the Stuxnet attackers were hoping to accomplish. The estimates of how long Stuxnet delayed the Iranian nuclear program vary from about one to three years, which still represents significant success.[61]

Based on the number of centrifuges taken offline and replaced at Natanz while the attack was operable, it is clear that Stuxnet was at least partially successful in destroying equipment. However, it appears that the destruction was not sufficient to stop completely the Iranian program as the Iranians introduced more than enough centrifuges to compensate and actually increased their production. The Iranian increase in production does not automatically imply that the attackers were unsuccessful. Stuxnet evidently affected uranium production significantly, as the Iranians should have been able to produce far more enriched uranium than they did with the number of centrifuges they were operating.

The final objective for Stuxnet was to remain hidden. Unfortunately for the attackers, Stuxnet was not only found by the defenders, but also got out into the wild where numerous researchers took it apart and analyzed it. Stuxnet did remain undetected for two to three years, but the decision to "swing for the fences" resulted in the attack having a shorter life span than desired.[62] Once researchers had discovered Stuxnet, the Iranians were able to get their nuclear program back on track.

The next step in analyzing the Stuxnet attacks is to determine the level of defensive success. The Iranians expected that their facilities would come under attack and so worked hard to protect their systems as much as possible. It is reasonable to assume that the Iranians had protected the Internet-enabled computers in the facilities with firewalls and intrusion systems. Given the high security present in the facility, coupled with the suspicions of sabotage, it is also likely that there were significant restrictions and controls on users. One of the methods relied upon by the Iranians to block attackers was reconstitution and recovery. Despite losing at least a thousand centrifuges and a major reduction in efficiency of production, they brought in many more centrifuges and actually managed to increase production.[63] Additionally, in Supervisory Control and Data Acquisition (SCADA) systems such as the one attacked by Stuxnet, air gapping is normally a key defense.

It also appears that the controllers running the centrifuges were air gapped and not directly connected to the Internet.[64] The structure and design of Stuxnet confirms the Iranian air gap, as the attackers clearly designed Stuxnet to jump an air gap utilizing multiple methods. Stuxnet has four propagation methods that include flash drives and various wireless and wired network attacks.[65] The designers of Stuxnet also used persistence to continue to hammer away at the air gap. Security researchers have found several versions of Stuxnet dating back as far as 2007 and it appears that the designers continued to make changes to increase the effectiveness of the attack.[66] Although the designers of Stuxnet were after the SCADA system, they understood that the road to it lay through the support system.

The two systems Iran was trying to defend in Natanz were the support system network of computers and the SCADA control systems themselves. The support system network consisted of the computers in the facility used to support the enrichment process and was the system Stuxnet needed to infiltrate to get to the SCADA system. The SCADA controllers ran the actual process, which was the point of the facility.

It appears that the attackers had riddled the support computer system with Stuxnet, which was also extremely hard to get rid of, as a single infected device missed by the defenders would rapidly infect the entire network all over again. The purpose of the support system was to keep the SCADA system operational and functioning. Instead of providing defense and support, the support system was the avenue through which the SCADA system was attacked and thus was not defended very successfully.

It is harder to assess the level of functionality of the Natanz SCADA system, as there is no reliable, unclassified data available. It does appear that the Iranians had a very difficult time getting Stuxnet out of their systems and they temporarily shut down enrichment operations at Natanz in November 2010.[67] I have to balance this data with the fact that overall enrichment numbers continued to rise over time due to a massive influx of new centrifuges so the system maintained at least some capability. However, given that the SCADA system was under the control of an enemy and was actively working to destroy centrifuges while allowing just enough enrichment to remain undetected, the level of functionality achieved by the defenders was low.

It appears that Stuxnet most likely represented a low level of cyberspace superiority for the U.S. and Israel, as they achieved some of their objectives, and $RCSI_{US/Israel} = 0.08$. The major objective for the attackers was to slow down Iran's enrichment program while remaining hidden to allow time for negotiation. These objectives were at best partially met. It is also possible that Stuxnet represented something closer to parity with neither side having superiority because of some of the uncertainty surrounding the level of success. A depiction of the Stuxnet attack utilizing the local cyberspace superiority model is shown in Figure 6.4.

Because Stuxnet is such a flexible piece of malware that has multiple propagation pathways, it is difficult to say with certainty which pathway was the effective one. The attackers may have initially inserted Stuxnet into Iran using a number of methods. Regardless, the designers clearly intended for it to spread across wireless networks. Once in place, it became a software Trojan and utilized multiple software flaws to execute SCADA attacks on industrial controllers. The attackers overcame Iranian attempts to block Stuxnet from interfering with their SCADA systems by using non-Internet based methods to jump the air gap combined with persistence by the attackers. Several of these characteristics are unique to Stuxnet so far, and important to cyberspace superiority.

Stuxnet was the first cyberspace weapon that demonstrated the capability to leverage cyberspace superiority to produce effects in the physical world. Researchers had generated physical effects in laboratory settings, but Stuxnet is the first case where attackers utilized such a weapon in the real world. Stuxnet will likely not be the last cyberspace attack to generate effects in the physical world and the fact that analysts discovered the weapon and propagated the source code makes it even more likely that lower level nation-state attackers can study Stuxnet and develop similar weapons to suit their objectives.

Stuxnet was also the first major cyberspace attack by a nation state to use cyberspace superiority to target Industrial Control Systems (ICS). ICS attacks on power grids and infrastructure have been a constant theme of authors trying to raise public interest, and public funding, for cyberspace; prior to Stuxnet, these

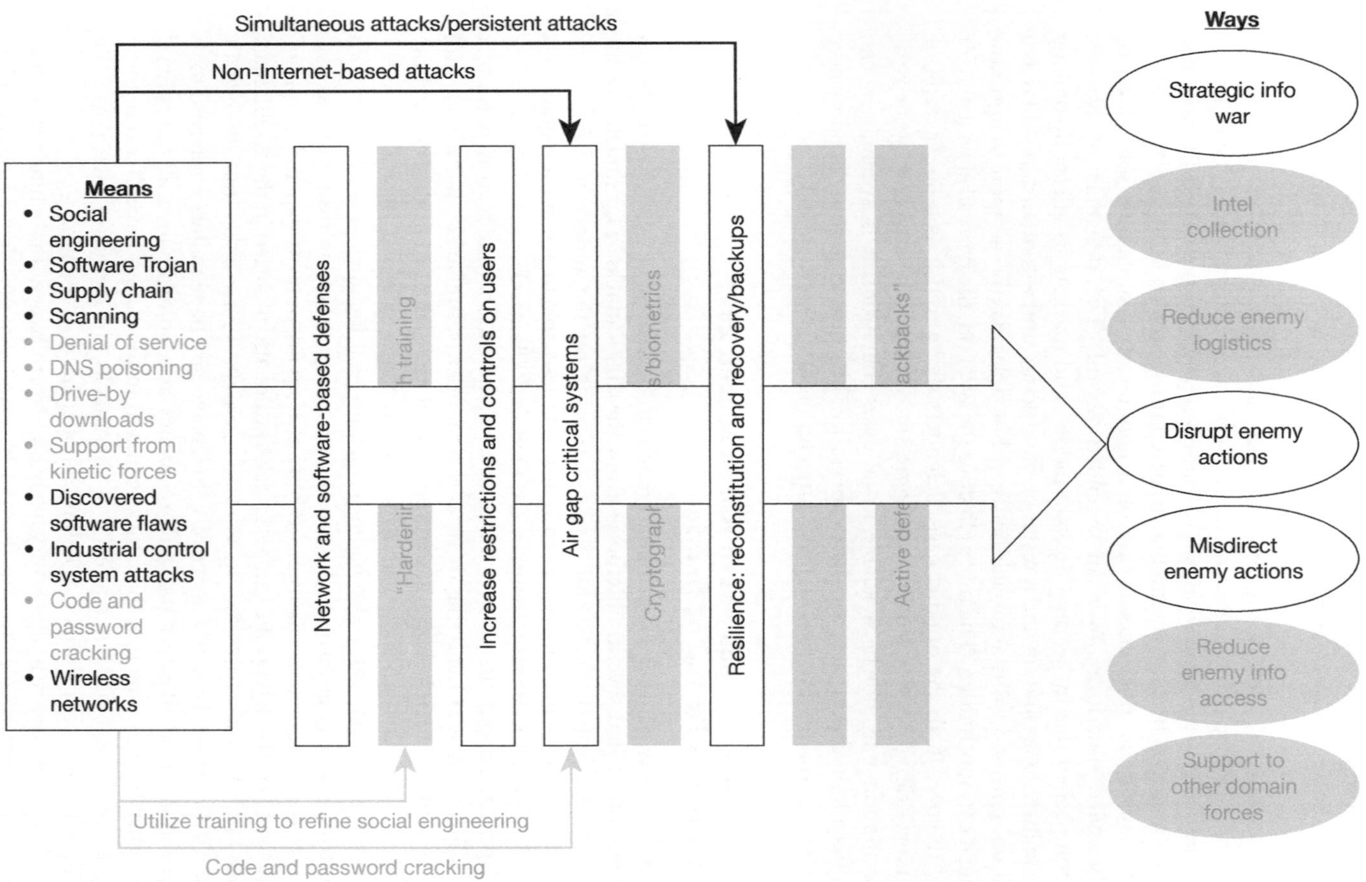

Figure 6.4 Stuxnet Local Cyberspace Model

Source: *Author's original work*

types of attacks were mostly theoretical. Stuxnet demonstrated that attacks on ICS are a real threat, even to the most highly guarded and defended systems.

In addition, Stuxnet was the first cyberspace weapon known to have successfully breached an air gap defense. Prior to Stuxnet, many analysts had considered air gaps an effective defense against attackers and a good way for defenders to maintain cyberspace superiority over their critical systems. Stuxnet demonstrated that there are ways around air gaps, and even provided the details for potential future attackers because researchers released the source code.

Stuxnet is the only known case of a nation-state maintaining some level of cyberspace superiority over an extended period. The designers of Stuxnet accomplished this by keeping Stuxnet hidden and masking its effects by making the failures look random and a result of poor design and workmanship. There is a natural tension in this approach between how effective the weapon is, and how long it can stay hidden. The more effective the weapon, the more likely a defender will discover it. In the Stuxnet case, defenders discovered it as a direct result of Stuxnet's designers releasing a more aggressive variant. The attackers' strategy of obscuration may not be available in all cases, but when it is available, it can produce long duration cyberspace superiority. The next case study is one where the North Korean attackers utilized a much noisier and open attack.

North Korea versus South Korea March 2011 Distributed Denial of Service

This case was another Distributed Denial of Service (DDoS) attack by North Korea, but it had several differences from the 2009 attacks. This attack was far more sophisticated underneath while appearing on the surface to be another simple DDoS attack. The North Koreans were also able to achieve a higher level of cyberspace superiority than they did in their 2009 attack.

North Korea did not admit to this attack, but there are several reasons to suspect their involvement. One is that there were a number of similarities in the code and method of the attack that made it appear as if the same group that created the 2009 attack on South Korea and the United States was also behind the 2011 attack.[68] The target set is also highly suspicious as it included sites affiliated with the South Korean government, military and civilian critical infrastructure as well as U.S. Forces Korea and Kunsan AB.[69] There was not only overlap in the types of targets, 14 of the 40 specific targets attacked were also attacked in the 2009 attack linked to North Korea.[70] Finally, McAfee researchers have linked the 2009, 2011 and 2013 attacks through a piece of cyberspace espionage malware referred to as Operation Troy.[71] Because the same reconnaissance software links all the attacks, it is sensible to assume that the attacks came from the same source. Because there is reasonably good evidence in each of the attacks, the cumulative weight of the evidence that North Korea was behind all of them is substantial.

All of this evidence makes is very likely that North Korea was behind the attacks and I will attribute all three to them. I have to infer the North Korean objectives, as they did not announce their motives. There are several clues in the characteristics of the attacks, these were not normal DDoS attacks such as were launched in 2009.

The attacks were an odd combination of technical sophistication and brute force. The attackers deliberately destroyed and wiped their botnets at the end of the 10-day attack window, which is very unusual for any sort of hacktivist or criminal organization. Those organizations protect their botnets to keep them for future use. The North Koreans instead went to great lengths to encrypt their botnets at multiple levels, then wipe them to make it more difficult for researchers to track. However, the weapon itself was an unsophisticated DDoS. McAfee Security sees this combination as evidence that the attacker's intent was to test the defender's response capabilities.[72]

The first objective appears to have been to test South Korean response and mitigation capabilities. I find the McAfee argument that this attack was primarily about reconnaissance compelling and so I placed the preponderance of the weight on that objective, which was very successful. As the targets of the attacks were websites located in South Korea, shutting down those websites appears to have been a secondary objective as well. Given the continuing animosity between North and South Korea, North Korea is always looking for any way to embarrass or damage South Korea, which makes that a likely final objective. There was not much press attention paid to these attacks and the South Korean response came across as competent and effective so this portion of the attack was only minimally successful.

On the defensive side, South Korea immediately launched mitigation measures and was able to utilize previously installed digital "bunkers" that were IP addresses set aside for organizations that come under DDoS attack.[73] The North Koreans attempted to make it difficult to respond to the attacks as, "several steps were taken to ensure that the mission was executed without interruption, within the predefined attack window—and following, ensuring that all vehicles of attack would be destroyed, thus limiting forensic analysis."[74] However, within a few days, McAfee and others were able to "detect, reverse engineer, and mitigate the attacks."[75]

The disruptions for South Korea and the U.S. military were short lived and both systems maintained a high level of functionality. The South Korean sites were slightly more effected by the attacks and the U.S. military sites only experienced negligible degradation. The analysis produced a $RCSI_{North\ Korea} = 0.03$, which is a very slight cyberspace superiority for North Korea bordering on neutrality.

Although North Korea only established a very low level of cyberspace superiority, this case represented a significant step forward for North Korea in capability from the 2009 attacks. The mechanism used was more sophisticated and if their primary goal was to obtain data on South Korean defense and reconstitution methods, they succeeded in that goal despite the low level of damage done. The local cyberspace superiority model applied to this attack is shown in Figure 6.5.

The North Koreans utilized social engineering to build the botnet that they subsequently utilized in the denial of service attack. They were attempting to utilize strategic information warfare to embarrass South Korea while gathering

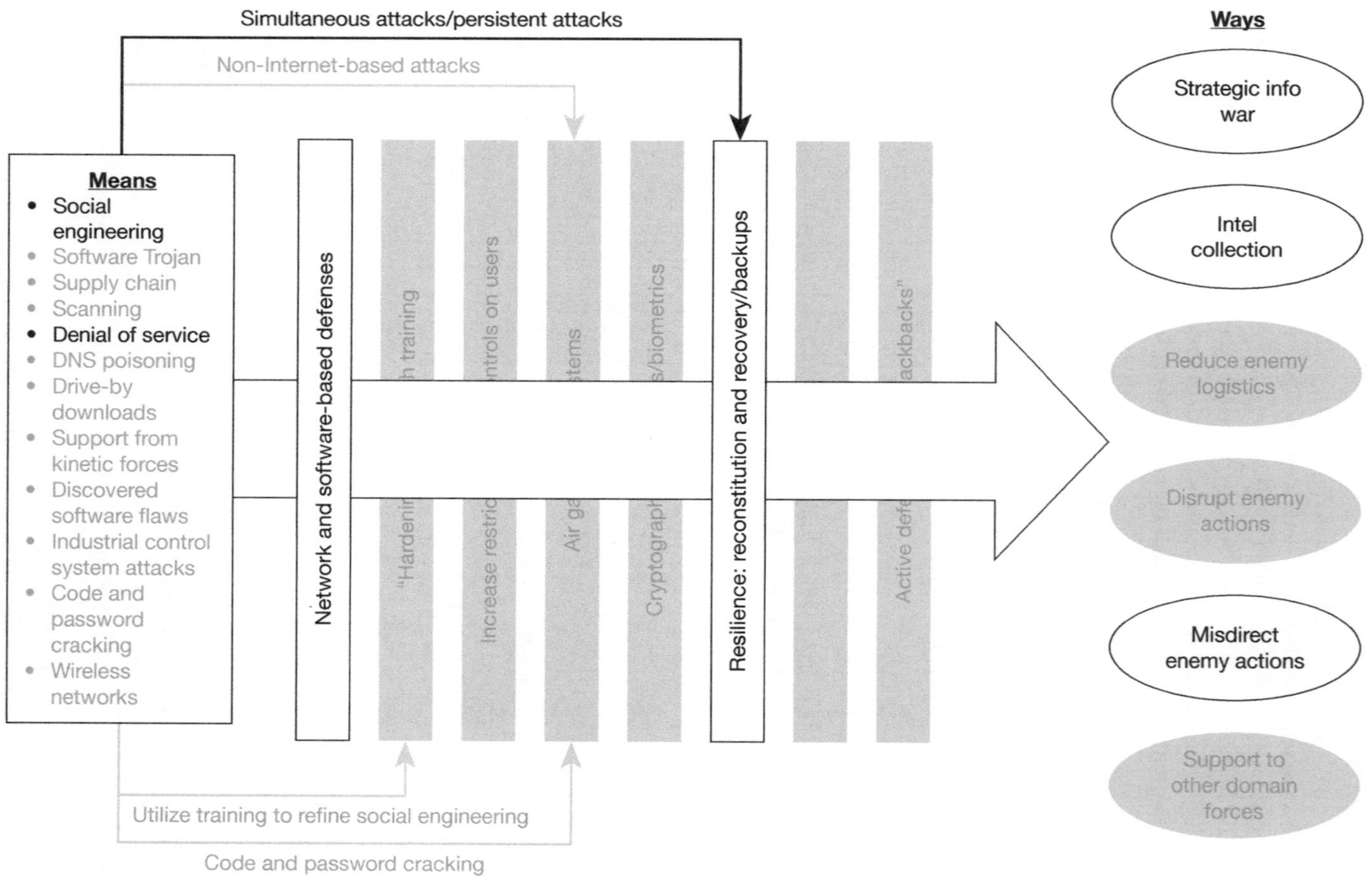

Figure 6.5 North Korea versus South Korea DDoS 2011 Local Cyberspace Model

Source: *Author's original work*

intelligence and misdirecting them into thinking that it was a simple denial of service. The South Korean blocks were partially successful, but the North Koreans were able to overcome them with simultaneous and persistent attacks to achieve a very slight level of cyberspace superiority.

This case is also interesting because the offender and defender were relatively successful as they were aiming at different things. The North Koreans were trying to learn about South Korean defenses, and the South Koreans were trying to keep their systems up and running. Both largely succeeded, which resulted in near neutrality that slightly favored North Korea in the overall cyberspace superiority. These attacks also set up the 2011 bank attacks, which were much more successful for North Korea.

North Korea versus South Korea April 2011 Bank Attack

Less than a month after the March DDoS attack, South Korea was under a major cyberspace attack again, and this time the North Koreans established a much higher level of cyberspace superiority.

Despite the accusations of South Korean prosecutors, North Korea flatly denied that it had anything to do with the attack, but there are again a number of reasons to doubt that claim. One is the linkage between the previous attacks; one of the IP addresses used by the attackers to break into Nonghyup's system was the same as one used in the March 2011 attack.[76] The software used in the attack was also similar to that used in the July 2009 attack on South Korean and U.S. websites, which I attributed to North Korea previously.[77] Finally, given that North and South Korea are still technically at war and North Korea has shown a long and enduring propensity to attack South Korea whenever possible, it is reasonable to assume that North Korea is behind this attack as well. North Korea's denials are also interesting because they state it is a false accusation, just like the accusation that they sunk the *Cheonan*, a South Korean ship that exploded in waters close to North Korea.[78] Given that the physical evidence convinced the international community, with the exception of North Korea's close allies, that North Korea was behind sinking the *Cheonan*, this denial also rings false. Accordingly, I will attribute this attack to the North Koreans.

Once again, I will infer the North Korean objectives from the attack itself. The attack was specific to Nonghyup bank rather than a wider attack against multiple banks or infrastructure. If the North Koreans' objective was to do the maximum damage and have the greatest disruption on the South Korean economy, they could have also launched DDoS attacks against other economic targets, even if they did not have the internal system access at other banks to do more destructive attacks. I therefore deduced a narrow primary objective of disrupting Nonghyup bank. North Korea will never pass up the opportunity to embarrass South Korea as well so I set that as a secondary objective.

North Korea was very successful in their objective to disrupt Nonghyup bank. On 12 April 2011, about half of the servers at Nonghyup bank crashed which resulted in approximately 30 million people who were unable to make online financial transactions or use the bank's ATMs.[79] The attackers launched the attack by implanting the weapon onto a Nonghyup subcontractor's laptop.[80] When the employee connected the laptop to the bank's network, the weapon implanted itself quietly throughout the network and waited for a preset triggering time. According to South Korean official Kim You-Kyung, when the weapon activated, it attempted to destroy the entire server system.[81] Some portions of the bank retained functionality and the defenders mitigated the attack over time, but overall the North Koreans were very successful in their attempt to disrupt the bank.

The North Koreans were also more successful against their secondary objective of embarrassing the South Korean government than they had been in the past. This attack received far more press attention and focus by the South Korean people than previous attacks. This attack affected slightly more than half of the population of South Korea, which stands at approximately 50 million. However, as the South Koreans mitigated the attack fairly quickly, it did not set up a "Watergate" type inquiry or bring down any politicians or the government of South Korea.

From the defensive perspective, the attackers did significant damage to Nonghyup bank who lost half their servers in the initial attack. 30 million account holders were unable to access their accounts for three days and 310,000 customers filed complaints with 1000 demanding compensation.[82] Some aspects of the Nonghyup system did manage to continue operation, but the overall system was minimally functional.

This case is the first attack where North Korea successfully established a high level of cyberspace superiority and $RCSI_{North\ Korea} = 0.51$. They were fundamentally successful in disrupting Nonghyup bank and dominating the news cycle in South Korea, thus successfully embarrassing the South Korean government. Although the attack was very successful, the South Koreans were able to mitigate it quickly and had restored most of the functionality at the bank after three days. The local cyberspace superiority model is shown in Figure 6.6.

North Korea utilized social engineering and a software Trojan through discovered software flaws to implant the weapon on a contractor's laptop. They then bypassed the air gap to the bank's system through the infected laptop to accomplish their ends through the way of strategic information war. South Korean resilience eventually overcame the attack but it did result in significant embarrassment and difficulties for the South Korean government. In the next attack, another air gap was attacked, but this time the block held.

Aramco

On 15 August 2012, attackers using a computer virus named Shamoon infected the Saudi Arabian national petroleum company Aramco.[83] This attack was not typical corporate espionage; the attackers intended to be as destructive as possible and ended up disabling 30,000 computers.[84] Shamoon did not have provisions for stealing information and it did not appear that the attackers were targeting specific

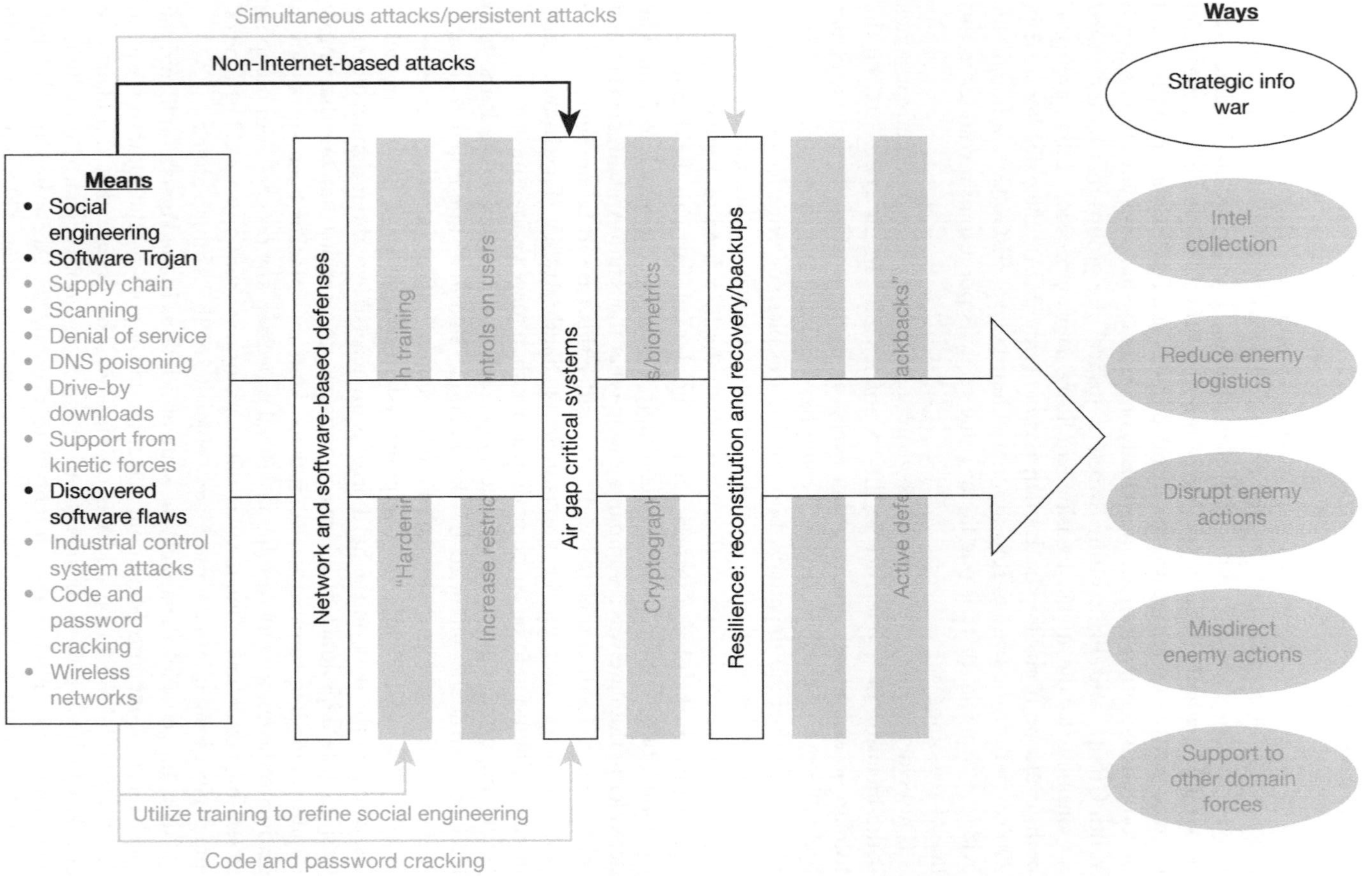

Figure 6.6 North Korea versus South Korea Bank Attack 2011 Local Cyberspace Model

Source: *Author's original work*

individuals. The characteristics of the attack provide important hints as to who was likely behind it.

The weight of the evidence suggests that Iran was behind the attack. The evidence is not conclusive, but the perennially nameless "American intelligence officials," have blamed Iran for the attack.[85] In addition, Secretary of Defense Leon Panetta made a number of veiled remarks interpreted as holding Iran responsible without directly accusing Iran.[86] Jeffrey Carr has done the most detailed analysis on attribution for Aramco that is available in the open press and he too concludes that Iran was most likely behind the Shamoon virus.[87] The "Arab Youth Group" and the "Cutting Sword of Justice" are groups that both claimed responsibility for the attack, accusing Saudi Arabia of oppression. Either group, or both, could be fronts for the Iranian Cyber Army (ICA), allegedly, "created in 2005 as part of the Iranian Revolutionary Guard Corps (IRGC)."[88] Although this evidence is strong, there is one factor some analysts point to as a counter to this line of reasoning.

The evidence that some experts use to argue that Iran was not behind the attack is the inclusion of a reference to the "Arabian Gulf" in the code.[89] Given the Iranian obsession with ensuring that everyone in the world calls that particular body of water the "Persian Gulf," some have claimed that this evidence shows Iran was not behind the attack. I do not find this piece of evidence persuasive, as it would have been very easy for the programers to include that reference for the specific reason of throwing off analysts given the high level of Iranian cultural significance in the phrase. Americans may not be familiar with the dispute over the name, but every Iranian is. Accordingly, I attribute the attack to Iran. The defender in this case was a company, but one that the Saudi Arabian government owns and is closely associated with; I consider this case to be an attack by the government of Iran on the government of Saudi Arabia. The Iranians also intended Shamoon to be far more destructive than mere vandalism.

One important clue to the Iranian objectives in the Aramco case is the high level of destruction intended by the weapon. Shamoon attempted to disable computers by erasing their master boot records.[90] If an attacker succeeds in deleting this information, the computer system cannot start. The computer is disabled and the data on the hard drive is un-accessible without significant effort by specialists. This attack could have been much more serious than one that simply requires reloading software on computers. Had the attacker been successful in getting to the computers running industrial processes, any process from pumping to refining could have gone haywire with catastrophic consequences. The type of attack gives insight into the most likely objective of the Aramco attack.

Given the scope of the attack, the state of relations in the Persian Gulf, and the mechanisms built into Shamoon, the most likely goal of the attackers was to disrupt Saudi-Arabian oil and gas production. The groups that did claim the attack, which were likely Iranian front groups, were not very clear on why they were attacking or what they intended to accomplish. According to Abdullah al-Saadan, Aramco's vice-president for corporate planning, "The main target in this attack was to stop the flow of oil and gas to local and international markets."[91]

Another possible motive was to damage the support system computers that the attacker infected with Shamoon. I needed to consider this objective, as the support system is the one that Shamoon ended up affecting. Although the attack appeared successful, it was only successful against one of the two objectives.

In some ways, the Aramco attack was a great success as the attacker damaged 30,000 computers, however, the attacker was unable to interfere with production. In this attack, it appears that the Iranians attempted to get past the air gap to the production computers. However, this attempt failed and no production computers were infected. At the opposite end of the spectrum, Shamoon disrupted 30,000 support system computers and brought the entire support system to a complete halt. Aramco appears to have been mostly off-line for about two weeks from 15 to 28 August 2012, which represents complete success during that timeframe.[92]

Aramco had significant defenses in place to protect their systems. According to Al-Saadan, the attack did not succeed because, "we had in place the processes and systems to manage, as well as sufficient incident response and business continuity plans to deal with such an attack."[93] He continued and said, "Built-in system architecture and protections for the primary components of our computer network, including firewalls and segmentation, meant that all our core operations continued smoothly."[94] Although their "core operations" ran smoothly, they were offline for approximately two weeks so there was significant impact to their support system as noted earlier.

The lack of success in crossing the air gap prevented Iran from achieving the bulk of their desired objectives. Therefore Saudi Arabia maintained cyberspace superiority and $RCSI_{\text{Saudi Arabia}} = 0.30$. Cyberspace superiority for Saudi Arabia makes intuitive sense given that the attack did not affect petroleum production. Aramco's aggressive defensive posture and a successful air gap helped them avert what could have been a catastrophic attack. This represents a moderate level of cyberspace superiority when compared to the other seven case studies; the local cyberspace superiority model is shown in Figure 6.7.

The principal dynamic apparent from this illustration is that Aramco's air gap prevented the attackers from obtaining their objectives. From some of al-Saadan's public statements, we know that Aramco had firewalls deployed as well as an air gap for their production system, which Al Saadan referred to as "segmentation." It is also clear that there was a reconstitution plan in place for resilience and the New York Times reported that Saudi Arabia flew in a dozen computer experts to help them mitigate the attack and reconstitute systems.[95] The attacker's attempt to use non-Internet propagation to get across the air gap failed, which is why it is still grayed out in Figure 6.7. Another attempted maneuver by the attackers was an additional attack launched on 22 August, one week after the first attack.[96] This second attack fizzled and appears to have done no significant damage, thus the persistence counter in the figure is still gray. One area that is unclear is what delivery mechanism was used by the attackers.

There are two theories of how the attackers introduced Shamoon into Aramco. The *Wall Street Journal* and *New York Times* reported sources that stated that an insider threat carried it into Aramco on a USB memory stick.[97] The fact that there

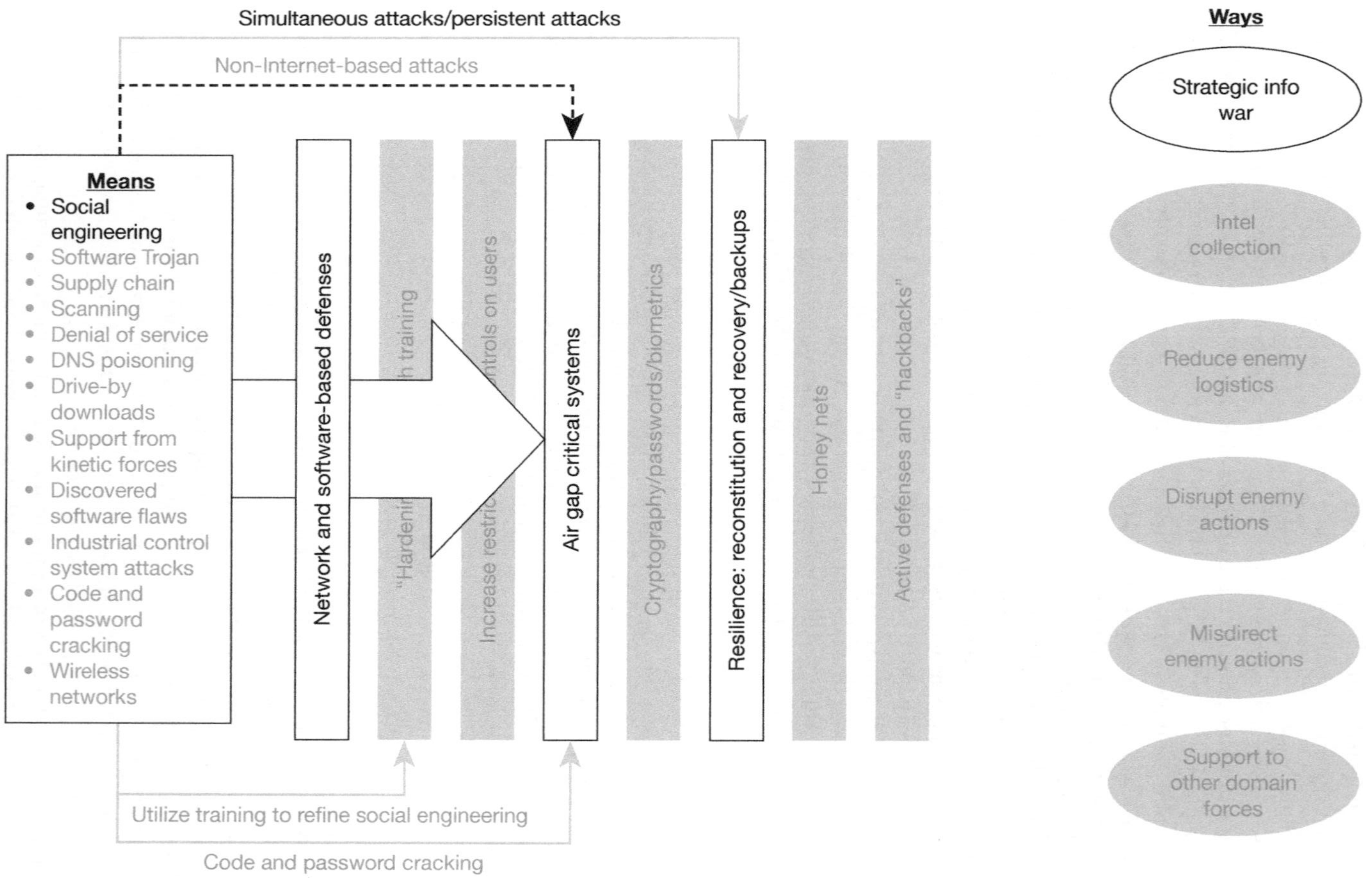

Figure 6.7 Aramco Attack Local Cyberspace Model

Source: *Author's original work*

were 70 Aramco employees Saudi Arabia was investigating for the attack supports this theory.[98] On the other hand, in an interview with *Arab News* al-Saadan denied that there was any insider threat and claimed that it was a "spear-phishing" attack where attackers target an individual with a legitimate looking e-mail that actually downloads malware.[99] Bloomberg also reported this same e-mail story.[100] It is impossible to tell, with the data available, which story is correct. It may be that they are both correct in that the virus was initially introduced by a "spear-phishing" attack, but it was designed to spread through USB flash devices in the hopes that it would cross the air gap to the computers that run oil and natural gas production. Like the Russian and Georgian conflict, as well as Stuxnet, there are several important elements of the Aramco attack for cyberspace superiority.

In a several ways, the Aramco attack was very similar to Stuxnet, but with a very different outcome. Shamoon attempted to cross an air gap, but unlike Stuxnet failed to do so. Shamoon was attempting to target an ICS, but unlike Stuxnet, it failed to get into the system. Shamoon was different from Stuxnet in that its designers used a less sophisticated approach.

Instead of attempting carefully to manipulate the ICS, Shamoon's designers intended it to disrupt the entire ICS by irrecoverably crashing individual computers. If Stuxnet was the cyberspace equivalent of a highly trained saboteur sneaking into a facility, Shamoon was an attempt to burn down the entire building. Burning down the facility can be effective, but it makes a lot of noise and is impossible to hide.

Shamoon's lack of success in achieving its objectives shows that a well-executed defense that maintains cyberspace superiority can stop a significant cyberspace attack. This lesson is perhaps the most significant finding from the Aramco case study. Disciplined defenders can gain a significant advantage for operations. In this case, they were able to protect significant Saudi Arabian oil and gas infrastructure and economic interests from serious disruption by an enemy state. The final case is another attack where the defenders managed to maintain the upper hand.

North Korea versus South Korea April 2013 Attack

Two years after the 2011 bank attacks, the North Koreans attacked again, this time against a broader target set during a time of heightened tensions. Analysts called these attacks the Dark Seoul attacks.

As before, the first step in determining who had how much cyberspace superiority is to determine the identity of the attacker. The same discussion earlier about attribution to North Korea applies, they denied any involvement but the circumstantial evidence is strong enough for me to attribute the attack to them anyway. McAfee had a team do extensive research on the Dark Seoul attacks and uncovered a covert espionage campaign called Operation Troy that linked all of the previous attacks to North Korea.[101] North Korea had also identified the specific broadcasters hit as potential targets, and "According to InformationWeek, the hacker responsible for the attack inadvertently exposed their IP address for a few minutes because of a technical problem. That address has been identified as being registered to the only Internet service provider in North Korea."[102] On top of that, in the international relations environment, South Korea was in the middle of a set of major exercises condemned by North Korea in a time of rising tensions. The evidence of attribution of the attack to North Korea is significant enough for this study.

To determine the North Korean objectives, I first examined their targets. Dark Seoul targeted three television broadcasters, YTN, MBC and KBS as well as three banks, Shinhan, Nonghyup, and Jeju as well as the telecommunications operator LG U+.[103]

The type of attack also provides evidence of what the attackers were seeking. Dark Seoul was very destructive and the attacker erased the master boot records of the 48,000 computers infected. The attacker also utilized other techniques clearly intended to affect Windows and Linux systems to broaden the attack's effects as much as possible.[104]

Based on Dark Seoul's targeting, the first objective of the North Koreans was to disrupt the South Korean banking system. However, Dark Seoul's bank attacks were only minimally successful. Some services were temporarily blocked, but restored after two hours, while some banks under attack suffered no damage at all.[105] The attacks against the broadcaster's computer networks were more successful although they did not force any of the stations off the air. However, the broadcasters lost most of their internal networks. Although there was some negative press in South Korea, the government did not end up looking weak or incompetent as they aggressively responded to the attacks and reconstituted the networks fairly quickly. McAfee's theory that the attackers intended to destroy evidence from Operation Troy is intriguing, although it is difficult to measure its success.[106] Security researchers discovered Operation Troy, but its connection to Dark Seoul was not discussed outside of Internet security circles in the broader media.

There were two systems that South Korea was trying to defend, the banks and the media companies. The banks were quite successful in defending their systems and only experienced minimal disruption. Some banks that North Korea attacked reported no damage, while other banks were back in operation after two hours.[107] On the media side, the broadcasters lost their internal networks but the attackers were unable to take them off the air. Therefore this represents only a partial success for the South Korean defenders.

North Korea did not achieve the same level of cyberspace superiority that they did in the bank attacks of 2011 and South Korea maintained cyberspace superiority with $RCSI_{South\ Korea} = 0.33$. This situation was due to apparent improvements in the South Korean capacity to mitigate, repair, and reconstitute; the local cyberspace superiority model is shown in Figure 6.8. This model is very similar to the 2011 bank attack except this time the resilience efforts were more effective and critical air gaps such as those protecting bank and broadcasting systems were more effective.

South Korea has chosen to take national cyberspace defense very seriously and has poured significant resources into this domain. The North Korean attacks have

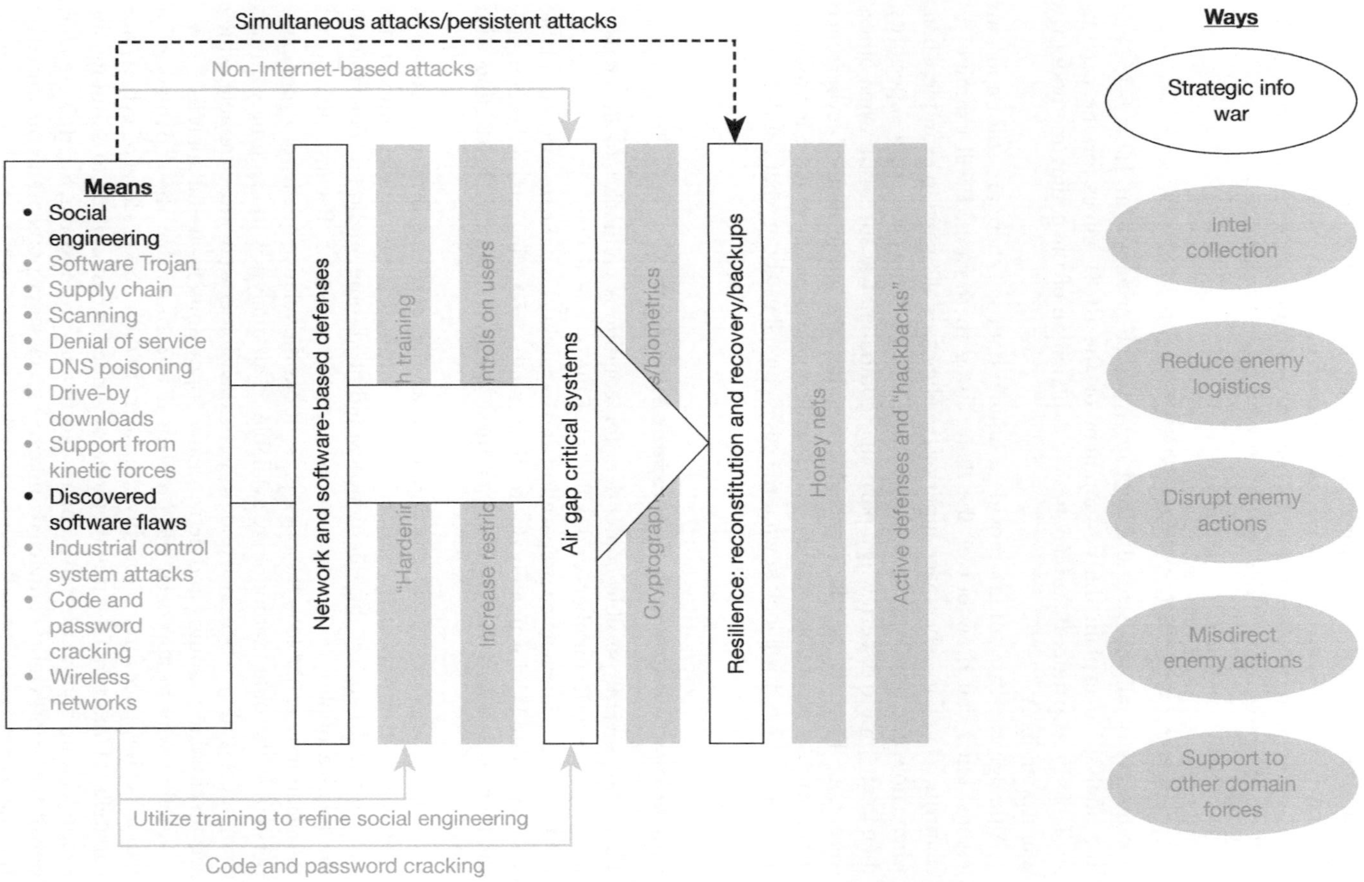

Figure 6.8 North Korea versus South Korea Bank Attack 2013 Local Cyberspace Model

Source: *Author's original work*

grown more effective over time, but the South Korean defenses have improved as well. In this case, the South Koreans were able to keep the North Koreans from gaining cyberspace superiority. This sequence of attacks by North Korea on South Korea shows that the offense does not have an insurmountable advantage over the defense. A prepared defender can defeat even sophisticated attacks.

Analysis of the Case Study Results

A summary of all the cases that met my research criteria is in Table 6.1. Note that analysis to explain the development of the RCSI values for the cases is available in Appendix B and a complete explanation of the coding methodology is in Appendix A.

Although the case studies provide a limited data set, there are still important lessons that I can draw out of the data. Using these cases, I will examine six elements related to cyberspace superiority. The cases allow me to examine when, where, how, and how long combatants managed to achieve cyberspace superiority, then to attempt to discern why a particular combatant was successful when others were not. Then I can then consider whether the possession of cyberspace superiority by a combatant truly did provide a significant advantage for military operations. First, I will look at what the cases can tell us about what conditions are conducive to cyberspace superiority.

Conditions Conducive to Cyberspace Superiority

There are several possible contenders for conditions conducive to cyberspace superiority. Is it the numbers and skill level of the people available to a combatant? Is it the level of intelligence preparation and capability? Is it the resources available to a combatant? Unfortunately, due to the secrecy surrounding national cyberspace capabilities it is very hard to answer these questions definitively, starting with people.

Libicki and others have maintained that the most important resource in cyberspace warfare is highly trained people, but do the case studies support this contention? To answer this question, I would need some method of determining the relative quality of various nations' cyberspace forces. Because little to no information is available in the open press about the relative quality of cyberspace personnel, the only methodology available to an analyst is to examine who was more successful in cyberspace and presume their forces were more capable, which sets up circular reasoning and destroys any opportunity for useful analysis.

Another way to approach the problem is to assume that the capability of a nation's cyberspace force is roughly equivalent to their nation's level of cyberspace capability. Unfortunately, this methodology does not stand up to scrutiny. For example, if an analyst were to compare North and South Korea, South Korea has one of the world's most connected and cyberspace savvy populations measured by Internet connectivity, broadband penetration, and a number of other measures. By any measure, North Korea is one of the world's least connected nations. On

Table 6.1 Cyberspace Superiority Case Studies

Year	*Case*	*Presumed Attacker*	*Objective*	*Defender*	*Outcome*
2007	Estonia	Russia	Replace statue, intimidate former USSR states	Estonia	$RCSI_{Russia} = (-0.15)$ $RCSI_{Estonia} = 0.15$
2008	Georgia	Russia	Seize South Ossetia and Abkhazia	Georgia	$RCSI_{Russia} = 0.61$ $RCSI_{Georgia} = (-0.61)$
2009	South Korean/U.S. DDoS	North Korea	Shut down U.S. and South Korean websites	South Korea/U.S.	$RCSI_{North\ Korea} = (-0.46)$ $RCSI_{US/South\ Korea} = 0.46$
2010	Stuxnet	U.S./Israel	Disrupt Iranian uranium enrichment	Iran	$RCSI_{US/Israel} = 0.08$ $RCSI_{Iran} = (-0.08)$
2011	March 2011 South Korean DDoS	North Korea	Shut down U.S./South Korean gov websites	South Korea	$RCSI_{North\ Korea} = 0.03$ $RCSI_{South\ Korea} = (-0.03)$
2011	April 2011 South Korean bank attack	North Korea	Disrupt Nonghyup bank/ embarrass South Korea	South Korea	$RCSI_{North\ Korea} = 0.51$ $RCSI_{South\ Korea} = (-0.51)$
2012	Aramco	Iran	Interrupt Aramco oil and gas production	Saudi Arabia/ Aramco	$RCSI_{Iran} = (-0.30)$ $RCSI_{Saudi\ Arabia} = 0.30$
2013	2013 South Korean bank attack	North Korea	Disrupt South Korean banks and media companies	South Korea	$RCSI_{North\ Korea} = (-0.33)$ $RCSI_{South\ Korea} = 0.33$

the surface, it appears that an analysis of the various cyberspace conflicts between the two might produce some useful information, but there is not a valid correlation between the cyberspace capability of a nation's population, and that of its cyberspace domain forces. North Korea has placed tremendous emphasis on cyberspace warfare, while South Korea appears to have put relatively less resources and people into cyberspace warfare. Therefore, it does not appear that "success" provides a reliable way to estimate the capabilities of a nation's cyberspace forces because circular reasoning seems the only likely outcome.

Without data on how capable various nations' cyberspace forces are independent from their success, it is impossible to determine whether the capability or number of people is an important determinant in achieving cyberspace warfare. In the second area of intelligence, we can draw at least a few qualified conclusions.

In several of the case studies where attackers achieved cyberspace superiority, they successfully prepared intelligence analysis on the adversary. Analysts have identified that building Stuxnet required significant intelligence preparatory work. In the unsuccessful attacks against Estonia, the Russians had no time for extensive intelligence preparation resulting in little success. In the Russian attacks on Georgia, it appears that there was significant intelligence preparation and the attacks were far more successful. I can infer successful intelligence preparation in the Georgian attack from the instantaneous timing of the attacks where the attackers hit multiple targets at the same time as the ground invasion. In the various North Korean attacks, the North Koreans did the intelligence preparation they thought was sufficient in preparation for each attack. However, the North Koreans were only successful in half of their attacks. In the Aramco attack, the Iranians did intelligence preparation, but the attack failed, as they did not solve the problem of crossing the air gap defensive block.

These cases lead me to conclude that successful intelligence preparation likely contributes to cyberspace superiority, but it does not completely determine who will be successful. A final area to examine is the physical resources available to an attacker.

As I noted earlier, there is no reliable way to compare the relative strength of cyberspace forces in all the cases, however, there are two cases where I can confidently say that one side had more resources committed. In all the North Korean attacks, it is impossible to say with certainty whether North Korean forces committed more resources than South Korea. With Russia and Estonia, it is also not clear who committed more resources in 2007 because the Estonians placed so much emphasis on cyberspace compared to their much larger neighbor, and it is likely that the Russian government relied on proxy "patriotic hackers" without using the state's full capabilities. It is also unclear how many resources the Iranians dedicated relative to the Saudis. The only two cases with a clearly stronger side are with the United States and Israel versus Iran in the Stuxnet case, and with Russia versus Georgia.

In both cases with a great disparity in resources and capability, the stronger combatant gained cyberspace superiority. However, the sample size is so small that the only conclusion I can draw is that I do not have any cases where a clearly weaker opponent definitively achieved cyberspace superiority. This finding is unsurprising, but at least allows me to state that I do not have any evidence to disprove the contention that the more capable, more heavily resourced force in cyberspace has an advantage.

This data limitation prevents me from making any firm conclusions about the contribution of physical resources to cyberspace superiority. As more cases of cyberspace conflict occur, it should be possible for researchers to determine the relative importance of the amount of physical resources and infrastructure available to combatants and compare that to other factors such as intelligence preparation. I next turn to analysis of the offense and defense in the case studies.

Offense versus Defense

Despite the predictions of some advocates, the cyberspace "bomber" does not always get through and the offense does not seem to have an overwhelming advantage. Out of eight case studies, the attacker had the cyberspace superiority advantage in four of them and the defender the advantage in the other four. In addition, there were wide differences among the cyberspace superiority gained for attackers and defenders.

There was great variation in the amount of cyberspace superiority gained by combatants on the offense and the defense. Russia achieved the highest cyberspace superiority of an attacker against Georgia with an $RCSI_{Russia}$ of 0.61, which is probably getting close to the Air Force Doctrine Document (AFDD) 3–12 definition of cyberspace supremacy, as the Georgians had little to no ability to interfere with what the Russians were doing in cyberspace. The United States and South Korea established the highest cyberspace superiority as a defender with an $RCSI_{US/South\ Korea}$ of 0.46 in 2009. There were also cases where attackers and defenders had very low levels of cyberspace superiority.

This limited data set does not support a strong advantage for either the attacker or defender. The details of the case studies do seem to indicate that if there is an advantage for the offense, it is short lived.

Persistence of Cyberspace Superiority

In seven of the eight cases, the persistence of the attack was less than two weeks. This finding has important implications because the persistence of cyberspace superiority has important implications for the utility of cyberspace attacks and the amount of advantage that an attacker has over a defender. Clearly, the cases here suggest that cyberspace superiority will not be persistent because defenders in most of the cases reacted to defend their systems with rapidly increasing success over time.

The one case where the attacker managed significant persistence measured in years was the Stuxnet attack. The Stuxnet attackers accomplished this persistence by carefully designing Stuxnet to keep the attack hidden, and instead to cause the Iranians to blame other issues, such as poor workmanship, for the continuing failure of their centrifuges. Once the Iranians realized that they were under cyberspace attack, they claim they were rapidly able to repair the damage. It is possible that Stuxnet still managed some persistence after discovery due to the way the designers program it to hide and re-propagate, but there is no data in the unclassified sources to determine how successful it was at persisting after being discovered. The short persistence of cyberspace superiority in most of the cases supports the theoretical expectation of short persistence in Chapter 3.

There are two tentative lessons that we can draw from this data on persistence. One is that the majority of cyberspace attacks only persist for approximately two weeks or less, and so attackers should plan around a limited timeframe. The second lesson is that if an attacker wants to achieve persistent effects, the only way that an attacker has been able to accomplish that goal is to mask that an attack is occurring at all. An attacker needs to hide the attack and make it appear as if something else is happening if the attack is to persist. Once defenders understand that they are under attack, they will react quickly and bring in the resources they need to stop the attack. In the Aramco case, Saudi Arabia quickly brought a team of computer security experts into the country to help stop the attack. Even less cyberspace-capable nations have this option. If something is important enough to attack, it is probably important enough to defend. The local character of the cyberspace superiority achieved in these cases also contributed to its lack of persistence.

Scope of Cyberspace Superiority

In none of the cases did a combatant achieve any significant level of universal cyberspace superiority. There is not even much evidence of a combatant achieving cyberspace superiority in multiple local areas simultaneously. The case that comes closest is that of Russia versus Georgia where the Russians attacked a number of systems and brought them down over the duration of the conflict, which was admittedly very short. If the conflict had turned into a stalemate in the land domain, would Russia have been able to maintain their cyberspace superiority and expand it? It is impossible to say with certainty because the Georgians were already seeking outside help to increase their capabilities when the conflict ended. On the Russian side, the Russian government used proxies, and not their full cyberspace forces. Had the Georgians been successful in bringing in outside help, the Russians had further capabilities they could have brought to bear as well.

The data simply cannot answer the question of the efficacy of universal cyberspace control, because no nation has yet attempted to achieve such superiority. No nation with a significant cyberspace capability has attempted seriously to disrupt the social fabric of a target country over a substantial timeframe. It is even questionable if disruption of a single country or theater of war would be truly universal because a nation can operate cyberspace capabilities from servers on the other side of the planet. It is likely that true universal cyberspace superiority would have to be worldwide. Although the data does not include attempts to gain universal cyberspace superiority, do the attempts to gain local cyberspace superiority in these cases demonstrate the ability to affect significantly military operations?

Cyberspace Superiority and the Physical Domains

In the Russia versus Georgia case, the Russians accrued advantages to their conventional forces they would not have had without the cyberspace attacks. This case is important as the only case in which an attacker used cyberspace operations in conjunction with physical domain forces. The Russians not only achieved a very high level of cyberspace superiority, they achieved a high level of success in their kinetic campaign. The Russians had overwhelming superiority in all domains and had planned for the attack and caught the Georgians unprepared for their onslaught.

The disruption of the Georgian communication networks did have a significant effect on the Georgian ability to resist the invasion. Russian forces would likely have conquered Georgia without the cyberspace attacks, but the lack of communications prevented the Georgians from mounting a more effective defense. Had the Georgians been able to mount a more effective initial defense it could have given them additional time to get the international community involved, and given them more leverage at the conference table. The lack of ability for the Georgian government to get their side of the story out further hampered them, and the Russian strategic information warfare attacks on the Georgian banking system put some pressure on Georgian elites to end the conflict. Russia clearly enjoyed some significant advantages from their cyberspace superiority. There is no definitive evidence of conventional military forces supporting cyberspace attacks from the physical domains in the case studies, but it may have occurred.

Military forces will likely not just receive support from cyberspace; they can provide support to cyberspace forces in conflicts as well. If a special operations soldier infected the notebook computer North Korea used in the April 2011 attack, then it would have been an example of conventional military forces supporting cyberspace warfare. It is not clear whether that is what happened, but it could have been the propagation pathway for the cyber weapon. One of the two potential propagation pathways for the Aramco attack also involved physical forces; they likely would have been Iranian Revolutionary Guard Corps (IRGC) operatives. What are not included in the case studies are overt physical attacks in support of cyberspace warfare, but combatants should still prepare for them.

Combatants can improve their cyberspace superiority through physical attacks on cyberspace related resources. The Russians could have done this in the Georgian case as they were accomplishing cyberspace attacks in conjunction with a physical military assault. The fact that they chose not to does not mean it will not happen in the future. The capability was there, but the Russians did not choose to utilize it. There are several possible reasons for the Russian choice including a low priority placed on the cyberspace aspects of the campaign by Russian forces, lack of targeting data on Georgian cyberspace sites, and the low level of capability demonstrated by Russian forces to attack targets deep in Georgian territory. Future cyberspace combatants should prepare for these types of physical attacks, while seeking to use cyberspace to produce advantage for military operations.

Cyberspace Superiority and Significant Advantage for Military Operations

The Russian attacks on Georgia discussed earlier, show one clear example of significant advantage for conventional military operations accruing to a successful cyberspace combatant. Even without large-scale conventional attack, there are other examples as well.

The small level of cyberspace superiority attained by the U.S. and Israel with Stuxnet was able to provide them some significant advantages they could not get from operations in the other domains. In the Stuxnet case, the United States and Israel did not achieve anywhere near the level of cyberspace superiority that Russia did against Georgia, but their superiority lasted for a longer time. As was noted previously, one of the distinguishing characteristics of the Stuxnet attack is the length of time the attackers were able to continue the attack by hiding its existence.

The United States was under increasing pressure by Israel to do something to stop the Iranian nuclear program. The Bush administration did not want kinetically to strike Iran because it felt that a strike would not be effective and would have significant negative consequences across the Middle East.[108] Had the Israelis kinetically attacked Iran, the outcome could have been even worse as the Israelis had less capability and all of the additional political baggage that went with their peculiar situation in the Middle East. Stuxnet was about buying time to allow sanctions and other political initiatives to work before Israel launched a kinetic strike that no one, including the Israelis, wanted.

The level of cyberspace superiority achieved by the United States and Israel, small as it was, proved sufficient to prevent a kinetic strike, as the attackers were able to slow the Iranian program without kinetic weapons. This accomplishment was a major achievement with significant consequences at the policy level. The next attack had less impact on the policy level, but was significant on the operational level.

Another case where a cyberspace combatant gained significant advantage for military operations through cyberspace superiority was the 2011 bank attack by North Korea. The attack was limited in scale, as the North Koreans only attacked one bank, but it was far more successful in its impact than previous North Korean attacks. The North Koreans managed to dominate the South Korean media cycle, cut 30 million South Koreans off from making financial transactions, and seriously embarrass the South Korean government, all while being able to claim that they had nothing to do with it.[109]

This situation represented significant advantage in military operations for the North Koreans, as it gave them a very low risk way to attack their enemies not available in the other domains. Had the North Koreans used special operations forces or aircraft physically to attack the bank and did the same level of damage, the North Koreans would have come under tremendous pressure from the international community. Instead, the North Koreans were able to deny they had anything to do with the attack, which gave their allies such as China the ability to block any proposed diplomatic action against them. Each of these cases shows significant advantage that accrued to the attacker due to his achievement of cyberspace superiority.

Even from the limited cases we have available, it can be seen that higher levels of cyberspace superiority correlate to advantages in military operations. This evidence supports the hypothesis that cyberspace superiority creates a significant advantage for military operations. Yet, due to the shortage of cases and the ambiguity of the evidence available, it is not possible from just these cases to say with certainty that cyberspace superiority creates a significant advantage for all military operations. However, when connected to the theory behind cyberspace superiority as presented in Chapters 2–4, there is strong evidence to suggest that indeed cyberspace superiority, when effectively achieved by a combatant, does create a significant advantage. In the final chapter, I will compare the evidence to my hypotheses and examine the conclusions that result from this study.

Notes

1 General James E. Cartwright, USMC, comments at Air Force Association Air Warfare Symposium, February 8, 2007, reported in Franklin D. Kramer, "Cyberpower and National Security: Policy Recommendations for a Strategic Framework." in *Cyberpower and National Security*, ed. Franklin D. Kramer, Stuart H. Starr and Larry K. Wentz (Washington, DC: Potomac Books, 2009), 14.

2 Alexander Gostev, "The Flame Questions and Answers," *Securelist*, 28 May 2012. www.securelist.com/en/blog/208193522/The_Flame_Questions_and_Answers

3 Kenneth Corbin, "Lessons From the Russia-Georgia Cyberwar," *Internet News*, 12 March 2009. www.internetnews.com/govern-ment/article.php/3810011/Lessons-From-the-Russia-Georgia-Cyberwar.htm

4 Stuart Fox, "Why Cyberwar is Unlikely," *Tech News Daily*, 2 July 2011. www.technewsdaily.com/6962-cyberwar-unlikely-deterrence-cyber-war.html

5 John Markoff, "Before the Gunfire, Cyberattacks," *The New York Times*, 12 August 2008, www.nytimes.com/2008/08/13/technology/13cyber.html?_r=0

6 Major General Mark Barrett, Dick Bedford, Elizabeth Skinner, and Eva Vergles. "Assured Access to the Global Commons." ed. by Supreme Allied Command Transformation. (Norfolk, VA: North Atlantic Treaty Organization, 2011), 41.

7 Even at the unclassified level, the Mandiant report provides substantial evidence that ties most Chinese origin attacks to a particular Chinese army unit, PLA Unit 61398. The report even provides pictures of the building that the Mandiant analysts believe is the source of these attacks. Across Western sources, no-one seems to take the Chinese denials very seriously. David E. Sanger, David Barboza and Nicole Perlroth, "Chinese Army Unit Is Seen as Tied to Hacking Against U.S." *New York Times*, 19 February 2013. www.nytimes.com/2013/02/19/technology/chinas-army-is-seen-as-tied-to-hacking-against-us.html?pagewanted=all&_r=2&

8 I excluded cases such as the Hezbollah, Hamas, and Palestinian attacks on Israel as there was only one nation state in the conflict. Granted that Hezbollah, Hamas, or the Palestinian Authority have some of the characteristics of nation states, but there is no evidence directly tying those organizations to the attacks on Israel. The attackers appeared to be "self-organizing" individuals outraged at Israel, rather than organized elements of a campaign undertaken by a central authority in pursuit of clear objectives.

9 Jared Moya, "Massive DDoS attacks target Estonia; Russia accused." Zeropaid, 14 May 2007, www.zeropaid.com/news/8759/massive_ddos_attacks_target_estonia_russia_accused
10 Dan Goodin, "Kremlin-backed youths launched Estonian cyberwar, says Russian official." *The Register*, 11 March 2009, www.theregister.co.uk/2009/03/11/russian_admits_estonian_ddos
11 Noah Shachtman, "Kremlin Kids: We Launched the Estonian Cyber War." *Wired*, 11 March 2009. www.wired.com/dangerroom/2009/03/pro-kremlin-gro
12 Meera Louis and Ott Ummelas. "Estonian Premier Says Internet Attacks Not Acceptable (Update2)" *Bloomberg*, 24 May 2007. www.bloomberg.com/apps/news?pid=newsarchive&sid=a9C66FjyCFBk&refer=europe
13 British Broadcasting Corporation, "Russia in Georgia separatist pact." *BBC*, 17 September 2008, http://news.bbc.co.uk/2/hi/europe/7620972.stm
14 Ariel Cohen and Robert E. Hamilton, *The Russian Military and the Georgia War: Lessons and Implications* (Carlisle, PA: Strategic Studies Institute, 2011), 1–4.
15 The Georgian military was goaded into attacking South Ossetia by attacks on Georgian villages, which gave the Russians the pretext they were looking for to invade Georgia. Paulo Shakarian, Jana Shakarian and Andrew Ruef, *Introduction to Cyber-Warfare: A Multidisciplinary Approach* (Amsterdam: Syngress, 2013), Kindle Location 940, chap. 3.
16 United States Cyber Consequences Unit, "Overview by the US-CCU of the Cyber Campaign Against Georgia in August of 2008," US-CCU Special Report, August 2009, 3.
17 United States Cyber Consequences Unit, "Overview by the US-CCU of the Cyber Campaign Against Georgia in August of 2008," 5.
18 Shakarian, et al., *Introduction to Cyber-Warfare*, Kindle Location 1043, chap 3.
19 Paul Rosenzweig, *Cyber Warfare: How Conflicts in Cyberspace are Challenging America and Changing the World* (Santa Barbara, CA: Praeger, 2013), Kindle Location 752, chap. 34.
20 United States Cyber Consequences Unit, "Overview by the US-CCU of the Cyber Campaign Against Georgia in August of 2008," 6.
21 For a complete definition and discussion of what constitutes strategic information warfare, see Chapter 4.
22 United States Cyber Consequences Unit, "Overview by the US-CCU of the Cyber Campaign Against Georgia in August of 2008," 7.
23 United States Cyber Consequences Unit, "Overview by the US-CCU of the Cyber Campaign Against Georgia in August of 2008," 7.
24 Shakarian, et al., *Introduction to Cyber-Warfare*, Kindle Location 1017, chap 3.
25 Robert Pape, *Bombing to Win: Air Power and Coercion in War* (London: Cornell University Press, 1996), 7.
26 Dan Goodin, "Georgian cyber attacks launched by Russian crime gangs: With help from Twitter, Facebook and Microsoft," *The Register*, 18 August 2009. www.theregister.co.uk/2009/08/18/georgian_cyber_attacks
27 Paulo Shakarian, "The 2008 Russian Cyber Campaign Against Georgia." Military Review, November–December 2011, 65.
28 United States Cyber Consequences Unit, "Overview by the US-CCU of the Cyber Campaign Against Georgia in August of 2008," 5.
29 United States Cyber Consequences Unit, "Overview by the US-CCU of the Cyber Campaign Against Georgia in August of 2008," 7.
30 Shakarian, et al., *Introduction to Cyber-Warfare*, Kindle Location 1014, chap. 3.
31 Shakarian, et al., *Introduction to Cyber-Warfare*, Kindle Location 1017, chap. 3.
32 Shakarian, et al., *Introduction to Cyber-Warfare*, Kindle Location 991, chap 3.
33 United States Cyber Consequences Unit, "Overview by the US-CCU of the Cyber Campaign Against Georgia in August of 2008," 7.
34 Rosenzweig, *Cyber Warfare*, Kindle Location 736, chap 3.

35 Cohen and Hamilton, *The Russian Military and the Georgia War*, 27.
36 Cohen and Hamilton, *The Russian Military and the Georgia War*, 19.
37 Associated Press, "North Korean army suspected in cyber attacks: Hackers told to 'destroy' South Korean communications, report says," *NBC News*, 11 July 2009. www.nbcnews.com/id/31866018/ns/world_news-asiapacific
38 Korea Times. "N. Korea Operates Cyber War Unit." The Korea Times. 5 May 2009. www.koreatimes.co.kr/www/news/nation/2010/04/113_44358.html
39 Colin Clark, "US Blew NK Cyber Attacks." *DoD Buzz*, 13 July 2009. www.dodbuzz.com/2009/07/13/7833
40 Korea Times, "Dreadful Cyber War." The Korea Times, 10 July 2009. www.koreatimes.co.kr/www/news/opinon/2009/07/137_48261.html
41 Lolita Baldor, "White House among targets of cyber attack: Other targets included NSA, Homeland Security and State Department," *NBC News*, 8 July 2009, www.nbcnews.com/id/31800532/ns/technology_and_science-security
42 Lolita Baldor, "White House among targets of cyber attack."
43 Associated Press, "N. Korea Suspected of Global Cyber Attack," *NBC News*, 8 July 2009. www.cbsnews.com/stories/2009/07/08/tech/main5143457.shtml
44 Jane Han, "Cyber Attack Hits Korea for Third Day," *Korea Times*, 9 July 2009. www.koreatimes.co.kr/www/news/biz/2009/09/123_48203.html
45 Jane Han, "Cyber Attack Hits Korea for Third Day."
46 Aleksandr Matrosov, Eugene Rodionov, David Harley, and Juraj Malcho, "Stuxnet Under the Microscope: Revisions 1.31," *eSeT*. Accessed 25 August 2013. http://go.eset.com/us/resources/white-papers/Stuxnet_Under_the_Microscope.pdf. 19
47 For a discussion of "zero-day" vulnerabilities, see chapter 4 in the section on discovered software flaws.
48 Paulo Shakarian, "Stuxnet: Cyberwar Revolution in Military Affairs," *Small Wars Journal*, 15 April 2011. 6.
49 Matrosov et al., "Stuxnet Under the Microscope: Revisions 1.31," 7.
50 Shakarian, "Stuxnet: Cyberwar Revolution in Military Affairs," 2.
51 Shakarian, "Stuxnet: Cyberwar Revolution in Military Affairs," 2.
52 David E. Sanger, "Obama Order Sped Up Wave of Cyberattacks Against Iran," *The New York Times*, 1 June 2012.
53 Rowan Scarborough, "In classified cyberwar against Iran, trail of Stuxnet leak leads to White House," *The Washington Times*, 18 August 2013.
54 Shakarian, et al., *Introduction to Cyber-Warfare*, Kindle Location 6972, chap. 13.
55 David E. Sanger, *Confront and Conceal: Obama's Secret Wars and Surprising Use of American Power* (New York: Broadway Books, 2013), 204.
56 Shakarian, "Stuxnet: Cyberwar Revolution in Military Affairs," 3.
57 Sanger, *Confront and Conceal*, 199.
58 Shakarian, et al., *Introduction to Cyber-Warfare*, Kindle Location 6943, chap. 13.
59 Sanger, *Confront and Conceal*, 207.
60 Shakarian, et al., *Introduction to Cyber-Warfare*, Kindle Location 6945, chap. 13.
61 Sanger, *Confront and Conceal*, 207.
62 Sanger, *Confront and Conceal*, 204.
63 Shakarian, et al., *Introduction to Cyber-Warfare*, Kindle Location 6945, chap. 13.
64 Sanger, *Confront and Conceal*, 194.
65 Matrosov et al., "Stuxnet Under the Microscope: Revisions 1.31," 24.
66 Jim Finkle, "Researchers say Stuxnet was deployed against Iran in 2007," *Reuters*, 26 February 2013. www.reuters.com/article/2013/02/26/us-cyberwar-stuxnet-idUSBRE91P0PP20130226
67 Shakarian, et al., *Introduction to Cyber-Warfare*, Kindle Location 7003, chap. 13.
68 Infosecurity, "North Korea likely source of DDoS attacks against South Korean sites, says McAfee," *Infosecurity*, 7 July 2011. www.infosecurity-us.com/view/19258/north-korea-likely-source-of-ddos-attacks-against-south-korean-sites-says-mcafee

69 Kevin Kwang, "S. Korea, US attacks possibly launched by N. Korea," *ZDNet*, 6 July 2011. www.zdnet.com/s-korea-us-attacks-possibly-launched-by-n-korea-2062301087
70 Kwang, "S. Korea, US attacks possibly launched by N. Korea."
71 Ryan Sherstobitoff and Itai Liba, "Dissecting Operation Troy: Cyberespionage in South Korea," White Paper developed by McAfee Labs, 2013, 8.
72 McAfee. "Ten Days of Rain: Expert analysis of distributed denial-of-service attacks targeting South Korea." White Paper developed by McAfee Security, 2011, 12.
73 Kwang, "S. Korea, US attacks possibly launched by N. Korea."
74 McAfee. "Ten Days of Rain," 3.
75 McAfee. "Ten Days of Rain," 3.
76 British Broadcasting Corporation, "North Korea 'behind South Korean bank cyber hack'," *BBC*, 3 May 2011. www.bbc.co.uk/news/world-asia-pacific-13263888
77 BBC, "North Korea 'behind South Korean bank cyber hack'."
78 Yonhap News Agency, "N. Korea claims Seoul making up stories to raise tension," *Yonhap*, 4 May 2011. http://english.yonhapnews.co.kr/national/2011/05/04/91/0302000000AEN20110504010700315F.HTML
79 Ryan Mauro, "Major North Korean Cyber Attack on South," *Frontpage Mag*, 1 September 2011. http://frontpagemag.com/2011/ryan-mauro/major-north-korean-cyber-attack-on-south
80 Yonhap News Agency, "S. Korea seeks int'l cooperation for further probe into cyber attack on bank." *Yonhap*, 15 May 2011. http://english.yonhapnews.co.kr/national/2011/05/15/25/0301000000AEN20110515002500320F.HTML
81 Finextra, "South Korean bank hit by cyber-attack." *Finextra*, 20 April 2011. www.finextra.com/News/Fullstory.aspx?newsitemid=22486
82 Finextra, "South Korean bank hit by cyber-attack."
83 Christopher Bronk and Eneken Tikk-Ringas, "Hack or Attack? Shamoon and the Evolution of Cyber Conflict," James A Baker III Institute for Public Policy Working Paper, 1 February 2013.
84 Shakarian, et al., *Introduction to Cyber-Warfare*, Kindle Location 1875, chap. 5.
85 Thom Shanker and David E. Sanger, "U.S. Suspects Iran Was Behind a Wave of Cyberattacks," *New York Times*, 13 October 2012. www.nytimes.com/2012/10/14/world/middleeast/us-suspects-iranians-were-behind-a-wave-of-cyberattacks.html?_r=2&pagewanted=all
86 Nicole Perlroth, "In Cyberattack on Saudi Firm, U.S. Sees Iran Firing Back," *The New York Times*, 23 October 2012. www.nytimes.com/2012/10/24/business/global/cyberattack-on-saudi-oil-firm-disquiets-us.html?pagewanted=all
87 To quote his analysis, "Iran is at the center of every significant aspect of this attack. It is the only nation with access to the original Wiper virus from which Shamoon was copied. Iran is angry at Saudi Aramco for off-setting Iran's drop in oil production due to the Embargo that started 45 days prior to the attack which gives it motive. It supports a militant organization (Hezbollah) that uses hackers and who allegedly has members employed at Saudi Aramco which gives it opportunity and access. Although the Arab Youth Group and the Cutting Sword of Justice involvement gives it the appearance of a mere hacktivist attack, I think that a careful analysis of the known facts points to a state-sponsored attack by Iran that was crafted to look like the work of hacktivists. Perhaps Iran has learned something from Russia about the strategy of misdirection by the government's recruitment of patriotic hackers." Jeffrey Carr, "Who's Responsible for the Saudi Aramco Network Attack?" *Infosec Island*, 28 August 2012. www.infosecisland.com/blogview/22290-Whos-Responsible-for-the-Saudi-Aramco-Network-Attack.html
88 Shakarian, et al., *Introduction to Cyber-Warfare*, Kindle Location 1856, chap. 5.
89 Perlroth, "In Cyberattack on Saudi Firm, U.S. Sees Iran Firing Back."
90 Shakarian, et al., *Introduction to Cyber-Warfare*, Kindle Location 1856, chap. 5.

91 Abdullah al-Saadan speaking to local media quoted in Camilla Hall and Javier Blas, "Aramco cyber attack targeted production," *Financial Times*, 10 December 2012. www.ft.com/intl/cms/s/0/5f313ab6-42da-11e2-a4e4-00144feabdc0.html#axzz2dfwhMlKi
92 Holden, "Cyber Attacks in the Spin Cycle: Saudi Aramco and Shamoon," *Analysis Intelligence*, 1 November 2012. http://analysisintelligence.com/cyber-defense/narrative-of-a-cyber-attack-saudi-aramco-and-shamoon
93 Siraj Wahab, "Cyber Attack on Aramco A 'Global Plot', says Saudi Arabia," *Arab News*, 10 December 2012. www.eurasiareview.com/10122012-cyber-attack-on-aramco-a-global-plot-says-saudi-arabia
94 Wahab, "Cyber Attack on Aramco A 'Global Plot', says Saudi Arabia."
95 Perlroth, "In Cyberattack on Saudi Firm, U.S. Sees Iran Firing Back."
96 Holden, "Cyber Attacks in the Spin Cycle."
97 Perlroth, "In Cyberattack on Saudi Firm, U.S. Sees Iran Firing Back."
98 Carr, "Who's Responsible for the Saudi Aramco Network Attack?"
99 Wahab, "Cyber Attack on Aramco A 'Global Plot', says Saudi Arabia."
100 Wael Mahdi, "Saudi Arabia Says Aramco Cyberattack Came From Foreign States," *Bloomberg*, 9 December 2012. www.bloomberg.com/news/2012-12-09/saudi-arabia-says-aramco-cyberattack-came-from-foreign-states.html.
101 Sherstobitoff and Liba, "Dissecting Operation Troy: Cyberespionage in South Korea," 28.
102 Thawte, "Cyberattack Traced to North Korea," *Thawte*, 2013. www.thawte.com/about/news/?story=423684
103 Japmarpaung, "Dark Seoul – Postmortem," 3 May 2013. http://japmarpaung.com/2013/05/03/dark-seoul-postmortem
104 Japmarpaung, "Dark Seoul – Postmortem."
105 Choe Sang-Hun, "Computer Networks in South Korea Are Paralyzed in Cyberattacks," 20 March 2013. www.nytimes.com/2013/03/21/world/asia/south-korea-computer-network-crashes.html
106 Sherstobitoff and Liba, "Dissecting Operation Troy: Cyberespionage in South Korea," 28.
107 Sang-Hun, "Computer Networks in South Korea Are Paralyzed in Cyberattacks."
108 Sanger, *Confront and Conceal*, 190.
109 Mauro, "Major North Korean Cyber Attack on South."

Bibliography

Associated Press. "N. Korea Suspected of Global Cyber Attack." *NBC News*, 8 July 2009. www.cbsnews.com/stories/2009/07/08/tech/main5143457.shtml

Associated Press. "North Korean army suspected in cyber attacks: Hackers told to 'destroy' South Korean communications, report says." *NBC News*, 11 July 2009. www.nbcnews.com/id/31866018/ns/world_news-asiapacific

Baldor, Lolita. "White House among targets of cyber attack: Other targets included NSA, Homeland Security and State Department." *NBC News*, 8 July 2009. www.nbcnews.com/id/31800532/ns/technology_and_science-security

Barrett, Major General Mark, Dick Bedford, Elizabeth Skinner, and Eva Vergles. "Assured Access to the Global Commons." Edited by Supreme Allied Command Transformation. Norfolk, VA: North Atlantic Treaty Organization, 2011.

British Broadcasting Corporation. "Russia in Georgia separatist pact." *BBC*, 17 September 2008. http://news.bbc.co.uk/2/hi/europe/7620972.stm

British Broadcasting Corporation. "North Korea 'behind South Korean bank cyber hack'." *BBC*, 3 May 2011. www.bbc.co.uk/news/world-asia-pacific-13263888

Bronk, Christopher and Eneken Tikk-Ringas. "Hack or Attack? Shamoon and the Evolution of Cyber Conflict." James A Baker III Institute for Public Policy Working Paper, 1 February 2013.

Carr, Jeffrey. "Who's Responsible for the Saudi Aramco Network Attack?" *Infosec Island*, 28 August2012.www.infosecisland.com/blogview/22290-Whos-Responsible-for-the-Saudi-Aramco-Network-Attack.html

Clark, Colin. "US Blew NK Cyber Attacks." *DoD Buzz*, 13 July 2009. www.dodbuzz.com/2009/07/13/7833

Cohen, Ariel and Robert E. Hamilton. *The Russian Military and the Georgia War: Lessons and Implications.* Carlisle, PA: Strategic Studies Institute, 2011.

Corbin, Kenneth. "Lessons From the Russia-Georgia Cyberwar." *Internet News*, 12 March 2009. www.internetnews.com/govern-ment/article.php/3810011/Lessons-From-the-Russia-Georgia-Cyberwar.htm

Finextra. "South Korean bank hit by cyber-attack." *Finextra*, 20 April 2011. www.finextra.com/News/Fullstory.aspx?newsitemid=22486

Finkle, Jim. "Researchers say Stuxnet was deployed against Iran in 2007." *Reuters*. 26 February 2013. www.reuters.com/article/2013/02/26/us-cyberwar-stuxnet-idUSBRE91P0PP20130226

Fox, Stuart. "Why Cyberwar is Unlikely." *Tech News Daily*, 2 July 2011. www.technewsdaily.com/6962-cyberwar-unlikely-deterrence-cyber-war.html

Goodin, Dan. "Kremlin-backed youths launched Estonian cyberwar, says Russian official." *The Register*, 11 March 2009. www.theregister.co.uk/2009/03/11/russian_admits_estonian_ddos

Goodin, Dan. "Georgian cyber attacks launched by Russian crime gangs: With help from Twitter, Facebook and Microsoft." *The Register*, 18 August 2009. www.theregister.co.uk/2009/08/18/georgian_cyber_attacks

Gostev, Alexander. "The Flame" Questions and Answers." *Securelist*, 28 May 2012. www.securelist.com/en/blog/208193522/The_Flame_Questions_and_Answers

Hall, Camilla and Javier Blas. "Aramco cyber attack targeted production." *Financial Times*, 10 December 2012. www.ft.com/intl/cms/s/0/5f313ab6-42da-11e2-a4e4-00144feabdc0.html#axzz2dfwhMlKi

Han, Jane. "Cyber Attack Hits Korea for Third Day." *Korea Times*, 9 July 2009. www.koreatimes.co.kr/www/news/biz/2009/09/123_48203.html

Holden. "Cyber Attacks in the Spin Cycle: Saudi Aramco and Shamoon." *Analysis Intelligence*, 1 November 2012. http://analysisintelligence.com/cyber-defense/narrative-of-a-cyber-attack-saudi-aramco-and-shamoon

Infosecurity. "North Korea likely source of DDoS attacks against South Korean sites, says McAfee." *Infosecurity*, 7 July 2011. www.infosecurity-us.com/view/19258/north-korea-likely-source-of-ddos-attacks-against-south-korean-sites-says-mcafee

Japmarpaung, "Dark Seoul – Postmortem." 3 May 2013. http://japmarpaung.com/2013/05/03/dark-seoul-postmortem

Korea Times. "N. Korea Operates Cyber War Unit." *The Korea Times*, 5 May 2009. www.koreatimes.co.kr/www/news/nation/2010/04/113_44358.html

Korea Times. "Dreadful Cyber War." *The Korea Times*, 10 July 2009. www.koreatimes.co.kr/www/news/opinon/2009/07/137_48261.html

Kramer, Franklin D. "Cyberpower and National Security: Policy Recommendations for a Strategic Framework." In *Cyberpower and National Security*, edited by Franklin D. Kramer, Stuart H. Starr and Larry K. Wentz, 3–23. Washington, DC: Potomac Books, 2009.

Kwang, Kevin. "S. Korea, US attacks possibly launched by N. Korea." *ZDNet*, 6 July 2011. www.zdnet.com/s-korea-us-attacks-possibly-launched-by-n-korea-2062301087

Louis, Meera and Ott Ummelas. "Estonian Premier Says Internet Attacks Not Acceptable (Update2)" *Bloomberg*, 24 May 2007. www.bloomberg.com/apps/news?pid=news archive&sid=a9C66FjyCFBk&refer=europe

Mahdi, Wael. "Saudi Arabia Says Aramco Cyberattack Came From Foreign States." *Bloomberg*, 9 December 2012. www.bloomberg.com/news/2012-12-09/saudi-arabia-says-aramco-cyberattack-came-from-foreign-states.html

Markoff, John. "Before the Gunfire, Cyberattacks." *The New York Times*, 12 August 2008. www.nytimes.com/2008/08/13/technology/13cyber.html?_r=0

Matrosov, Aleksandr, Eugene Rodionov, David Harley, and Juraj Malcho. "Stuxnet Under the Microscope: Revisions 1.31." *eSeT*. Accessed 25 August 2013. http://go.eset.com/us/resources/white-papers/Stuxnet_Under_the_Microscope.pdf

Mauro, Ryan. "Major North Korean Cyber Attack on South." *Frontpage Mag*, 1 September 2011. http://frontpagemag.com/2011/ryan-mauro/major-north-korean-cyber-attack-on-south

McAfee. "Ten Days of Rain: Expert analysis of distributed denial-of-service attacks targeting South Korea." White Paper developed by McAfee Security. 2011.

Moya, Jared. "Massive DDoS attacks target Estonia; Russia accused." *Zeropaid*, 14 May 2007. www.zeropaid.com/news/8759/massive_ddos_attacks_target_estonia_russia_accused

Pape, Robert. *Bombing to Win: Air Power and Coercion in War.* London: Cornell University Press, 1996.

Perlroth, Nicole. "In Cyberattack on Saudi Firm, U.S. Sees Iran Firing Back." *The New York Times*, 23 October 2012. www.nytimes.com/2012/10/24/business/global/cyberattack-on-saudi-oil-firm-disquiets-us.html?pagewanted=all

Rosenzweig, Paul. *Cyber Warfare: How Conflicts in Cyberspace are Challenging America and Changing the World.* Santa Barbara, CA: Praeger, 2013. Kindle edition.

Sang-Hun, Choe. "Computer Networks in South Korea Are Paralyzed in Cyberattacks." 20 March 2013. www.nytimes.com/2013/03/21/world/asia/south-korea-computer-network-crashes.html

Sanger, David E. "Obama Order Sped Up Wave of Cyberattacks Against Iran." *The New York Times.* 1 June 2012.

Sanger, David E. *Confront and Conceal: Obama's Secret Wars and Surprising Use of American Power.* New York: Broadway Books, 2013. Kindle edition.

Sanger, David E., David Barboza and Nicole Perlroth. "Chinese Army Unit Is Seen as Tied to Hacking Against U.S." *New York Times*, 19 February 2013. www.nytimes.com/2013/02/19/technology/chinas-army-is-seen-as-tied-to-hacking-against-us.html?page wanted=all&_r=2&

Scarborough, Rowan. "In classified cyberwar against Iran, trail of Stuxnet leak leads to White House." *The Washington Times*, 18 August 2013.

Shachtman, Noah. "Kremlin Kids: We Launched the Estonian Cyber War." *Wired*, 11 March 2009. www.wired.com/dangerroom/2009/03/pro-kremlin-gro

Shakarian, Paulo. "Stuxnet: Cyberwar Revolution in Military Affairs." *Small Wars Journal*, 15 April 2011.

Shakarian, Paulo. "The 2008 Russian Cyber Campaign Against Georgia." *Military Review*, November–December 2011, 63–68.

Shakarian, Paulo, Jana Shakarian and Andrew Ruef. *Introduction to Cyber-Warfare: A Multidisciplinary Approach.* Amsterdam: Syngress, 2013. Kindle edition.

Shanker, Thom and David E. Sanger. "U.S. Suspects Iran Was Behind a Wave of Cyberattacks." *New York Times*, 13 October 2012. www.nytimes.com/2012/10/14/world/middleeast/us-suspects-iranians-were-behind-a-wave-of-cyberattacks.html?_r=2&pagewanted=all

Sherstobitoff, Ryan and Itai Liba. "Dissecting Operation Troy: Cyberespionage in South Korea." White Paper developed by McAfee Labs. 2013.

Thawte. "Cyberattack Traced to North Korea." *Thawte*, 2013. www.thawte.com/about/news/?story=423684

U.S. Cyber Consequences Unit. "Overview by the US-CCU of the Cyber Campaign Against Georgia in August of 2008." US-CCU Special Report, August 2009.

Wahab, Siraj. "Cyber Attack on Aramco A 'Global Plot', says Saudi Arabia." *Arab News*, 10 December 2012. www.eurasiareview.com/10122012-cyber-attack-on-aramco-a-global-plot-says-saudi-arabia

Yonhap News Agency. "N. Korea claims Seoul making up stories to raise tension." *Yonhap*, 4 May 2011. http://english.yonhapnews.co.kr/national/2011/05/04/91/0302000000AEN20110504010700315F.HTML

Yonhap News Agency. "S. Korea seeks int'l cooperation for further probe into cyber attack on bank." *Yonhap*, 15 May 2011. http://english.yonhapnews.co.kr/national/2011/05/15/25/0301000000AEN20110515002500320F.HTML.

7 Conclusion

The existence of cyberspace superiority has important implications for warfare in the twenty-first century. Without an understanding of the framework underlying conflict in cyberspace, nation-states will be less successful in utilizing and exploiting this new domain. Cyberspace superiority, with its linkages between local and universal, connections between means and ways, blocks by enemy combatants, and the continuing dynamic of struggle, provides such an organizing framework. Combatants can measure cyberspace superiority, analyze it, and use it for planning. In the end, cyberspace combatants should utilize cyberspace superiority as a concept for the simple reason that it is useful, and can lead to better outcomes in warfare.

Unfortunately, there has been little academic work done on cyberspace superiority. Many authors have dismissed it quickly as unattainable, largely because they did not make a distinction between universal and local cyberspace superiority. Although global "command of the cyber" may be unobtainable, varying levels of cyberspace superiority are possible in specific local areas of cyberspace with enough persistence to accomplish a combatant's objectives. Cyberspace superiority is useful as a concept because it can help to focus and connect a combatant's efforts in cyberspace.

To build an understanding of what constitutes superiority in cyberspace, it is necessary to start with a definition of what constitutes cyberspace. Cyberspace is a domain created by the connections between computing devices. The Joint Staff has defined cyberspace as, "a global domain within the information environment consisting of the interdependent network of information technology infrastructures and resident data, including the Internet, telecommunications networks, computer systems, and embedded processors and controllers."[1]

Cyberspace superiority is fundamentally about achieving enough control of the cyberspace domain to enable the successful completion of your objectives, while blocking your enemy from accomplishing his objectives. Domain specific forces always attempt to control their domains, as they have to establish some minimal level of control to operate effectively.[2] Cyberspace operators are no different, nor should they be. According to Air Force Doctrine Document (AFDD) 3–12, cyberspace superiority is, "The operational advantage in, through, and from cyberspace to conduct operations at a given time and in a given domain without prohibitive interference."[3]

The heart of this book was to determine whether a meaningful level of cyberspace superiority was achievable and would provide a significant advantage in military operations. This question brought up several supporting questions that I had to answer. First, is cyberspace superiority a local or universal concept? In other words, does cyberspace superiority only apply in small areas or across entire theaters? The second question dealt with the issue of persistency with regard to cyberspace superiority. Once gained, was cyberspace superiority likely to last for years, months, weeks, or minutes? The third question sought to determine whether analysts could reliably measure cyberspace superiority. Without an analytically sound and repeatable method of measuring cyberspace superiority, its presence could become merely a matter of opinion not useful for rigorous analysis.

To determine whether cyberspace superiority was meaningful as a concept, I first examined superiority concepts in the land, maritime, and air domains. Next, I delved into the cyberspace domain itself and looked at its characteristics to see how cyberspace superiority would be similar to, and different from, the other warfighting domains. Finally, I analyzed eight case studies to test the theory and draw out the conclusions of this study. To lay the foundation, I first turned to the other domains to see what elements of domain superiority I could usefully apply to cyberspace.

Elements of Domain Superiority

Combatants have fought in each of the other domains almost as soon as mankind discovered how to operate within each domain. Humans have sought superiority on the land, in the maritime domain, air domain, space domain, and cyberspace domain. I excluded space from this analysis, as there is not yet a consensus on how domain superiority operates in space, or enough case studies for an analyst to examine.

One of the important elements that came out of my survey of domain superiority in the other domains is the importance of universal and local domain superiority and the interactions between them. Each domain was different in this regard, with some, such as the maritime domain, placing more importance at the universal level, and others such as the cyberspace domain placing more importance at the local level. A lack of clarity on whether the superiority under discussion is at the universal or local level generates much of the confusion that results when analysts argue past each other about domain superiority.

Universal and local domain superiority interact in all of the domains and do not stand separate. In most of the domains, this interaction occurs in the same two ways. First, combatants generate the forces at the universal level before moving those resources to the appropriate local area where they will fight. Second, the losses sustained by those combatants in conflict reduce the forces available at the universal level. That reduction then impacts what forces a combatant has available to allocate among all the local areas. In cyberspace, combatants still generate resources at the universal level before pushing them to local areas, but the feedback mechanism is different. In cyberspace, losses do not normally occur through physical destruction such as an attacker sinking a ship or shooting down an aircraft. Instead, they occur when the enemy learns how to defeat the tools and weapons used by a cyberspace combatant. The feedback produced has a similar outcome, but there is a different mechanism behind it.

Another difference in the operation of domain superiority across the domains is the amount of overlap between the offensive and defensive sides of superiority. In some domains, such as the land and maritime domains, most forces can operate effectively in offensive and defensive roles. In the air domain there is a mixture, with only some forces able to undertake offensive or defensive missions. In the cyberspace domain, however, tools and weapons are normally very specific and combatants cannot shift them from offense to defense or vice versa, which reduces their flexibility. I wove the offensive/defensive split, and the universal/local separation throughout all of my analysis of the elements of domain superiority.

In my analysis of each of the domains, I looked at six areas. I examined the domain's geography and characteristics, offensive or defensive primacy, the method of gaining domain superiority, the use of domain superiority, the persistence of domain superiority, and measurement concepts of superiority in the domain. I will follow the same pattern as I pull out the most important elements from all of the domains.

Geography and Characteristics of the Domains Related to Superiority

The land domain is the one most unlike the cyberspace domain. Physical features, such as mountains and rivers dominate the land domain and as a result, geography dominates superiority in the land domain. This normally produces a sequential approach to land domain superiority because land-based forces have to protect their lines of communication and must move sequentially toward their objectives. The maritime domain shares more characteristics with the cyberspace domain than the land domain.

The maritime domain consists of a bounded maneuver space accessed by technology that is principally important due to the sea lines of communication that carry most of the world's cargo. Like the land domain, the maritime domain has distinct edges with the other domains, however, unlike land, the maritime domain produces its most significant effects in the other domains. The interaction of the land domain with the maritime domain produces a large number of chokepoints that are important strategic terrain in the maritime domain. These chokepoints have similarity to cyberspace chokepoints and produce some similar effects. Another similarity to the cyberspace domain is that the maritime domain is vast and open and humans do not live there, so normally no one has superiority in most of the maritime domain; it is "uncommanded." Combatants access the maritime domain through technology and expensive infrastructure such as ships and ports. In this way, the maritime domain is similar to the air domain.

The geography of the air domain is very different from that of land or sea and gives the domain its unique characteristics, including that the air domain is mostly open and less constrained. The air domain differs from the land and maritime domains in that air domain forces can more easily bypass defenses to target directly civilians and infrastructure, which can make air domain warfare much less sequential. The great speed, long range, and flexibility of modern aircraft also make it very easy for air domain forces to concentrate rapidly on a mission or location. Combatants access the air domain through technology much as combatants access the maritime, space, and cyberspace domains. Although still very distinct, a combination of characteristics from the air and maritime domains apply to the cyberspace domain.

The fact that cyberspace is man-made, but connected to the physical world drives the geography of cyberspace. There are chokepoints in cyberspace that we can consider as roughly analogous to mountain ranges or other features in the land domain, but cyberspace operators create them and they can be rapidly changed, moved, or entirely deleted. This mutability has significant implications for cyberspace superiority and the continuing rapid improvement of hardware across cyberspace further accentuates this constant mutability. As cyberspace grows and expands, its network structure gives it a high level of built-in resilience to attacks. As hardware improves, the cost of entry into cyberspace continues to decrease.

An entry-level capability for a nation-state in cyberspace can be very economical, however, significant capability is still expensive. It seems counter intuitive for a domain that derives its very existence from technology, but well trained and capable people are more important in the battle for cyberspace superiority than equipment. However, even the largest cyberspace forces are miniscule compared to the vastness of cyberspace and so, like the maritime domain, no nation will have cyberspace superiority in most areas of cyberspace. Part of the reason for this characteristic is the specialization of cyberspace weapons that cannot simply seek out and destroy enemy forces autonomously.

Offensive cyberspace weapons have no ability to detect enemy offensive cyberspace weapons and so they cannot destroy them in opportune "meeting engagements." This makes cyberspace forces very different from land, maritime, or air forces, who can all detect and react to the unexpected presence of enemy forces. In this respect, cyberspace forces are most like the satellites of the space domain that fly past each other while continuing to do their individual missions unless specifically instructed to do something else. An area of great divergence among the domains is whether the offensive or defensive has primacy in the domain.

Offensive or Defensive Primacy in the Domains

Colin Gray has identified that the advantage for offense or defense in a given domain is dependent upon the "tactical-technical logic" of that domain.[4] The advantage can shift within a given domain due to changes in either tactics or technology, but the advantage does not normally shift rapidly.

In the land domain, the defensive currently has the advantage in the tactical-technical logic. The reason for the defender's advantage is that normally, the defender can remain hidden and undercover, while the attacker has to move forward in the open and is exposed. This situation is what accounts for the military maxim that an attacker should outnumber the defender three to one if he is going to be successful.

In the maritime domain, neither the offensive nor defensive has clear primacy; it depends on the specifics of the engagement. This is because, unlike the land domain, in maritime surface warfare the attacker and defender can see each other at the same time and have an equal opportunity to fire first. There are several exceptions to this general rule, in undersea combat, the advantage goes to the one who stays hidden, which gives a benefit to the defense as it is easier to stay silent and hidden while remaining motionless. In addition, a fleet operating within range of friendly land-based defenses gains a significant advantage over an attacking fleet. Like the maritime domain, the air domain also does not have clear primacy for the attacker or defender.

While earlier air domain theorists favored the offensive, whether the defensive or offensive had primacy in the air domain has shifted over time with technological change. Right now, there is no clear primacy to the offense or defense; the more effective operational and tactical force is likely to defeat its foe on either the offense or defense. The Israeli Air Force has demonstrated this principle by defeating its foes whether on the offensive or defensive through superiority in equipment, tactics, and strategy.

The advantage in the cyberspace domain goes to the attacker who can be proactive, as he can remain hidden and anonymous, while the defender is out in the open and reactive. In the land domain, attackers have to unmask to attack; in the cyberspace domain it is the defenders who are out in the open, and it is the attackers who have the advantage of stealth. Offensive cyberspace weapons striking the inside of an enemy system attack in a two-stage process, first they gain access, then they execute the mission. Most cyberspace weapons rely on deception to get in, and stealth to persist and accomplish their missions, which means defenders will be unable to see them coming and gives an advantage to the offense. This advantage is not strong enough to overwhelm other factors, and the defense can be, and often is, successful in gaining and maintaining superiority in cyberspace.

Method of Gaining Domain Superiority

There is great variation among the various domains in how a combatant attains domain superiority. One reason for this difference is that in each of the domains the importance of the local and universal levels of superiority changes. In the land domain, there is a balance between the local and universal levels.

Physical presence is the key to establishing land domain superiority but it is not sufficient; a combatant also needs population acceptance to make his superiority secure. For the United States, establishing physical presence has been easier than population acceptance in the last few conflicts. Successful combatants have most often established physical presence by defeating the enemy army in battle and occupying his territory. Combatants can also gain control through some form of negotiated settlement or peace treaty that transfers land from one combatant to another. In the maritime domain, there are several competing theories of how to gain superiority.

Maritime theorists have disagreed on the relative importance of the local or universal level in gaining maritime superiority. For Mahan, the only way to gain maritime superiority was to destroy the enemy's fleet, while Corbett saw other possibilities. For Corbett, combatants could establish a form of maritime superiority through a blockade, or commerce warfare and avoiding the enemy fleet completely. The reason for these different theories of gaining superiority is that Mahan saw maritime superiority as universal and Corbett saw it as local. The air domain is a mixture of universal and local.

The universal level of air superiority is more significant than the local level due to the excellent mobility of airpower, the concentrated character of the airpower instrument and the vulnerability of universal airpower to attack. To gain air domain superiority at the universal level a combatant needs to attack the enemy's offensive and defensive air domain forces. An enemy can normally shift forces in the air domain rapidly so defeating all the forces in one local area may not bring sustained advantage if the enemy can simply shift forces from another area to fight for the same local area again. Local air superiority involves defeating only those enemy forces required to attain a specific objective in a local area whether that objective is offensive or defensive. This local superiority may be all that is required if the objectives sought by a combatant are limited. For cyberspace combatants, local superiority will normally be all that is achievable.

One method of achieving a form of universal cyberspace superiority could be to focus on chokepoints to control the flow of information and degrade the enemy's ability to use cyberspace, but at the current time, policy and technical limitations make successfully controlling all chokepoints in cyberspace unlikely. The network design of cyberspace enables most traffic seamlessly and rapidly to divert around attempted blocks with no active intervention by the user. Also, because of the problems with attribution, it will not be clear to a combatant which streams of information belong to the enemy. In addition, the enormous amount of data passing across chokepoints such as major undersea cables makes filtering it very difficult with current technology. As controlling chokepoints is not practical with the current technology and structure of cyberspace, combatants should pursue whatever universal superiority is attainable, while focusing on the fight for local cyberspace superiority.

In cyberspace, the local level of superiority is far more important than the universal when compared to the other domains. There are a number of reasons for this situation. First, it is difficult to move cyberspace weapons from one local area to another. Second, offensive and defensive forces in cyberspace are very different, which prevents combatants from moving them between offensive and defensive missions. Next, attackers design specialized cyberspace weapons, which typically affect a single system. Finally, cyberspace superiority tends to be local in that it is extremely difficult for combatants to find and attack enemy cyberspace "fleets" and "armies." These factors suggest that combatants should focus on gaining local cyberspace superiority.

An attacker will gain local cyberspace superiority by successfully accessing enemy systems to accomplish desired objectives, while a defender will gain local cyberspace superiority by blocking the attacker from achieving his offensive objectives, while protecting friendly access to cyberspace systems. The constant maneuvering between attackers and defenders sets up a dynamic in cyberspace akin to Clausewitz's wrestlers as the maneuvers of each side effect the options available to the other. Once a combatant has gained a measure of domain superiority, what can combatants do with it?

Use of Domain Superiority

As we saw in the gaining of domain superiority, the use of superiority across the different domains varies. At its heart, the use of domain superiority is about a combatant accomplishing the goals and objectives they have set in that domain. In the land domain, combatants often connect these objectives to the purpose of the conflict.

Once a combatant establishes superiority in the land domain to include the acceptance of the situation by the population, he can normally dictate terms to the enemy. If the conflict continues in other theaters, a combatant can utilize the portion where the combatant has superiority to produce resources and continue to pursue overall victory. World War II provides numerous examples of combatants utilizing conquered terrain to produce the resources needed to continue the war. In the maritime domain, combatants most often utilize superiority to protect sea lines of communication.

Once a combatant gains maritime superiority, they can protect friendly sea lines of communication and attack those of the enemy, while enabling friendly power projection ashore and preventing enemy power projection. Some theorists, such as Mahan, viewed maritime superiority as critical to a nation because of its potential control of commerce. Corbett agreed that seaborne commerce was vital, but he also saw the importance of being able to utilize the maritime sphere to influence the land domain. As the maritime domain cannot be owned and occupied in the same manner as the land domain, Corbett saw that the principal contribution of maritime superiority was to influence the land domain through sea lines of communication or power projection ashore. Although there are lines of communication in the air domain as well, combatants normally focus the use of superiority on the accomplishment of objectives.

There are three major ways that airpower analysts have suggested a combatant can use air superiority to achieve campaign objectives. The first is to attack the enemy population to put pressure on enemy decision makers. The second is to attack infrastructure or industry to prevent the enemy from constructing weapons. The third is to use airpower to support surface forces. This support to surface forces can include attacking enemy forces engaged in combat with friendly forces, attacking enemy forces in reserve, and resupply of friendly forces. Combatants have used all three approaches at various times in the air domain; they are not mutually exclusive and often reinforce each other. For example, bomber attacks on railway targets in France prior to the Normandy invasion affected the German war economy and prevented the rapid transfer of troops to the front. Although these approaches can be combined, punishment of enemy populations has normally not produced decisive results and I agree with Robert Pape that normally the best approach is to attack the enemy's military strategy.[5] If the enemy is attempting to achieve his objectives with his army, this will often take the form of attacking the enemy army. In cyberspace, like the air domain, combatants focus their use of superiority on the accomplishment of their objectives.

One of the most common ways that cyberspace combatants attempt to use cyberspace superiority is strategic information warfare where they try to achieve effects directly through cyberspace. These can include physical effects such as the destruction of infrastructure, or psychological effects such as attempting to coerce an enemy to take, or refrain from taking, some action.

Intelligence collection is probably the most common use of cyberspace superiority but it is also the most difficult to pin down and analyze as when it is done right, no-one knows about it. Combatants do have to be careful with intelligence collection as even the most innocent collection for defensive purposes, can easily be seen as preparation for an offensive attack and generate the hostility and attack that the intelligence collector was trying to avoid in the first place.

Combatants can also use their cyberspace superiority to target an enemy logistical system, or more broadly, to disrupt or misdirect any enemy action or plan. However, cyberspace superiority for a combatant is not merely focused on what can be done to the enemy.

Perhaps the most important contribution of cyberspace superiority at the current time for a combatant is the support provided to enable other domain forces. This support has become so ubiquitous that combatants often do not even realize how dependent they are upon cyberspace to enable their communications and other systems.

For a defender, their use of cyberspace superiority is focused on preventing the enemy from achieving any of the offensive cyberspace ways, while preserving access to friendly systems and providing the maximum benefit from their own cyberspace superiority. Those benefits will be significantly affected by the persistence of cyberspace superiority.

Persistence of Domain Superiority

The persistence of domain superiority varies widely with land superiority being the most persistent and cyberspace superiority the least. The characteristics of the various domains and the timescales associated with action within them drive these differences.

Land domain superiority tends to be persistent due to greater influence of the universal level of superiority as well as the sequential tendencies of land combat, the inertia of populations whose support changes slowly, and the current primacy of the defensive. All of these factors combine to make changing land superiority very difficult. Persistence of superiority in the maritime domain is more variable.

Whether the maritime superiority gained is local or universal will greatly affect the persistence of maritime superiority. According to Mahan, who focused on universal maritime superiority, superiority should be persistent based on major fleet actions that would affect universal superiority. If the enemy refuses to fight a major fleet action for universal control, then control will not only be localized, but also fleeting as the enemy can dash out of port to raid convoys and establish local control in an area, then retreat into port when threatened by the main adversary fleet. Persistence in the air domain is similar to the maritime domain with long persistence only available with universal air superiority.

Because of the high mobility of air domain forces to move from one local area to another, a combatant will be able to achieve persistence of superiority in the air domain only if he is able to achieve universal, not local, air superiority. Airpower theorists, who saw that air superiority could be local, also recognized that local superiority would tend to be transient. Air superiority will tend to be local and transient unless one side has an overwhelming abundance of superiority that they can achieve across the entire theater of operations as the Coalition did in the 1991 Gulf War. Unfortunately for cyberspace operators, they normally can only achieve local domain superiority, which also limits them to short persistence of that superiority.

The persistence of offensive cyberspace superiority will be very short for an attacker due to the replicability of cyberspace, its great speed of action, and the rapid degradation of offensive cyberspace weapons once defenders discover them. Software and data in cyberspace are replicable, which makes software- and data-based attacks easier to recover from quickly. The short timescales of action in cyberspace produce great speed and rapidly changing dominance, which reduces persistence. Another reason attacker's cyberspace superiority will not tend to be persistent is the rapid degradation in the effectiveness of offensive cyberspace weapons once defenders discover them. Once a defender finds an enemy weapon, the defender will be able to inoculate their other systems and the weapon will lose most of its utility for future attacks. To verify any of these findings against real world case studies, analysts have to have some reliable methodology to measure domain superiority, which is where we turn next.

Measurement Concepts of Domain Superiority

Because there is such breadth in the characteristics of domain superiority across the domains, there is also great variation in how it is measured. Several of the domains though, have elements of measurement that have great utility in cyberspace.

Land domain superiority consists of territorial control and acceptance of that control; analysts use a range of metrics to measure territorial control by which combatant's soldiers overtly occupy terrain and control populations. Determining whose soldiers occupy which portion of the contested terrain is by far the easier task. James Clancy and Chuck Crossett identify three main types of population control metrics they label measures of sustainability, legitimacy, and stability.[6] Analysts can think of sustainability as supply and resources getting to the insurgent enemy, legitimacy focuses on the effectiveness of the friendly government in the eyes of the population, and stability measures the level of security and ability to function of a local society. Measuring maritime domain superiority requires a very different set of tools.

Measures of maritime superiority include the balance of forces between the two fleets, metrics to measure the openness of sea lines of communication, and the ability of combatants to project power from the maritime environment into other domains. Metrics to compare fleets should focus on combat effectiveness, which can be difficult to measure. Simple comparisons of tonnage or types of ships will likely be inadequate. Metrics that measure how much friendly shipping is reaching its destination and how much enemy shipping is not, will provide a picture of how open the sea lines of communication are. Finally, if a maritime combatant can utilize the maritime environment to project power into the air or land domains at will through amphibious assaults or carrier borne aviation, it demonstrates a high level of maritime superiority. Like the maritime domain, the ability of cyberspace to project power into the other domains will be a key component of measurement, but the air domain measurement techniques have more applicability.

Measuring air domain superiority is a question of assessing how effectively an attacker or defender is accomplishing their objectives in the domain. Common indicators include how often strike aircraft have to jettison their bombs before getting to their targets, how often targets are struck successfully, how many enemy sorties get into friendly territory, and what their effectiveness was. Many of the indicators used in the air domain such as strike effectiveness and number of successful enemy air attacks transfer readily into the cyberspace domain. Like with air domain superiority, cyberspace superiority measurement will also focus on a combatant's achievement of objectives, on the offensive and defensive sides.

Cyberspace domain superiority is fundamentally about a combatant being able to achieve his objectives in cyberspace while preventing the enemy from achieving his objectives, thus both combatant's objectives will be key to measurement. On the offensive side, an analyst can best accomplish this by measuring the attacker's success against whatever objectives he was pursuing. On the defensive side, an analyst can measure success by examining the level of functionality of critical systems under cyberspace attack. The most effective way to combine and properly weight these multiple objectives and inputs is through a weighted preference model. A summary of all the domain superiority characteristics is in Table 7.1.

Modeling Local Cyberspace Superiority

Within any domain, combatants seek to connect their means and ways, while at the same time their adversary is attempting to block them from achieving their objectives. A defender can interfere with an attacker's means or ways, and an

Table 7.1 Summary of Domain Characteristics and Domain Superiority

Geography and Characteristics	
Land	• Physical terrain such as mountains, rivers, and swamps dictate lines of communication and which forces are most effective where. • Combat tends to be sequential with forces excluding each other from areas of their control while protecting their own lines of communication.
Maritime	• Maneuver space is bounded by land masses and ports which form chokepoints. • Sea lines of communication are the key element worth fighting over. • Accessed via expensive technology (ships) and expensive entry points (ports).
Air	• Open and relatively unbounded without natural chokepoints. • No clear front line involves civilians directly in combat operations. • Characterized by great speed of action. • Dependent upon technology for access. • Accessed via expensive technology (aircraft) and expensive entry points (airfields). • Dominance in this domain is not sufficient for victory, it enables the land and maritime domains.
Cyberspace	• Manmade but connected to the physical world. • Can usefully be modeled by Libicki's three layers of physical, syntactic, and semantic. • An entry-level capability for a nation-state in cyberspace can be very economical, however, significant capability is still expensive. • The network structure of cyberspace gives it a high level of built-in resilience to attacks that focus on interfering with communication between nodes. • There are chokepoints in cyberspace that we can consider as roughly analogous to mountain ranges or other features in the land domain. • Combatants can connect, disconnect, or change the linkages between the components that create cyberspace. • Designers continue rapidly to make the individual hardware more capable. • Because of the small number of military cyberspace forces in relation to the vast amount of civilian cyberspace, normally no nation-state will have superiority in most areas of cyberspace. • Combatants may restrain themselves in cyberspace to avoid crossing perceived global norms of cyberspace as a global common. • Offensive cyberspace weapons have no ability to "see" and react to each other, thus there is no analog to a meeting engagement in cyberspace.
Offensive or Defensive Primacy	
Land	• With modern weapons the defensive has primacy as the defender can stay undercover while the offender must unmask to advance.

Maritime	• There is no clear offensive or defensive primacy in the maritime domain
	  ◦ Normally both offensive and defensive forces can see each other at the same distance.
	  ◦ Exceptions include submarine warfare which favors the offender and a fleet in a defended port which favors the defense.

Air	• Older theorists favored the offensive, advantage has shifted back and forth over time depending on technology.

(Continued)

Table 7.1 (Continued)

Offensive or Defensive Primacy	
Cyberspace	• The advantage in the cyberspace domain goes to the attacker who can be proactive as he can remain hidden and anonymous, while the defender is out in the open and reactive.
Method of Gaining Superiority	
Land	• Universal: defeat enemy army to allow physical access to the terrain and then gain control and support of the population. • Local: defeat local regular or insurgent forces.
Maritime	• Universal: defeat enemy fleet or blockade them in port; weaker combatant can contest by keeping a "fleet in being" and executing small counter attacks. • Local: disrupt enemy shipping while protecting your own.
Air	• Offensive universal: degrade enemy strategic IADS. • Defensive universal: degrade enemy offensive airpower. • Offensive local: defeat enemy local IADS. • Defensive Local: defeat enemy local offensive airpower.

Cyberspace	• Controlling chokepoints is one way of establishing universal cyberspace superiority, however, it will normally not be possible.
	• There are a number of reasons local cyberspace superiority will normally be all that is achievable
	  ○ It is difficult to move cyberspace weapons from one local area to another.
	  ○ Offensive and defensive forces in cyberspace are very different, which prevents combatants from moving them between offensive and defensive missions.
	  ○ The specialization of cyberspace weapons that attackers design for a single system.
	  ○ It is extremely difficult for combatants to find and attack enemy cyberspace "fleets" and "armies".
	• An attacker will gain local cyberspace superiority by successfully accessing enemy systems to accomplish desired objectives.
	• A defender will gain local cyberspace superiority by successfully blocking the enemy from achieving his offensive objectives, and protecting friendly access to cyberspace systems.

Use of Superiority	
Land	• Often, control of the land domain will terminate the conflict; if not, combatants can extract resources for continued combat in other areas and domains.
Maritime	• Enable shipment of military and commercial goods. • Project power into the land domain while preventing the enemy from doing the same.
Air	• Offensive: directly striking enemy centers of gravity either to affect enemy capabilities or change enemy decisions; support other domain forces. • Defensive: prevent enemy from striking friendly centers of gravity.
Cyberspace	• Offensive: accomplish operational objectives through strategic information warfare, intelligence collection, reducing enemy logistics, disrupting enemy actions, misdirecting enemy actions, and support to other domain forces. • Defensive: prevent enemy from accomplishing their offensive objectives while protecting friendly systems and maintaining their effectiveness.

Persistence	
Land	• Land domain superiority tends to be persistent due to greater influence of the universal level of superiority, as well as the sequential tendencies of land combat, the inertia of populations whose support changes slowly, and the current primacy of the defensive.
Maritime	• Whether the maritime superiority gained is local or universal will greatly affect the persistence of maritime superiority ◦ If a combatant can achieve universal maritime superiority through defeating the enemy fleet, then persistence can be high. ◦ If the enemy refuses to fight a major fleet action for universal control, then control will not only be localized, but also fleeting as the enemy can dash out of port to raid convoys and establish local control in an area, but then retreat back into port when threatened by the main adversary fleet.
Air	• Because of the high mobility of air domain forces to move from one local area to another, a combatant will be able to achieve persistence of superiority in the air domain only if he is able to achieve universal versus local air superiority.
Cyberspace	• The persistence of cyberspace superiority will be very short due to the replicability of cyberspace, its great speed of action, and the rapid degradation of offensive cyberspace weapons once defenders discover them.
Measurement Concept	
Land	• Whose soldiers are in possession of the terrain? • Metrics to determine the level of support of the population.
Maritime	• Universal: remaining capability of enemy fleet. • Local: metrics to measure friendly and enemy utilization of sea lines of communication; ability to project power into other domains.
Air	• Ability to achieve objectives in the air. • Relative measurement and trends of resources.
Cyberspace	• Offensive success is measured by summing the level of objective achievement. • Defensive success is measured by summing the level of functionality of key systems and the prevention of enemy success.

attacker in turn can attempt to interfere with the defender's blocks. A simple way of illustrating this dynamic interaction is shown in Figure 7.1.

A defender can react to the attacker's maneuvering and so on, but this model provides a glimpse of the complex and continuing interaction between the two combatants as each tries to accomplish its objectives and adjusts to what the enemy is doing. To bring the model into the cyberspace domain, the specific means, ways, and ends currently applicable in cyberspace can be added, as shown in Figure 7.2.

Details of all these tools can be found in Chapter 4, and they are likely to change slowly with time and technology development, but the concept that both parties will continue to maneuver in relation to the other will continue as long as conflict continues in any domain.

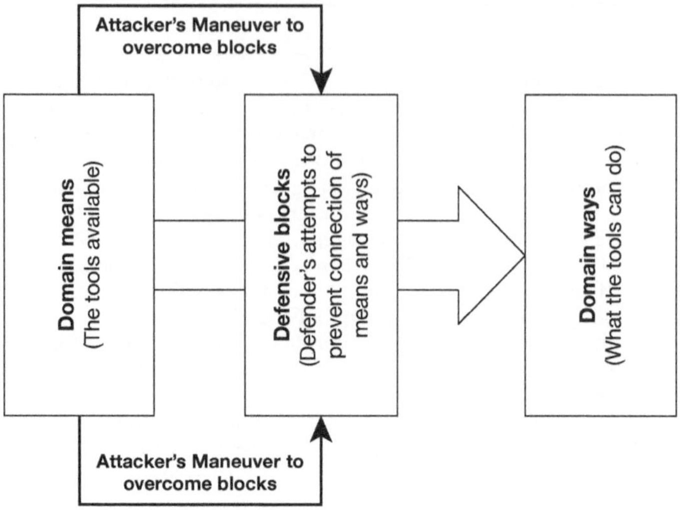

Figure 7.1 Domain Conflict Model
Source: *Author's original work*

Findings from the Case Studies

I analyzed nation-state cyberspace conflict for which there was sufficient information available in unclassified sources. It was very important that I coded the inputs using a consistent and repeatable methodology and I have placed the details of the coding methodology in Appendix A. The analysis of the case studies can be found in Chapter 6, with the detailed breakdown of the measurement inputs in Appendix B. I have placed the results below in Table 7.2.

Despite the predictions of some advocates, the cyberspace "bomber" does not always get through and the offense only seems to have a slight advantage. Out of eight case studies, the attacker had greater cyberspace superiority in four of them and the defender had greater cyberspace superiority in the other four. There was also a wide range in the superiority combatants achieved on the offensive and defensive sides. There are no cases where a clearly weaker attacker succeeded, but I cannot conclude that either the offensive or defensive has clear primacy based on case study evidence. I can conclude that neither the offense nor defense has overwhelming dominance, as offenders and defenders both had varying levels of success. In addition, from the previous study of cyberspace characteristics, I expect that the offense will have a slight advantage, but the advantage will normally be very short lived.

The persistence of any level of offensive cyberspace superiority was less than two weeks in seven of the eight cases, leading to a conclusion that offensive cyberspace superiority will not normally be persistent. The one case where the attacker managed significant persistence measured in years was the Stuxnet

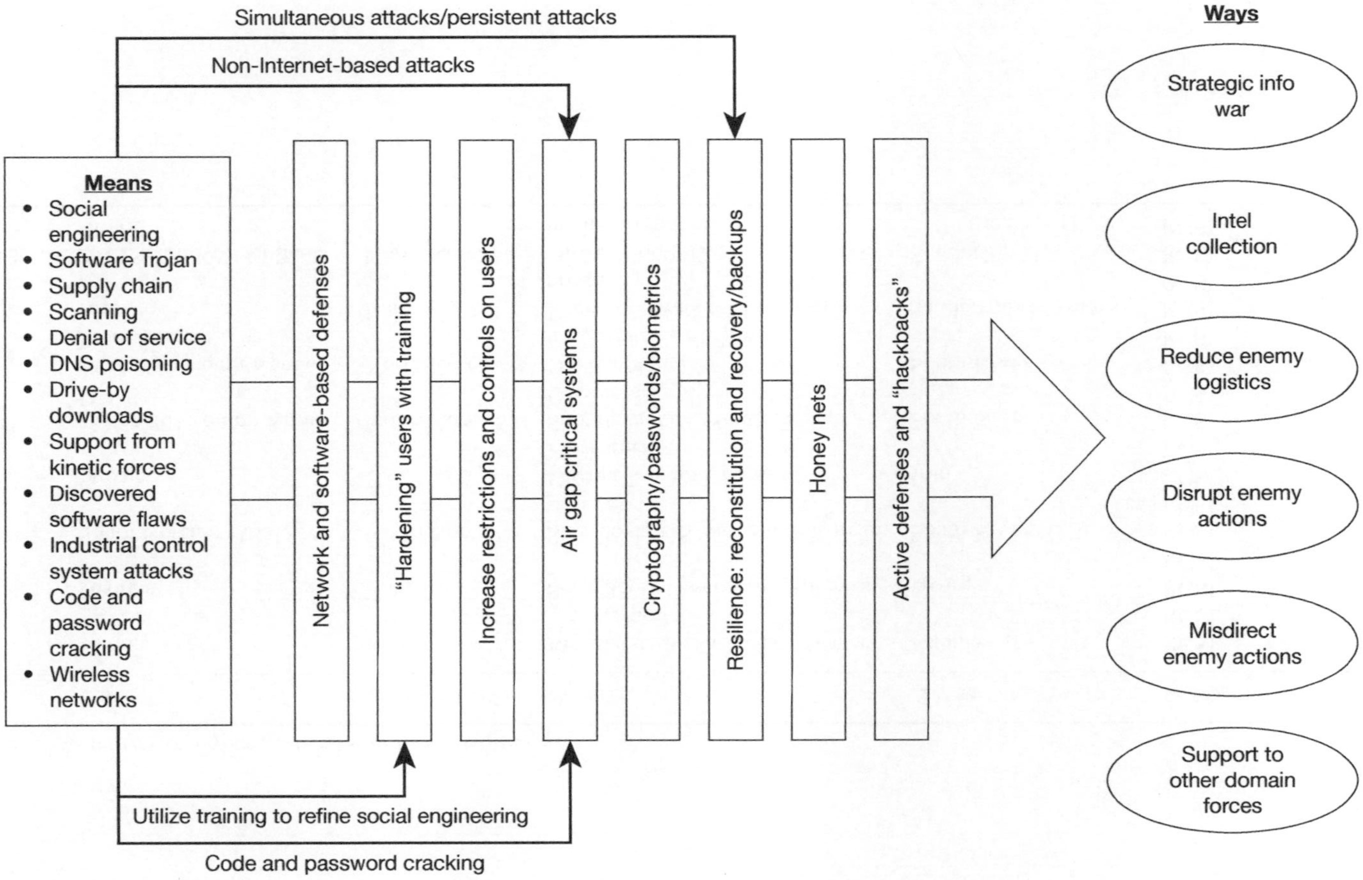

Figure 7.2 Local Cyberspace Superiority Model

Source: *Author's original work*

Table 7.2 Summary of Cyberspace Superiority Case Studies

Year	*Case*	*Presumed Attacker*	*Objective*	*Defender*	*Outcome*
2007	Estonia	Russia	Replace statue, intimidate former USSR states	Estonia	$RCSI_{Russia} = (-0.15)$ $RCSI_{Estonia} = 0.15$
2008	Georgia	Russia	Seize South Ossetia and Abkhazia	Georgia	$RCSI_{Russia} = 0.61$ $RCSI_{Georgia} = (-0.61)$
2009	South Korean/U.S. DDoS	North Korea	Shut down U.S. and South Korean websites	South Korea/U.S.	$RCSI_{North\ Korea} = (-0.46)$ $RCSI_{US/South\ Korea} = 0.46$
2010	Stuxnet	U.S./Israel	Disrupt Iranian Uranium Enrichment	Iran	$RCSI_{US/Israel} = 0.08$ $RCSI_{Iran} = (-0.08)$
2011	March 2011 South Korean DDoS	North Korea	Shut down U.S./South Korean Gov websites	South Korea	$RCSI_{North\ Korea} = 0.03$ $RCSI_{South\ Korea} = (-0.03)$
2011	April 2011 South Korean Bank Attack	North Korea	Disrupt Nonghyup Bank/ Embarrass South Korea	South Korea	$RCSI_{North\ Korea} = 0.51$ $RCSI_{South\ Korea} = (-0.51)$
2012	Aramco	Iran	Interrupt Aramco oil and gas production	Saudi Arabia/Aramco	$RCSI_{Iran} = (-0.30)$ $RCSI_{Saudi\ Arabia} = 0.30$
2013	2013 South Korean Bank Attack	North Korea	Disrupt South Korean banks and media companies	South Korea	$RCSI_{North\ Korea} = (-0.33)$ $RCSI_{South\ Korea} = 0.33$

attack. The attackers managed long persistence in this case because the defenders did not know they were under attack and the designers of Stuxnet worked very hard to keep the weapon hidden.

I can draw two conclusions from this data on persistence. One is that the majority of cyberspace attacks only persist for approximately two weeks or less, and the second is that a weapon that can remain hidden is the only proven method of achieving long persistence of cyberspace superiority. Once defenders understand that they are under attack, they will react quickly and bring in the resources they need to stop the attack. Another conclusion I can pull from the case studies involves universal cyberspace superiority.

Universal cyberspace superiority is not achievable, and combatants should not pour significant resources into pursuing it. In none of the cases did a combatant achieve any amount of universal cyberspace superiority. There is not even much evidence of a combatant achieving cyberspace superiority in multiple local areas simultaneously. Cyberspace is fragmented into countless local areas, not just based on geographic location, but multiple local areas that can exist in the same physical location through various systems. In a single command center, for example, there are normally numerous systems at different levels of classification that are separate local areas of cyberspace. In addition, universal superiority in cyberspace would need to be global. In the air domain, it is possible for a combatant to have universal superiority in a theater of operations such as the Persian Gulf. In cyberspace this geographic separation of theaters is not possible and a combatant may have servers and nodes spread over the entire planet. Thus, to achieve universal cyberspace superiority a combatant would have to achieve global cyberspace superiority over all of cyberspace, which is not attainable by any combatant. What a combatant can achieve is significant advantage for military operations through local cyberspace superiority.

Despite the relatively limited number of cases available, there are at least three cases that show cyberspace superiority providing significant advantage for military operations. In the Russia versus Georgia case, Russia accrued advantages to their conventional forces they would not have had without the cyberspace attacks. The disruption of the Georgian communication networks had a significant effect on the Georgian ability to resist the invasion, and the other Russian attacks increased the pressure on Georgia to concede. The Russians achieved a high level of cyberspace superiority, but even a small amount of cyberspace superiority can bring some advantage, as with Stuxnet.

The small level of cyberspace superiority attained by the U.S. and Israel with Stuxnet was able to provide them some significant advantages they could not have gotten from operations in the other domains. The level of cyberspace superiority achieved by the United States and Israel, small as it was, was sufficient to prevent a kinetic strike, as the attackers were able to slow the Iranian nuclear program without kinetic weapons. The strategic effect was to prevent kinetic operations that would likely have gone very badly, and to buy time for negotiations to find a solution. There is one other case where it is easy to see a combatant accruing a significant advantage for military operations.

The third case where a cyberspace combatant gained significant advantage for military operations through cyberspace superiority was the 2011 bank attack by North Korea. This attack resulted in significant advantage in military operations for the North Koreans as it gave them a very low risk way to attack their enemies that was not available in other domains. If the North Koreans had accomplished the same damage from a physical domain, they would not have been able to escape punishment by the international community. Because they used cyberspace, they were able to do significant damage, and still avoid serious consequences. Even with the limited cases available, there is good evidence that higher levels of cyberspace superiority correlate to advantage in military operations.

Final Conclusions

If a nation achieves cyberspace superiority during a conflict, then it gains a significant advantage for military operations. Cyberspace superiority provides advantages at the tactical, operational, and strategic levels.

Although the number of cases of nation-state warfare in cyberspace is small, theory and practice in the other domains also leads to the expectation that cyberspace superiority should provide significant operational advantage. Domain forces have always first attempted to achieve superiority their domain before they were able to utilize that superiority to have effects in other domains.[7] Although armies have not often seen land warfare in these terms, both marine and air domain operators understand the need to establish superiority in their domain before they can provide support to the other domains. Cyberspace operators face the same situation, although superiority in their domain has different characteristics than the maritime and air domains as discussed previously. One area where these different characteristics stood out was in the interplay between the universal and local levels of superiority in the different domains.

One of the important insights that came out of this study of superiority in the different domains was the connection between universal and local domain superiority. The details change for each of the domains, but in general, local superiority is what matters when determining who can accomplish their objectives without prohibitive interference. Local superiority tends to be much more transitory than universal superiority, but local and universal superiority feedback into each other. The level of universal superiority determines the forces that are available in the conflict for local superiority and the losses incurred in the local engagement then feed back into the level of universal superiority. This finding leads directly into one of the questions I examined in this study.

The first supporting question was whether domain superiority in general and cyberspace superiority in particular was a universal or local phenomenon. As I discussed earlier, the answer borne out by my research is yes, it is both a universal and local phenomenon but for cyberspace superiority, the local level is far more important. On the universal level are the assets that have theater-wide impact such as main armies, battle fleets, or strategic air defenses. On the local level are the smaller units and tools that only have reach to affect some smaller segment of the overall theater. The universal and local levels interact, and there is more importance to universal or local depending on the domain. In the cyberspace domain, the universal level is very hard to influence so attackers and defenders will do the majority of their work on the local level. The answer to my second supporting question largely flowed from the answer to the first that cyberspace superiority will normally be limited to the local level.

The second supporting question was how persistent domain superiority would be. The answer is that in the cyberspace domain, the persistence for an attacker is very low. From a theoretical perspective, I have demonstrated why local cyberspace superiority tends to be so transitory. Universal superiority is more difficult to achieve in the cyberspace domain than in the land, maritime, or air domains and in each of the domains, it is the universal domain superiority that tends to be persistent. Although local superiority is the one that will determine whether an attacker achieves a particular objective, the universal domain superiority is what produces the resources used in the local conflicts. Because universal domain superiority is so difficult to achieve, most conflicts in cyberspace will be determined at the local level, which tends to produce transitory effects. I can provide further corroborating evidence for this theoretical finding from the case studies. Out of eight case studies, seven of the conflicts lasted two weeks or less. Whatever level of offensive cyberspace superiority that an attacker achieved was either lost by the termination of the conflict, or by the defense developing countermeasures that made the offensive weapons in use ineffective. Measuring the level of cyberspace superiority during a conflict was the next challenge.

My final supporting question was how a combatant could measure the level of cyberspace superiority. A weighted preference methodology is the right tool to measure offensive success by summing the level of objective achievement along with the weight of those objectives, and to measure defensive success by summing the level of functionality of key systems with along with their criticality. When I coded the inputs according to the methodology in Appendix A and applied it to the case studies, the measurement system generated useful results.

Cyberspace is a unique domain, but not so unique that the logic of war and strategy applicable in the other domains does not apply. To repurpose Clausewitz, "Its grammar, indeed, may be its own, but not its logic."[8] Cyberspace warriors need to guard against a tendency toward technological determinism and the dynamic interaction with the enemy will be impossible to predict with accuracy. Strategy's paradoxical nature explained by Luttwak, where combatants often get the opposite of what they are trying to achieve due to the enemy's responses, applies fully to cyberspace as well.[9] Both sides will be actively pursuing cyberspace superiority in an interactive manner, but they will each likely only be able to achieve local and transitory superiority.

Superiority in cyberspace is achievable and desirable, although it will be difficult to attain in more than a local and temporary form. Unlike the land, maritime, and air domains, offensive cyberspace forces do not engage in combat if they cross paths in cyberspace. Losses are normally only produced in local fights between offensive and defensive forces. The defensive forces also do not "destroy" offensive weapons; they render them impotent by patching vulnerabilities and updating detection systems. In some ways, the medical analogy suggested by Paul Rosenzweig is a better mental template than traditional combat.[10] Good cyberspace defenses have more similarity to vaccines and medical care than infantrymen and artillery. Cyberspace defenses fight the current infection and restore the patient to good health, while inoculating him from any further infection. Also, like medicine, if there are opportunities to drain swamps and decrease the total number of diseases in the world, cyberspace warriors should attempt to reduce the enemy's universal capability when possible.

Just because it will be difficult to achieve universal cyberspace superiority does not mean that combatants should not seek and attack universal cyberspace targets whenever possible, as degrading the enemy's universal cyberspace resources will make the local fights easier. The connection between the two goes both ways, and while a nation should not put too many resources into chasing difficult universal cyberspace superiority targets, there will be times when those targets are accessible. A kinetic strike in the physical domains is the easiest path to lasting effects, but only if the targets are expensive and hard to replace. Simple servers and computers will not normally be productive targets. Even if attacks on infrastructure and cyberspace personnel are wildly successful, it does not guarantee a combatant's victory in the overall conflict.

Cyberspace superiority is neither necessary, nor sufficient for success in conflict, but it is important and will provide significant advantage to a combatant who achieves it. The ability successfully to execute cyberspace operations is only part of a balanced national security portfolio for any nation. Offensive cyberspace operations can play two major roles, it can directly attack targets to produce effects, and it can provide support to other domain forces. At the current time and for the foreseeable future, the support cyberspace forces provide to the other domains is more important than the ability to produce direct effects. Nations should not neglect strategic information warfare, and there will be cases where it is the only or best option, but cyberspace operators need to remember the lessons of the early airpower theorists and not focus so much on producing strategic effects that they overpromise and under-deliver. In the United States, cyberspace operations have many of the same organizational and institutional issues that made the rise of airpower so difficult within the defense establishment. A balanced focus on what cyberspace can provide to the other domains with the ability to produce strategic effects will help ease the transition.

Cyberspace is here to stay from toilets to tanks. A modern nation should thoroughly study the past and build capable forces to contest and create superiority in the new domain of cyberspace.

Notes

1 Joint Chiefs of Staff, Joint Operations, Vol. 3–13, *Information Operations*, 2012.
2 Thomas David McCarthy, "Traveling Domain Theory: A Comparative Approach for Cyberspace Theory Development" (PhD diss., Fletcher School of Law and Diplomacy, 2012), 188.

3 Air Force Doctrine Document (AFDD) 3–12, *Cyberspace Operations. Change 1*, 15 July 2010, 2.
4 Colin S. Gray, *Modern Strategy* (Oxford: Oxford University Press, 1999), 110.
5 Robert Pape, *Bombing to Win: Air Power and Coercion in War* (London: Cornell University Press, 1996), 15.
6 James Clancy and Chuck Crossett, "Measuring Effectiveness in Irregular Warfare," *Parameters*, Summer 2007, 96.
7 McCarthy, "Traveling Domain Theory," 188.
8 Carl von Clausewitz, *On War*, ed. and trans. by Michael Howard and Peter Paret (Princeton, NJ: Princeton University Press, 1976), 605.
9 Edward N. Luttwak, *Strategy: The Logic of War and Peace* (Cambridge, MA: Belknap Press, 2003), 2.
10 Paul Rosenzweig, *Cyber Warfare: How Conflicts in Cyberspace are Challenging America and Changing the World* (Santa Barbara, CA: Praeger, 2013), Kindle Location 3727, chap. 16.

Bibliography

Air Force Doctrine Document (AFDD) 3–12, *Cyberspace Operations*, Change 1. 30 November 2011.

Clancy, James and Chuck Crossett. "Measuring Effectiveness in Irregular Warfare." *Parameters*, Summer 2007, 88–100.

Clausewitz, Carl von. *On War*. Edited and Translated by Michael Howard and Peter Paret. Princeton, NJ: Princeton University Press, 1976.

Gray, Colin S. *Modern Strategy*. Oxford: Oxford University Press, 1999.

Luttwak, Edward, N. *Strategy: The Logic of War and Peace*. Cambridge, MA: Belknap Press, 2003.

McCarthy, Thomas David. "Traveling Domain Theory: A Comparative Approach for Cyberspace Theory Development." PhD Dissertation, Fletcher School of Law and Diplomacy, 2012.

Pape, Robert. *Bombing to Win: Air Power and Coercion in War*. London: Cornell University Press, 1996.

Rosenzweig, Paul. *Cyber Warfare: How Conflicts in Cyberspace are Challenging America and Changing the World*. Santa Barbara, CA: Praeger, 2013. Kindle edition.

U.S. Department of Defense, Joint Chiefs of Staff. Joint Operations. Vol. 3–13, *Information Operations*. Washington, DC: U.S. Government Printing Office, 2012.

Appendix A
Coding of Measurement Inputs

One of the greatest difficulties with measuring cyberspace is that an analyst cannot easily quantify the inputs. An analyst can construct an elegant and complex weighted preference model, but if they do not carefully code the inputs into the model, the output will not be useful for analysis or study.

The purpose of this appendix is to detail the definitions used in coding the various inputs that went into the measurement system developed in Chapter 5. The intent of a coding system is that analysts could use these definitions to get similar inputs given similar data for a case study. There will be some variation, but I will provide examples to illustrate each of the levels for the input variables where appropriate, along with an explanation of how the weighing factors and system criticality variables can be determined. The first variable to examine is the level of success.

Level of Success (S)

The first critical input to the measurement model is level of success (S), which is the amount of success an attacker achieves against a particular cyberspace objective. To determine the value of this variable, a researcher needs to understand what objective an attacker is attempting to achieve from whatever data sources are available. Then the analyst can quantify that data as an input from 0.00 to 1.00 as shown in Table A.1.

A researcher can extrapolate between two levels of success to assign a 0.25, for example, but this extrapolation will rarely be required as the ten levels available provide sufficient discrimination. Researchers should avoid making the inputs look more precise than they actually are as these values are normally going to represent quantification of incomplete and ambiguous data sets.

To assign $S = 1.00$, every part of an objective must have been reached. This category is easy to comprehend, yet one of the more difficult to achieve for a protagonist. For example, if the objective was to take down a power grid, $S = 1.00$ would imply that the power grid was completely non-functional and was not providing any power anywhere to any customer. If the objective were to disrupt cellular communications, then $S = 1.00$ would imply that there was no cell phone service operable anywhere in the targeted area.

Table A.1 Level of Success (S) Coding

Description of Level of Success Coding	*Level of Success (S)*
Complete success, objective accomplished	1.00
Extremely successful against objective	0.90
Very successful against objective	0.80
Successful against objective	0.70
Mostly successful against objective	0.60
Achieved approximately half of objective	0.50
Somewhat successful against objective	0.40
Little success against objective	0.30
Minimally successful against objective	0.20
Almost no success against objective	0.10
Complete failure, no objectives achieved	0.00

To assign S = 0.90, an attacker must have been extremely successful against the desired objective. In this case, the attacker must have accomplished almost his entire objective with a negligible reduction in some minor area. For example, if the objective was to disrupt cellular communications, and one cellular tower was partially functional allowing a handful of calls in an unimportant remote area, that would be assigned S = 0.90.

To assign S = 0.80, the attacker had to have been very successful against the desired objective. The difference between S = 0.80 and S = 0.90 is that although the attacker still achieved what he intended to achieve, there are minor areas where success was not complete. For example, if an attacker was attempting to disrupt the operations of a bank, but 10% of the bank's ATM machines still worked, that would represent S = 0.80. The attacker has fully disrupted the target; the bank will suffer large losses in revenue and public trust despite the ability of some of the bank's customers to access their accounts.

To assign S = 0.70, an attacker must have been successful against the desired objective. In this case, the attacker has achieved what they set out to achieve, although they may not have been successful in all areas. For example, if the attacker's objective was to disrupt a command and control system, and 25% of the system was still functional, S = 0.70 would be appropriate if the overall system could not function effectively. As another example, if an attacker was attempting to disrupt a logistics system, and elements of the system stayed functional, but the system could not effectively move resources across the theater, that would represent S = 0.70.

To assign S = 0.60, an attacker must have been mostly successful against the desired objective. For example, if an attacker was trying to take down a power grid to disrupt an area, and 30% of the grid stayed functional, then that would represent S = 0.60. In this case, the attacker has not completely met his system objective. Some relatively unimportant part of the enemy system is operational despite the attack affecting the majority of the system as intended.

To assign an S = 0.50, the attacker must have achieved approximately half of the desired objective. In some cases, this circumstance will be easy to measure. For example, if an electrical grid is attacked and is still providing power to 50% of its customers, that would represent S = 0.50. Other cases will depend more on a qualitative analysis, suggesting that an attacker accomplished only half of a desired objective. An example of this situation might be a North Korean objective to embarrass the South Korean government. If public opinion and news coverage seems to be split, assigning S = 0.50 would be appropriate.

To assign S = 0.40, the attacker must have only achieved partial success against his objective. The attacker should have accomplished less than half of what he wanted, but he still accomplished something of significance. For example, in an attack against a bank, the attacker might have been able to force some branches in a limited number of cities to close, but the majority of the bank's branches were able to remain open and serve customers. The attacker did real damage to the bank, but the bank was still able to function at a reduced capacity.

To assign S = 0.30, the attacker had little success against his objective. For example, in an attack against a power grid, the attacker was able to shut down 10% of the power grid's customers. The attack still accomplished something of value to the attacker, but the effects achieved were disappointing.

To assign S = 0.20, the attacker had to have minimal success against his objective. For example, an attack against a communications system might have slowed the system somewhat, but the enemy is still able to utilize the system. A real world example is the North Korean attempt to take down a number of South Korean Government websites in 2011. Only a few websites were affected, and only for a short period of time.

To assign S = 0.10, the attacker must have had almost no success against his desired objective. An example of this circumstance might be if an attacker was attempting to take down a power grid, and succeeded in knocking out a few substations, but defenders were able to reroute with no loss of power to customers. The attacker successfully disrupted some elements of the system, but the overall system continued to function effectively. As another example, a rating of S = 0.10 would be appropriate if an attacker attempted to disrupt a communications system but only succeeded in negligibly slowing traffic. There was some effect, but it did little to advance the attackers agenda.

To assign S = 0.00, the attacker had to have no success at all against the desired objective. Some elements of the attack might have been technically successful, but the attacker achieved none of his goals. The Russian attacks against Estonia in 2007 provide an example of this situation. Although some of the cyberspace attacks produced various effects, the statue that the Russian government wanted returned to its former site remained in place in its new location. The next factor that we need to consider on the offensive side is the weighing factor that accounts for the importance of each level of success in the model.

Weighting Factor (W)

I use the weighting factor to account for the different levels of importance that an attacker has for his various objectives. The mathematical sum of all the weighting factors must always equal 1.00, which represents 100%. If an attacker has only one objective, then W = 1.00. If there is more than one objective, a researcher should determine the weighting factors by considering how important each objective is to the attacker in relation to each other. For example, if an attacker had two objectives and objective 1 was three times more important than objective 2, then $W_1 = 0.75$ and $W_2 = 0.25$. If there are multiple objectives, an analyst compares the relative importance of all objectives against the other objectives. The weighting factor says nothing about the absolute importance of the objective to the attacker, only the relative importance in relation to the other cyberspace objectives the attacker pursued as part of the same conflict.

Level of Functionality (L)

On the defensive side, analysts should think of the level of functionality (L) in a similar way as the level of success (S) on the offensive side of the measurement construct. Level of functionality captures how effectively defenders are protecting their systems. L is a measurement of the health of the friendly system, not how strong or weak the enemy attack was. A strong attack that a defender was successful against and a weak attack that was an attacker was less successful against would receive the same rating if the system functionality was the same in both cases. The level of functionality ranges from 0.00 to 1.00 in accordance with Table A.2.

Just as with level of success on the offensive side, researchers can extrapolate between the levels, although this extrapolation will often not be either useful or required, given the typical issues with the data set. If the attacker had no measurable effect on the defended system, then L = 1.00 is the appropriate rating. Assigning this value can be appropriate even if the attacker had some success against other areas, but not the system under consideration. As a real world example, when the Iranians attempted to shut down oil and gas production at Aramco, they disrupted a large number of support computers, but oil and gas production was not affected so the oil and gas production system still maintained L = 1.00.

Table A.2 Level of Functionality (L) Coding

Description of Level of Functionality Coding	*Level of Functionality (L)*
System is fully functional with no degradation	1.00
System is functional with negligible degradation	0.90
System is functional with minimal degradation	0.80
System is functional with little degradation	0.70
System is functional with some degradation	0.60
System has half of its normal functionality	0.50
System functional with significant disruption	0.40
System is functional with major disruption	0.30
System is minimally functional	0.20
System is barely functional	0.10
System is completely inoperative with no functionality	0.00

If the attacker only produced negligible disruption to the defended system, then L = 0.90 is appropriate. The attacker may have had limited success against peripheral or unimportant parts of the defended system, but it was barely noticeable. An example of this situation is the North Korean attacks of 2009 against U.S. Government websites. The attack slightly affected a few poorly-defended websites, such as some at the Department of Transportation, but the attack did not affect more important sites such as those at the White House and Department of Defense.

To assign L = 0.80, the defended system should be functional with only minimal degradation. You can see a real world example of this circumstance in the North Korean 2013 attacks against several South Korean banks. Although the banks suffered some systems degradation, they were able to continue to function with little disruption for their customers.

To assign L = 0.70, the defended system should be functional with little degradation. In the North Korean 2013 bank attacks, had South Korean banks been forced to close a few branches for a short period of time affecting a small percentage of their customers, then L = 0.70 would be appropriate. At L = 0.70 there has been disruption, but it is not yet of much significance.

To assign L = 0.60, the defended system should have experienced some disruption, but it is still more than 50% functional. For example, if a power grid were attacked and 75% of the power grid's customers still had power, that would represent L = 0.60. There was real disruption, but the system overall continued to function well above 50% effectiveness.

To assign L = 0.50, the defended system should be at approximately 50% effectiveness. This rating applies to easily quantified systems such as power grids and telecommunications, as well as systems that are more difficult to quantify. A real world example of a system at 50% is the South Korean broadcasters in 2013, who did not go off the air, but lost many of their support systems, which significantly affected their ability to produce material and cover news events.

To assign L = 0.40, the defended system should be experiencing significant disruption and be operating at less than 50% efficacy. For example, a command and control system that had lost the ability to communicate with more than 50% of its nodes, but still could effectively control some areas would be at L = 0.40.

To assign L = 0.30, the defended system should be experiencing major disruption. To return to the power grid example, a power grid that is only providing power to 25% of its customers would be at L = 0.30. The system still has some capability, but it is well less than 50% functional.

To assign L = 0.20, the defended system should be minimally functional. As a real world example, Georgia in 2008 could relay government communications, but only with great difficulty and through abnormal channels. The regular communications links between the Georgian government and its military forces were under significant attack and only functioning intermittently.

To assign L = 0.10, the defended system should be almost completely non-functional. Some elements of the system may still be operational, but as a complete system, it has barely any useful functionality.

To assign L = 0.00, the defended system has lost all ability to perform any part of its designed functionality. The support system network in the Aramco attack is an example of this situation where the attacker successfully destroyed the entire network, which Aramco had to rebuild completely from the ground up. In the power grid example, to assign an L = 0.00, the power grid should not be providing any power to any portion of its customers. This level of effectiveness is one of the important defensive inputs, the second is system criticality.

System Criticality (C)

System criticality (C) fulfills the same function on the defensive side that the weighting factor (W) does on the offensive side and operates in a similar way. System criticality brings into the model the importance of the various defended systems to the defender and it must add up to 1.00, or 100%, for a particular conflict under study. If there are multiple systems under attack, then their relative importance to the defender sets the values. If a defender has three systems under attack and one of them is twice as important as the other two then $C_1 = 0.50$, $C_2 = 0.25$, and $C_3 = 0.25$. The final measurement system input we should consider is a nation's reliance on cyberspace.

Reliance on Cyberspace (R)

Reliance on cyberspace (R) brings a relative measurement of the importance of cyberspace into each member of the dyad under consideration. It is a relative measurement to the two nations under consideration so a nation's R will change depending on who the other nation is that an analyst is comparing. For example, if nation A with a moderate level of reliance on cyberspace was paired with nation B, which was extremely dependent upon cyberspace, the values might be $R_A = 0.30$ and $R_B = 0.70$. However, if nation A was paired in a different conflict with nation C that had minimal reliance upon cyberspace then the values could be $R_A = 0.80$ and $R_C = 0.20$. Both R values in a dyad must always add up to 1.00 or 100%. The reason R is relative is that the output of the measurement system is also relative. Cyberspace superiority in a conflict is a relative measurement between two combatants, and their absolute reliance on cyberspace is not as important as their relative reliance on cyberspace.

Appendix B
Cyberspace Superiority Case Study Measurement

This appendix will provide the details of the inputs put into the measurement model developed in Chapter 5 for each case study to produce the Relative Cyberspace Superiority Index (RCSI) in each instance.

Russia versus Estonia 2007

Offensive Level of Success (S) and Weighting Factor (W) in Russia vs. Estonia 2007

The main Russian objective was to coerce Estonian into replacing a World War II Soviet memorial. The attacks occurred after the Estonian government moved the memorial and ethnic Russians in Estonia rioted.

The second Russian objective was to use the conflict with Estonia to demonstrate to the other former Soviet republics that they should give in to Russian demands. This objective was always in the background of the conflict given that Estonia had recently joined the EU and NATO over Russian objections. The Russians saw this situation as an opportunity to flex their muscles and demonstrate that there would be a price to pay for going against their wishes. Unfortunately for the Russians, their attempted intimidation was not very successful.

Russia made little progress toward its objectives. The statue stayed where it was and the Estonian government refused to back down so I set $S_1 = 0.00$. The Russians were also only minimally successful in intimidating neighboring states. The Baltic States continued to move further out of the Russian orbit and Georgia continued refuse to bow to Russian pressure, which led to the Georgian conflict a year later. Russia was minimally successful in at least showing that there would be a price for going against her interests and so I set $S_2 = 0.20$.

It was unclear exactly how to weight these objectives. On the one hand, from a geopolitical perspective, the location of the statue was not very important compared to the respect shown to Russian interests by neighboring countries. On the other hand, the statue became a powerful symbol that received an immense amount of attention in Russian media. I therefore assigned equal weight to both objectives and $W_1 = W_2 = 0.50$. The Russian offensive inputs into the cyberspace superiority measurement model are in Table B.1.

Table B.1 Russian Objectives in Estonian Attack

	Objective	*Level of Success (S)*	*Weighting Factor (W)*
1	Get the statue replaced	0.00	0.50
2	Intimidate other former Soviet states	0.20	0.50

These inputs yield $OCSI_{Russia}$ = 0.10, which represents the lowest level of offensive cyberspace superiority of the eight case studies. As Estonia did not attack any Russian targets, $OCSI_{Estonia}$ = 0.00.

Defensive Level of Functionality (L) and Criticality (C) in Russia vs. Estonia 2007

The second step in determining cyberspace superiority is to look at the defended systems and their functionality. Although there were a number of different systems attacked across Estonia, the two that were most important were government and banking websites.

The attacks initially affected the Estonian systems significantly, however, the defenders were able rapidly to reconstitute and so mitigated much of the damage. The attacks were simple Distributed Denial of Service (DDoS) with some website vandalism and the attackers did not target critical information such as banking transactions. However, over the period of time that the attacks continued, the disruptions were initially very severe until Estonian defenses became more effective. Both systems appear to have had similar levels of functionality over time. In accordance with the coding matrix in Appendix A, both systems were functional with major disruption so $L_1 = L_2 = 0.30$.

The banking system was more important in the daily life of Estonians than being able to access government websites. As a result, I weighted the banking system four times heavier than government websites, which gives $L_1 = 0.80$ and $L_2 = 0.20$. The defensive inputs are in Table B.2. With these inputs, $DCSI_{Estonia}$ = 0.30 and as there were no Estonian attacks to defend against, $DCSI_{Russia}$ = 0.00.

Table B.2 Estonian Systems Under Attack in 2007

	System	*Level of Functionality (L)*	*System Criticality (C)*
1	Banking system	0.30	0.80
2	Government Internet	0.30	0.20

Relative Cyberspace Superiority Index in Russia vs. Estonia

The final major input into the model is how important cyberspace was to both nations. In 2007 Estonia was one of the most highly wired and connected countries in the world earning it the nickname "e-stonia." If Russia had experienced the same level of Internet attacks, it would have been less disruptive for most Russian citizens because their dependence on cyberspace was much less. As a result, I set Estonia's reliance on cyberspace three times higher than Russia's reliance and assigned $R_{Russia} = 0.25$ and $R_{Estonia} = 0.75$.

All of these inputs combined gives:

$$OCSI_{Russia} = 0.10$$
$$DCSI_{Russia} = 0.00$$
$$R_{Russia} = 0.25$$
$$OCSI_{Estonia} = 0.00$$
$$DCSI_{Estonia} = 0.30$$
$$R_{Estonia} = 0.75$$

$CSI_{Russia} = 0.08$ and $CSI_{Estonia} = 0.23$, which yields:

$$RCSI_{Russia} = -0.15$$
$$RCSI_{Estonia} = 0.15$$

Russia versus Georgia 2008

Offensive Level of Success (S) and Weighting Factor (W) in Russia versus Georgia 2008

I utilized the methodology in Appendix A to code the Russian offensive objectives and weighting. I identified four Russian objectives, the first of which was to cut Georgian internal communications. The attacks were extremely successful in achieving this objective as it, "was almost impossible for citizens and officials alike to communicate about what was happening on the ground during the military invasion."[1] Russia also successfully shut down Georgian cell phone service, further reducing the capability of Georgians to communicate internally about what was happening.[2] Overall, the Russians were extremely, but not completely, successful in this area, which equates to $S_1 = 0.90$.

The next Russian objective was to sever Georgian communications with the international community, most likely in an attempt to get their overall campaign objectives achieved before the international community could bring much pressure to bear. Accordingly, they attacked the BBC and CNN with some success.[3] However, with the multiplicity of international communications, Russia was only minimally successful at cutting off information to the international community, which equates to $S_2 = 0.20$.

The third Russian objective was to shift customers from Georgian to Russian pipelines, I deduce from the order in which the Russians attacked areas of Georgia coupled with the pressure brought on Georgian pipelines through mysterious insurgent attacks in addition to the cyberspace attacks. There was some damage to Georgian credibility and some oil and gas producers did look for alternate routes, but there was not long term impact and the Russians were minimally successful against this objective with $S_3 = 0.20$.[4]

I can infer the final Russian objective from the banking target set. Georgian banks were flooded with fraudulent transactions, which caused international banks to cut Georgia off from the international banking system.[5] This action had the effect of shutting down Georgia's banking system for 10 days, which produced hardship for regular Georgians, but special concern for the Georgian elites who were most affected by banking disruption, and also had the most voice with the government.[6] Although technically successful, this attack was only minimally successful in accomplishing the Russian objective, as there was no discernable pressure by either elites or regular Georgians on the Georgian government. Accordingly, $S_4 = 0.20$.

I tilted the weighting of the Russian offensive objectives toward cutting internal Georgian communications. I did this because Russian operational success on the ground was of primary importance and if the Georgians had thrown back the Russians, none of the other objectives would have been very important. Accordingly, I gave cutting internal Georgian communication half of the weighting with $W_1 = 0.50$.

Cutting external Georgian communications and putting pressure on the Georgian government were less important objectives that received less emphasis in the attacks. I weighted these two objectives as twice the weight of the final objective of shifting customers to Russian pipelines. The final pipeline objective only received a limited amount of effort from the Russian cyber attackers and was peripheral to the key issues in the Russian and Georgian conflict. Therefore I set W_2 and $W_4 = 0.20$ each, and $W_3 = 0.10$. Table B.3 shows the Russian offensive inputs. When input into the measurement system, these objectives and weights yield $OCSI_{Russia} = 0.55$, which represents a successful offensive campaign by Russian forces and is the third highest OCSI of the eight cases I examined.

The Georgians were not completely idle on the offensive front, although they did not have nearly the success of the Russians. The Georgians launched two documented attacks of their own, one against South Ossetia in the week before the conflict. In addition, they attempted one known "counter-cyberspace" attack trying to make the Russian attack blowback on Russia by posting a counterfeit attack tool. This tool acted as if it was attacking Georgian sites while actually attacking Russian ones.[7]

Table B.3 Russian Offensive Objectives in Russian/Georgian Conflict

	Objective	*Level of Success (S)*	*Weighting Factor (W)*
1	Cut internal Georgian communications	0.90	0.50
2	Cut external Georgian communications	0.20	0.20
3	Shift customers to Russian pipelines	0.20	0.10
4	Punishment/pressure Georgia	0.20	0.20

Table B.4 Georgian Offensive Objectives in Russian/Georgian Conflict

	Objective	*Level of Success (S)*	*Weighting Factor (W)*
1	Degrade South Ossetian communications	0.10	0.50
2	Divert Russian cyber attacks to Russian targets	0.10	0.50

Both Georgian attacks had minimal impact against their targets and had almost no success against their objectives. Thus, in accordance with the coding methodology in Appendix A, both S_1 and $S_2 = 0.10$.

It was unclear how much importance the Georgians put into their two objectives of degrading South Ossetian communications and diverting Russian attacks. In the absence of good data, I gave each objective equal weighting so W_1 and $W_2 = 0.50$. In this particular case, the weighting has no real effect on the OSCI since S_1 and S_2 have the same value. Table B.4 gives the Georgian levels of success and weighting. This weighting yields an $OCSI_{Georgia} = 0.10$ and illustrates that Georgia had little offensive success in this conflict. The offensive side of cyberspace superiority is only half of the story; next, we turn to the defensive aspect.

Defensive Level of Functionality (L) and Criticality (C) in Russia versus Georgia 2008

On the defensive side of the conflict, the Russians appeared to have little difficulty dealing with Georgian attacks. Only two of their systems came under any Georgian attack at all: their conventional military command and control and their command and control of their cyberspace forces. There is no indication at all that the Georgians had any effect on Russian military command and control so $L_1 = 1.0$. As for the Russian command and control of their cyberspace forces, there was a counterfeit Georgian attack tool operative on some Russian bulletin boards used to control the Russian forces. Although there is no evidence that this counterfeit tool had any effect on Russian control of their cyberspace operators, it is likely that the Georgians fooled at least a few. I therefore set $L_2 = 0.90$ which represents negligible degradation in the Russian cyberspace command and control system.

Command and control of their conventional forces was overwhelmingly more important to the Russians than control of their cyberspace assets and I weighted it much heavier when calculating cyberspace superiority. Therefore I set $C_1 = 0.95$ and $C_2 = 0.05$. The Russian side's defensive inputs are in Table B.5.

Table B.5 Critical Russian Systems in Russian/Georgian Conflict

	System	*Level of Functionality (L)*	*System Criticality (C)*
1	Conventional military command and control	1.00	0.95
2	Cyberspace command and control	0.90	0.05

These inputs yield a $DCSI_{Russia} = 0.995$ and with rounding to two decimal places, $DCSI_{Russia} = 1.00$, which represents total success for the Russians on the defensive side. The Georgians were far less successful in their defensive efforts.

The Georgians were very ineffective in defending their systems, which contributed to their lack of cyberspace superiority. Georgian cyberspace defenses fell into two broad categories, normal firewall type defenses, and system resilience. The Georgians had normal firewalls and intrusion detection systems in place. These systems were not adequate to stop even the initial wave of Russian attacks. The Georgians sought technical assistance from Estonia and other NATO countries to enhance their defenses but it soon became apparent that they were unable to defend successfully their systems. Georgia then shifted to a reconstitution and resilience mode where they moved their key websites to servers in Estonia and the United States. Although this attempt was marginally more successful, they still had great difficulty in keeping their websites accessible.[8] The Russian attackers overcame this attempted block through persistent and simultaneous attacks from multiple botnets, or groups of remotely controlled computers. At one point, the website of the Georgian president was under attack from 500 IP addresses simultaneously.[9] I have captured the success of these Russian attacks in the Georgian defensive inputs into the measurement system.

The attackers severely curtailed Georgian internal communications with all Georgian cell phone service as well as much of the e-mail system collapsing. As a result I coded the system as barely functional, which equates to $L_1 = 0.10$.

Although international communications came under pressure, Georgia was still able to get out some elements of its message. It is clear that international communications were neither completely functional nor completely nonfunctional, but I was unable to find any data detailed enough to develop specific percentages. In the absence of comprehensive data, I assigned $L_2 = 0.50$.

The banking system collapsed completely during the conflict. This makes coding simple, and $L_3 = 0.00$.

The Georgian government lost most of its ability to communicate with its various components through cyberspace and telecommunications. In accordance with the coding matrix in Appendix A, the communications system was minimally functional since some orders still got through and so $L_4 = 0.20$.

Finally, the Georgian infrastructure that came under attack experienced disruption but I was unable to find detailed information about how much. In the absence of detailed data, I estimated a 50% degradation and set $L_5 = 0.50$.

In weighting the system criticality of the Georgian cyberspace systems that came under attack, internal communication was the most important. The lack of internal communication greatly hampered Georgian conventional forces as they attempted to meet the Russian attack. Had the Georgian military been able to mount any sort of effective defense, it would have purchased time and maneuver space for the Georgian government to involve the international community and weakened the bargaining position of the Russians. Accordingly, I set the criticality of the internal communications system at $C_1 = 0.50$ to give it the same weight as the other four systems combined.

Table B.6 Critical Georgian Systems in Russian/Georgian Conflict

	System	*Level of Functionality (L)*	*System Criticality (C)*
1	Georgian internal communications	0.10	0.50
2	International communications	0.50	0.20
3	Banking	0.00	0.10
4	Government communication	0.20	0.10
5	Georgian infrastructure	0.50	0.10

The next most important system was international communications. Had the Georgians been able to communicate clearly to the outside world, they could potentially have been able to rally support and international pressure to their assistance. Increased international support would have provided more benefit to the Georgians than improved access to their other cyberspace systems so I gave international communications twice the weight of the remaining systems with $C_2 = 0.20$.

The remaining three systems of banking, government communication, and infrastructure I gave equal weighting at $C_3 = C_4 = C_5 = 0.10$. Although each of these systems was important, none of them had the impact of international or internal communications on the outcome of the conflict. The Georgian systems that came under attack are in Table B.6. With these inputs, the measurement system produces a $DCSI_{Georgia} = 0.22$. This is on the low end of the eight case studies and represents a relatively unsuccessful defense.

Relative Cyberspace Superiority Index in Russia versus Georgia

Cyberspace systems were of approximately equal importance to both parties in the Russian/Georgian conflict so I set both R to 0.50. There was not a clear distinction between Russia and Georgia in what they use cyberspace for, or how reliant they were upon it.

When I enter all of the previous information into the RCSI equation, it yields:

$OCSI_{Russia} = 0.55$
$DCSI_{Russia} = 1.00$
$R_{Russia} = 0.50$
$OCSI_{Georgia} = 0.10$
$DCSI_{Georgia} = 0.22$
$R_{Georgia} = 0.50$

$CSI_{Russia} = 0.77$ and $CSI_{Georgia} = 0.16$, which yields:

$RCSI_{Russia} = 0.61$
$RCSI_{Georgia} = -0.61$

North Korea versus United States and South Korea in 2009

Level of Success (S) and Weighting Factor (W) in 2009 North Korean Attacks

As North Korea did not take responsibility for the attack, I have to infer their objectives from the target set. All of the attacks were Distributed Denial of Service (DDoS) attacks which attack access to Internet based websites or services, but do not access information on the targeted systems.[10] The targets included government sites in the United States and South Korea as well as the party website of the conservative party in South Korea, and finally what can best be characterized as economic targets in South Korea and the U.S. such as South Korean banks and the NASDAQ stock exchange.[11] The objective of the attacker appeared to be to damage U.S. and South Korean governmental and economic websites. Inferring what North Korea intended to gain from the attacks if they were successful is more challenging. Possibilities range from simply trying to damage adversaries, to continuing the normal cycle of escalation, to establishing Kim Jong Un as a military leader who could damage North Korea's enemies.

The attacks on U.S. government websites were only marginally successful. Major targets such as the Pentagon and White House successfully defended themselves with no loss of capability. Some, less well-defended federal agencies such as the Department of Transportation and the FTC experienced some difficulty, but the overall effect on the U.S. government was barely noticeable.[12] In accordance with the coding matrix in Appendix A, I therefore assigned $S_1 = 0.10$.

The attacks on the South Korean government websites were more successful with the official Presidential website and the defense ministry paralyzed during the initial attacks.[13] Some of the South Korean websites under attack were able to continue functioning so I set the overall $S_2 = 0.50$.

U.S. economic sites experienced little disruption while some South Korean banking sites and an online auction system experienced difficulty.[14] As the North Koreans achieved almost no success against the U.S. economic sites I set $S_3 = 0.10$. The attackers had slightly more success against the South Korean economic sites and achieved minimal success against this objective so I set $S_4 = 0.20$.

The relative weights were set to emphasize the government sites rather than the economic ones as that was where the initial attacks focused. The attacks shifted to economic sites in the second wave after the attackers appeared not to get the results for which they had been hoping.[15] I started by giving South Korea and the United States half of the weighting, then I weighed each nation's government sites at four times the weight of the economic sites. I give the resulting weights in the objective Table B.7. These inputs yield an $OCSI_{\text{North Korea}} = 0.27$, which is the third lowest of the eight cases. South Korea and the United States had no offensive objectives so $OCSI_{\text{US/South Korea}} = 0.00$.

Table B.7 North Korean Offensive Objectives in 2009

	Objective	*Level of Success (S)*	*Weighting Factor (W)*
1	Shut down U.S. government websites	0.10	0.40
2	Shut down South Korean government websites	0.50	0.40
3	Shut down U.S. economic websites	0.10	0.10
4	Shut down South Korean economic websites	0.20	0.10

Level of Functionality (L) and Criticality (C) in 2009 North Korean Attacks

The next step is to determine the defensive inputs for the cyberspace superiority measurement system. On the defensive side, the United States and South Korea were very active. Computer security firms bolstered the systems under attack, attacking IP addresses were cut off, and South Korea went so far as have the Korean Communications Commission (KCC) order service providers to deny access to 30,000 South Korean computers that were part of the attacking botnet.[16] These defensive measures were largely successful.

The attacks against U.S. government websites were largely ineffectual, and the only sites affected at all were not critical ones. Therefore in accordance with the coding matrix in Appendix A, I set $L_1 = 0.90$.

The attacks against South Korean government websites were more effective. However, the attacks had relatively short duration due to effective countermeasures by the defenders and the attacks only significantly affected some government sites so I assigned $L_2 = 0.50$.

U.S. economic websites continued at full functionality during the period of the attacks. Therefore, deciding on coding is relatively simple and $L_3 = 1.00$.

A few, relatively unimportant South Korean economic websites experienced some minor issues. However, the overall system experienced negligible degradation and $L_4 = 0.90$.

To weight the system criticality of the various systems, I mirrored the same technique I used in the offensive inputs of giving half the weight to each nation, then weighting the government systems as four times the weight of the economic systems. The results are shown in Table B.8. With these inputs, $DCSI_{US/South\ Korea} = 0.75$, which represents the third highest DCSI of the eight

Table B.8 Critical U.S. and South Korean Systems in 2009

	System	*Level of Functionality (L)*	*System Criticality (C)*
1	U.S. government websites	0.90	0.40
2	South Korean government websites	0.50	0.40
3	U.S. economic websites	1.00	0.10
4	South Korean economic websites	0.90	0.10

cases. As South Korea and the United States were not attacking North Korean systems, $DCSI_{North\ Korea} = 0.00$.

Relative Cyberspace Superiority Index in 2009 North Korean Attacks

North Korea does not rely nearly as heavily on cyberspace as the U.S. and South Korea. There is minimal cyberspace connectivity in North Korea, and in 2009 it was only for government use. Accordingly I set $R_{North\ Korea} = 0.05$ and $R_{US/South\ Korea} = 0.95$. All of these inputs give:

$$OCSI_{North\ Korea} = 0.27$$
$$DCSI_{North\ Korea} = 0.0$$
$$R_{North\ Korea} = 0.05$$
$$OCSI_{US/South\ Korea} = 0.0$$
$$DCSI_{US/South\ Korea} = 0.75$$
$$R_{US/South\ Korea} = 0.95$$

$CSI_{North\ Korea} = 0.26$ and $CSI_{US/South\ Korea} = 0.71$, which yields:

$$RCSI_{North\ Korea} = -0.46$$
$$RCSI_{US/South\ Korea} = 0.46$$

Stuxnet

Offensive Level of Success (S) and Weighting Factor (W) in the Stuxnet Case

Based on American and Israeli policy and messaging, it appears that the overall objective of Stuxnet was to slow the Iranian nuclear program to provide time for sanctions and negotiation to solve the problem. Thus, the first objective was to delay enrichment activities at Natanz as much as possible by sabotaging the enrichment system. It also appears the attackers wanted effects beyond temporary disruption.

The attackers did not just want to stop current enrichment activities; they wanted physically to destroy equipment to prevent future enrichment. As evidence of this, it appears that Stuxnet escaped "into the wild" because the attackers began to utilize a more aggressive attack method when they were not achieving a high enough level of destruction.[17] It appears that the more aggressive version of Stuxnet got out in the wild when an Iranian scientist inadvertently interrupted Stuxnet in the middle of a process. This interruption resulted in Stuxnet spreading beyond the nuclear system the designers intended it exclusively to infect.[18] This mistake resulted in the attacker's failure to accomplish their third objective of secrecy.

A third objective was clearly to remain undetected as long as possible. One of the most impressive aspects of Stuxnet was that it not only destroyed centrifuges, it made it look like the centrifuges were dying of "natural causes." Stuxnet periodically changed the speed of the centrifuges in a specific manner designed to produce eventual failure, but continued to report to the controller that everything was fine and the centrifuge was spinning exactly as it should.[19] Part of the objective of Stuxnet was not just to delay, but also to confuse and mystify the Iranians as to why their centrifuges were not working, which would produce even more delay.[20] This was only possible as long as the weapon itself remained hidden.

The attackers only had mixed success against these objectives. On the one hand, it appears that there was damage done to Iranian centrifuges. Iran decommissioned and replaced about 1,000 IR-1 centrifuges at the Natanz Fuel Enrichment Plan in late 2009 or early 2010.[21] Stuxnet could easily have been responsible for the destruction of these centrifuges. It is also verifiable that while the Iranians designed Natanz for 50,000 centrifuges, there were only about one fifth of that number running after ten years of work.[22] On the other hand, the Iranians apparently responded to the reduction in efficiency by significantly ramping up the number of centrifuges they were running. The Iranians managed to increase their daily production by 20%, although the Institute for Science and International Security (ISIS) report considered this a significant underperformance given the number of new centrifuges the Iranians added.[23]

The delay in the enrichment program was significant, but it also was not everything the Stuxnet attackers were hoping to accomplish. The estimates of how long Stuxnet delayed the Iranian nuclear program vary from about one to three years, which still represents significant success.[24] Therefore, I coded $S_1 = 0.50$ in accordance with the coding methodology in Appendix A.

Based on the number of centrifuges taken offline and replaced at Natanz while the attack was operable, it is clear that Stuxnet was at least partially successful in destroying equipment. However, it appears that the destruction was not sufficient to stop completely the Iranian program as the Iranians introduced more than enough centrifuges to compensate and actually increased their production. The Iranian increase in production does not automatically imply that the attackers were unsuccessful. Stuxnet evidently affected uranium production significantly, as the Iranians should have been able to produce far more enriched uranium than they did with the number of centrifuges they were operating. Thus, Stuxnet's success against destroying equipment is mixed with $S_2 = 0.50$.

The final objective for Stuxnet was to remain hidden. Unfortunately for the attackers, Stuxnet was not only found by the defenders, but also got out into the wild where numerous researchers took it apart and analyzed it. Therefore I set $S_3 = 0.0$ as a complete failure of the objective. This coding might seem unduly harsh as Stuxnet did remain undetected for two to three years, but the decision to "swing for the fences" resulted in the attack having a shorter life span than desired.[25] Once researchers had discovered Stuxnet, the Iranians were able to get their program back on track.

As delaying the Iranian nuclear program was the main strategic purpose behind Stuxnet, I gave it as much weight as the other two objectives combined. Therefore, I set $W_1 = 0.50$.

Table B.9 U.S./Israeli Objectives with Stuxnet versus Iran

	Objective	*Level of Success (S)*	*Weighting Factor (W)*
1	Delay current Iranian nuclear enrichment	0.50	0.50
2	Destroy Iranian nuclear enrichment equipment	0.50	0.30
3	Remain undetected	0.00	0.20

Of the two remaining objectives, doing damage was apparently more of a priority than staying hidden. I can deduce this from the fact that Stuxnet was "torqued-up" in order to do more damage despite the fact that the upgrade would increase the risk of exposure.[26] Accordingly I set $W_2 = 0.3$ and $W_3 = 0.2$. The inputs on the offensive side of the Stuxnet attack are shown in Table B.9.

Given these inputs, $OCSI_{US/Israel} = 0.40$. This value is in the lower range of OCSIs in the case studies among those nations who were actively attacking. As the Iranians were not actively attacking as part of this conflict during this timeframe, I set $OCSI_{Iran} = 0.00$.

Defensive Level of Functionality (L) and Criticality (C) in the Stuxnet Case

The next step in analyzing the Stuxnet attacks is to determine the defensive inputs for the cyberspace superiority measurement model. The Iranians expected that their facilities would come under attack and so worked hard to protect their systems as much as possible. It is reasonable to assume that the Iranians had protected the Internet-enabled computers in the facilities with firewalls and intrusion systems. Given the high security present in the facility, coupled with the suspicions of sabotage, it is also likely that there were significant restrictions and controls on users. One of the methods relied upon by the Iranians to block attackers was reconstitution and recovery. Despite losing at least a thousand centrifuges and a major reduction in efficiency of production, they brought in many more centrifuges and actually managed to increase production.[27] Additionally, in Supervisory Control and Data Acquisition (SCADA) systems such as the one attacked by Stuxnet, air gapping is normally a key defense.

It also appears that the controllers running the centrifuges were air gapped and not directly connected to the Internet.[28] The structure and design of Stuxnet confirms the Iranian air gap, as the attackers clearly designed Stuxnet to jump an air gap utilizing multiple methods. Stuxnet has four propagation methods that include flash drives and various wireless and wired network attacks.[29] The designers of Stuxnet also used persistence to continue to hammer away at the air gap. Security researchers have found several versions of Stuxnet dating back as far as 2007 and it appears that the designers continued to make changes to increase the effectiveness of the attack.[30] Although the designers of Stuxnet were after the

SCADA system, they understood that the road to the SCADA system lay through the support system.

The two systems Iran was trying to defend in Natanz were the support system network of computers and the SCADA control system. The support system network consisted of the computers in the facility used to support the enrichment process and was the system Stuxnet needed to infiltrate to get to the SCADA system. The SCADA controllers ran the actual process, which was vital to the mission of the facility.

It appears that the attackers had riddled the support computer system with Stuxnet, which was also extremely hard for the Iranians to remove, as a single infected device missed by the defenders would rapidly infect the entire network all over again. The purpose of the support system was to keep the SCADA system operational and functioning. Instead of providing defense and support, the support system was the avenue through which the SCADA system was attacked, thus I set $L_1 = 0.00$.

It is harder to assess the level of functionality of the Natanz SCADA system, as there is no reliable, unclassified data available. It does appear that the Iranians had a very difficult time getting Stuxnet out of their systems and they temporarily shut down enrichment operations at Natanz in November 2010.[31] I have to balance this data with the fact that overall enrichment numbers continued to rise over time due to a massive influx of new centrifuges so the system maintained at least some capability. However, given that the SCADA system was under the control of an attacker who was actively working to destroy centrifuges while allowing just enough enrichment to remain undetected, I set the level of functionality of the system as barely functional with $L_2 = 0.10$.

Of the two systems, the SCADA system was the heart of the uranium enrichment process and the support system was less important in the day-to-day process. I put four times the weight on the SCADA system than the support system and so set $C_1 = 0.20$ and $C_2 = 0.80$. The inputs on the defensive side are shown in Table B.10. Given these inputs, $DCSI_{Iran} = 0.08$. This is a very low level of defensive cyberspace superiority when compared to the other case studies. As the Iranians were not directly counterattacking the U.S. and Israel had a $DCSI_{US/Israel} = 0.00$.

Table B.10 Iranian Systems in Stuxnet Attack

	System	*Level of Functionality (L)*	*System Criticality (C)*
1	Support system network	0.00	0.20
2	SCADA control system	0.10	0.80

Relative Cyberspace Superiority Index in the Stuxnet Case

I set $R_{US/Israel} = 0.75$ and $R_{Iran} = 0.25$ based on the greater level of importance of cyberspace in U.S. and Israeli society. The complete list of variables is as follows:

$OCSI_{US/Israel} = 0.40$
$DCSI_{US/Israel} = 0.00$
$R_{US/Israel} = 0.75$
$OCSI_{Iran} = 0.00$
$DCSI_{Iran} = 0.08$
$R_{Iran} = 0.25$

$CSI_{US/Israel} = 0.10$ and $CSI_{Iran} = 0.02$, which yields:

$RCSI_{US/Israel} = 0.08$
$RCSI_{Iran} = -0.08$

It is interesting to note that giving Stuxnet full credit for remaining undetected and setting $S_3 = 1.0$ only changes the overall $RCSI_{US/Israel}$ slightly to 0.13. Either way, this RCSI represents a very low level of cyberspace superiority by the U.S. and Israel, which makes sense given that despite whatever damage the attackers did, Iran's production of enriched uranium appears to have actually increased slightly.

These numbers represent a "best case" scenario for the U.S. and Israel. Because the level of success is not clear, I also ran a case with:

Iranian $L_1 = 0.50$
Iranian $L_2 = 0.50$

This scenario represents a more successful defense by Iran with them maintaining 50% effectiveness in both their support and SCADA systems. It is not likely that the Iranians achieved more than 50% system functionality given the evidence of disruption discussed previously. In this case, the variables become:

$OCSI_{US/Israel} = 0.40$
$DCSI_{US/Israel} = 0.00$
$R_{US/Israel} = 0.75$
$OCSI_{Iran} = 0.00$
$DCSI_{Iran} = 0.50$
$R_{Iran} = 0.25$

$CSI_{US/Israel} = 0.10$ and $CSI_{Iran} = 0.13$, which yields:

$RCSI_{US/Israel} = -0.03$
$RCSI_{Iran} = 0.03$

In this case, Iran has a very slight cyberspace superiority. It appears that Stuxnet most likely represented a low level of cyberspace superiority for the U.S. and Israel, as they achieved some of their objectives, but it is possible that it represented something closer to parity with neither side having superiority.

North Korea versus South Korea March 2011 Distributed Denial of Service

Level of Success (S) and Weighting Factor (W) in North Korean 2011 DDoS Attacks

The attacks were an odd combination of technical sophistication and brute force. The attackers deliberately destroyed and wiped their botnets at the end of the 10-day attack window, which is very unusual for any sort of hacktivist or criminal organization. Those organizations protect their botnets to keep them for future use. The North Koreans instead went to great lengths to encrypt their botnets at multiple levels, then wipe them to make it more difficult for researchers to track. However, the weapon itself was an unsophisticated DDoS. McAfee Security sees this combination as evidence that the attacker's intent was to test the defender's response capabilities.[32]

The first objective appears to have been to test South Korean response and mitigation capabilities. The North Koreans were completely successful in this objective and were able to monitor the South Korean response. I therefore set $S_1 = 1.00$.

As the targets of the attacks were websites located in South Korea, shutting down those websites appears to have been an objective as well. That portion of the attack was only minimally effective and most of the targeted websites were able to continue operating so I set $S_2 = 0.20$.

Given the continuing animosity between North and South Korea, North Korea is always looking for any way to embarrass or damage South Korea, which makes that a likely final objective. Unlike the 2009 attack, every site attacked was physically located in South Korea. There was not much press attention paid to these attacks and the South Korean response came across as competent and effective so this portion of the attack was also minimally successful and I set $S_3 = 0.20$.

I find the McAfee argument that this attack was primarily about reconnaissance compelling, so I placed the preponderance of the weight on that objective. I put four times the weight on the reconnaissance objective as the other two objectives combined, which gives $W_1 = 0.80$. I placed equal weight on the remaining two objectives, which gives $W_2 = W_3 = 0.10$. The offensive inputs for cyberspace superiority are shown in Table B.11. These inputs yield an $OCSI_{\text{North Korea}} = 0.84$. As South Korea and U.S. Forces Korea had no offensive objectives, $OCSI_{\text{South Korean}} = 0.00$.

Table B.11 North Korean Offensive Objectives in 2011 DDoS Attack

	Objective	*Level of Success (S)*	*Weighting Factor (W)*
1	Determine South Korean response and recovery capabilities	1.00	0.80
2	Shut down South Korean websites	0.20	0.10
3	Embarrass South Korean government	0.20	0.10

Level of Functionality (L) and Criticality (C) in North Korean 2011 DDoS Attacks

The second step in determining who had how much cyberspace superiority is to develop the defensive inputs. On the defensive side, South Korea immediately launched mitigation measures and was able to utilize previously installed digital "bunkers" that were IP addresses set aside for organizations that came under DDoS attack.[33] The North Koreans attempted to make it difficult to respond to the attacks as, "several steps were taken to ensure that the mission was executed without interruption, within the predefined attack window—and following, ensuring that all vehicles of attack would be destroyed, thus limiting forensic analysis."[34] However, within a few days, McAfee and others were able to "detect, reverse engineer, and mitigate the attacks."[35]

The disruptions for South Korea and the U.S. military were short lived and both systems maintained a high level of functionality. The South Korean sites were slightly more effected by the attacks so I coded them as functional with minimal degradation and set $L_1 = 0.80$. The U.S. military sites only experienced negligible degradation and so $L_2 = 0.90$.

The North Koreans attacked a far greater number of South Korean sites compared to a relative handful of U.S. military sites so I weighted the South Korean sites much more heavily. I placed 90% of the weight on the South Korean sites and only 10% on the U.S. military sites in South Korea. Accordingly, I set $C_1 = 0.90$ and $C_2 = 0.10$. The defended systems are in Table B.12. With these inputs $DCSI_{\text{South Korea}} = 0.81$, which is the most successful level of defense achieved among the eight case studies. North Korea did not come under attack and so $DCSI_{\text{North Korea}} = 0.00$.

Table B.12 Critical U.S. and South Korean Systems in 2011 DDoS Attack

	System	*Level of Functionality (L)*	*System Criticality (C)*
1	South Korean government and military websites	0.80	0.90
2	U.S. military websites	0.90	0.10

Relative Cyberspace Superiority Index in North Korean 2011 DDoS Attacks

North Korea does not rely nearly as heavily on cyberspace as the U.S. and South Korea so $R_{\text{North Korea}} = 0.05$ and $R_{\text{South Korea}} = 0.95$. All of these inputs give:

$$OCSI_{\text{North Korea}} = 0.84$$
$$DCSI_{\text{North Korea}} = 0.00$$
$$R_{\text{North Korea}} = 0.05$$
$$OCSI_{\text{South Korea}} = 0.00$$

$DCSI_{South\ Korea} = 0.77$
$R_{South\ Korea} = 0.95$

$CSI_{North\ Korea} = 0.80$ and $CSI_{South\ Korea} = .77$, which yields:

$RCSI_{North\ Korea} = 0.03$
$RCSI_{South\ Korea} = -0.03$

North Korea versus South Korea April 2011 Bank Attack

Level of Success (S) and Weighting Factor (W) in North Korean 2011 Bank Attack

Once again, I will infer the North Korean objectives from the attack itself. The attack was specific to Nonghyup bank rather than being a wider attack against multiple banks or infrastructure. If the North Korean's objective was to do the maximum damage and have the greatest disruption on the South Korean economy, they could have also launched DDoS attacks against other economic targets, even if they did not have the internal system access at other banks to do more destructive attacks. I therefore deduced a narrow primary objective of disrupting Nonghyup bank. North Korea will never pass up the opportunity to embarrass South Korea as well so I set that as a secondary objective.

North Korea was very successful in their objective to disrupt Nonghyup bank. On 12 April 2011, about half of the servers at Nonghyup bank crashed which resulted in approximately 30 million people who were unable to make online financial transactions or use the bank's ATMs.[36] The attackers launched the incident by implanting the weapon onto a Nonghyup subcontractor's laptop.[37] When the employee connected the laptop to the bank's network, the weapon implanted itself quietly throughout the network and waited for a preset triggering time. According to South Korean official Kim You-Kyung, when the weapon activated, it attempted to destroy the entire server system.[38] Some portions of the bank retained functionality and the defenders mitigated the attack over time, but overall the North Koreans were very successful in their attempt to disrupt the bank. Accordingly, I set $S_1 = 0.80$.

The North Koreans were also more successful against their secondary objective of embarrassing the South Korean government than they had been in the past. This attack received far more press attention and focus by the South Korean people than previous attacks. This attack affected slightly more than half of the population of South Korea, which stands at approximately 50 million. However, as the South Koreans mitigated the attack fairly quickly, it did not set up a "Watergate" type inquiry or bring down any politicians or the government of South Korea. I therefore coded $S_2 = 0.50$.

Because the North Koreans directed this attack specifically at Nonghyup bank without additional DDoS attacks that were clearly within the North Koreans' capability, I gave more weight to the bank objective. If the primary purpose of the attack was to embarrass the South Korean government, North Korea could have

Table B.13 North Korean Offensive Objectives in 2011 Bank Attack

	Objective	*Level of Success (S)*	*Weighting Factor (W)*
1	Disrupt Nonghyup bank	0.80	0.80
2	Embarrass South Korean government	0.50	0.20

added additional DDoS attacks, which would have increased the pressure considerably. Therefore, I weighed the bank objective as four times the weight of embarrassing the South Korean government. I set $W_1 = 0.80$ and $W_2 = 0.20$. The offensive inputs are shown in Table B.13.

These inputs give a respectable $OCSI_{North\ Korea} = 0.74$, which is the second highest among the eight case studies. South Korea did not attack any North Korean systems so $OCSI_{South\ Korea} = 0.00$.

Level of Functionality (L) and Criticality (C) in North Korean 2011 Bank Attack

The attackers did significant damage to Nonghyup bank who lost half their servers in the initial attack. 30 million account holders were unable to access their accounts for three days and 310,000 customers filed complaints with 1000 demanding compensation.[39] Some aspects of the Nonghyup system did manage to continue operation, but I coded the overall system as minimally functional, which gives $L_1 = 0.20$.

As Nonghyup bank was the only institution to come under attack, the system criticality is simple at $C_1 = 1.00$. The defensive inputs are in shown Table B.14. These inputs yielded a $DCSI_{South\ Korea} = 0.20$. North Korean systems did not come under attack and so $DCSI_{North\ Korea} = 0.00$.

Table B.14 Critical South Korean System in 2011 Bank Attack

	System	*Level of Functionality (L)*	*System Criticality (C)*
1	Nonghyup Bank	0.20	1.00

Relative Cyberspace Superiority Index in North Korean 2011 Bank Attack

North Korea does not rely nearly as heavily on cyberspace as South Korea so $R_{North\ Korea} = 0.05$ and $R_{South\ Korea} = 0.95$. All of these inputs give:

$OCSI_{North\ Korea} = 0.74$
$DCSI_{North\ Korea} = 0.00$
$R_{North\ Korea} = 0.05$
$OCSI_{South\ Korea} = 0.00$

$DCSI_{South\ Korea} = 0.20$
$R_{South\ Korea} = 0.95$

$CSI_{North\ Korea} = 0.70$ and $CSI_{South\ Korea} = 0.19$, which yields:

$RCSI_{North\ Korea} = 0.51$
$RCSI_{South\ Korea} = -0.51$

Aramco

Offensive Level of Success (S) and Weighting Factor (W) in the Aramco Case

One important clue to the Iranian objectives in the Aramco case is the high level of destruction intended by the weapon. Shamoon attempted to disable computers by erasing their master boot records.[40] If an attacker succeeds in deleting this information, the computer system cannot start. The computer is disabled and the data on the hard drive is un-accessible without significant effort by specialists. This attack could have been much more serious than one that simply requires reloading software on computers. Had the attacker been successful in getting to the computers running industrial processes, any process from pumping to refining could have gone haywire with catastrophic consequences. The type of attack gives insight into the most likely objective of the Aramco attack.

Given the scope of the attack, the state of relations in the Persian Gulf, and the mechanisms built into Shamoon, the most likely goal of the attackers was to disrupt Saudi-Arabian oil and gas production. The groups that did claim the attack, which were likely Iranian front groups, were not very clear on why they were attacking or what they intended to accomplish. According to Abdullah al-Saadan, Aramco's vice-president for corporate planning, "The main target in this attack was to stop the flow of oil and gas to local and international markets."[41]

Another possible motive was to damage the support system computers that the attacker infected with Shamoon. I needed to consider this objective, as the support system is the one that Shamoon ended up affecting. Although the attack appeared successful, it was only successful against one of the two objectives.

In some ways, the Aramco attack was a great success as the attacker damaged 30,000 computers, however, the attacker was unable to interfere with production. It appears that the Iranians attempted to get past the air gap to the production computers. However, this attempt failed and no production computers were infected. Coding the inputs in this case is straightforward. Because the production system remained untouched, petroleum production was unaffected by the attack and $S_1 = 0.00$, as a complete failure. At the opposite end of the spectrum, Shamoon disrupted 30,000 support system computers and brought the entire support system to a complete halt. Aramco appears to have been mostly off-line for about two weeks from 15 to 28 August 2012.[42] Therefore, I assigned $S_2 = 1.00$, as a complete success. With such wide disparity in success between the two objectives, weighting becomes even more important.

Table B.15 Iranian Objectives in Aramco Attack

	Objective	*Level of Success (S)*	*Weighting Factor (W)*
1	Interrupt Aramco petroleum production	0.00	0.80
2	Damage Aramco support network	1.00	0.20

Success against the petroleum production system would have brought Iran far greater strategic benefits than what they got from the support system attack; therefore, I weighted the petroleum production objective much more highly. I assigned four times the weight to disrupting petroleum production as I did to disrupting the support system. Thus $W_1 = 0.80$ and $W_2 = 0.20$. The offensive inputs in the Aramco attack are shown in Table B.15.

With these inputs $OCSI_{Iran} = 0.20$, which represents a low level of success and cyberspace superiority. This OCSI is the second lowest of the eight cases I examined. On the Saudi Arabian side, the lack of offensive cyberspace objectives yields an $OCSI_{Saudi\ Arabia} = 0.00$. Aramco's defenders had some effective tools in place to protect their systems and now we turn to the defensive inputs.

Defensive Level of Functionality (L) and Criticality (C) in the Aramco Case

The next main input into the cyberspace superiority measurement model is the level of functionality and criticality of the defended systems. Aramco had significant defenses in place to protect their systems. According to Al-Saadan, the attack did not succeed because, "we had in place the processes and systems to manage, as well as sufficient incident response and business continuity plans to deal with such an attack."[43] He continued and said, "Built-in system architecture and protections for the primary components of our computer network, including firewalls and segmentation, meant that all our core operations continued smoothly."[44] Although their "core operations" ran smoothly, they were offline for approximately two weeks so there was significant impact to their support system as noted earlier. This data gives straightforward coding of the defensive inputs.

As the petroleum production computer system appeared to be untouched by the attack and operating at full efficiency, I coded $L_1 = 1.00$. Although Aramco had motive to cover up any damage done to their production systems, there was no drop in production apparent to analysts so it appears that Shamoon truly did not reach the production system. This outcome is in stark contrast to that for the support system.

Aramco's support computer system completely collapsed for about two weeks and so the coding of its functionality is relatively simple as well. I coded the support system at $L_2 = 0.00$. Due to the large disparity in functionality between the two systems under consideration, once again the weighting largely determined the output.

Table B.16 Saudi Arabian Systems in Aramco Attack

	System	*Level of Functionality (L)*	*System Criticality (C)*
1	Petroleum production system	1.00	0.80
2	Support network system	0.00	0.20

From a defensive perspective, the petroleum production computer system was far more important to Aramco than their support system. I therefore gave it a similar weight as on the offensive side and I weighted the petroleum production system at four times the importance of the support system. This gives $C_1 = 0.80$ and $C_2 = 0.20$. Although the damage to the support system was embarrassing, it did not cause investors to flee Aramco or delay the delivery of any of their product, which would likely have been the case if the attack had affected production. The Saudi Arabian systems inputs in the Aramco attack are shown in Table B.16.

These inputs combined yield a $DCSI_{Saudi\ Arabia} = 0.80$. This represents a very successful defense and is the second highest DCSI of the eight cases I analyzed. Iran did not have to defend their systems from Saudi Arabia during this attack and so $DCSI_{Iran} = 0.00$.

Relative Cyberspace Superiority Index in the Aramco Case

Iran and Saudi Arabia are dependent on cyberspace at roughly the same level so R_{Iran} and $R_{Saudi\ Arabia}$ were each set to 0.50. The inputs and final result was:

$OCSI_{Iran} = 0.20$
$DCSI_{Iran} = 0.00$
$R_{Iran} = 0.50$
$OCSI_{Saudi\ Arabia} = 0.0$
$DCSI_{Saudi\ Arabia} = 0.25$
$R_{Saudi\ Arabia} = 0.50$

$CSI_{Iran} = 0.10$ and $CSI_{Saudi\ Arabia} = 0.40$, which yields:

$RCSI_{Iran} = -0.30$
$RCSI_{Saudi\ Arabia} = 0.30$

North Korea versus South Korea April 2013 Attack

Level of Success (S) and Weighting Factor (W) in North Korean April 2013 Attack

To determine the North Korean objectives, I first examined their targets. Dark Seoul targeted three television broadcasters, YTN, MBC and KBS as well as three banks, Shinhan, Nonghyup, and Jeju as well as the telecommunications operator LG U+.[45]

The type of attack also provides evidence of what the attackers were seeking. Dark Seoul was very destructive and the attacker erased the master boot records of the 48,000 computers infected. The attacker also utilized other techniques clearly intended to affect both Windows and Linux systems to broaden the attack's effects as much as possible.[46]

Based on Dark Seoul's targeting, the first objective of the North Koreans was to disrupt the South Korean banking system. However, Dark Seoul's bank attacks were only minimally successful. Some services were temporarily blocked, but restored after two hours, while some banks under attack suffered no damage at all.[47] I therefore set $S_1 = 0.20$.

The attacks against the broadcaster's computer networks were more successful although they did not force any of the stations off the air. The broadcasters lost most of their internal networks so I set $S_2 = 0.50$.

Although there was some negative press in South Korea, the government did not end up looking weak or incompetent as they aggressively responded to the attacks and reconstituted the networks fairly quickly. As a result, I also set $S_3 = 0.50$ to represent approximately half success against the objective of embarrassing the South Korean government.

McAfee's theory that the attackers intended to destroy evidence from Operation Troy is intriguing, although it is difficult to code its success.[48] Security researchers discovered Operation Troy, but its connection to Dark Seoul was not discussed outside of Internet security circles in the broader media. I therefore set $S_4 = 0.50$ as half-success.

I considered disrupting the banks and broadcasters as the primary purpose of the attackers based upon their target set. Therefore, I assigned each of those objectives equal weight, and gave each four times the weight of the remaining two objectives of embarrassing the South Korean government and erasing Operation Troy. The offensive inputs are shown in Table B.17. These inputs give an $OCSI_{North\ Korea} = 0.38$, which is around the mid-range of the eight case studies I examined. South Korea had no offensive objectives and so $OCSI_{South\ Korea} = 0.00$.

Table B.17 North Korean Offensive Objectives in April 2013 Attack

	Objective	*Level of Success (S)*	*Weighting Factor (W)*
1	Disrupt banks	0.20	0.40
2	Disrupt broadcasters	0.50	0.40
3	Embarrass South Korean government	0.50	0.10
4	Erase evidence of espionage	0.50	0.10

Level of Functionality (L) and Criticality (C) in North Korean April 2013 Attack

South Korea was attempting to defend two systems; the banks and the media companies. The banks were quite successful in defending their systems and only

Table B.18 Critical South Korean Systems in April 2013 attack

	System	*Level of Functionality (L)*	*System Criticality (C)*
1	South Korean banking systems	0.80	0.75
2	South Korean media internal systems	0.50	0.25

experienced minimal disruption. Some banks that North Korea attacked reported no damage, while other banks were back in operation after two hours.[49] Therefore I set $L_1 = 0.80$. On the media side, the broadcasters lost their internal networks but the attackers were unable to take them off the air. This represents a middle ground and so I set $L_2 = 0.50$. The defended systems are shown in Table B.18. This coding gives a $DCSI_{South\ Korea} = 0.73$. As North Korea was not attacked, $DCSI_{North\ Korea} = 0.00$.

Relative Cyberspace Superiority Index in North Korean April 2013 Attack

North Korea does not rely nearly as heavily on cyberspace as South Korea so $R_{North\ Korea} = 0.05$ and $R_{South\ Korea} = 0.95$. All of these inputs give:

$OCSI_{North\ Korea} = 0.38$
$DCSI_{North\ Korea} = 0.00$
$R_{North\ Korea} = 0.05$
$OCSI_{South\ Korea} = 0.00$
$DCSI_{South\ Korea} = 0.73$
$R_{South\ Korea} = 0.95$

$CSI_{North\ Korea} = 0.36$ and $CSI_{South\ Korea} = 0.69$, which yields:

$RCSI_{North\ Korea} = -0.33$
$RCSI_{South\ Korea} = 0.33$

Notes

1 Dan Goodin, "Georgian cyber attacks launched by Russian crime gangs: With help from Twitter, Facebook and Microsoft," *The Register*, 18 August 2009. www.theregister.co.uk/2009/08/18/georgian_cyber_attacks
2 Paulo Shakarian, "The 2008 Russian Cyber Campaign Against Georgia." Military Review, November–December 2011, 65.
3 United States Cyber Consequences Unit, "Overview by the US-CCU of the Cyber Campaign Against Georgia in August of 2008," US-CCU Special Report, August 2009, 5.
4 United States Cyber Consequences Unit, "Overview by the US-CCU of the Cyber Campaign Against Georgia in August of 2008," 7.
5 Paulo Shakarian, Jana Shakarian and Andrew Ruef, *Introduction to Cyber-Warfare: A Multidisciplinary Approach* (Amsterdam: Syngress, 2013), Kindle Location 1014, chap. 3.

6 Shakarian, et al., *Introduction to Cyber-Warfare*, Kindle Location 1017, chap. 3.
7 Shakarian, et al., *Introduction to Cyber-Warfare*, Kindle Location 991, chap 3.
8 United States Cyber Consequences Unit, "Overview by the US-CCU of the Cyber Campaign Against Georgia in August of 2008," 7.
9 Paul Rosenzweig, *Cyber Warfare: How Conflicts in Cyberspace are Challenging America and Changing the World* (Santa Barbara, CA: Praeger, 2013), Kindle Location 736, chap 3.
10 Korea Times, "Dreadful Cyber War." The Korea Times, 10 July 2009. www.koreatimes.co.kr/www/news/opinon/2009/07/137_48261.html
11 Lolita Baldor, "White House among targets of cyber attack: Other targets included NSA, Homeland Security and State Department," *NBC News*, 8 July 2009, www.nbcnews.com/id/31800532/ns/technology_and_science-security
12 Lolita Baldor, "White House among targets of cyber attack."
13 Associated Press, "N. Korea Suspected of Global Cyber Attack," *NBC News*, 8 July 2009. www.cbsnews.com/stories/2009/07/08/tech/main5143457.shtml
14 Jane Han, "Cyber Attack Hits Korea for Third Day," *Korea Times*, 9 July 2009. www.koreatimes.co.kr/www/news/biz/2009/09/123_48203.html
15 Lolita Baldor, "US officials eye North Korea in cyber attack," *Tulsa World*, 8 July 2009. www.tulsaworld.com/article.aspx/US_officials_eye_North_Korea_in_cyber_attack/20090708_13_0_seouls64065
16 Jane Han, "Cyber Attack Hits Korea for Third Day."
17 Shakarian, et al., *Introduction to Cyber-Warfare*, Kindle Location 6972, chap. 13.
18 David E. Sanger, *Confront and Conceal: Obama's Secret Wars and Surprising Use of American Power* (New York: Broadway Books, 2013), 204.
19 Paulo Shakarian, "Stuxnet: Cyberwar Revolution in Military Affairs," *Small Wars Journal*, 15 April 2011. 3.
20 Sanger, *Confront and Conceal*, 199.
21 Shakarian, et al., *Introduction to Cyber-Warfare*, Kindle Location 6943, chap. 13.
22 Sanger, *Confront and Conceal*, 207.
23 Shakarian, et al., *Introduction to Cyber-Warfare*, Kindle Location 6945, chap. 13.
24 Sanger, *Confront and Conceal*, 207.
25 Sanger, *Confront and Conceal*, 204.
26 Sanger, *Confront and Conceal*, 204.
27 Shakarian, et al., *Introduction to Cyber-Warfare*, Kindle Location 6945, chap. 13.
28 Sanger, *Confront and Conceal*, 194.
29 Aleksandr Matrosov, Eugene Rodionov, David Harley, and Juraj Malcho, "Stuxnet Under the Microscope: Revisions 1.31," *eSeT*. Accessed 25 August 2013. http://go.eset.com/us/resources/white-papers/Stuxnet_Under_the_Microscope.pdf. 24
30 Jim Finkle, "Researchers say Stuxnet was deployed against Iran in 2007," *Reuters*, 26 February 2013. www.reuters.com/article/2013/02/26/us-cyberwar-stuxnet-idUSBRE91P0PP20130226
31 Shakarian, et al., *Introduction to Cyber-Warfare*, Kindle Location 7003, chap. 13.
32 McAfee. "Ten Days of Rain: Expert analysis of distributed denial-of-service attacks targeting South Korea." White Paper developed by McAfee Security, 2011, 12.
33 Kevin Kwang, "S. Korea, US attacks possibly launched by N. Korea," *ZDNet*, 6 July 2011. www.zdnet.com/s-korea-us-attacks-possibly-launched-by-n-korea-2062301087
34 McAfee. "Ten Days of Rain," 3.
35 McAfee. "Ten Days of Rain," 3.
36 Ryan Mauro, "Major North Korean Cyber Attack on South," *Frontpage Mag*, 1 September 2011. http://frontpagemag.com/2011/ryan-mauro/major-north-korean-cyber-attack-on-south
37 Yonhap News Agency, "S. Korea seeks int'l cooperation for further probe into cyber attack on bank." *Yonhap*, 15 May 2011. http://english.yonhapnews.co.kr/national/2011/05/15/25/0301000000AEN20110515002500320F.HTML

38 Finextra, "South Korean bank hit by cyber-attack." *Finextra*, 20 April 2011. www.finextra.com/News/Fullstory.aspx?newsitemid=22486
39 Finextra, "South Korean bank hit by cyber-attack."
40 Shakarian, et al., *Introduction to Cyber-Warfare*, Kindle Location 1856, chap. 5.
41 Abdullah al-Saadan speaking to local media quoted in Camilla Hall and Javier Blas, "Aramco cyber attack targeted production," *Financial Times*, 10 December 2012. www.ft.com/intl/cms/s/0/5f313ab6-42da-11e2-a4e4-00144feabdc0.html#axzz2dfwhMlKi
42 Holden, "Cyber Attacks in the Spin Cycle: Saudi Aramco and Shamoon," *Analysis Intelligence*, 1 November 2012. http://analysisintelligence.com/cyber-defense/narrative-of-a-cyber-attack-saudi-aramco-and-shamoon
43 Siraj Wahab, "Cyber Attack on Aramco A 'Global Plot', says Saudi Arabia," *Arab News*, 10 December 2012. www.eurasiareview.com/10122012-cyber-attack-on-aramco-a-global-plot-says-saudi-arabia
44 Wahab, "Cyber Attack on Aramco A 'Global Plot', says Saudi Arabia."
45 Japmarpaung, "Dark Seoul – Postmortem," 3 May 2013. http://japmarpaung.com/2013/05/03/dark-seoul-postmortem
46 Japmarpaung, "Dark Seoul – Postmortem."
47 Choe Sang-Hun, "Computer Networks in South Korea Are Paralyzed in Cyberattacks," 20 March 2013. www.nytimes.com/2013/03/21/world/asia/south-korea-computer-network-crashes.html
48 Sherstobitoff and Liba, "Dissecting Operation Troy: Cyberespionage in South Korea," 28.
49 Sang-Hun, "Computer Networks in South Korea Are Paralyzed in Cyberattacks."

Bibliography

Associated Press. "N. Korea Suspected of Global Cyber Attack." *NBC News*, 8 July 2009. www.cbsnews.com/stories/2009/07/08/tech/main5143457.shtml

Baldor, Lolita. "US officials eye North Korea in cyber attack." *Tulsa World*, 8 July 2009. www.tulsaworld.com/article.aspx/US_officials_eye_North_Korea_in_cyber_attack/20090708_13_0_seouls64065

Baldor, Lolita. "White House among targets of cyber attack: Other targets included NSA, Homeland Security and State Department." *NBC News*, 8 July 2009. www.nbcnews.com/id/31800532/ns/technology_and_science-security

Finextra. "South Korean bank hit by cyber-attack." *Finextra*, 20 April 2011. www.finextra.com/News/Fullstory.aspx?newsitemid=22486

Finkle, Jim. "Researchers say Stuxnet was deployed against Iran in 2007." *Reuters*. 26 February 2013. www.reuters.com/article/2013/02/26/us-cyberwar-stuxnet-idUSBRE91P0PP20130226

Goodin, Dan. "Georgian cyber attacks launched by Russian crime gangs: With help from Twitter, Facebook and Microsoft." *The Register*, 18 August 2009. www.theregister.co.uk/2009/08/18/georgian_cyber_attacks

Hall, Camilla and Javier Blas. "Aramco cyber attack targeted production." *Financial Times*, 10 December 2012. www.ft.com/intl/cms/s/0/5f313ab6-42da-11e2-a4e4-00144feabdc0.html#axzz2dfwhMlKi

Han, Jane. "Cyber Attack Hits Korea for Third Day." *Korea Times*, 9 July 2009. www.koreatimes.co.kr/www/news/biz/2009/09/123_48203.html

Holden. "Cyber Attacks in the Spin Cycle: Saudi Aramco and Shamoon." *Analysis Intelligence*, 1 November 2012. http://analysisintelligence.com/cyber-defense/narrative-of-a-cyber-attack-saudi-aramco-and-shamoon

Japmarpaung, "Dark Seoul – Postmortem." 3 May 2013. http://japmarpaung.com/2013/05/03/dark-seoul-postmortem

Korea Times. "Dreadful Cyber War." *The Korea Times*, 10 July 2009. www.koreatimes.co.kr/www/news/opinon/2009/07/137_48261.html

Kwang, Kevin. "S. Korea, US attacks possibly launched by N. Korea." *ZDNet*, 6 July 2011. www.zdnet.com/s-korea-us-attacks-possibly-launched-by-n-korea-2062301087

Matrosov, Aleksandr, Eugene Rodionov, David Harley, and Juraj Malcho. "Stuxnet Under the Microscope: Revisions 1.31." *eSeT*. Accessed 25 August 2013. http://go.eset.com/us/resources/white-papers/Stuxnet_Under_the_Microscope.pdf

Mauro, Ryan. "Major North Korean Cyber Attack on South." *Frontpage Mag*, 1 September 2011.http://frontpagemag.com/2011/ryan-mauro/major-north-korean-cyber-attack-on-south

McAfee. "Ten Days of Rain: Expert analysis of distributed denial-of-service attacks targeting South Korea." White Paper developed by McAfee Security. 2011.

Rosenzweig, Paul. *Cyber Warfare: How Conflicts in Cyberspace are Challenging America and Changing the World*. Santa Barbara, CA: Praeger, 2013. Kindle edition.

Sang-Hun, Choe. "Computer Networks in South Korea Are Paralyzed in Cyberattacks." 20 March 2013. /www.nytimes.com/2013/03/21/world/asia/south-korea-computer-network-crashes.html

Sanger, David E. *Confront and Conceal: Obama's Secret Wars and Surprising Use of American Power.* New York: Broadway Books, 2013. Kindle edition.

Shakarian, Paulo. "Stuxnet: Cyberwar Revolution in Military Affairs." *Small Wars Journal*, 15 April 2011.

Shakarian, Paulo. "The 2008 Russian Cyber Campaign Against Georgia." *Military Review*, November–December 2011, 63–68.

Shakarian, Paulo, Jana Shakarian and Andrew Ruef. *Introduction to Cyber-Warfare: A Multidisciplinary Approach*. Amsterdam: Syngress, 2013. Kindle edition.

Sherstobitoff, Ryan and Itai Liba. "Dissecting Operation Troy: Cyberespionage in South Korea." White Paper developed by McAfee Labs. 2013.

U.S. Cyber Consequences Unit. "Overview by the US-CCU of the Cyber Campaign Against Georgia in August of 2008." US-CCU Special Report, August 2009.

Wahab, Siraj. "Cyber Attack on Aramco A 'Global Plot', says Saudi Arabia." *Arab News*, 10 December 2012. www.eurasiareview.com/10122012-cyber-attack-on-aramco-a-global-plot-says-saudi-arabia

Yonhap News Agency. "S. Korea seeks int'l cooperation for further probe into cyber attack on bank." *Yonhap*, 15 May 2011. http://english.yonhapnews.co.kr/national/2011/05/15/25/0301000000AEN20110515002500320F.HTML

Index